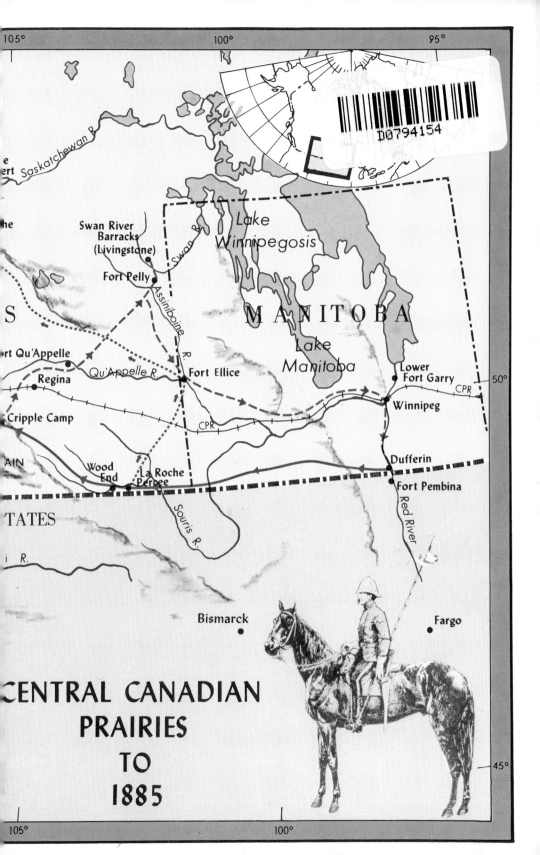

105°   100°   95°

Saskatchewan R.

Swan River
Barracks
(Livingstone)

Fort Pelly

Swan R.

Lake
Winnipegosis

M A N I T O B A

Lake
Manitoba

S

Assiniboine R.

rt Qu'Appelle

Qu'Appelle R.

Regina

Fort Ellice

Cripple Camp

CPR

Lower
Fort Garry

CPR

Winnipeg

50°

AIN

Wood
End

La Roche
Percee

Dufferin

Fort Pembina

TATES

Souris R.

Red River

i R.

Bismarck

Fargo

CENTRAL CANADIAN
PRAIRIES
TO
1885

105°   100°

45°

The Royal Canadian Mounted Police
A Century of History

from Brad
1914

The Royal Canadian Mounted Police
A Century of History
1873-1973

Nora and William Kelly

Hurtig Publishers, Edmonton, Alberta

Hurtig Publishers
10560 105 Street
Edmonton, Alberta

ISBN 0-88830-069-7

Designed, typeset, printed and bound in Canada

To those
who have lost
their lives
in the service
of the Force

Contents

Royal Canadian Mounted Police 1920 – 1973

Illustrations

Appear between pages 160/161

Maps

Preface

This book is an attempt to show the evolution of the Royal Canadian Mounted Police and to place it in the perspective of Canadian history. Obviously the full story is not possible here. The main developments and outstanding events demanded inclusion. But recorded history covers so many details that the material in this book was chosen from available material many times that amount. Unrecorded history contains much more. For every incident and every individual mentioned here, hundreds are equally worthy of mention. Similarly, but by no means to the same extent, the book contains less criticism of the Mounted Police than history records.

One point of criticism stems from the belief that the Force is acquiring too much police power through its commitments on three levels—federal, provincial and municipal. In assessing the role of the Force, however, it is necessary to remember that it is not an autonomous body in any one of these three areas. In federal policing and general administration the Force is responsible to the federal government and to the solicitor general, who is the minister directly in control. In provincial policing it is responsible to the provincial governments to which it is under contract, and to the attorneys general. Similarly, in municipal policing in some 150 municipalities in which it is under contract, it is responsible to the municipal authorities. Thus at each of these three levels the Mounted Police report to and are under the control of the elected representatives of the people. And thus, as is required in our democratic system, it is the electorate which indirectly has control, not only of the manner in which the Force performs its duties but also of the laws which it enforces.

Under these circumstances, members of the public have the responsibility of becoming knowledgeable about the working of the Force. Similarly they have the right to criticize when they see fit and the duty to make their views known. The well-being of a police force, no less than the well-being of our political system, depends on the interest and involvement of the public.

One purpose of this book is to help Canadians to become better acquainted with our national police force. Obviously the incidents depicted are mainly the spectacular and the dramatic. However, the favourable reputation of the Force could not have been established without the work and the dedication of the men performing its day-to-day duties. It is largely to their credit that the organization has acquired worldwide renown.

It is impossible to thank, by name, everyone who has assisted us during the preparation of this book. Instead we thank Commissioner W.L. Higgitt of the Royal Canadian Mounted Police for permitting us to deal with any member of the Force who could assist in any way, and we thank those members in particular. We gratefully acknowledge permission to use copyrighted material from the *RCMP Quarterlies*, and we thank the authors of articles and other material in those *Quarterlies*. We are grateful for the many photographs provided by the Force for inclusion in this book. All except those otherwise indicated are Royal Canadian Mounted Police photographs. We also thank ex-members for their generosity in providing information.

Nora Kelly
William Kelly

11

Prologue

Whisky traders and nomadic Indians dominated the Canadian West during the late 1860s and the early 1870s. From outlaw trading forts dotting the prairies the traders doled out whisky to the Indians in exchange for buffalo robes, furs and horses. Plied with whisky, the Indians, who had never known alcohol before the white men introduced it to them, ran wild. They stole horses and traded them for still more firewater. They burned the legitimate trading posts of the Hudson's Bay Company on the Bow and the Red Deer rivers, forcing that company out of the district. They robbed, tortured and murdered at will, so that no traveller dared to venture into the foothills of the Rockies without an armed escort.

The most notorious outlaw trading post, Fort Whoop-Up, stood in the foothills of the Rockies about forty miles north of the American border, near the present site of Lethbridge, Alberta. It was operated by whisky trader Alfred B. Hamilton and a score of fellow Americans, and flew its own flag, which resembled the United States flag but had no stars. The traders got their supplies from across the border, from Hamilton's uncle Isaac G. Baker, who operated the largest trading company at Fort Benton, Montana.

One basic recipe for "Whoop-Up Bug Juice" called for a quart of whisky, a pound of rank chewing tobacco, a handful of red pepper, a bottle of Jamaica ginger, and a quart of molasses. This was diluted with water, heated to the boiling point and traded by the cupful. Some Indians demanded an undiluted firewater that could be ignited by a match. Perhaps it was only ironic justice that in his first trading year Hamilton's customers burned down his cluster of eleven log huts.

The rebuilt Fort Whoop-Up was better able to withstand attack. It was a real fort, 130 feet by 140 feet, with heavy-timbered, mud-chinked walls loopholed for musketry. Two opposite corners were fortified with bastions, and two three-pounder guns stood ready for action. Lining the inner walls were storerooms, living quarters, a kitchen, a blacksmith shop and stables, all with massive log walls. The roofs, also of great logs, were covered with sod in case Indians tried to set fire to the fort by shooting flaming arrows into the roof. Chimneys were crossed with iron bars as protection against thirsty or bloodthirsty Indians.

Even those Indians coming to Fort Whoop-Up purposely to trade were not usually allowed to enter the fort's fifteen-foot oak gate. They simply pushed their buffalo robes through a small wicket-like opening in the wall to a trader inside the fort. He handed back whisky from the tub beside him, two tin cupfuls for an ordinary buffalo robe. A first-grade buffalo pony traded for four gallons of whisky, and a rifle for a pile of furs to the height of the gun.

Outlaw whisky traders pushed as far north as Fort Edmonton. When Hudson's Bay Company factors there remonstrated with them, they replied that since there was no force to restrain them, they would do as they pleased. They did just that. The few white men in the territory outside the trading posts did not dare introduce farm animals or culti-vate the land to any extent.

Sir John A. Macdonald, the prime minister of Canada since Confederation in 1867, was well aware of the situation. But from 1869, when Canada purchased the vast north-west from the fur-trading Hudson's Bay Company which formerly owned it through British charter, he had confidently anticipated its settlement. As S.W. Horrall, the present historian of the Royal Canadian Mounted Police, recently revealed, in the same year that Canada acquired the Bay's territory Macdonald began planning a mounted police force for that vast area.

As Macdonald knew, while the Hudson's Bay Company was in control, justice was maintained by justices of the peace who were located at its scattered posts, and by a criminal and civil court centred at Fort Garry. This fort, north of the present city of Winnipeg, lay in what was then known as the Red River Settlement, but later became the Province of Manitoba.

However, the company's influence had never penetrated the far south-western part of its sprawling territory. And after the American Civil War, when the United States federal authorities began to succeed in stopping the whisky trade in Montana, traders from that state pushed north into Hudson's Bay Company land to trade with the Indians. By contrast with the legitimate trade goods of calico, pots, beads, blankets, knives, hatchets and so on, the free traders bartered with liquor, rifles and ammunition. Of these, liquor brought the greatest profit.

Liquor demoralized the Indians. Violence and disorder increased. And to make matters worse, the buffalo were being hunted to extinction. On both sides of the border they were slaughtered by Indians and whites for their hides for trade, and by whites even for their tongues, a gastronomical delicacy. Thus the Indians were losing their main source of food, shelter and clothing, and also their fuel—buffalo chips.

As Sir John A. knew, it was natural that the Indians would resent settlers who would further disrupt their historic way of life, and that they would fight to the death to try to retain for their own use the land on which their survival depended. Therefore he decided to create a mounted police force for that area. Its duties would be to provide general law enforcement, and especially to prevent the violent conflict between Indians and settlers that had characterized the settlement of the American West.

Macdonald decided that the police force he visualized would first maintain law and order where there were already settlers, at Red River. He gave specific instructions to William McDougall, the lieutenant-governor designate of the north-west, who left Ottawa for that area in September of 1869, in anticipation of December 1, when Canadian authority was scheduled to replace that of the Hudson's Bay Company.

The force was to be organized during the winter of 1869–70. It would be of "mounted rifles," and patterned after the Royal Irish Constabulary, which had developed out of the social unrest and civil strife of nineteenth century Ireland. It would be a police and not a military organization, although its members would be trained as cavalry and instructed in the use of rifles and artillery. Also, to minimize possible conflict of races, the mounted police force was to be a "mixed one of pure white and British and French half-breeds."

But the Red River Rebellion broke out before McDougall arrived at his destination. Louis Riel and his Métis supporters seized control of Fort Garry, the most vital point in the Red River settlements, and set up a provisional government. As a result, an enabling Act was passed in May, 1870, for the Red River area to enter the Dominion as the Province of Manitoba, responsible for its own policing.

The remainder of the vast western area was to be designated the North-West Territories. It would be governed as an unorganized tract, with the lieutenant-governor of Manitoba as ex officio lieutenant-governor of the Territories acting on orders from Ottawa, with assistance from a council. Sir John A., who was minister of Justice as well as prime minister, would organize a mobile police force of two hundred mounted men. Justice would be dispensed by the justices of the peace already appointed by the Hudson's Bay Company, and by a judge and other justices of the peace appointed later by the council.

Recruiting for the mounted police force had actually begun earlier that year by way of an order-in-council. Now it was resumed and continued for some time. But four days after Sir John A. had announced his plan to the House of Commons he became critically ill. By the time he resumed his official duties in September, the organization of the new police force had been discontinued.

Meanwhile, whisky traders continued to operate in the vast West. The Indians continued to trade with them, to their own disadvantage. Violence and unrest continued, and many Indians were now armed with rifles. American officials reported that Blackfoot Indians were crossing the border to steal horses and murder white settlers in Montana.

The small Province of Manitoba and the North-West Territories beyond it had been incorporated into the Dominion of Canada on July 15, 1870. At the first meeting of the council in October, an ordinance was passed forbidding the importation or sale of spirituous liquors, but there was no way of enforcing the legislation.

Also in October of the same year, Lieutenant-Governor Adams George Archibald commissioned a British army officer, Lieutenant William F. Butler, to investigate the conditions on the western frontier. Butler's report, made in 1871 after a journey of 2,700 miles by wagon, on horseback and by dog team, and later published as *The Great Lone Land*, indicted the whisky trade and its demoralizing effect on the Indians. Lieutenant Butler recommended sending a military force of from one hundred to 150 mounted riflemen to establish law and order in the West. But the federal government merely sent its specially chosen observer, Colonel P. Robertson-Ross, the adjutant-general of the Canadian militia, to investigate further.

In December, 1872, Robertson-Ross reported back to Macdonald personally, stressing that he agreed with Butler's estimate of the situation. His report included such facts as that within one year eighty-eight Blackfeet were murdered in drunken brawls. A half-breed mutilated an Indian woman by cutting the tendons of her arms. Later the same half-breed murdered his wife not far from the gate of Fort Edmonton, in what would be Alberta, but he could not be arrested because no one had the legal power to make the arrest.

The adjutant-general noted that United States traders imported rifles, revolvers, whisky and other goods into Canada, not only against the import and export laws of the two countries, but also without paying the customs duties. He recommended that a military force of five hundred mounted rifles should be established at once. He suggested that their uniforms should include red coats because many Indians had told him that their tribes had grown to trust their "old brothers" the red-coated soldiers formerly stationed in the Red River district (H.M. 6th Regiment of Foot, at Fort Garry, 1846-48).

But still the federal government did not organize a law-enforcement body for the West, although the building of the Canadian Pacific Railway, which the government had promised to British Columbia at Confederation, could proceed only through territory where law and order reigned. Probably the cost held the government back. Canada was a new country with limited revenues, and it was still maintaining a large military force at Fort Garry. Surveying the international boundary was expensive, and the proposed railway would be even more so. Besides, Sir John A. had planned only that his police force should accompany settlement, not precede it.

Then in March, 1873, the Robertson-Ross report was made public. Criticism about the North-West Territories followed in the House of Commons. Macdonald responded by announcing the government's intention to ask for money to organize a police force "similar to the Irish Mounted Constabulary" and with military discipline.

On May 23, 1873, the enabling bill was given royal assent. It provided for the establishment of "a Police Force in the North-West Territories," and also for criminal courts, common jails and the appointment of magistrates. The police force would be a civil force of not more than three hundred police in uniform, headed by a Commissioner and several officers, who would also be ex officio justices of the peace. Other members would include a paymaster, a veterinary surgeon, and various ranks of constables and sub-constables. Armed simply but effectively, and mounted on "the hardy horse of the country," the police would patrol the frontier, collect customs, prevent whisky trading with the Indians and generally maintain law and order. The force would be responsible to Ottawa, and not to the local authorities as were the police in the provinces. The bill carried no reference to a multi-racial force, perhaps because the Red River Rebellion had convinced the prime minister that the Métis could not be trusted, but it did not specifically exclude half-breeds.

During the summer of 1873, in spite of alarming reports from Lieutenant-Governor Alexander Morris about the serious situation at Fort Whoop-Up, the government still made no move to send police to the north-west. But on August 30, Sir John A. made the precautionary move of having the Force officially constituted by order-in-council.

A few days later the government learned from American authorities in Washington that in May a party of Assiniboine Indians had been murdered in a "horrible massacre" in the Cypress Hills, North-West Territories, by whites from Fort Benton in Montana. The American authorities stated that they could take no action because the murders had been committed on British territory. But they offered to help in the arrest and extradition of those involved.

Accounts of the massacre vary, but Abel Farwell, a respectable American trader with a post nearby, reported later that he watched the slaughter of the Assiniboines, powerless to prevent it. About two hundred Assiniboines, he said, were camped near Farwell's post. Some fifteen wolf hunters from Fort Benton arrived and camped nearby. The wolfers, who included not only Americans but also several French Canadians and at least three English Canadians, were out in pursuit of Cree Indians who had stolen some of their horses. The Assiniboines had nothing to do with the theft of the horses, but the white men got drunk and vowed to attack them anyway. They also got the Indians drunk by giving them liquor. The next day, after more carousing, the wolfers opened fire on the unprepared Indians. Farwell reported that they murdered more than thirty men, women and children, wounded many others, and forced all able-bodied Indians to flee to the hills.

Lieutenant-Governor Morris's report of the same incident arrived in Ottawa soon after the American report. But Morris had mistakenly assumed that the murders had been committed by whisky traders from Fort Whoop-Up. He stressed that unless the government took immediate action, the killing of the Assiniboines could lead to a major Indian war. He pleaded that the police be sent west before the Dawson route was closed for navigation about the middle of October and frozen in for the winter.

Now the government was forced to move. It had already arranged with Gilbert McMicken, commissioner of the Dominion police in Manitoba, to go to Fort Benton to start extradition proceedings against the murderers. An order-in-council of September 25, 1873, appointed nine commissioned officers to the "Mounted Police Force for the North-West Territories." The Commissioner was still to be appointed, but these first members of the organization immediately began recruiting. At last the formation of Sir John A. Macdonald's long-planned Force was underway.

North-West
Mounted
Police
1873 – 1904

Chapter 1
The Old Originals
1873 – 1874

Recruiting for the Mounted Police Force for the North-West Territories began in September, 1873, at centres in Ontario including Ottawa and Toronto, in the Eastern Townships of Quebec, and in the Maritimes. Every man accepted would have to be of sound constitution, able to ride, active and able-bodied, of good character, between the ages of eighteen and forty years, and able to read and write either the English or the French language.

But after Sir John A. Macdonald's three years of on-again, off-again planning, only about a month remained for recruiting, organizing, equipping the Force with uniforms, arms and supplies, and getting it to Fort Garry before the freeze-up. The resulting haste and confusion led to difficulties which hampered the Force for many months as it struggled to become operational.

Even many of the recruits would probably not have been accepted if there had been time to secure more suitable ones, although from the first there was a solid core of men who had had military training. By the time the first objective of 150 men was reached, the recruits included former clerks, tradesmen, farmers, telegraph operators, professors, gardeners, sailors, lumbermen, planters, students, surveyors and even a bartender. Most of the men were glad there were no riding tests.

According to S.W. Horrall, among the original members were a few who were bilingual, as well as a small party from the Province of Quebec who spoke French only. Their pay would be low even at 1873 values. Salaries ranged from the Commissioner's "not exceeding $2,600 a year" to seventy-five cents a day for a sub-constable. Rations and living quarters, however, would be provided for all ranks.

But impatient recruits probably thought less of pay and more of adventure when in October three Divisions—"A," "B" and "C"—set sail from Collingwood on Lake Huron, to cross the Great Lakes by steamer. These Divisions, commonly called Troops, of about fifty men each, were heading westward for Lower Fort Garry in Manitoba, where they would train during the coming winter.

The voyage to the head of the lakes was not too difficult for the first two contingents, which left on October 10. But the third contingent steamed up Lake Superior against a severe storm that made most of the men violently seasick, for which none had bargained in connection with police service on the North-West plains.

From Prince Arthur's Landing (Port Arthur) to the Manitoba prairies, except for some miles in wagons and carts, all contingents travelled in small boats over the notorious Dawson route. This route included dozens of lakes and rivers and almost fifty back-breaking portages, some as long as two miles.

West of Lake of the Woods the third contingent endured an early winter blizzard, not unusual for that part of the country. It soaked their tents, then froze them so hard that they could not be unpacked for several days. In below-zero weather this contingent made a twenty-mile march through deep snow. The men had not been provided with uniforms to wear en route, although each had been issued with a great-coat. But even the coats over their regular clothing failed to keep out the bitter cold, and their boots froze solid, forcing some men to march with their feet wrapped in underwear and shirts.

At Lower Fort Garry, twenty miles north of Winnipeg, the three Divisions of slightly more than 150 men established themselves at the Stone Fort, which the government had leased from the Hudson's Bay Company for their use. Immediately the officers began to purchase horses, most of them unbroken western broncos, in accord with Sir John A.'s stipulation regarding the "hardy horse of the country." Soon after their arrival at the Stone Fort the troops were dismayed to learn that their uniforms, clothing, arms, accoutrements and stores were frozen in somewhere along the Dawson route. Nevertheless they had to begin training.

On November 3, 1873, they were sworn in. Actually, this was the day on which the North-West Mounted Police became a vital entity. But although its members referred to the Force by this name, it was not the official title, as the Act referred only to the "Mounted Police" or the "Police Force for the North-West Territories." The government, the press, and the public called them, in addition, the "Dominion Mounted Police" and the "Manitoba Mounted Police."

Two weeks before the swearing-in date, Prime Minister Macdonald had appointed the Force's first Commissioner. He was Lieutenant-Colonel George Arthur French, thirty-two years old, and Irish. Before his appointment he had been an officer of the Royal Artillery and commandant of the Canadian School of Gunnery at Kingston in Ontario, and before that he had served briefly in the Royal Irish Constabulary. But the tall, vigorous French had not yet arrived at Lower Fort Garry.

So on that cloudy, cold Monday morning in November, 1873, when the whole Force was paraded for the first time, the commanding officer was not Commissioner French. Instead he was Lieutenant-Colonel W. Osborne Smith, the commanding officer of the militia in Manitoba, whom Sir John A. had appointed to act as Commissioner. In the chill of a gray stone room Divisions "A," "B" and "C" stood stiffly to attention while Smith administered the oath of office to all officers and men present.

Then the men signed a paper headed "Mounted Police Force of Canada," promising for three years to obey and perform all lawful orders and to reimburse the government for any damage to its property. The first to sign was Arthur Henry Griesbach, a veteran of the Cape Mounted Rifles, who in 1870 had helped prepare for the organization of the prime minister's proposed riflemen-police. The second was Percy R. Neale. The third was twenty-two-year-old Samuel B. Steele, who had taken military training at Canada's first School of Gunnery at Kingston. Later each man was issued with a warrant of appointment with his name and rank. The officers did not sign, as they received their commissions from Queen Victoria.

Soon Commissioner French arrived at the Stone Fort, having travelled there via the United States. Lieutenant-Colonel Smith had already supplied the Force with fatigue uniforms, warm clothing and arms from the militia stores at Fort Garry, and training had begun. Now French speeded up training and organization toward his dream of "an immense, unbridled realm policed by a thoroughly organized and fully equipped body of troopers."

Early in December, after word reached the Stone Fort that several whisky traders were operating among Indians on the west shore of Lake Winnipeg, Commissioner French instigated the Force's first patrol. He assigned Inspector J.F. Macleod to investigate and if possible to arrest the traders and take them in for trial. To accompany him Macleod chose a constable and three sub-constables, one from each of the three troops. Then the inspector, who himself was an expert, gave the others instruction in snowshoeing, and supervised their practice.

The little party set out in horse-drawn bobsleighs, followed by two dog teams hauling toboggans loaded with a tent, blankets and food. On reaching the mouth of the Red River, they strapped on their snowshoes. After several days of hard travelling, camping by night in the shelter of the woods, they reached the small log shack used as the whisky traders' headquarters.

There they took six men into custody. They also confiscated about ten gallons of liquor they found on the premises. Then they took their prisoners back to the Stone Fort, arriving there the day before Christmas. The first patrol by the North-West Mounted Police had been successfully accomplished.

The Force was less successful in clearing the confusion caused by the rank names of the early years. Officers below the Commissioner were classified as "superintendent-and-inspector" and "superintendent-and-sub-inspector." Usually the latter were referred to as "sub-inspector," but the former became either "superintendent" or "inspector," which was awkward. NCOs were constables, and the men were sub-constables, which seemed clear enough. But a senior constable was also classified as a staff constable, with rank corresponding to troop sergeant major, and another constable could be at the same time a quartermaster sergeant or a paymaster sergeant. There were also such ranks as "paymaster acting as quartermaster," "surgeon," and "veterinary surgeon." Adding confusion, many members used former military rank names, or were addressed by military rank names in accord with the duties to which they were assigned.

All during that first winter the police received riding instruction from Regimental No. 3, Staff Constable Steele, who was tall, fair-haired, and so embarrassingly slim-waisted that he wore a sash under his tunic to give him a less girlish appearance.

"Our work was unceasing from 6:00 A.M. until after dark," he wrote later in *Forty Years in Canada*. "I drilled five rides per day the whole of the winter in an open *manège*, and the orders were that if the temperatures were not lower than thirty-six below zero the riding and breaking should go on." Even after he had gentled the wild broncos so as to let the recruits mount, "the men were repeatedly thrown with great violence to the frozen ground; but no one lost his nerve . . . when spring opened they were very fine riders, laying the foundation of Canadian horsemanship in the wild and woolly west."

While the NCOs and men shivered through a perpetual round of riding, rifle practice, and foot and arms drill, their officers were equally busy. From one reveille to the next they inspected men and barracks, supervised the weighing of food rations, and checked hospital management. They also ordered the mounting of the guard, always making sure that the men detailed for various duties were not only present but also sober, this last task sometimes the most difficult of all. They checked attendance at "retreat," at "tattoo" and at "lights out," and turned in detailed written reports by 10:00 A.M. the next day.

However, police of all ranks also found time for balls, parties, rifle matches and a Quadrille Club. On one occasion Steele and a comrade rode the twenty miles to Winnipeg in twenty degrees below zero weather to attend a grand ball. Their ride on American trotters, said Steele, was one of the warmest he had ever experienced, as "the seat was a military one, every stride raising us several inches off the saddle, and bringing us down with a bump which would have been fatal to anyone with a weak heart."

Commissioner French exerted the strictest discipline in an effort to shape his men into the ideal troopers he visualized. But the Force was a civil organization, so a fine was the only punishment allowed until French persuaded the government to rectify the matter, which it did during the next session of Parliament. The order book of 1873 set the price of a trooper's angry remark to his NCO at $5.00, an argument at $10.00. Sleeping on duty cost two weeks' pay; the first case of drunkenness cost $3.00, the second $6.00; all very expensive diversions for men earning seventy-five cents a day.

"All individuals of the police force can please themselves as to wearing whiskers, moustaches or beards," stated the order book, "but those who prefer to shave must do so daily." "Many of the NCOs and men, being under the impression that they are permitted to finish their stable work and return to barracks long before the stable hour expires, are labouring under a great mistake; for the future they will occupy the whole stable hour in grooming their horses with the exception of the time employed in feeding and watering. . . . "

"Constables who are in the habit of drinking or card-playing with sub-constables, or having money transactions of a questionable nature with them, or who by their general conduct do not endeavour to inspire the sub-constables with proper respect for the position of constable, will be unfit for the rank they hold."

A few weeks later the order book recorded a notice which aptly summarized the duties of the Mounted Police, and which has held equally true ever since. "It is notified for general information that the government will make use of any person connected with the Force at any work that may be considered desirable."

Yet no matter how well the enthusiastic Commissioner might discipline his men, he soon realized that 150 were utterly inadequate to police 300,000 square miles of north-west prairies. So he went to Ottawa early in 1874 to persuade the government of the urgent need to increase the strength of the Force to the maximum of three hundred.

When French reached Ottawa he faced an awkward situation. Two days after the inauguration of the Force on November 3 of the previous year, the Conservative government of Sir John A. Macdonald had been defeated in the House of Commons over the Pacific scandal. The government had resigned, and Alexander Mackenzie became the next prime minister. Mackenzie was a strong advocate of prohibition. Whereas Macdonald's chief aim had been to prevent war between settlers and Indians, Mackenzie's was to suppress the whisky traffic in the Whoop-Up country. For a time Mackenzie contemplated using a military expedition instead of the police, and once again the fate of the Force hung in the balance. However, the organization continued, still under the authority of the minister of Justice, although in later years it would sometimes be controlled by other government departments.

It was March, 1874, when the new minister of Justice was given the authority to complete the organization of the Mounted Police at Lower Fort Garry, and to supply its three hundred members with the necessary equipment for an expedition into the North-West Territories.

By now the idea of scarlet-tunicked Mounted Police had captivated public fancy. In the spring of 1874 thousands of men responded to "recruits wanted" advertisements in eastern Canadian newspapers. From this swarm of eager applicants the recruiting officers chose a splendid group of two hundred well-developed men. The extra fifty were allowed to make up for the drop-outs and dismissals likely to occur in the three Divisions so hastily recruited a few months earlier. Most of this second group had some military experience, and some of them had served with the Royal Irish Constabulary. Their average age was about twenty-five years, with only one under twenty-one, fifteen-year-old Frederick A. Bagley, a trumpeter from Kingston.

Divisions "D," "E" and "F" were assembled at Toronto, on the site of the present Canadian National Exhibition grounds. In order to avoid the prairie rainy season they stayed on the Toronto lakefront during April and May. There the men were trained in mounted drill and in foot and arms drill, while Commissioner French himself did much of the organizational work.

On June 6 two special Grand Trunk Railway trains left Toronto, carrying the Commissioner, fifteen other officers, 201 constables and sub-constables, and 244 exceptionally fine horses. In order to avoid the laborious Dawson route the police had obtained permission to travel through the United States, on condition that they wear civilian clothes and that carbines, ammunition and officers' swords be packed in boxes. So the trains headed for Fargo, North Dakota, about 1,300 miles distant. From Fargo Divisions "D," "E" and "F" would march 160 miles north to Camp Dufferin, now Emerson, Manitoba, where they were scheduled to meet "A," "B" and "C."

As the troop trains pulled out of Toronto, military bands blared and cheering crowds waved an enthusiastic farewell to the civilian-clothed recruits, some of whom, fearful of Indian scalping, had shaved their heads. This unnecessary precaution cancelled out the initial glamour. All along the way people stared at the shorn heads protruding from train windows, and boys shouted, "Yoo-hoo, you jail birds!"

The second day out of Toronto, when the police stopped at the Chicago stockyards to allow their horses to feed in open corrals overnight, the trip became even less glamorous. Thousands of pigs wallowed in sties nearby as two officers and thirty men stood guard all night in a ceaseless rain and an almost unbearable stench.

En route from Toronto the troop trains picked up two cars of horses and nine cars of wagons, mowing machines and hayrakes, in addition to flour, bacon, pork and biscuits. Commissioner French also took on extra recruits, mostly at Chicago and St. Paul, in case of drop-outs at Dufferin. By this time the North-West Mounted Police included not only men from Canada (both English-speaking and French-speaking), from the British Isles and from the United States, but also from France, the Channel Islands, Jamaica, Germany and Bohemia.

Meanwhile, recruits recruited dogs. At one town a constable picked' up a stray dog. Immediately scores of others had to have dogs. At the next few train stops they combed streets and alleys, leaving the canine population of several towns somewhat depleted.

On the morning of June 12 the troop trains reached Fargo, North Dakota, and the Mounted Police seemed destined to remain there for some time. As they unloaded the freight cars they presented a picture of utter confusion. The transport wagons, the harness and even the saddles had been shipped in sections; the harness was of different makes; and sections of the knock down wagons had been distributed hapha- zardly along the line of freight cars. A huge field was strewn with a formidable jumble of parts, while men with little or no experience of horses and wagons tried in vain to assemble odd-sized boards as wagons, or to fit innumerable mismatched pieces of leather and metal rings into complete sets of harness.

But the Fargo traders, who by evening were calculating their profits from a police stop-over of at least a week, were disappointed. At four o'clock the next morning Commissioner French detailed squads to work at clearly defined tasks in four-hour shifts. At five o'clock that afternoon "D" Division left Fargo and headed for Dufferin with twenty-nine loaded wagons. Two hours later "E" Division left, and the next day "F" followed with all but the heaviest of the remaining stores, which would be shipped to Dufferin by Red River steamer.

As the Mounted Police moved northward, other troubles beset them. The horses were riding-horses, and many had never been hitched to vehicles. Some kicked and bucked, refusing to pull the wagons till the men soothed them and put their own shoulders to the wheels. Others galloped wildly over the prairie, their inexperienced drivers unable to stop them till troopers on horseback rounded them up.

The men suffered from the unusual heat of early summer and from prairie cholera. Two horses died of sunstroke. The mosquitoes fiercely attacked both men and horses. In fact Henri Julien, a Montreal correspondent-artist for the *Canadian Illustrated News* who was accompanying the police, reported facetiously that the insects were so fierce they could tear a mosquito net to pieces or put out a fire.

Nevertheless, on the evening of June 19 the three Divisions and their transport wagons reached Dufferin. This small border settlement consisted of a Hudson's Bay Company store, a depot of the International Boundary Commission, a few half-breed shacks, and as many saloons.

Divisions "A," "B" and "C" were already there, under the command of the former Inspector Macleod, who now held the recently created rank of assistant commissioner. Macleod, Scottish-born and Canadian-educated, had had both military experience and experience as a practising lawyer, and so was exceptionally well fitted for service with the Mounted Police. His Divisions had their own wagons, supplies and animals, as well as some half-breed guides and cattle herders.

At ten o'clock the night after "D," "E" and "F" arrived, a fierce thunderstorm suddenly burst on the police encampment. Forked lightning lit up the sky and deafening thunder shook the earth, while high winds lashed hail and rain to a stinging velocity. The scrawny western ponies, tethered in their usual picket lines, merely turned their backs to the prairie storm. But the sleek eastern horses, in their protective zareba of loaded wagons, were unaccustomed to such weather. They plunged about, terrified by the lightning and the storm noises, especially by the incessant flapping of the canvas wagon covers which had been ripped open by the first strong gusts of wind.

Steele, who was riding near the large corral, saw the whole incident. Lightning suddenly struck in the middle of the eastern horses. They snapped their halter ropes and charged wildly through the circle of heavily loaded wagons, trampling several to kindling. Dashing through a row of tents, they headed for the gate of the large field in which the police were camped. Nothing could halt them. The six guards who tried were trampled underfoot, one with his scalp gashed and pulled down over his forehead.

As the frenzied animals charged the gate they clambered over one another in horrible confusion, the screams of the injured rising above the howling cyclonic wind. The helpless police watched as they galloped across the Pembina bridge into North Dakota. Steele wrote later that the unforgettable night had "a weird and romantic complexion, typically suggestive of the Wild West." It might also have been the end of the Mounted Police if the horses had not been recaptured.

Sub-Inspector James Walker, Chief Constable J.B. Mitchell and others hurriedly saddled western broncos and rode with Steele all night after the stampeding creatures in the hope of recapturing them before the Sioux got them. Fortunately the eastern horses were still tired from their 160-mile march from Fargo. But even so, the police found some of them fifty miles from the camp. Within twenty hours they had herded most of them back to camp, and all but one of them were recovered later. Young trumpeter Bagley had ridden with the older men and was fast asleep in the saddle when his horse delivered him back to camp, so exhausted from twenty-four hours without food or rest that he had to be lifted down and put to bed.

During the next few days, while the eastern horses lay about scarcely moving, the police made final preparations for the great march west. Men who knew something of the unmarked wilderness to which they were going had warned Commissioner French that he would be forced to turn back, defeated. It was one thing for a small party to travel north-west over the well-travelled trails to the established Hudson's Bay Company posts. It was quite different for a large pioneer police force to head west into the wild, uncharted plains. French, however, refused to be daunted.

"Some of the Fort Garry croakers say we won't be back till Christmas, and experienced ones say we will lose forty percent of our horses!" he reported to Ottawa. "Be prepared!"

So the police continued to sort uniforms, arms, saddlery and stores and to pack them in wagons and oxcarts. They bought cattle to be slaughtered en route, others for breeding purposes, and about a hundred oxen for transport and farming. Extra troops from Divisions "D," "E" and "F" were transferred to bring "A," "B" and "C" up to strength. Finally each Division was assigned horses of a distinctive colour, and every man was detailed to look after a particular horse.

Bagley coveted an unusual buckskin with a black streak along its back, although he knew that another man had chosen it first. When the horses were assigned the young trumpeter arranged to be "guarding" it. He got the animal, also the reputation of being a horse thief.

During this period of final preparation Commissioner French ordered full-dress parades to help whip each Division into shape. Bagley wrote later describing one of them: "The parade was an inspiring sight with every man in new scarlet tunic; white, puggree-bound helmet, the loose ends hanging down each man's back, giving a rather 'Indian Mutiny' effect; the horses fresh and in splendid condition; the metal parts of the accoutrements burnished and glittering in the sun, and the artillery troop "C" with its nine-pounder M.L., steel guns and bright chestnut horses conspicuous in the middle of the column. ... This was the one and only occasion in the entire history of the Force that it was to be seen thus on ceremonial parade in full strength, fully equipped and every officer and man present (with the exception of the several left at the Stone Fort and those stationed at Fort Ellice), for within a few months the troops were scattered to the four points of the compass never again to be thus united."

The police mentioned by Bagley as being at Fort Ellice were Sub-Inspector A. Shurtliff and about ten men, sent from the Stone Fort to that prominent Hudson's Bay Company post to establish a detachment on the site chosen by the government for the headquarters of the new Force. According to the best available map, it was at the junction of the Assiniboine and the Qu'Appelle Rivers, approximately 190 miles north-west of Fort Garry and one hundred miles north of the international boundary. Fort Ellice was a converging point of important trails leading into the Territories, notably to Forts Carlton, Pitt and Edmonton. It also had the advantage of being connected to Winnipeg by a well-travelled cart trail.

Meanwhile, not everyone was as enthusiastic as Bagley. Many men had become despondent because of the badly cooked food, the mosquitoes, the heat, the news of Sioux scalpings just across the border, the rumours of danger ahead, and the nerve-racking wait for revolvers and other supplies. One by one they began to desert and cross into the U.S.

When the number of desertions reached thirty-one, Commissioner French called a full-dress parade. He addressed his men. Any who chose might leave at once, without reproach, but of those who stayed he would demand the utmost loyalty, even in the face of death. A few misfits left. But with the decision of the rest to stay, the Force took on new life. Desertions stopped, and the spirit of adventure reappeared. The aggravations continued, but they did not seem to matter as much.

At the beginning of July the revolvers ordered from England arrived at last, and Commissioner French set July 6 as the starting date for the march west. But departure was postponed when on that day he received a message from a United States army official saying that a large band of Sioux had raided the Métis settlement of St. Joseph (usually called St. Joe) in Dakota. The army official asked for the cooperation of the Mounted Police in cutting off the Indians if they attempted to cross into Canada.

In their first mounted patrol a large section of the Force, fully armed, rode to the place where the Sioux were most likely to cross the border. But the anticipated action did not occur. After a few hours they learned that the Indians had dispersed. Nevertheless, the men enjoyed the short-lived excitement, and morale was high as they rode back to camp to make final preparations during the next two days for the great march west.

Chapter 2
The Great March West
1874

To the accompaniment of bugle calls, cracking of whips and shouts of command, the astonishing two-mile-long cavalcade of North-West Mounted Police pulled out of Dufferin toward evening on July 8, 1874, and headed into the late afternoon sun for the foothills of the Rockies some eight hundred miles westward.

Division "A" took the lead, mounted on prancing dark bays. The men's scarlet Norfolk jackets, white helmets and white gauntlets contrasted vividly with the drab prairie background, while the officers' colourful helmet plumes and gold embroidery added further splendour. Swords, brass buttons and highly polished boots gleamed, while lance pennants fluttered in the breeze. After "A" rumbled thirteen supply wagons covered by great tarpaulins. The other five Divisions followed, equally glamorous and also followed by wagons, seventy-three in the whole cavalcade. "B" rode dark brown horses, "C" had bright chestnuts, "D" were on grays and buckskins, "E" on blacks, and "F" on light bays.

But the 275 officers and men of the North-West Mounted were pioneers as well as police. During their great march, and later wherever they settled, they would have to protect and provide for themselves. Two nine-pounder field guns, two mortars, and artillery and munition wagons augmented "C" Division. At the rear of the procession came 114 creaking Red River carts drawn by oxen; a large herd of cattle for slaughter; cows and calves; clanking mowing machines, ploughs and harrows; portable forges and field kitchens. The half-breed drivers, miraculously at least partly sober after a final spree in Dufferin, urged the plodding oxen forward with flamboyant curses.

The "pull-out" or "Hudson's Bay start" of July 8 allowed the police to make sure they had forgotten nothing important and that they were not too heavily loaded. After three miles they made camp by a little lake and satisfied themselves on the first point. But the next day Commissioner French sent two wagonloads of unnecessary baggage back to Dufferin, where oats were substituted. He also sent back under arrest an insubordinate officer, a political appointee, who threatened to acquaint Ottawa with the "deplorable handling of the Force."

That first night out, fifty oxen strayed away, and a number of still-nervous eastern horses stampeded. Meanwhile, with a heavy guard on duty in case of Indian attack, one over-zealous sentry paraded back and forth with carbine cocked. "Sir," he explained to an irate officer, "in such circumstances one cannot be too well prepared to fire."

During the next five months not only Commissioner French but others too kept diaries. John Peter Turner, the first official historian of the Force, organized them into a composite, vividly descriptive narrative in *The North-West Mounted Police*.

On July 9, both men and horses were tortured by clouds of mosquitoes, one horse died, and three broken-down wagons were left behind. On July 10, the mowing machines cut hay along the way, but the horses had to be sent across the Pembina River in United States territory for water. On July 11, the men had no dinner at noon, but the horses were watered at a creek. When they camped that evening, the nearest water was said to be fifteen miles away, so they did without any.

On July 12, Bagley, who with his buckskin pony was officially part of "D" Division, sounded reveille at 3:00 A.M. The men had no breakfast, and still no water. They started marching at 5:00 A.M., again beset by mosquitoes. Later in the day they endured a heavy thunderstorm with hail. Then an enormous swarm of grasshoppers, one of the many plaguing Manitoba that year, blackened the air to a height of several hundred feet. The ravenous insects devoured all grass, flowers and leaves, attacked the paint and wood of the wagons and carbines, penetrated the blanket rolls, and covered the drinking pools.

The next day the cavalcade got away soon after 3:00 A.M. Now the carts and wagons began to break down, causing many delays. The men tried to make up for it by travelling till eight in the evening. Then they camped at Calf Mountain, fifty-nine miles from Dufferin, and cut hay with the mowers before turning in.

The next day Pierre Léveillé, a well-known Métis and experienced plainsman, joined the column, accompanied by five other Métis. They brought with them six carts of presents sent as gifts to the Indians by Lieutenant-Governor Morris. Léveillé, hired in Dufferin as chief guide and interpreter for the march west, was a remarkable man, over six feet in his moccasins and weighing about three hundred pounds without an ounce of spare flesh. He was reputedly so strong that if his horse got stuck in the mud, he merely raised it by the tail and propelled it forward.

As the march continued, so did entries in the diaries. "Started at 4:00 A.M. and travelled twelve miles before breakfast. . . . Buffalo trails and wallows on all sides. . . . Left at 3:00 A.M. and twelve miles without water. . . . Many wagons and carts far behind. . . . Oat supply almost gone. . . . Two horses left behind, unfit for further travel. Rain all night; mosquitoes bad."

By July 19 many horses were too exhausted to go on. So for two days the dusty, travel-weary troops camped at their first crossing point of the meandering Souris River, where wood, water and grass were abundant. All oxen and carts reached camp by nightfall of the first day, but two more horses were left behind and two more died. The men repaired carts, shod horses at their portable forges, and enjoyed the luxury of bathing and washing their clothes.

Then they resumed the march, with progress possible chiefly because Commissioner French's insistence on strict discipline had made difficult things a habit. Often they got drinking water from muddy prairie sloughs by sinking a barrel with holes bored in its bottom. Even after the liquid was filtered it was the colour of ink. Frequently it was alkaline, and caused prairie cholera among men and animals. The men also became deathly ill from eating the flesh of tired cattle. Occasional hailstorms, actual and attempted stampedes by the still-nervous eastern horses, and numerous prairie fires added to the hardships. The two field guns made much extra work at every hill and river. The eastern horses, not used to prairie travel and food, failed so rapidly that the men dismounted and walked every alternate mile. Even then some animals had to be abandoned, or tended individually by sub-constables.

One youth, alarmed when his invalid charge lagged far behind the column, shot him. On overtaking the others he explained breathlessly that five blood-thirsty Sioux had attacked him and shot his horse. Commissioner French did not believe him, but there was no time to investigate.

On July 22 the Force made a second crossing of the Souris. Two days later, once more at the same river, Commissioner French called a halt just beyond La Roche Percée, near the present site of Estevan, Saskatchewan, 270 miles from Dufferin. Here the men again spent several busy but refreshing days, this time firing their forges with coal found on the river bank. On Sunday, July 26, they held their first church parade. "I was much pleased to hear many of the men singing hymns in the evening; unfortunately the language of many is by no means scriptural," French wrote.

The day after they made camp Assistant Surgeon R.B. Nevitt and a constable arrived from Dufferin with letters and papers, which included American newspaper reports that the North-West Mounted Police had been exterminated by the Sioux. French immediately wrote a careful report to the government, to be carried back to Dufferin. He stressed that his command was in "good health and high spirits," a pardonable inaccuracy under the circumstances.

At this camp near La Roche Percée, the Commissioner held a consultation with his senior officers. They reviewed the government's four-fold proposal. First, the whole Force was to march straight west to the foothills of the Rockies and to establish order there. Then one group of police would remain; a second group would march north to Fort Edmonton; and a third would return east to establish police headquarters at Fort Ellice, about a hundred miles north-north-east of La Roche Percée. Thus, the government had planned, the Canadian prairies could be thoroughly patrolled and policed by three groups of policemen, from three points forming an immense triangle.

Now, however, the Commissioner and his officers agreed that, burdened by dysentery-weakened men, failing horses and weary cattle, they could not accomplish even the march to the Rockies before winter set in, let alone the entire government plan. They decided that the experienced and popular Inspector W.D. Jarvis should take the greater part of Division "A" north-west to Edmonton by way of Fort Ellice, while the rest of the Force marched westward.

Most of the healthy men and horses of "A" were transferred to other Divisions. In their places Jarvis received some of the youngest and weakest men and the sickest horses. His "parade state" listed thirty-two police in all, including Sub-Inspector Shurtliff who had recently arrived from Fort Ellice detachment; Chief Constable Steele; and Sub-Inspector Sévère Gagnon, who kept a comprehensive account of the whole march in his French-language diary.

On August 1, with the sick men driving the wagons, and thirteen half-breeds driving the carts, the depleted Division "A" set out for Fort Edmonton, almost nine hundred miles away by trail. In addition to the fifty-five sick horses there were five in reasonably good condition, seventy-four oxen and cattle, fifty-seven oxcarts, twenty-six wagons, fifty-two cows and forty-five calves. There were also agricultural implements and general stores not deemed essential to the main body of the Force, one item of the latter being more than 25,000 pounds of flour.

At first, although the police changed horses twice each morning and afternoon, Jarvis and his contingent sometimes made only eight to ten miles a day. The foot-sore cows and calves lay down every few yards and had to be prodded on. Horses collapsed and two had to be abandoned. But as the half-breed guide, walking beside his little pony and cart, led them farther north, they came to gently rolling country covered with luxuriant grass, and the animals gained strength.

At Fort Ellice, Inspector Jarvis left the very sick men, some exhausted horses, most of the cows and calves, and a large quantity of supplies. Sub-Inspector Shurtliff and his detachment also stayed, under orders to build detachment quarters there on the north bank of the Assiniboine River. Incidentally, because Fort Ellice was so accessible to "civilization," Mrs. Shurtliff was there with her husband.

On August 18, after a few days rest, Jarvis, Gagnon, Steele and the others pushed on with their carts, wagons and animals. This part of Division "A"'s journey was the only one of the whole march west in which any of the police met many travellers. Jarvis and his men were now travelling along the sole "highway" between Red River and the Rockies, the main cart trail from Fort Garry (Winnipeg) to Forts Carlton, Pitt and Edmonton. As was usual for that time of year, most of the travellers they met were going east in anticipation of winter. There were brigades of carts loaded with buffalo robes, dried meat and pemmican, all driven by hunters, freighters and traders heading for Fort Garry. Other chance-met east-bound travellers included the Reverend George McDougall, noted pioneer Methodist minister, and his wife, and some Roman Catholic priests. One of the latter had visited Commissioner French's west-going column a few weeks earlier, and he told Jarvis that French's horses were in no better condition than his own.

In spite of all difficulties, however, Jarvis's contingent had its lighter moments. For instance, after the evening meal one of the half-breeds would get out his fiddle, and the others would take turns dancing the "Red River Jig" on a door they had carted along for the purpose.

Among the police considerable amusement revolved about an Irish sub-constable who had been brought up by two maiden aunts and who made a note in his diary of any strong language he overheard. One morning as his team struggled up a steep hill, the fiery-tempered Inspector Jarvis came along and encouraged them with a few earthy phrases. The Irishman sprang from the driver's seat, dropped to one knee and scribbled furiously in his little book. The other men laughed uproariously, but luckily the inspector had moved on.

The men needed such touches of humour. On September 8 they took all day to cross the south branch of the Saskatchewan River with the aid of a cable-ferry already established there. The cattle were forced to swim. Three days later, on reaching Fort Carlton, about three hundred miles from Fort Ellice, some of the horses were completely exhausted. "If they were not government property, but my own, I would shoot the worst," Jarvis said.

It took from September 15 to September 20 to cross the north branch of the Saskatchewan, using a scow ferry, and with some of the cattle swimming again. By early October the cold nights of approaching winter stiffened the horses so critically that the men had to get up several times each night to rub them, losing their own sleep and becoming exhausted in the process.

On October 19 Jarvis and his pitiful procession reached Victoria, about eight hundred miles from La Roche Percée. There they left behind all the cows and calves and eleven oxen, arranging with the trader in charge of the post there to care for them during the winter.

Then "A" Division forced itself to continue the march, with Fort Edmonton still one hundred miles distant. Constant rain turned the trail to mud, then under Sub-Inspector Gagnon's leadership they built corduroy roads before them. Where the lowest spots became sloughs, the men unloaded the wagons and hauled them across by hand. Then they carried the supplies over on horseback, reloaded the wagons and pushed on. In other places Gagnon and his men built bridges over impassable waters.

For five hundred miles the animals had had almost no grain and very little pasture, and now the failing horses could not rise in the morning, or they collapsed as they marched. One fell at least a dozen times, and each time Steele and two other men raised him with a pole under his belly. Other horses, crazed with fever, staggered to the ponds to drink, then fell motionless at the edge and could only be dragged out with ropes.

"They were living skeletons," Jarvis reported later.

Some of the men, too, were little better than skeletons. But during the last few days of October and the first two days of November, 1,255 miles from Fort Garry, Division "A" of the North-West Mounted Police straggled into Fort Edmonton. There they obtained warm winter quarters from the Hudson's Bay Company, which had a substantial post there. And gradually men and animals regained health and vigour.

Meanwhile, Commissioner French and the other five Divisions, plus the remainder of "A," freed of invalids and cattle, had continued their westward march from La Roche Percée, 270 miles west of Dufferin.

As they left on the evening of July 29 their destination was, in general, the foothills of the Rockies some four hundred miles distant. More specifically, they aimed for the junction of the Bow and Belly

(South Saskatchewan) rivers. There, the Commissioner had been led to believe, he would find the notorious Fort Whoop-Up and the outlaw whisky traders who had finally sparked the formation of his police force. There, too, he had been told, he would find plenty of rich grazing land, suitable to support a strong police post.

A few miles out of La Roche Percée the Boundary Road crossed into the United States. It was a sore point with French that although the government had originally told him to follow this road, they had changed his instructions just as he was about to leave Dufferin. Even the Palliser map he had been told to follow had proved to be inaccurate. And now the police had the additional problem of blazing their own trail through Canadian territory. Guided by Léveillé and other Métis they headed north-west to miss the border mountains. Then on August 3 Léveillé reported that they had reached territory the guides did not know.

Fortunately the Commissioner had studied navigation, so he continually checked the direction of march by stars and compass. He also checked his mileage by the odometer which was fastened to a wheel of his own vehicle. This cross-country navigation meant much extra work, as he had to take angles at every turn of the route from dawn to dark. At noon halt, when most men dozed to make up for their lack of sleep caused by the early starts, Commissioner French had to be on the alert to take the altitude of the sun and to find his latitude. At night he often had to wait up till one or two in the morning to obtain the magnetic variation by the polestar.

This main contingent of the Mounted Police, like Jarvis and his men, suffered constant hardships. Dust and overpowering heat plagued both men and animals. Bagley's lips became so parched and swollen that he could not sound the bugle calls. Worn-out horses lagged far behind the main column, which was often strung out for four or five miles. One night rockets were fired as a signal to a missing man who had wandered too far in search of ducks, and this set off a brief stampede among some of the eastern horses.

By the beginning of August twenty-two men suffered from dysentery. The wood supply for kitchen use began to give out. One night a violent storm blew most of the tents down. On August 6 they reached hilly country, and the next day, when the temperature was ninety-one degrees, a party of men with oxen had to go back to pull up the guns, which were too much for the weakened horses.

During the next few days, in the region of Old Wives Lakes and Old Wives Creeks, some 150 miles from La Roche Percée, the five Divisions met double trouble. Alkaline water caused such severe dysentery that the Commissioner left invalid men and horses behind at Cripple Camp. Also, the troops became infested with lice while camping on a deserted Indian campsite, and since it takes only a few days for a louse to become a great-grandparent, no one escaped the plague.

Here, too, the police were disillusioned at the sight of their first band of Indians, a dejected, verminous tribe of Sioux with matted hair and filthy blankets, probably the Indians whose campsite they had occupied. Nevertheless the police and the Sioux met at a formal pow-wow, and later Surgeon J. Kittson held a sick parade and treated about twenty Indians.

As the main body of the Force continued westward over undulating plains covered with the ashes of recent prairie fires, the only scenery was an occasional small bush or a scattering of buffalo bones. At night they camped by water holes swarming with mosquitoes, and used buffalo chips for fuel.

By August 24 they were on the borders of the Blackfoot country, which the Métis warned them was dangerous. "Among the men there was now keen anticipation of adventure, attended by the zest of potential danger," wrote Turner. "Except for the staccato cries of the Métis cart drivers, the thud of hoofs and creak of saddlery, there were long spells of silence in which no one spoke, but rode with reins lying loose, each turning his head slowly from side to side as he searched the plain for any hostile moves."

Then, in sight of the Cypress Hills, about 590 miles from Dufferin, they stopped to repair equipment and to shoe horses and oxen. While halting at this place, the men's anticipation of adventure was heightened still more when several half-breeds visited the police camp and told hair-raising stories of Fort Whoop-Up. This halt also gave Assistant Commissioner Macleod and Sub-Inspector Walker time to return from their trip with twenty-seven oxcarts and Métis drivers to a nearby depot of the Boundary Commission survey party for that party's surplus oats and provisions.

Marching on again, the men thrilled to their first close-up of great herds of buffalo. In the hunt that followed, the Commissioner, Pierre Léveillé, Julien and others each killed one, thus producing 1,720 pounds of meat. Soon the men were enjoying their first boiled buffalo steak, of which digestible meat they each ate ten pounds daily for the next few days. Assistant Commissioner Macleod was so impressed by the majestic animals, picturesque as well as palatable, that he suggested using the buffalo head on the North-West Mounted Police uniform buttons, a suggestion which was adopted a few years later.

But the buffalo were also a menace. Their immense, ever-moving herds were almost impenetrable, and for days the police cavalcade travelled precariously among them. Sometimes they were forced to line up transport wagons to head off a stampede of the ponderous creatures. Besides, the great animals ate every blade of grass and trampled the water holes to a thick paste of gumbo.

The consequent scarcity of water and grass weakened the already weary horses. Each day more horses died, while exhausted and dying oxen lay strewn far behind the plodding cavalcade. One bitterly cold and rainy night in early September, five horses dropped dead and three others almost collapsed. After that the Commissioner ordered every officer and man to give up one blanket to a horse and to double up with a comrade to keep warm. But still the animals wasted away and died. The march was becoming a disaster.

To make matters worse, a new guide who had insisted he knew the way had misled the Force. Many of the men thought he was a spy for the whisky traders, deliberately misleading them. In any case, the cavalcade did not reach the forks of the Bow and Belly rivers as he had promised, and for all practical purposes could be considered lost. When Commissioner French turned to his own carefully kept records, he discovered that the guide had led them one day's march off course, too far to the north. From that point the Commissioner himself did the guiding and got them back on course. But the difficulties continued.

"I am beginning to feel very much alarmed for the safety of the Force," Commissioner French wrote in his diary. It was the first time he had admitted it.

A few days later, however, they did reach the forks of the Bow and Belly rivers. But contrary to expectation, the place contained neither Fort Whoop-Up nor any rich grazing land. Obviously it would be futile to establish a police post there. French decided, rightly, that the information he had been given, like the map, was incorrect. He sent out reconnaissance parties which reported the alarming news that for eighty miles north-west and for thirty miles west there was neither grass nor trail. Also, the buffalo were approaching from the west in thousands.

The only possible route was south to the well-wooded Sweet Grass Hills some fifty miles away, near the American border. There men and animals could rest. And while the Divisions rested, Commissioner French could go to Fort Benton, Montana, to buy supplies and to contact the Canadian government by telegraph. Then, refreshed and re-supplied, Divisions "B," "C" and "F" could continue west, and "D" and "E" could return east to establish police headquarters.

So the cavalcade of tattered men, jaded horses and dying oxen turned south, aiming toward the Sweet Grass Hills. By now the men were walking most of the time to spare the horses, and some whose boots had fallen apart had wrapped their feet in sacks. Rations consisted of little more than fresh game, flour, and dried sliced potatoes. Fats and grease were so scarce that one man who found a can of machine oil left by the boundary surveyors doled it out to himself a few precious drops at each meal, adamantly refusing to share it with his comrades.

By mid-September ice covered the prairie ponds. The men dreaded that an early snow would cover the dried buffalo chips and deprive them of fuel. Worse still, a severe cold spell would kill the weakened animals and the men would have no transport. Now the ragged command plodded forward desperately on sheer nerve, while horses and oxen staggered woodenly forward or dropped out along the trail, nine horses dead and five oxen abandoned in one thirty-six hour period. And always, except for the three conspicuous landmarks of the Sweet Grass Hills in the distance, the same unbroken horizon seemed to move ahead of them. Sub-Inspector Cecil E. Denny wrote in his diary: "Can't go much farther."

Yet still the motley procession of weakened men and animals crept forward, and on September 18 they neared the Sweet Grass Hills. Hope revived even the most exhausted men as they had their first view of the glittering snow-capped Rockies a hundred miles westward.

"Haggard, tired and thirsty, the dismounted, weary horsemen . . . strained forward," says Turner. "Shouldering and pulling at the labouring wheels, stumbling and lurching, swearing and cheering . . . the vanguard of ordered sovereignty on the plains lashed its dying energy to final effort."

Later that day, except for the oxen left behind to rest, the last stragglers of the eight-mile stretch of "tattered divisions of the once brilliant array" arrived at the Sweet Grass Hills. As young Bagley limped toward the inviting spot he pulled off his worn, stiffened boots to relieve his painfully blistered feet. Sub-Inspector Walker heaved the boy to his huge shoulders and carried him pickaback the rest of the way.

There at the Sweet Grass Hills the exhausted contingent rested for a few days. Then, according to plan, Assistant Commissioner Macleod, Divisions "B," "C" and "F," plus the remnants of "A," prepared to continue westward to set up a police post in the vicinity of the whisky traders. Later, when it was convenient, the men of "A" Division would go north to Edmonton to rejoin Inspector Jarvis.

Also according to plan, Commissioner French and Divisions "D" and "E" prepared to return east to establish police headquarters at Fort Ellice. So French selected the best horses and oxen for "D" and "E" in anticipation of hundreds of miles more of a grueling march, and assigned all unnecessary stores and equipment to "B," "C" and "F."

A few days after reaching the Sweet Grass Hills the Commissioner, the assistant commissioner, Léveillé and seven others, plus several Métis with empty carts, left for Fort Benton some 160 miles to the southeast in Montana. Their large purchases of oats, provisions, socks, gloves and moccasins there were no surprise to the trading companies. For although the police had watched in vain for the notorious and powerful Blackfeet, those Indians had stalked them for weeks, then had spread the news of the red-coat pony-soldiers "thick as ants on a hill."

While at Benton, Commissioner French learned from Ottawa that when he returned east he was to establish headquarters not at Fort Ellice, but about one hundred miles north of it, at Livingston on the Swan River, where contractors were already erecting police buildings. Also while at Benton, he learned from the I.G. Baker Trading Company that Fort Whoop-Up was at the forks of the Belly and St. Mary's rivers, some seventy miles north-west of the Sweet Grass Hills. That trading company, probably anticipating more profitable returns from a large party of police than from a few whisky traders, urged French to "clean up" Fort Whoop-Up. Commissioner French left Fort Benton ahead of the others to join Divisions "D" and "E" which had already begun the trek back east, heading for Livingston and the Swan River.

As the other police left Benton to return to Canada they were accompanied by Jerry Potts, a half-Peigan, half-Scots plainsman with an uncanny sense of direction even in country he scarcely knew. Commissioner French had engaged him as scout and interpreter, chiefly to guide the police to Fort Whoop-Up, but Potts subsequently served with the police for twenty-two years. He now led Assistant-Commissioner Macleod and his party back to the Sweet Grass Hills. En route, Denny and twenty men camped at the Milk River crossing to await the coming of the I.G. Baker Company's bull teams with the supplies purchased at Benton.

A few days later Potts led Macleod and Divisions "B," "C" and "E" on an easy march to Fort Whoop-Up. At last three Divisions of the Mounted Police were in the depths of the untamed west. But Jerry Potts soon dispelled their expectations of daring whisky traders and wild Indians. Most of the trading outfits, he said, had left for winter quarters in Missouri when they had learned that the Force was approaching. And the Blackfeet, in opulence after the season's trading, were not inclined to fight, except perhaps their hereditary enemies, the Crees and the Assiniboines.

On October 9, Potts led Macleod and his men to the high ground overlooking the notorious fortress between the two rivers. There was no sign of life below, where the palisaded, bastioned Fort Whoop-Up was flying what the men thought was the Stars and Stripes. But Macleod ordered the two nine-pounder field guns and the two mortars to be placed in strategic positions. Then with rifles loaded and ready, and everyone silent and intent, Macleod's horsemen moved toward the fort. They expected soon to receive an order to dismount and deploy.

"But," wrote Turner, "Macleod rode straight ahead, Potts at his side. There were murmurs of amazement as the assistant commissioner dismounted and strode toward the open main gate. Entering and going to the nearest building within the enclosure, he rapped on the door."

After Macleod's continued knocking, the door was opened by an uncouth, gray-haired man. Dave Akers nonchalantly invited the police to "come right in" and make themselves at home. All the whisky traders had left the place long ago, he said, and the northern manager of the I.G. Baker Company was using the old fort as his own base. The manager was away, but they were very welcome.

It was an anticlimax. Actually, long before Macleod and his men drew near the ill-reputed fort, a party of buffalo hunters had warned the traders that a large party of horsemen wearing red coats was approaching. The style of trading had been altered accordingly, and a thorough police search of the building revealed no liquor.

From Whoop-Up, Jerry Potts led Divisions "B," "C" and "F" to a place on the Old Man's River which he advised would be suitable for a permanent police post. There at ten o'clock on the morning of October 13, Macleod ordered the troops to make camp.

"If you want to write home," a staff constable announced, "now is your chance. Your address is c/o North-West Mounted Police, Camp Macleod, North-West Territories, via Benton, Montana." Then, letters written, the men began chopping down cottonwood trees with which to build Fort Macleod.

By this time Commissioner French and Divisions "D" and "E" had marched several hundred miles back eastward, headed for the forks of the Swan and Snake Rivers, and spurred on by the Commissioner's fear that an early winter would overtake the weary troops dressed mostly in threadbare summer clothing. At Cripple Camp, they had picked up the former invalids, by then completely recovered, and in spite of continuing difficulties they neared the Swan River toward the end of October.

But when the Commissioner rode ahead to Livingston, to inspect the new Swan River barracks about which Ottawa had notified him, he was utterly dismayed. He found unfinished buildings strung out for a thousand feet on top of the biggest ridge of granite boulders in the district. The unseasoned wood had shrunk, and daylight filtered through the innumerable cracks. Not a tree protected the place from biting north winds. Besides there was neither accommodation nor equipment for all the men, and Shurtliff, who had arrived from Fort Ellice, reported that half the hay which had been cut for winter use had been burned by prairie fires.

French ordered the men to remain nearby at the Hudson's Bay Company post at Fort Pelly where there was good grass, while he and his senior officers held a board of inquiry. As a result, Division "E," the sick men, and all the weak animals remained to winter as best they could at Fort Pelly or at Swan River barracks.

Then on October 24 the Commissioner and the rest marched on again, heading for Winnipeg, where French presumed he could conveniently winter his men and animals. By now the prairie was covered with wind-driven snow, but "D" Division and the strongest horses and oxen marched steadfastly on, by way of Fort Ellice. By the time they arrived in Winnipeg on November 7, one man had worn out two pairs of boots and twelve pairs of moccasins since he left Dufferin in July.

French was very bitter about the Swan River barracks scandal, especially when he heard that the government had paid the contractors $30,000, a huge sum in 1874, while the Mounted Police had been forced to practise the strictest economy. His cutting remarks made him so unpopular at Winnipeg that the authorities there decided there was no accommodation available. They sent him on to Dufferin.

"D" Division was back where it started. Its oxen and horses had died. Its men had gone hungry, had drunk filtered mud, had worn their clothes to shreds and had grown desperately weak from dysentery. Yet they had maintained admirable discipline and in four months had marched 1,959 miles, an average of slightly more than nineteen miles a day. They had done this at first stifled by the dust and ashes of prairie fires in temperatures reaching one hundred degrees in the shade, and finally trudging through snowdrifts at thirty degrees below zero.

The achievements of the other five Divisions were similarly remarkable. Although the "Old Originals" had not accomplished precisely what the government had proposed, they had accomplished an amazing amount of it. Moreover, the march itself was a unique achievement.

In Commissioner French's first Annual Report to the government he commented with feeling on the details of the great march, the longest on record of a force carrying its own supplies. It was all the more notable since, as he pointed out, its members were "tied down by no stringent rules or articles of war, but only by the silken cord of a civil contract."

"Of such a march, under such adverse circumstances," he wrote, "all true Canadians may well be proud."

Chapter 3
The Prairie Outposts
1874–1875

Toward the end of October, 1874, less than two weeks after they camped beside the Old Man's River and began to build Fort Macleod, Divisions "B," "C" and "F" struck their first blow at the liquor traffic in the North-West Territories.

Assistant Commissioner Macleod learned from the Indian Three Bulls that he had given two horses in exchange for two gallons of whisky from a trader operating from a post about fifty miles north. The trader, William Bond, was described by Macleod as a "coloured man" who also acted as guide and interpreter, and later by Turner as a Mexican half-breed. Macleod told Jerry Potts to get all the information he could and to arrange to meet Three Bulls on the road the next evening.

The following day at dusk Inspector N.L.F. Crozier, with ten picked men and with Jerry Potts as guide, rode out of Fort Macleod. They kept the rendezvous with Three Bulls, then they all headed north along trails covered by the snow of early winter. Although Crozier had chosen the best horses from the three Divisions, they were in such poor condition that one broke down after only a few miles and had to be sent back to the camp, where it later died from paralysis. But the rest of the little party pushed on for forty-five miles. Then, turning to follow a trail which the keen-eyed Potts had detected, they came upon Bond and four white men with sixteen horses and two heavily loaded wagons.

"Halt! In the name of the Queen!" Crozier shouted.

Cursing, the outnumbered traders obeyed. Then the police searched the wagons and found several cases of alcohol, five Henry rifles, five revolvers and 116 buffalo robes.

The police took the traders and their wagons to Fort Macleod and charged all five with possession of intoxicating liquor. Assistant Commissioner Macleod tried them, while all the inspectors sat with him on the cases to profit by his experience as a lawyer. All five accused were found guilty and fined heavily. Later the police destroyed their whisky, and Macleod confiscated their illegally obtained robes in accord with previous instructions from Commissioner French.

The next day a Fort Benton trader paid the fines of the white men, but not of Bond, who had been found guilty of the additional charge of selling liquor to Three Bulls. So Bond, who could not pay the full amount of his fine even after the police sold his horse, rifle and revolver, all of which they had confiscated, had to stay at the police post to serve a jail term. But the police had no jail to put him in, and they were too busy building the fort to keep a strict guard. So the first convicted prisoner of the Mounted Police was also the first to escape. Macleod refused to risk ill-conditioned horses in pursuing him. But he did not get far. In the spring his frozen body was found nearby. Meanwhile, those policemen responsible for Bond's escape were sentenced to a term of imprisonment.

Although the police began their drive against whisky traders so soon after arriving at the site of Fort Macleod, their chief concern during the first few weeks was to erect the fort itself. For this they used the only materials at hand, cottonwood logs and mud.

When early November blizzards set in, Macleod ordered the makeshift buildings for the sick men to be finished first. Such an order was necessary, since the men had not yet recovered from the strain of the great march and fell easy prey to sickness, especially to severe colds. As many as forty-five men, almost one-third of the total, were certified by the police surgeon as unfit for duty in one day. After the sick men's temporary quarters were completed, stables for the horses were to be built, then men's quarters and, finally, shelter for the officers.

So men and officers, then officers alone, lived in tents in the woods in below-zero weather, while seven days a week they chopped, hauled, hammered and plastered. Chinking between the logs with mud had to be done without gloves, but only if the temperature dropped lower than ten degrees below zero did the police-pioneers leave mudding for another job.

Threadbare clothes added to the general discomfort. Sentries belted blankets about themselves and tied raw buffalo skin around their boots to hold them together. Then an ex-tailor saw Indian women making moccasins from buffalo hides and volunteered to try to make clothes the same way. The first outfit of coat and pants, moccasins, cap and mitts for the guard, was made of the buffalo robes confiscated from Bond and his comrades. Soon many officers and men were wearing similar warm garments made of skins confiscated from whisky traders or purchased from the Indians, and with caps and mitts lined with red flannel transferred for this purpose from "Indian Supplies" to "Police Stores."

Meanwhile the thirty-eight-year-old Macleod held friendly meetings with the Indians, paving the way for the forthcoming treaties. For several weeks, lesser chiefs of the Bloods and Peigans visited Fort Macleod, but the powerful Blackfeet held aloof. The police made no advance to them, but merely continued the fort's construction, dealt fairly with any cases of crime, raided whisky traders' posts, and began to collect customs duties on traders' imported goods.

Then on December 1 Chief Crowfoot of the Blackfeet called on Stamixotokan, or Bull's Head, as the Indians had already named the assistant commissioner (because of the buffalo head over his door or because of the Macleod crest in the Glengarry cap he sometimes wore). The noble chieftain in the deerskin jacket covered with black lines recording battle victories was favourably impressed by the gracious officer in scarlet and gold. And when Macleod reported the meeting to Commissioner French he wrote: "All the Indians I have so far met appear to be a very intelligent lot of men."

A few days later Crowfoot returned, bringing all the chiefs of the Blackfeet, Bloods and Peigans for a pow-wow. Interpreter Jerry Potts introduced each blanketed, befeathered chief in turn to the assistant commissioner. After a series of handshakes and formal greetings they sat in a circle, then Potts used the traditional buffalo chip to light the peace pipe. The Indians solemnly puffed it and passed it all round, then turned expectantly to the tall, erect officer.

"I come from the Great White Queen," Macleod told them via Potts. "I come in friendship." Then he explained that the police would remain at Fort Macleod and would establish law and order over the prairies. They had not come to steal the Indians' land, he said, and when the government wanted any land it would send men to discuss the matter with the Indians and to make treaties.

Crowfoot, reputedly the wisest and mightiest of the chiefs, expressed approval. Others said they were glad the redcoats were driving away whisky traders who robbed them of their wives, their horses and their robes, and whose fire-water caused much trouble.

"Before you came the Indian crept along in fear," one chief said, crouching down and moving along awkwardly. "Now," he continued, springing upright, "he is not afraid to walk erect." And when the Indians left the fort they spread the news that the stalwart officer of the White Queen was truly the red man's friend.

Jerry Potts's unique background made him invaluable at such pow-wows. He was the son of an educated Scots trader at Fort Benton and a Peigan woman. When he was about sixteen a vagrant Blackfoot Indian killed his father. The boy galloped deep into Blackfoot country after the murderer and stabbed him to death in revenge. The Blackfeet, greatly impressed, accepted Jerry as one of themselves. He became a leader, emerging from one bloody battle with nineteen scalps dangling at his belt.

Yet Potts spoke little of his adventures or, indeed, of anything else.

"What's beyond that hill?" an inquisitive officer asked him as he guided the police effortlessly through the foothills to the site of Fort Macleod.

"'N'udder hill," Potts answered.

As a trailer and scout, however, Potts was superlative. The short, slope-shouldered plainsman could find his way through blinding storms or blackest night, and seemed able to smell water at five miles. Above all, his priceless value to the police came from his integrity and loyalty. No matter how difficult or dangerous a situation might be, Potts was always on hand to help, and his influence among the Indians often suppressed bickering that might easily have led to bloodshed and war.

By mid-December, Fort Macleod was almost completed, and a village had grown up nearby. There were stores and even a log billiard room set up by the I.G. Baker Company, by T.C. Power and Brother, and by others. Supplies and mail arrived, irregularly but surely, in great wagons drawn by long lines of oxen or mules, and mail went out the same way. Now that the police had arrived, a more orderly existence was possible. Plainsmen travelled freely with peace of mind, missionaries pushed into new territory, and the first settlers arrived.

The varied and scattered populace beyond the limits of the village depended mainly on the buffalo for their livelihood. Large herds of these shaggy creatures still provided both Indians and whites with their chief sustenance, and the traders with skins and robes for the Benton market.

On Christmas Day, 1874, the police at Fort Macleod demonstrated their friendliness to the Indians by inviting the chiefs and headmen of the district to a great feast. Then they entertained their guests with an exhibition of military skills. When they made a tree disappear by shooting a cannon at it, the Indians were impressed by their great medicine. The festivities ended with a dance.

"Fiddles, harmonicas and voices joined in light-hearted celebration," wrote Turner. "High boots and beaded moccasins swept the hard earth floors, and in reel and jig the extremes of life were forgotten amid an unburdening of frontier mirth." Draped in decorations above the mess room door hung a motto which, if used a century later in a film, would have been scoffed at as "too Hollywood." The motto read: "The Pioneers of a Glorious Future."

On New Year's Eve the officers of Fort Macleod gathered in their low-ceilinged mess room across whose mud floor the indentation of a buffalo trail could still be traced. As they waited to welcome the New Year they considered the achievements of Divisions "B," "C" and "F."

They had completed Fort Macleod. Like many trading posts of the time it was built as a nearly square enclosure, with heavy-timbered living quarters, workshops, stores, stables, a hospital and a blacksmith's shop, all facing inward. Inside the square stood the two nine-pounder guns from the East, a powder magazine and a flag staff.

In addition to Fort Macleod they had established two outlying detachments which had collected $3,000 in customs duties. They had won the Indians' friendship and respect. And their diligence had driven the whisky peddlers at least temporarily from the great southern plains of Canada.

But Assistant Commissioner Macleod was still beset by troubles. The government had sent neither pay-money nor the promised new clothing. Uniforms had been patched and patched again until they had worn to shreds. Underwear was now in rags. Sentries wrapped themselves in blankets as protection from the bitter cold. Men were forced to go into debt to the traders, who sold clothing at exorbitant prices. Lice were such a plague that one evening the men had refused to "fall in" until excused from fatigues long enough to sterilize their clothes, which they did by boiling them in salt water and hanging them out to freeze. The men grew more disgruntled because they had received no mail from home since leaving Dufferin the previous summer.

In vain Macleod sent letters and telegrams by police riders to Benton for relay to Ottawa. It seemed that the government in its comfortable and civilized surroundings had completely forgotten the police. At last, in desperation, men began to desert.

"Eighteen have deserted for want of pay," Macleod wired to Ottawa. Then paradoxically, to stress the grimness of the situation, he added: "If paid many more will desert."

Only then did Ottawa reply. In mid-March they instructed the exasperated assistant commissioner to go to Helena, Montana. In that frontier town, colourful mining centre and state capital, he could get money from a certain bank. While there he should also make plans for the possible apprehension and extradition of the men who had massacred the Assiniboine Indians in the Cypress Hills in 1873.

Helena, three hundred miles to the south, could be reached only by crossing the forbidding Bad Lands. Worse still, it was a particularly bad time of the winter, the season the Blackfeet believed invoked evil. The government at Ottawa had no way of knowing conditions, and if it had known it would probably have expected Macleod to wait until later.

But the hardy pioneering Scot, who cared intensely for his men, decided not to wait. He, Sub-Inspector Denny, two other police and Jerry Potts mounted their native saddle horses and set out. Two pack horses carried blankets, buffalo robes, boiled bacon, hardtack, tea and oats. The first night they halted at Fort Whoop-Up, and in the morning two brilliant "sundogs" foretold bad weather. Their host Dave Akers warned them to wait, but Macleod and Potts preferred to move on.

The whole trip was a nightmare. A fierce blizzard blew up, and they would have frozen in their saddles if Jerry Potts had not led them to a deep ravine with a cut bank. There they used their hunting knives to dig a cave in the hard-banked snowdrifts and huddled in it for thirty-six hours.

Bitter cold of fifty-five degrees below zero forced the police party on. The wind blew so furiously that even after the snow stopped they often could not distinguish one another or even see their horses' heads. Macleod's face froze badly. The exhausted and stiffened sub-constable wanted to be left behind and had to be urged forward constantly. Denny went snowblind and froze a foot. It was impossible to make a fire so they ate cold bacon. But somehow they staggered after Potts, who led them uncannily on through the swirling snow even after he went partially snowblind.

At last the storm broke. They reached a traders' outpost, then the American military post Fort Shaw. Denny stayed there until he recovered. The others moved on to Helena and took rooms at a hotel, where they were later joined by Denny.

After spending several weeks at Helena while telegrams sped back and forth between Macleod and Ottawa, the little police party travelled homeward in the comparative comfort of approaching spring. Macleod had obtained $30,000 from the bank and the mail from the post office. The money probably accounted, at least partly, for the fact that a few of the earlier deserters willingly went back with him. As for the men at Fort Macleod, they soon felt happier, jingling coins in their pockets and exchanging gossip which had come in the mail from home.

While Macleod was in Helena he had reported to Ottawa what he had learned since reaching the West about the Hardwick gang, the Benton murderers of the Assiniboine Indians at the Cypress Hills. He also had planned for their arrest and extradition. Soon afterwards, in accord with Macleod's plans, the government specially appointed Lieutenant-Colonel A.G. Irvine, formerly commandant of the garrison of Red River, as an inspector in the Mounted Police. Then they sent him to work undercover in Montana to accumulate more evidence and witnesses.

Subsequently the government laid extradition charges against fourteen of the alleged murderers. In July a hearing of five of them took place in Helena, with Macleod and Irvine present.

Although the American authorities were keen to bring the murderers to justice, feeling in Montana ran high against the Canadians. In fact, many white Montanans seemed to believe that the massacre had been necessary to keep the Indians in their place. Inside and outside the courtroom, rough, threatening frontiersmen seemed ready to riot on behalf of their local heroes. Even the district attorney, hired by Canada to conduct the prosecution, openly favoured them. But the greatest difficulty arose from the fact that although the witnesses for Canada, including Abel Farwell and his Indian wife, told horrible stories of the killings, the accused swore that they had been attacked by the Indians and forced to defend themselves. With such conflicting evidence, United States Commissioner Cullen had no choice but to refuse extradition.

Then one of the accused, probably exhilarated by the verdict as well as by the ever-flowing liquor, charged Macleod with false imprisonment. The assistant commissioner was arrested and placed in custody. But he immediately applied to Chief Justice D.S. Wade of Helena for his own discharge. The chief justice ruled that Macleod had acted correctly on behalf of the Canadian government and with the approval of the United States government. Macleod was released and the police party returned to Canada.

Later that year, when several others of the same Hardwick gang imprudently crossed into Canadian territory, the police from Forts Walsh and Macleod arrested them. Then Inspector Irvine, accompanied by Pierre Léveillé as guide and Abel Farwell as witness, escorted three of them across the vast plains to distant Winnipeg for trial. But again conflicting testimony resulted in acquittals.

In May, 1875, "B" Division left Fort Macleod and headed for the Cypress Hills, with saddles arranged to accommodate blankets and overcoats, and with supply wagons well loaded. Three weeks later, under the command of the forceful Inspector J.M. Walsh, they founded Fort Walsh, almost on the exact spot where the Assiniboine Indians had been massacred.

The other three Divisions of the Force were working out their own problems elsewhere.

Division "A" at Fort Edmonton, like "B," "C" and "F" at Macleod, had given a successful party at Christmas, 1874. The men had voted a month's pay each toward the party in return for the generous hospitality of the Edmonton people. Practically every settler, hunter and trader within a hundred miles went to the two-day festivities. These included a church service, two dances, and an enormous dinner of fresh buffalo tongues, venison, roast chicken, goose, plum puddings, mince pies and countless gallons of tea. Also like the police farther south, Division "A" had cleared its district of whisky traders. And as soon as spring weather permitted, Inspector Jarvis and his men built their own police post at Fort Saskatchewan, some twenty miles east of Edmonton.

At Swan River meanwhile, Division "E" had helped the contractors to finish the buildings intended as permanent headquarters for the North-West Mounted Police. But as Commissioner French had foreseen, conditions were most unsatisfactory. To make a place to drill the men had to remove huge boulders, using the primitive method of building fires on the rocks and then pouring on cold water to split them apart. The men were almost as cold in the drafty barracks as out. They often got out of their bunks in the morning to step on floors covered in snow which had blown in through holes in the roofs.

"It's just as well," one officer wrote, reporting faulty thermometers, "that the men don't know how cold it is when they are out working. But when they go to bed they should know if it is cold enough to freeze their ears, as was the case with Sub-Constable McCrum."

At Swan River, as at Fort Macleod, the men's clothing had worn out, and they wore the ragged remnants of uniforms plus assorted garments bought from the Hudson's Bay Company at Fort Pelly ten miles away. Many men had been ill. And the scarcity of food resulted in a monotonous diet of fat pork, biscuits, bread and tea. Yet "E" Division, like the others, gave a successful Christmas party. The Hudson's Bay Company staff from Fort Pelly and the half-breed settlers and their families for many miles around attended a grand dance and a dinner which included such purchased delicacies as "berry pemmican" and bear meat. Most important of all was that "E," like the others, had cleared its district of illegal traders, and had established law and order, dealing fairly and impartially with both Indians and whites.

Unexpected problems arose, however, as when an Indian, one of the first prisoners at Swan River, was sentenced to thirty days for wife-beating. He served his time wearing one of the six convict suits the police had brought from Toronto, and was bitterly disappointed to have to give it up. "I come back to jail again soon," he said. So the police stopped using the suits.

Commissioner French and "D" Division had spent the winter of 1874-75 in Dufferin. In the spring of 1875 they began to march back to Swan River, where they arrived early in July.

By then French was in considerable disfavour. The government resented the embarrassment he caused them by his continued scathing remarks about the Swan River scandal. At the same time the Opposition party struck out at the government, the Mounted Police and the Commissioner. A few weeks after French reached Swan River and established North-West Mounted Police headquarters there, Major-General E. Selby Smyth, head of the Canadian militia, arrived. He had come on government instructions to tour all Mounted Police posts and to report back on conditions.

To the disappointment of the Opposition in the House of Commons at Ottawa, Major-General Smyth's report on the Mounted Police mostly expressed approval and admiration. He did, however, recommend that the police should grow their own oats and should establish a training depot, both of which recommendations were later put into effect.

Also, later, uniforms were approved or changed. This was partly because of what Smyth criticized as "a want of uniformity in the dress." For instance, the original Bedford cord breeches were of flesh colour or steel gray (not blue), and sometimes corduroy trousers were substituted for these. Also, Smyth recommended greater distinction between the clothing of officers and other ranks.

Among other things, the tunic pattern of jacket was adopted in place of the "frock" for constables and sub-constables. An elaborate uniform was approved for the officers, with swords which, according to Smyth, had "a great effect upon the Indian mind," and gold embroidered sword belts. Hanging from each belt was a sabretache, or leather pouch, edged with gold and bearing the badge of the Force—a buffalo head surrounded by maple leaves, with a garter inscribed with the words *Maintien le Droit*. This misspelled motto, meaning "Maintain the Right," was later corrected to *Maintiens le Droit*. Incidentally, although the helmet and "pillbox" were generally disliked by the men as unsuitable, they were not officially discarded until about 1900.

Meanwhile the Mounted Police continued to strengthen their position on the Canadian prairies. By the end of 1875, in addition to the police posts at Swan River Barracks, Fort Saskatchewan, Fort Macleod and Fort Walsh, they had established Fort Calgary on the Bow River halfway between Forts Saskatchewan and Macleod, and also several minor posts at strategic points.

They were growing stronger in other ways too. For instance, an esprit-de-corps was developing. When a Manitoba newspaper charged that an officer of "D" Division was tyrannical, his men signed and presented him with a memorial expressing sympathy for him. Also indicating strength was the policy of silence concerning police matters, instituted at Fort Macleod to preclude the possibility of outside interference with the administration of justice. "Nothing concerning the Force or the business of the Force to be in any way discussed with outsiders," declared an order posted there in December, 1875.

After little more than a year in their prairie outposts, the accomplishments and development of the North-West Mounted Police augured well for the future of the country they served.

Chapter 4
The Police and the Indians
1876–1877

In the spring of 1876 the American Sioux, who were engaged in a bitter struggle against the American army, sent a message and some tobacco to the Canadian Blackfeet. The message requested the Blackfeet to help fight the Long Knives, as the Sioux called the United States Cavalry. In return the Sioux would help the Blackfeet later to exterminate the whites north of the Medicine Line, as they called the border. The tobacco, when smoked, would seal the bargain.

"We cannot smoke your tobacco on such terms," Crowfoot said, refusing the symbolic gift. "The white men are our friends."

The belligerent Sioux resented his attitude and threatened reprisals. Later, Crowfoot told this to Sub-Inspector Denny at Calgary. Denny promised that the police would protect the Blackfeet if they were attacked, and in return Crowfoot pledged two thousand warriors if the Sioux should invade Canada. This agreement gave the Mounted Police considerable peace of mind, as the rebellious Sioux continued to fight in the United States, and the danger of their invasion of Canada remained.

In June, at the time of the Sioux victory at the Little Big Horn, Inspector Walsh was on sick leave at Hot Springs, Arkansas. The Canadian government ordered him to return to his post. As he did so, by way of Chicago and the Missouri River, he had the job of escorting thirty-five recruits on their way west from eastern Canada. But his party was stranded at Bismarck, North Dakota, in the heart of the Sioux country, because the American army had commandeered every available boat to supply troops searching for Sioux Chief Sitting Bull.

Walsh knew he was urgently needed in the Cypress Hills. But it seemed that he and his party would have to stay in Bismarck all summer, and if the summer perhaps the winter too. He decided to hire the next steamer before the American quartermaster did so. Even when the *Peninah's* captain asked a presumably prohibitive $6,000 for the trip to Fort Benton, Walsh agreed, resourcefully determined to get and load freight orders to help pay the high tariff.

Arriving at the telegraph office just before closing time on Saturday evening, the inspector wired Ottawa for permission. There was no time for an answer, but all night he cornered likely prospects on the street, in trading posts and in saloons, and by dawn his thirty-five recruits had begun loading the *Peninah*. When the telegraph office reopened on Sunday evening, Walsh was there waiting for permission to do what he had already done. The moment the wire granting permission came he set sail, before the protesting American quartermaster could contact Washington.

Twelve days after leaving Bismarck, still far from Fort Benton, Walsh's part-way destination, the *Peninah* grounded on a sand bar. The inspector and his men shouldered blankets and suitcases and struck out across country for Fort Walsh about 180 miles away. One of the recruits, nineteen-year-old Daniel Davis, later known as "Peach," recorded details of the trek.

First they headed for a house in view about three miles away. There they met Slippery Ann, a long-haired tough-looking frontiersman wearing a fringed buckskin suit. He told them that Big Bear and his band of Crees were heading for Fort Walsh, planning to attack it. Walsh, more anxious than ever to reach the fort, hired Slippery Ann as guide. Then his strange-looking party pushed forward through the sickening summer heat of the arid, cactus-sprinkled American prairie.

En route they met a large band of Crows who told of having refused Big Bear's offer of fifty ponies, plus a squaw for each brave who would help to attack the whites across the Medicine Line. The police passed around hardtack in appreciation. But when some of the recruits paid special attention to the young women, a fight seemed inevitable, with the police likely to lose their scalps.

Slippery Ann, who had seen a recruit named Andy Grogan perform sleight-of-hand tricks, saved the day by announcing that the police medicine man would make medicine. The Indians, not daring to offend a medicine man, stood still to watch. Grogan stepped up to a warrior on horseback.

"Ask him what his pony eats," the recruit said to interpreter Slippery Ann.

"Grass," the Crow answered.

"This pony has eaten something else," Grogan said, and from the animal's mouth he withdrew a dozen pocket knives.

Davis finished his story. "This feat astonished the Indians so much that they cheered, saying that they had often heard of the devil but had never seen him. They would not even take the horse that the trick was played on. . . . Slippery Ann remarked that we had Grogan to thank for saving our scalps."

On arriving at Fort Walsh, the inspector immediately ordered "B" Division to prepare defences against the hundreds of Crees camped nearby in readiness for attacking the fort. The police strengthened the stockades, buried excess ammunition, called the guards inside, and stacked bags of flour to form shooting boxes. Then Walsh sent a half-breed scout, disguised as an Indian, to the Cree camp. There he spread the news that the police had been greatly strengthened by reinforcements. The Crees decided not to attack at dawn as planned. Instead Big Bear merely visited the fort later that day, and the police lectured him about obeying the law.

Meanwhile, unrest among the border Indians had made southern police posts temporarily more important than posts elsewhere, so that they received the most attention from the government.

This created a doubly awkward situation for Commissioner French, far away to the north-east at Swan River. On the one hand, regular and frequent communication between Swan River Barracks and Fort Macleod was impossible, so the Commissioner had no effective control of the border police. On the other hand, the assistant commissioner in charge at Fort Macleod could contact Ottawa via Fort Benton, so he dealt directly with the government. Copies of all correspondence were sent to Swan River, but they travelled very slowly. Thus the Commissioner, besides lacking control of the southern police, was often in ignorance of their work and whereabouts. French felt that such divided command was intolerable.

This situation, plus the continuing friction between him and the government, led to his resignation in July, 1876. The government he had so bluntly criticized voiced no regret. Yet this man, who would later become Major-General Sir George Arthur French, had laid the foundation of a great federal police organization. Moreover, he had established it on a non-partisan basis by refusing to allow political interference in a system of promotion based on merit. In appreciation the senior ranks of police at Swan River presented him with a $200 gold watch and chain, a remarkable gift considering the police pay at that time, and the others presented Mrs. French with a service of silver plate. Both gifts were ordered by telegraph from Winnipeg.

Earlier that year Assistant Commissioner Macleod had resigned to become western Canada's first stipendiary magistrate, a civil post he alone was capable of filling. Inspector Irvine had succeeded him as assistant commissioner, but the government did not appoint Irvine as French's successor. Instead it considered the disturbances so prevalent among the Indians, and recalled Macleod from civil life. So Stamixotokan Macleod, whom the Indians trusted as one who "never spoke with a forked tongue," became the second Commissioner of the North-West Mounted Police.

Commissioner Macleod's first move, with government approval, was to transfer police headquarters from Swan River to Fort Macleod.

He himself went to Swan River to supervise the transfer of Divisions "D" and "E," arriving at 6:00 A.M. on August 6. He ordered the whole establishment, except for a few men remaining at Swan River, to be ready by 9:30 A.M. for the 1,150-mile trek to Fort Macleod via Forts Carlton and Pitt. Moreover, the troops must be prepared to spend the winter en route if necessary, for they would be delayed by attending to certain Indian treaties at the latter two forts. Preparations included even the shoeing of horses, but thanks to the efficiency established by Commissioner French, the march began half an hour ahead of schedule.

The column filing out of the barracks square that sunny August morning was led by the first band of the North-West Mounted Police. It belonged to "D" Division, and had been organized at Swan River in February, 1876. A winter patrol going to Winnipeg had placed the order, and the volunteer bandsmen, among whom was seventeen-year-old bugler Bagley, had themselves paid for the instruments, which were delivered in April by dog team.

Two notables riding in the column that followed the band were Chief Constable Steele and Sub-Inspector Francis Dickens. Dickens, the third son of the famous novelist, had previously served in the office of district superintendent of the Bengal Police in India. After returning to England because of his father's death he had emigrated to Canada. He joined the North-West Mounted Police in November, 1874, then marched to Swan River with French the following spring. Now, as he moved on again, he carried with him one of his few souvenirs of home and family: a gold watch engraved with the name of Charles Dickens.

After a march of twelve days, Commissioner Macleod and his cavalcade reached Fort Carlton. There at the end of August, and at Fort Pitt early in September, the Mounted Police acted as escorts for the government representatives during their signing of Treaty No. 6, a treaty in which the Plain and Wood Crees deeded 120,000 square miles of territory to the government.

As the almost one hundred scarlet-tunicked riders approached the Indian encampment at Carlton, they were led by the unmounted band. On hearing the brassy blare of martial music, the women and children fled to their teepees. But the braves were greatly impressed, particularly by the drum, for which they offered a good horse.

After leaving Fort Pitt, Divisions "D" and "E" marched southward. When they came to a point where they had to cross the South Saskatchewan River, they found the water very deep and about a quarter of a mile wide. Again and again the strong current of icy water drove the horses back to shore. The guides swore that only a miracle would persuade the animals to cross the river.

Staff Constable Mitchell and a sub-constable performed the miracle. Stripping off their clothes and mounting two of the more docile horses they rode into the river. A few yards from shore they slipped from their seats. Swimming close to the horses' heads they coaxed and guided the animals through the strong currents. The sub-constable finished the frigid crossing clinging to his horse's tail. The other horses, apparently satisfied that the feat could be accomplished, followed without much persuasion.

Getting supplies and equipment over presented another problem. The men improvised a raft of two wagon-beds lashed together, with wagon sheets drawn underneath to prevent leaking. At each crossing these rafts were swept downstream a mile or so and had to be towed that distance upstream to be unloaded. But in three days of ceaseless toil, "D" and "E" got all their supplies safely across and the contingent marched on to Fort Walsh.

"E" Division remained there, while the Commissioner and "D" marched on to Fort Macleod, arriving late in October.

These reinforcements for the southern detachments of the North-West Mounted Police arrived none too soon. Ever since Custer's defeat the Sioux had been harassed so effectively by American cavalry that they had begun to cross into Canada seeking refuge. By the end of December a large group of 500 braves, 1,000 women, 1,400 children and 3,500 horses were camped near Wood Mountain.

That same month, accompanied by twelve police and three scouts, Inspector Walsh made the eight-day trip from Fort Walsh to Wood Mountain. First he reassured the Canadian Indians in the area that they need have no fear of the American newcomers. Then he called a council meeting of the Sioux. He sternly explained the laws they must obey, and told them that they would not be allowed to attack any Americans from Canadian soil. Finally, seeing the pitiful truth of their protestations that they were starving because they had no ammunition to hunt the buffalo, he allowed the traders to sell them some. Then the police party returned to Fort Walsh, nearly freezing to death en route in a below-zero storm of bitter winter.

As the Sioux spread over the prairie hunting buffalo that winter, the Mounted Police, understaffed, overworked, and still short of sturdy horses in good condition, patrolled ceaselessly to keep the Sioux and other American Indians under control.

In May of the following spring, scouts reported to Walsh at Fort Walsh that Sitting Bull and his large camp were approaching the border. Walsh took three police and two scout-interpreters, one of whom was Louis Léveillé, brother of Pierre, and set out across the hilly country to meet the formidable chief.

On the third day the little patrol party found itself surrounded by Indians in the hills, but the men calmly advanced to the edge of a large camp and dismounted. A chief came forward. This was Sitting Bull's camp, he said, and this was the first time any white man, soldier or scout, had dared to march into it like this.

Walsh arranged for an interview with the notorious Sioux chief and his lesser chiefs. Turner wrote that, after a series of handshakes all round, "All seemed eager to recite the oft-told story that their forefathers were English, that they had been raised on English soil." The same story prevailed throughout the Sioux: they were originally *Shaganosh* (British). During the War of 1812, sixty-five years earlier, the Sioux had found themselves under the Americans. A chief of their *Shaganosh* Father (King George III) had told them that if they did not want to live under the Americans they could move northward.

Then Walsh and Sitting Bull spoke together, through an interpreter as the others had also done. First Walsh explained the Canadian laws and asked for obedience to them. Then he promised ammunition for shooting buffalo, as he had done with the other American Indians.

Sitting Bull responded at length, vowing to do no wrong in the country of the White Mother. And although Walsh realized that he must be constantly alert in case Sitting Bull's attitude changed, he believed that for the moment the great warrior appreciated sanctuary on Canadian soil.

That night Walsh and the other five of the police party slept in Sitting Bull's camp, the first white soldiers or scouts ever to do so. The next morning they set out for the return ride to Fort Walsh, now the main centre of police and Indian activity in the Canadian West.

On the whole the Indians behaved well. But troublesome incidents arose from time to time, partly because more Indians shared in hunting the noticeably fewer buffalo. One such incident occurred in late May, soon after Walsh returned from meeting Sitting Bull.

About 250 lodges of American Assiniboines crossed into Canada to hunt buffalo, and set up their tents near the fifteen lodges of a small band of Canadian Salteaux. The Assiniboine warrior Crow's Dance, who had formed a war lodge of about two hundred young braves, invited the Salteaux to join his camp and to hunt as he directed. When the Salteaux Chief Little Child refused, Crow's Dance threatened to force him to obey. Little Child protested that he would obey only the White Chief at Fort Walsh, meaning Inspector Walsh, and the Salteaux began to break camp.

The Assiniboines immediately attacked them, firing guns, killing nineteen train or sleigh dogs, slashing teepees, upsetting travois, and knocking down any Salteaux who got in their way. "And if the redcoats come," Crow's Dance boasted, "we'll cut out the White Chief's heart and eat it."

But later in the day the Salteaux did move southward, while the Assiniboines moved toward the east. And that night Little Child slipped away to the police fort about fifty miles distant. Thirty hours later he was back, accompanied by Inspector Walsh, Sub-Inspector E. Allen, Surgeon Kittson, fourteen other police and scout Louis Léveillé.

As Walsh's party neared the Assiniboine camp at dawn, they halted about a mile away from the great cluster of lodges which nestled in the valley clearing fringed with cottonwoods. In the centre they could see the war lodge, where they knew Crow's Dance would be.

After inspecting all arms and ordering pistols and carbines loaded, the inspector detailed Dr. Kittson, two police and Léveillé to go to a small butte half a mile from the camp and to begin building a breastwork of stones.

Then Walsh led his other few horsemen silently down a ravine toward the Assiniboine camp. On nearing it the police broke into a sharp trot and surrounded the war lodge. Crow's Dance and his braves, like all the others in the camp, were sleeping soundly after performing a war dance until a late hour the previous night. Before the sleepy Assiniboines realized what was happening, the police had seized Crow's Dance, Chief Crooked Arm and the braves with them, and carried them off to Dr. Kittson's emergency station at the butte. There, while the rest of the camp still slept soundly, the troopers handcuffed their prisoners and hurriedly fortified the breastwork of rocks and earth.

Walsh described the next move in his official report, a laconic masterpiece of traditional Mounted Police understatement. "It was now 5:00 A.M.; I ordered breakfast," he wrote.

Then instead of returning immediately to Fort Walsh the inspector sent Léveillé to the Assiniboine camp to summon the chiefs to council. When they arrived at the butte, followed by a crowd of angry braves, Walsh told them sharply that under the White Mother's law every person had the privilege of leaving camp when he chose, and that they must never again behave as they had toward the Salteaux. Also, he said, the police were taking Crow's Dance and twelve of the other prisoners to Fort Walsh for trial.

Walsh's self-assurance so impressed the American Indians that they did not interfere as the police and their prisoners set out for Fort Walsh. There the offenders were tried by the inspector and Assistant Commissioner Irvine sitting together on the case. Eleven were released with a warning, while Crow's Dance and Chief Crooked Arm got short terms with hard labour.

A few months later, members of the North-West Mounted Police took part in an event which involved Canadian Indians, and which was probably the most important to this time in the transitional period of western Canada.

On the afternoon of September 4, 1877, Commissioner Macleod and a guard of honour of one hundred mounted men rode out from Fort Macleod to meet a distinguished visitor. He was David Laird, lieutenant-governor of the North-West Territories, a distinct political unit since the signing of Treaty No. 6. He had come as a treaty commissioner representing the government, to act with Commissioner Macleod to negotiate Treaty No. 7 with the Indians of the Blackfoot country. These Indians, who roamed the plains from the North Saskatchewan River to the international boundary in what is now the Province of Alberta, were the only powerful group that had not yet signed such an agreement.

At Chief Crowfoot's request the treaty meeting was to be held at the Blackfoot Crossing on the Bow River, and on September 12 Divisions "C" and "D" set out for that point, some eighty miles north of Fort Macleod. The column, under the personal command of Commissioner Macleod, comprised about a hundred mounted men, "D" Division band, a small artillery unit in charge of the two field guns taken west in the great march of 1874, and a baggage train of six light wagons. Lieutenant-Governor Laird was escorted north two days later by Assistant Commissioner Irvine.

At the Blackfoot Crossing, or "Ridge under the Water," the police camped in a beautiful wooded valley, pitching their tents opposite the thousands of painted Indian teepees already set up. Traders arriving with large supplies of goods in anticipation of the Indians' treaty money pitched their tents nearby.

Treaty negotiations, which had been postponed two days to allow for the attendance of distant Indian chiefs, opened formally on Wednesday, September 19, at 2:00 P.M. As Lieutenant-Governor Laird and Commissioner Macleod approached the white council marquee and the assembled Indians, they were escorted by the assistant commissioner and fifty scarlet-tunicked police on prancing horses. The police band welcomed them with patriotic airs and the artillery fired a salute. Also present were Mrs. Macleod, Mrs. Shurtliff, Mrs. Winder, wife of Inspector W. Winder, various white settlers who had come from as far as Fort Edmonton to witness the unique ceremony, and a few missionaries and priests who later gave valuable assistance as interpreters.

Crowfoot, greatest of all the Blackfeet, and Old Sun, influential among the North Blackfeet, with other splendidly dressed chiefs of the Blackfeet, Blood, Peigan, Sarcee and other tribes, sat on the ground in front of the council tent. Beyond them in a huge semicircle squatted the rest of the Indian community of about four thousand men, women and children. Autumn colours blazed in the background, and the silvery ripples of the blue-green Bow shimmered in the sunshine.

In opening the proceedings the lieutenant-governor explained that the Great White Queen loved both her white and her red children, that she wanted them to live peaceably together, and that she wanted to help the Indians farm and raise cattle so that they could survive without the rapidly disappearing buffalo.

"If you will let the Queen have part of your land for settlers," he said in effect through an interpreter, "she will set some land aside for you, and will give you farm equipment or cattle, just as you choose. Also, she will pay each man, woman and child twelve dollars this year and five dollars every year forever. The chiefs and councillors will get more money, and in addition each chief will get a suit of clothes, a medal and a flag. The Queen will also give you potatoes and ammunition. And when you settle in one place she will send teachers to teach your children to read books like this," and he showed them a Bible.

During the next few days Lieutenant-Governor Laird and Commissioner Macleod answered questions and discussed various details with the Indians concerning actual ownership of Indian reserves, timber and coal rights, and the Indians' rights to hunt anywhere over the prairies.

By Friday, September 21, the Indians decided to sign the treaty that would deed their land to the government and would grant them certain privileges and reserves of land in exchange, especially as their friends the redcoats advised it.

"If the police had not come to this country, where would we all be now?" asked the aristocratic Crowfoot at a final council meeting. "Bad men and whisky were killing us so fast that very few of us, indeed, would have been left today. The police have protected us as the feathers of the bird protect it from the frosts of winter. I am satisfied. I will sign the treaty."

"Three years ago I met and shook hands with Stamixotokan," said Red Crow. "Since that time he made me many promises. He kept them all. I entirely trust Stamixotokan, and will leave everything to him. I will sign with Crowfoot." About fifteen other chiefs spoke in the same vein, with a freedom of expression that the taciturn Jerry Potts termed remarkable.

That night the lieutenant-governor drafted the treaty. Meanwhile Commissioner Macleod visited the head chiefs in the separate camps to learn which locality each preferred for his reservation, succeeding so promptly in his mission that the places chosen were named in the treaty.

The next day, September 22, 1877, Treaty No. 7 was signed, with each chief making his mark under the signatures of the treaty commissioners, and with the Mounted Police officers, Mrs. Macleod and the other officers' wives, the missionaries, priests and settlers signing as witnesses. Then a salute of thirteen guns announced the conclusion of a vital step toward pacifying and colonizing the Canadian West, a step possible at that early date chiefly because of the presence of the North-West Mounted Police.

The lieutenant-governor duly presented medals, flags and uniforms to the chiefs, and the band played "God Save the Queen." Then the Mounted Police distributed the treaty money, a task which, incidentally, the Indian chiefs asked that the Mounted Police should continue to perform in future years.

Distribution of the money was somewhat complicated by the difficulty of determining the number in each family. Many Indians after receiving their money would return saying they had counted wrong. Each had apparently discovered that he had another wife or two more children, or would ask payment for a child not yet born. Eventually, 4,392 payments were made.

For a short time the traders did a brisk business. Then the Indians dispersed. The traders moved on. The lieutenant-governor returned to Battleford, recently designated capital of the North-West Territories. And Macleod and his men returned to their posts to continue to maintain order among the Indians on the vast Canadian plains.

Chapter 5
The Ending of an Era
1878–1882

The chief concern of the North-West Mounted Police from 1878 to 1880, as it had been during the two preceding years, was to maintain order among the Canadian and American Indians roaming the Canadian prairies, while at the same time continuing to establish themselves as prairie pioneers.

Settlement of the West was proceeding, but not nearly as fast as Sir John A. Macdonald had hoped. The buffalo were now being slaughtered indiscriminately by the same Indians who would suffer most from their disappearance. Turner, describing conditions in 1879, reported: "Thousands of beasts were killed and left untouched by knives, or merely shorn of tongues and choice cuts. For miles and miles over this last, tragic hunting ground, the air stank with the festering wreckage, made the more ghastly by flocks of crows, carrion vultures and bloated wolves." Those settlers who started cattle ranching in what would become southern Alberta complained that Indians were constantly killing their stock, which was not surprising when semi-starving Indians could no longer find buffalo.

Fort Macleod and the little village surrounding it had developed considerably by 1878–79. Not only were there more stores and small traders' huts, but there were also cottages in which several police officers and their wives lived rather than continue to live in the barracks inside the fort. The first public school in that future southern Alberta district was built in 1878. The earliest scholars included the son of Inspector Winder and the son and daughter of Jerry Potts.

Trading companies from Fort Benton still brought in supplies in large ox wagons or in prairie schooners fastened together in threes and hauled by ten pairs of huge oxen. By this time there were regular mail services to and from Forts Calgary and Edmonton, and to Ottawa via Fort Shaw in the United States. Mail-carrying contracts were let out by the police who themselves did the sorting in their orderly room. Since the nearest post offices were at Forts Benton and Shaw, all letters had to bear United States stamps.

The I.G. Baker Company contracted to supply the police post with forage and rations. Also, in the absence of chartered banks, they acted as bankers for the police. The men deposited their pay with the company and received a large percentage of interest per annum, which saved the firm the trouble and risk of bringing large sums of money into the country, and was thus profitable to both parties.

The Fort Macleod police were busy from dawn to dusk with the barracks routine of a cavalry regiment, guarding prisoners, "busting" broncos (under the direction of Steele), and carrying out various pioneer tasks. In the summer of 1879 they raised their own potatoes and one hundred acres of oats, put up 325 tons of hay and cut 28,000 fence rails. The next winter they hauled the hay and rails to the fort, and put up a new saw mill and mill dam, for which they cut and hauled their own timbers. Also, they constantly improved or repaired their log buildings. By this time they had floored their living quarters with planking, and at their own expense they had lined the mud-chinked walls with factory cotton to keep out the dust. They still made their own furniture, including wooden bunk beds.

Actual police work usually kept them up till midnight and often all night. They constantly visited Indian camps and traders' posts, intercepted whisky traders, and arrested other lawbreakers for assault, theft, larceny, and so on. This work in turn created the additional work of producing the necessary witnesses and holding court.

In 1878, because of the many Canadian and American Indians in the Cypress Hills district, North-West Mounted Police Headquarters had been transferred from Fort Macleod to Fort Walsh, even though the latter was unhealthfully situated and caused an alarming amount of sickness among the police. The Fort Walsh men, in spite of their arduous duties, went in for ceremony, particularly when the guard was mounted at 2:00 P.M. each day. Full dress in that spit-and-polish era included white buckskin breeches, kept clean, as were belts, gauntlets and helmets, with pipe clay dug from a nearby hill. Competition to have the smartest man was so keen that rival barracks used to carry their representative over the dusty square to the parade ground.

The men at Walsh, like those at all other police posts, still celebrated Christmas and the New Year with banquets and dances. Sometimes they gave concerts and amateur theatricals. One group of actors hurried back from arresting "Four Jack Bob" Everson for assaulting an Indian, then presented their first play, "Dick Turpin." The police also mixed companionably with the traders who set up posts nearby, and with the early settlers, many of whom were former Mounted Police who had taken advantage of the grant of 160 acres of free land offered at the expiration of three years' service with the Force.

In summer the Mounted Police played cricket, tennis and football. One football match between police and Indians almost resulted in a fatality. A constable shouldered an Indian and sent him flying. The Indian drew his scalping knife and headed for the constable. The constable headed for the fort and stayed there until the danger had passed.

For a few years during this period Fort Walsh boasted a band, which had first made its appearance when "F" Division was transferred there from Fort Calgary in 1878, bringing its band instruments with it. But in 1881, to celebrate a British military victory in Afghanistan, Commissioner Macleod authorized a special issue of grog to the bandsmen giving a concert before the officers' mess. Stimulated, the musicians volunteered to give a patriotic program that evening. But they must have had more than their official ration of liquor, for by evening they so annoyed one another with discordant wails that a free-for-all developed. Musical instruments became weapons, and the career of the first and only Fort Walsh band was ended.

In 1879 at Fort Saskatchewan, the general pattern of Mounted Police life was shockingly interrupted. A sleek, well-fleshed Indian aroused the suspicion of Inspector Jarvis's men when he reported that his wife, children, brother-in-law and mother-in-law had all died of starvation during the winter. He himself, said Swift Runner, had managed to keep alive by boiling and eating his teepee.

"Geev 'eem the strong medicine, mon capitaine, an' 'e weel tell you everyt'ing," the half-breed interpreter suggested to Sub-Inspector Sévère Gagnon.

The strong medicine, a plug of tobacco soaked in strong tea, loosened the suspect's tongue considerably. When Gagnon questioned him as to where he had buried his relatives' bodies, the Indian threw back his head, howled like a wolf, and led the police to a camp in the bush. There they found his teepee neatly folded and stowed away in the branches of a tree. His campfire ashes were strewn with human skulls and bones to which clung bits of teeth-marked flesh. "This is my wife," Swift Runner said later, poking his finger into the eyesocket of one skull and laughing.

Eventually he confessed that he had "made beef of them all," although in fact he had had plenty of dried animal meat in his possession when he had committed cannibalism. Almost to the end he joked about his crime and kept telling one plump guard what fine eating he would make. He seemed especially attracted to the youthful and presumably tender Bagley, although perhaps this was merely because Bagley could talk to him in Cree.

Evidence at Swift Runner's trial indicated that he had formerly been known as mild and trustworthy, a good husband and fond of his children. But for years he had suffered abnormally from troubled dreams of an Indian spirit which had urged him to become a cannibal, and eventually he had obeyed that spirit. Presumably today he would be judged insane. As it was, however, a jury pronounced him guilty and he was sentenced to be hanged.

Bagley was one of the death watch, and the night before the execution Swift Runner presented him with his beaded and furred war club and his smoking pipe. Years later, Bagley described the case in an article.

"Early in the morning of December 20, 1879, Kak-Kee-See-Koo-Chin [Swift Runner] was hanged. In the biting forty-two-degrees-below-zero weather his surviving relatives and a number of specially invited chiefs sat in a circle within the fort furiously drumming and singing the death song to speed their departing brother on his way to the happy hunting grounds. As he stood on the scaffold, the murderer expressed his thanks to the Mounted Police and the priests (who had received him into the Roman Catholic church after the trial) for their kindness to him and urged his own people to take warning from his fate." (The execution, incidentally, was not conducted by the police but by an old army pensioner.)

The year 1879 also witnessed three other notable events. First, the Act which in 1873 had established "a Police Force in the North-West Territories" was amended to designate that Force officially as "The North-West Mounted Police," with the official French version as "La Police à cheval du Nord-Ouest." Second, police rank names were changed to do away with the confusion the original ones had caused. From July, 1897, the various classifications of constable became constable, corporal, sergeant, staff sergeant and sergeant-major. The officers became inspectors and superintendents, except that the assistant commissioner and the Commissioner retained their original titles. With minor variations these rank names have applied ever since. Third, in November, 1897, the first murder of a Mounted Policeman occurred.

Constable Marmaduke Graburn did not return to the camp near

Fort Walsh after riding alone on a short errand, and patrols sent out in all directions from the fort failed to find him. The next morning as Jerry Potts led a search party over his trail, by then partly covered with snow, their anxiety proved to be well-founded.

First Potts pointed out the solitary hoofprints of Graburn's horse, then the track of an unshod Indian pony as Graburn and an Indian rode side by side. Next the tracks of a second Indian pony appeared over the others, as if a second Indian had trailed Graburn and the first Indian. Farther on the search party found blood on the trail, then Graburn's hat, then his dead body with two bullet wounds in the back of the head. Apparently the first Indian had engaged Graburn in conversation while the second Indian rode up behind and shot him. But unfortunately at that point a Chinook wind had melted the snow, so that even the eagle eyes of Potts could find no further sign of a trail. So for the time being the investigation came to a halt.

Almost six months later two Blood Indians, in jail at Fort Walsh for horse stealing, feared they might also be charged with the Graburn murder. They decided to tell what they knew. At midnight they asked to see Superintendent Crozier in his quarters. After persuading the police to cover the windows with blankets they gave the name and description of Graburn's murderer, explaining that the crime had been committed to avenge a supposed insult, with the second Indian an unwilling accomplice. Later it was reported that the Indians had mistaken Graburn for another policeman.

The murderer, a Blood Indian named Star Child, had fled to the Bear Paw Mountains across the border, they said. Commissioner Macleod asked the United States authorities to arrest him, but the sheriff of the district demanded $5,000 in cash to cover his risk. So Star Child remained at large.

However, a year later he recrossed the border and joined Blood Indians near Fort Macleod. Four policemen were detailed to arrest him, so Potts guided them to the Blood camp. There Corporal Patterson and his men attempted a surprise attack at dawn. But Star Child heard the police and before they could handcuff him he discharged his rifle, arousing the camp. Patterson picked him up bodily and the police party galloped away. The other Bloods swung to their ponies in pursuit, but the police won the twenty-five mile race to Fort Macleod.

During the trial which followed, Star Child admitted his guilt and the police produced corroborating evidence. But the jury of white settlers, perhaps fearing that the Bloods would slay their cattle or even begin an Indian war, declared him "Not guilty!" So the first murder of a Mounted Policeman went unavenged, and the official report of

Graburn's death read: "Murdered by person or persons unknown, thought to be Indians."

Yet the murdered youth's confrères showed no less concern than formerly for the welfare of either white man or red. For instance, in the winter of 1880-81 when smallpox swept through the Qu'Appelle district, Constable Holmes, who had studied medicine for several years, risked his life to bring the epidemic under control. He travelled hundreds of miles by snowshoe and slept in snowdrifts in thirty-degree-below-zero weather in order to visit and vaccinate all the Indians and half-breeds as well as many white settlers in the district. For days at a time he lived in foul-smelling wigwams while treating Indians dying of the dreaded disease. At last he won out and no new cases developed. Inspector Steele recommended him for promotion and a small bonus, but neither recommendation was put into effect.

In general the American Sioux appreciated Canadian sanctuary and were law-abiding. But some, especially those under Sitting Bull, continued to clash with the police.

On one occasion Sitting Bull's braves stole several Mounted Police horses from the herd at Wood End tended by a lone policeman. He made the only possible gesture of protest and fired warning shots over the heads of the departing thieves. The temperamental Sitting Bull, who happened to be in a bad mood, sent word to the police that he was displeased at the attack on his warriors. Sub-Inspector E. Allen rode to the Sioux camp and demanded the horses. Sitting Bull, who was mounted on a fine pony at the time, scornfully made it clear that the police could do nothing to get the horses back.

"I would take even the horse you are riding if I thought it stolen," Allen replied.

"It is," Sitting Bull challenged.

The officer, apparently taken aback, sidled his horse closer to the other. Suddenly he leaned over, lifted Sitting Bull from his saddle, grabbed the horse's bridle, and pulled the animal aside. As the Indians stared dumbfounded, Allen's men closed in to protect him. Then the police party, with Sitting Bull's horse in tow, raced for their fort.

That evening the Sioux approached, yelling, evidently planning an attack. In the meantime the police had prepared for a siege and had even written letters of farewell and buried them in an iron box. But they knew their only possible salvation lay in a show of nonchalance, so they put out the lights as if going to bed as usual, and waited in suspense. Fortunately, the Sioux Chief Broad Tail strongly resented Sitting Bull's autocratic rule. He persuaded the others to call off the attack, and the police were saved.

Such incidents convinced the police that the north-west would never have true peace till the Sioux left the country. Remembering Chief Broad Tail's resentment of Sitting Bull's power, they began to deal with individual chiefs separately. One by one they persuaded them to return home, till Sitting Bull was almost deserted. Very poor hunting and the resulting famine during the winter of 1880–81 convinced him that he, too, had better accept the reservation awaiting him across the border. In July, 1881, Sitting Bull went back to the United States.

Meanwhile, by the fall of 1880, most of the Sioux had withdrawn and nearly all the Canadian Indians had signed treaties. The Canadian government realized that Commissioner Macleod's restraining presence among the Indians was no longer required. So they allowed him to resign from the Force and to resume his civic post as stipendiary magistrate for the North-West Territories.

In November, 1880, the former Assistant Commissioner Acheson Gosford Irvine, Canadian by birth and educated in Quebec, became the third Commissioner of the North-West Mounted Police. Now that Indian problems no longer predominated, he was free to turn his attention to conditions in the Force itself.

Irvine, slight, gentlemanly, and still in his early forties, had recently returned from Ireland and a study of the efficient Royal Irish Constabulary. With this substantial background he recommended to the government changes in the North-West Mounted Police. The government agreed to several, including three of outstanding importance: an increase in the strength of the Force to five hundred; the use of more efficient rifles and equipment; and the establishing of a central depot that would contain permanent headquarters and a training school for recruits.

Early in 1882, Mounted Police strength stood at 474. To offset the expense of the extra police, however, the government economized by drastically cutting police pay, and by withdrawing the free land grant for those police who had served their full term. Also, the government issued two Divisions with Winchester repeaters. But they refused to pay for beds of any kind, so the police still slept on boards.

In approving the establishment of permanent headquarters, the government kept in mind the fact that somewhere along the proposed route of the Canadian Pacific Railway they would choose a site for a new capital of the North-West Territories to succeed the original capital at Battleford, which was not on the route of the railway. The permanent headquarters of the Mounted Police, the government decided, should be located in the new capital. During 1881 it became generally understood that the site of the new capital would be near the point at which the railway crossed Pile O' Bones (Wascana) Creek, later named Regina in honour of Queen Victoria. The Mounted Police training depot which would be established there was destined to change completely the early situation so aptly summed up by the officer who told an angry whisky trader, "We make up the law as we go along."

The "Indian period" of Mounted Police history was drawing to a close, a peaceful close, thanks in part to the sincerity, tact and fair dealing of Commissioner Macleod. And as it did so, Macleod's successor, Commissioner Irvine, was directing the Force in its first step toward modern police efficiency.

Chapter 6
The Canadian Pacific Railway
1882–1885

Before the North-West Mounted Police could leave their southern detachments, either to transfer their headquarters to the site of the new capital or to police the construction of the Canadian Pacific Railway through the North-West Territories, provision had to be made for the thousands of Canadian Indians living in the Cypress Hills. The Indians might cause trouble if left unsupervised. Worse still, they would probably starve if left to their own devices now that the buffalo had almost disappeared from the plains.

The government offered them reservations farther north, at Qu'Appelle, Battleford and Fort Pitt, hoping that they would accept them in place of the reservations they had chosen when signing the various Indian treaties. Some accepted and moved. But the Assiniboines in particular were understandably reluctant to leave the lands that had been their homes for many generations, even though their friends the redcoats advised it.

In May, 1882, however, Assiniboine Chiefs Poor Man and Grizzly Bear's Head agreed to move their 1,100 followers two hundred miles north to Battleford. Only one policeman could be spared from Fort Walsh as escort: young Constable Daniel "Peach" Davis, who now had more than five years' service with the Force. Under his supervision the procession of squeaking Red River carts, horse travois and Indian families headed north.

Davis soon realized that the twenty-five provision carts leading the column held the key to his success in delivering the already homesick Assiniboines to Battleford. When some of the resentful braves looted the carts, Davis explained to the chiefs that any food left at the end of the journey would be theirs, and they made the braves return the loot. When the Indians refused to cross the South Saskatchewan River, the constable himself crossed with provisions. He made a campfire and a huge kettle of tea, then appealed to the women. They crossed and the braves soon followed.

After twenty-five exasperating days Davis delivered his charges to the Indian agent at Battleford, having earned the Assiniboine name meaning "God Mad All the Time."

By July all the Indians had left the Cypress Hills, and the Mounted Police prepared to evacuate Fort Walsh. But in August Big Bear and his Crees returned, saying they could not make the long trek north to Fort Pitt because of poor hunting en route. And in September Piapot and his Crees returned from Qu'Appelle.

"No like Qu'Appelle," Piapot explained. "Back here to stay."

That winter the police had a troublesome time with braves who turned to horse stealing for excitement. They also had to feed the Indians from their limited police supplies. But by December, 1882, when Commissioner Irvine set out for the new headquarters at Regina, the Indians had promised that they would return north in the spring.

Before Chief Piapot left the south, however, he tried to prevent further construction of the Canadian Pacific Railway. He, like many Indians, saw the railway as the visible symbol of their multiple tragedy. They had already lost their traditional freedom, well-being, and way of life which had developed over the centuries on the buffalo-covered plains. And now, not only had the buffalo disappeared, but the Indians were being driven from their traditional homeland. Moreover, the new reserves they were offered were in the north, on land considered best for agriculture rather than for hunting. And the railway would lie between the new reserves and their traditional hunting grounds to the south.

But the ribbon of steel that so distressed the Indians was of vital importance to Canada. It would link the eastern provinces and British Columbia, which had joined Confederation in 1871 after Sir John A. Macdonald had pledged to start a Pacific railway in two years and finish it in ten. Moreover, the government was especially conscious of the fact that during the years in which no railway construction had been started, British Columbia had demanded secession. At last, in February, 1881, the Canadian Pacific Railway had been organized under an Act of Parliament. The construction that soon got underway was heralded not only as a vital East-West link, but also as the forerunner of settlement and eventual prosperity for the whole country.

So in May, 1882, when Piapot and his tribe tried to halt track-laying by camping on the railway right-of-way, it was the duty of the Mounted

Police to make them move off.

Corporal W.B. Wilde and a constable rode out to investigate from the Maple Creek detachment, which by this time was replacing Fort Walsh in importance. They found Piapot's lodge directly on the right-of-way. The chief himself sat at his tent door smoking his pipe, while scores of braves shouting war cries wheeled their ponies about and shot rifles in the air, urged on by shrieking women and yelping dogs.

"I'll give you just fifteen minutes to move," the corporal said, taking out his watch.

The braves rode near enough to jostle the police, trying to make them fight. But the scarlet-tunicked men sat motionless on their horses.

"Time's up!" Wilde declared, throwing his reins to the constable and springing off his horse. He strode to Piapot's teepee and kicked down the centre pole, so that the painted buffalo-skin covering collapsed. Then he did the same with the other teepees.

The nonplussed Indians moved on. But, as Pierre Berton commented in *The Last Spike*: "This incident . . . helped to bolster the tradition of the redcoats as fearless upholders of the law. Yet, in the light of the Indians' tragedy, it is inexpressibly sad."

Meanwhile, resentful Indians back east along the CPR, knowing that game would disappear as settlers followed the railway, desperately blockaded the tracks with huge logs or tried to derail the "fire-devils" by wedging tomahawks between the ends of the rails. Hideously painted warriors stood menacingly between the workers and the trees they needed to cut to make ties. They stole the company's supplies and stampeded their cattle and horses.

The railway's own workers caused much trouble, too. Many of them were foreigners who scarcely understood English. It was not strange that they failed to realize the importance of the work they were doing and that they showed no concern for the country they passed through. They carelessly caused prairie fires, and resented enforcement of the law.

Whisky peddlers found a ready market among the construction workers. Some peddlers from across the United States border smuggled liquor in fake bibles and in eggs with their centres removed. Others sold mincemeat and preserved peaches soaked in brandy. All were intent on relieving the workers of their wages, either by outright sales or by getting them drunk and stealing from them.

But the Mounted Police determinedly upheld the law. All along the line of construction NCOs and men arrested lawbreakers on charges of theft, receiving stolen property, being drunk and disorderly, shooting with intent to cause bodily harm, destroying property, peddling liquor in the North-West Territories, gambling in the North-West Territories, and so on. Then Mounted Police officers tried the cases, holding court wherever they found it convenient, often out in the open.

In August, 1882, the railway nosed past Regina. At that time it was merely a canvas town on a bare plain, and the portable buildings intended as police headquarters had not yet arrived from eastern Canada. A month later Inspector Steele, by now deep-chested and muscular, was sent to Regina to lay out the ground for the buildings, and to be in charge of the detachments as far west as Swift Current. He would also act as magistrate for that district.

Steele's courtroom at Regina was a marquee sixteen feet by fourteen feet, which also served as mess room and sleeping apartment. On several occasions at what later became the prosperous town of Swift Current, he held court in the open, sitting on a Red River cart with a plank across his knee and taking down evidence on the flap of his dispatch bag.

The year 1883 began with a commendation for the Mounted Police. On January 1, William Van Horne, general manager of the CPR, wrote gratefully to Commissioner Irvine. "Without the assistance of the officers and men of the splendid force under your command, it would have been impossible to have accomplished as much as we did," he wrote regarding the construction accomplished in the previous year. "On no great work within my knowledge where so many men have been employed has such perfect order prevailed."

During the rest of the year, while construction pushed on westward from Medicine Hat, the Mounted Police carried on as before. From time to time they met many of the important persons who travelled on excursion trains to see the line. On one occasion when Van Horne travelled on such a train he wanted to demonstrate how practical they were. He himself took the lever and Superintendent Walsh worked the brakes.

In the spring of 1884, Inspector Steele was ordered to choose a strong party and go to British Columbia to police the CPR line of construction through the Rocky Mountains. Everyone knew that it was likely to be a hazardous job, but every man under his command volunteered. Steele chose the twenty-five best shots with rifle and revolver.

On arriving at Laggan, British Columbia, Steele found several diffi-culties in the way of efficient police work. For one thing, liquor sales were prohibited under the Act for the Preservation of Peace on Public Works. But unless the police found a bar in the tent or cabin they searched, they were not allowed to confiscate even a suspiciously large amount of liquor, and in any case penalties were light.

As Steele said later, the police found it a "detestable duty" to enforce prohibition. Also, some of the police themselves indulged in occasional drinking. The basic fact was that prohibition had originally been set up in the North-West Territories to protect the Indians. Now it was still being enforced, against the wishes of the local residents who resented the police enforcing the law.

However, the police had no choice. They were charged with enforcing whatever law existed, and they did so to the best of their ability. As Berton wrote: "The Mounties did not have to stand for election (as did the American marshalls), they were relatively incorruptible, and they were fair; that was one of the reasons why the Canadian West lacked some of the so-called colour of its American counterpart."

Another difficulty facing the Mounted Police lay in the fact that their jurisdiction, being federal, was limited to ten miles each side of the surveyed railway line. So thirsty labourers walked beyond the ten-mile limit, especially after pay day, got the liquor they wanted, and returned drunk and disorderly. Also, the government of British Columbia wanted the extra revenue from the sale of liquor licenses. So in spite of the federal ruling of prohibition, the province enthusiastically issued liquor licenses within the twenty-mile belt.

At Steele's suggestion, however, the twenty-mile belt was widened to forty. Also, the regulation about the police having to find a bar was withdrawn, and penalties were stiffened. These three changes helped the police to keep the situation under control.

In addition to enforcing the liquor regulations the Mounted Police escorted the railway paymaster, settled quarrels, and prevented thefts and holdups. Above all they constantly watched the "large numbers of ruffians, gamblers and murderers" who, according to Steele, had been plying their trade on the Northern Pacific Railway in the United States, and who, now that the American railway had been completed, flocked to the CPR.

As the head of steel pushed farther into the mountains, so did the Mounted Police, and that fall the construction company erected winter quarters for the police at the Beaver River. The strong log building had a courtroom and cells for thirty prisoners. Some of the cells stood apart from the others, in anticipation of women prisoners expected from among the prostitutes and other camp followers who moved westward with the construction gangs. The police buildings also had some rooms for the inspector in charge, men's quarters and stables.

It was not difficult to keep the cells occupied. As soon as construction reached the Beaver, gangs of toughs also moved there. Then they built their saloons, dance halls and disorderly houses opposite the Mounted Police post. When the cells were not filled with other prisoners they contained drunks put there to protect them from pickpockets.

In April, 1885, Inspector Steele quelled a disturbance that might easily have led to rioting, bloodshed and murder. The trouble began when the 1,200 navvies went on strike, claiming that they had not been paid for weeks, and threatening to beat CPR officials and to destroy company equipment and property. Steele was critically ill with mountain (typho-malarial) fever, yet he managed to sit in a chair to receive a delegation of the strikers. He persuaded them to meet the construction manager, who promised to do his best for them. Several hundred men returned to work. But many others refused and stayed at the Beaver, egged on by the gamblers and whisky peddlers who were understandably eager for the men to be paid.

Steele had only eight men at the Beaver then, since most of his men had been sent to maintain order at other points. He knew that because of the North-West Rebellion he could not expect reinforcements from elsewhere. But he also knew that he must keep the situation under control. So when he heard that about three hundred strikers, many armed with revolvers, were ordering other workers to stop work, he sent Sergeant Fury and a small party to guard a track-laying gang.

The strikers surged up, shooting as they came, but the tracklayers were in a protected position and kept on working. Fury drew his party in a line from side to side of the narrow cutting that separated the workers from the strikers, and threatened to shoot the first man crossing it. The strikers withdrew.

Later that day they gathered in the streets of the town to listen to an agitator urging them to attack the Mounted Police barracks. Constable Kerr, who was out getting medicine for Steele, stepped up and tried to arrest the agitator. But the mob closed in and rescued the man. They threw the constable to the ground, then forced him to retreat across the little bridge between the barracks and the town.

Steele, who had been sitting in a camp chair waiting for Kerr's return, learned of the incident from Sergeant Fury. He realized that he must not let the crowd get the upper hand and that the agitator must not go free.

"Take what men you require," he told the sergeant, "and arrest him."

Fury and two constables found the man in a saloon, but again a mob rescued him.

"Take your revolvers!" Steele snapped at the three dishevelled policemen who reported back to him. "And shoot anyone who interferes with the arrest."

Fury set off again, this time with three constables, Craig, Fain and Walters. After a few minutes Steele heard a shot. Going to the window, he saw Craig and Walters dragging the struggling prisoner across the little bridge. A woman followed them, cursing wildly, while Fury and

Fain formed a rear guard, brandishing their revolvers at an infuriated mob of about seven hundred men, many of them armed.

Steele wrote later that he felt an astonishing surge of strength in spite of his illness. He rushed out, calling to a justice of the peace who was with him to follow with the Riot Act, and snatching a rifle from the constable on guard at the jail. He reached the little bridge just as Walters hit the struggling prisoner with his fist and knocked him senseless. Steele faced the crowd about to rush the bridge.

"Halt or I'll fire!" he shouted, covering them with his rifle.

They halted, all but the still shrieking woman, who pushed forward.

"Take her in, too!" he shouted.

By this time the justice of the peace had arrived with the Riot Act from the police office.

"Listen to this!" Steele ordered the crowd. "And keep your hands off your guns or I'll shoot the first man who makes a hostile movement! And I warn you," he added as the justice finished reading, "that if I find more than twelve of you standing together I will open fire. Now disperse and behave yourselves."

By this time a considerable number of responsible persons—engineers, merchants, contractors—all well armed, had come to the barracks to support the police, so the uneasy mob moved off.

That night Steele sent the prisoner by train to a nearby detachment at Palliser. The next morning, which he described as "quiet as a country village on Sunday," he ordered the arrest of all the ringleaders who had broken the law by trying to prevent the other man's arrest. When they pleaded guilty, he sentenced them to $100 fines or six months' imprisonment with hard labour. Then he went by locomotive to Palliser, tried the prisoner there, and sentenced him to the same punishment.

About a week later the North-West Rebellion caused Inspector Steele and his men to be posted to other stations. By that time the labourers were all paid, and no further trouble developed. After the rebellion was suppressed Steele returned to British Columbia and resumed his duties along the CPR.

When the railway was completed in November, 1885, he was a guest at the ceremony of driving the last spike. Then he rode with other special guests on the train that went through the mountains to the Pacific coast. They rushed along at an amazing fifty-seven miles an hour, roaring through tunnels and whirling around sharp corners, till Steele and two others were the only men in the car not suffering from train sickness. His comments on the wild ride explain the satisfaction many Mounted Policemen knew in those early days.

"It was the exultant moment of pioneer work," he said, "and we were all pioneers."

Chapter 7
Rebellion and Reconstruction
1885 – 1895

Half-breed rebellion liable to break out at any moment. Troops must be largely reinforced. If half-breeds rise Indians will join them."

This message, sent by Superintendent Crozier from Fort Carlton on March 13, 1885, so alarmed the government that it ordered Commissioner Irvine to take all available men from Regina to assist Crozier. Yet the message was no surprise. For more than eight months Crozier had been warning the government of the half-breeds' unrest.

The chief immediate grievance of these Métis descendants of French hunters and Indians was understandable. They wanted to retain their long, narrow homesteads fronting the Saskatchewan River in French Canadian style. But government surveyors were re-mapping the land in square sections and quarter sections, and threatening the Métis with eviction. And the government, instead of trying to settle the dispute, had merely established a police post at Fort Carlton and substantially increased the police strength at Prince Albert, Battleford and Fort Pitt.

Both half-breeds and Indians, still in the majority in that northern area which Turner called the "Métis principality of Gabriel Dumont," had other legitimate grievances. Since the seat of territorial government had been transferred from Battleford to Regina, there was almost no work available, hence very little money. Only poor schools existed, and none in some areas, while hunger and poverty scourged Métis settlements and Indian reservations alike. Many Indians were actually starving, yet the government, in a move the Mounted Police found incomprehensible, had in 1884 reduced their rations. The complaints of the English half-breeds had at least partly been remedied in 1884, but those of the Métis had been ignored because the investigator did not understand French. There seemed no hope for either Indians or Métis.

Now Louis Riel, leader of the Red River Rebellion in 1869–70, was back on the scene, having returned from exile in the United States in the summer of 1884. He had come at the invitation of Dumont and the other Métis, and was now organizing the second rebellion of his career. According to Turner's account of Wandering Spirit's testimony after the North-West Rebellion, Riel's background was revealed. As early as 1881 Riel, then trading whisky along the Missouri River, had given whisky to influential leaders among Big Bear's Crees and had asked their future help in wiping out all Canadians if the government failed to give Riel the money he intended to demand. In the fall of 1884 he had notified the Crees, by then moved from the southern district to the north, that "when the leaves come out" the half-breeds would rise and kill the whites. The Americans, he said, would then buy the land from the Indians for "lots of money," and all tribes who wished to benefit would have to help rid the country of Canadians.

On March 18, 1885, five days after Crozier's warning message, and two days after his own eclipse-of-the-sun trick, Riel held a mass meeting of half-breeds, many of them armed, at Batoche. There he planned a provisional government. Later he himself headed a board of strategy, while Gabriel Dumont, eager to lead his wretched people to a better life, became commander-in-chief. The rebels chose ten troop captains and obtained food supplies by seizing two general stores. Riel declared that the Mounted Police would be wiped out of existence in a week. The rebellion had begun.

Meanwhile, also by coincidence on March 18, Commissioner Irvine and a sleigh column of ninety police had left Regina to march north in the bitter cold of a prairie winter to reinforce Crozier's detachment. Some men suffered frostbite and others went snowblind. But an urgent message came through from Crozier, saying that Indians were joining the half-breed rebels in robbing stages and looting, and in planning an attack on Prince Albert or Fort Carlton. They were also cutting the wires of the Dominion Telegraph line which had been extended from Port Arthur on Lake Superior to Battleford in 1878. In spite of hardships Irvine and his men hurried on, travelling 291 miles in seven agonizing days, and arriving at Prince Albert in the evening of March 24.

Two days later Irvine's party left for Fort Carlton. But before they arrived there, Crozier and a party of fifty-six Mounted Police and forty-three Prince Albert volunteers (local townsmen and farmers) had tried to retrieve supplies and ammunition left behind by a trader who had abandoned his store at Duck Lake. About two miles from that point

Crozier's party was intercepted by some 350 half-breeds under Gabriel Dumont. The rebels sent out a flag of truce, but soon began moving their forces to outflank the police-volunteer party.

Crozier realized their ruse before his men were completely surrounded, and they fought their way out through the enemy ranks. But they were outnumbered more than three to one. Besides, as the police and volunteers manoeuvred with difficulty in the deep-crusted snow, the half-breeds were able to snipe at them from the cover of a wooded ridge and a log building near the trail. Both police and volunteers, working as separate groups, lost heavily. There were twelve killed and twelve wounded, five horses dead and several disabled, and the seven-pounder gun was left in the field but brought in later. Leaving behind some of the Prince Albert dead who, according to Turner, had fallen near the log building and could not be reached without incurring suicidal risks, they retreated.

The defeat of the police party proved to the Indians and the Métis that the police were not invincible, as they had seemed to be until this time. But because Dumont was wounded, his men failed to pursue the retreating column and finish it off as he expected them to, presumably because of an order from Riel, who was averse to actual bloodshed. So the police and volunteers reached Carlton without further loss.

When Commissioner Irvine arrived there later in the day, everyone agreed that Prince Albert, a well-established settlement surrounded by pioneer farmers, and the only white settlement in the district, was the logical centre of defence. Fort Carlton, on the other hand, was merely a Hudson's Bay Company post without settler population. Also it was on the river's edge below a three-hundred-foot bank, and especially vulnerable to attack from above.

That night, in preparation for evacuating Carlton, men loaded sleighs with supplies and sank surplus material through holes cut in the river ice to keep it from the rebels. They also stuffed hay into mattresses for the wounded men in the sleighs. Then in the early hours of the morning some of the loose hay leaped into flame from contact with an overheated stove pipe. The men, helpless, watched the fort burn. Police and volunteers evacuated it at 4:00 A.M.

Hours earlier, the flames had attracted the attention of the Métis nearby. They galloped up to investigate, then galloped back to report to Riel and Dumont. Again Dumont wanted to attack and wipe out the retreating party. But again Riel refused, preferring to wait till later. So the straggling two-mile column, which took two hours to climb the steep hill outside the fort, marched on unmolested and reached Prince Albert later that same evening.

The panic-stricken townsfolk welcomed them with great relief, not knowing how near to panic the newcomers themselves had been not long ago. Irvine chose the Presbyterian church and manse as a central refuge and ordered a loop-holed, nine-foot stockade of cordwood built around them. Some men carried in stores, blocks of river ice, and big supplies of arms and ammunition. Others pulled down all the buildings immediately surrounding their make-shift citadel. Then the 1,800 townsfolk and refugee settlers moved in or near the church fortress. When the dreaded attack came, they would all crowd in.

Meanwhile the government was organizing military relief, and toward the end of March it wired Commissioner Irvine: "Major-General Commanding Militia proceeds forthwith. . . . On his arrival, in military operations when acting with militia, take orders from him."

Before Major-General Frederick Middleton and his two thousand troops arrived in the Saskatchewan district via the CPR, however, the massacre of Frog Lake occurred.

The officer in charge of about twenty-five police at Fort Pitt, some thirty-five miles from Frog Lake, was Inspector Francis Dickens, then serving his eleventh year with the Force. To the people of the district this slight little man with the distinctive reddish beard seemed silent and morose, though his obvious introspection was undoubtedly enhanced by the growing affliction of deafness. Dickens, like Superintendent Crozier, had for several months been alarmed at the half-breeds' unrest. Now, as it became apparent that the Indians were in sympathy with the half-breeds, he grew convinced that the white people of the district were in danger from Big Bear and his Crees.

On March 20, Dickens sent a message to Indian agent Tom Quinn at Frog Lake. He urged either that the settlers should go to Fort Pitt for protection or that the Indian agent should accept an extra guard of Mounted Police to reinforce Corporal R.B. Sleigh and the small guard already serving under Quinn's orders. But Quinn, himself a Minnesotan of mixed Sioux blood, dreaded antagonizing the Indians, and refused both offers. Moreover, he felt that the presence of any police offended Big Bear. He ordered the police to return to Fort Pitt. Reluctantly they withdrew.

On the morning of April 2 the Crees, led not by Big Bear who protested against it, but by war chief Wandering Spirit, attacked Frog Lake. At first the braves, in full war paint, merely looted, but later they killed Quinn and seven other men. Only at the intervention of the half-breeds did they spare the lives of the other whites, taking them instead as prisoners to the Indian camp.

Eleven days after the Frog Lake massacre, Big Bear, with 250 Crees, camped near Fort Pitt. He explained to Inspector Dickens that his young braves were getting out of hand, and he tried to persuade him to abandon the police fort and so avoid more bloodshed. But instead of complying, Dickens accepted the offer of the Hudson's Bay Company factor, W.J. Maclean, to go out and negotiate with the Indians.

The next day, however, with negotiations still under way, the Crees opened hostilities. Constables D.L. Cowan and C. Loasby and Special Constable H. Quinn, nephew of the Indian agent, inadvertently rode near the parley camp after a scouting expedition to Frog Lake, and the Indians fired on them.

The three men galloped toward the fort amid a hail of bullets. Cowan's horse, excited, began to buck. Cowan swung from the saddle and ran for the fort, but was shot dead. Loasby continued to gallop straight for the fort, a stream of blood flowing from a serious thigh wound. Then his horse, shot in the neck, fell, and Loasby rolled with him. Big Bear's son-in-law Lone Man, close in pursuit, shot him in the back as he got to his feet, then, thinking him dead, galloped away. But Loasby staggered to his feet and lurched toward the fort, where he was met and carried in by one of the Hudson's Bay clerks. Quinn, who tried a roundabout way, was taken prisoner. His life was spared at the insistence of an Indian who knew and liked him.

Later that day the Crees sent word to Fort Pitt that they were holding Maclean prisoner. The messenger also carried a letter from Maclean which Big Bear had commanded him to write to his family, advising them to join him in the Indian camp for safety. They decided to do so, and the score of Hudson's Bay Company men went with them, all of them subsequently held by the Indians till the end of hostilities. Again Big Bear insisted that the police should abandon the fort, promising them safe conduct, and warning them that his followers were determined to burn the fort that night.

Inspector Dickens knew that about two dozen police could not possibly defend Fort Pitt against several hundred well-armed Indians. Surrender was equally out of the question. He decided to retreat to Battleford, where he could join the fight against Cree Chief Poundmaker.

That night, April 14, it snowed heavily. Under cover of the storm, the police stole out of the fort, carrying the wounded Loasby. Ahead of them lay a hundred-mile journey down the ice-filled Saskatchewan River, and the only craft available was a scow that Dickens had had built during the past few days. It leaked, flooded and almost sank when the men crowded into it. But they bailed desperately and managed to cross the river, then camped till dawn. For seven wretched days they travelled down the river, constantly bailing, their wet clothing freezing to their bodies in the bitter cold. At night, with no relief from the ceaseless north wind and with no way of drying clothes or blankets, they camped on the shore.

On the morning of April 22, Dickens and his suffering, exhausted party arrived at Fort Battleford. Scouts from that point had seen them coming, and they were welcomed by a Mounted Police band directed by Sergeant Bagley. Incidentally, Dickens' health, weakened by the stresses of his previous ten years with the Force, was ruined by the journey.

At Fort Pitt, Indians galloped up almost as soon as the police had left. Suddenly confronted with an abundance of goods free for the taking, the starving, impoverished Indians smashed windows and doors. Then they fought among themselves for anything movable—kegs of nails, bolts of calico, woollen shawls and so on. Most important were the supplies of food, which helped them to keep the rebellion going. Dickens' gold watch, which he had left behind, was eventually offered for sale by a half-breed, and so was recovered many years later.

Meanwhile, two parallel columns of militia, each reinforced by a substantial body of Mounted Police, were marching north from the CPR line. The main column, under General Middleton, clashed unsuccessfully with the rebels at Fish Creek and was forced to halt and await reinforcements.

The western column, under Lieutenant-Colonel W.D. Otter, reached Battleford then set out to attack Poundmaker at Cut Knife Hill some thirty miles farther west. Almost one-third of the attacking force were seventy-five Mounted Police under Superintendents W.M. Herchmer and Percy R. Neale, second of the Old Originals to sign on at Lower Fort Garry in 1874. The police occupied the most dangerous positions throughout, acting as advance, rear and flank guards. Otter's clash with the rebels, however, was no more successful than Middleton's, and he ordered a retreat to Battleford. Again the police took up their positions on the exposed parts of the column.

When General Middleton resumed his advance from Fish Creek he was more successful. On May 12, he won a decisive victory by capturing the half-breed headquarters at Batoche. Several days later Louis Riel surrendered to a scout, and was soon on his way with twenty-four other prisoners, by steamer, wagon and train, to North-West Mounted Police headquarters at Regina. Gabriel Dumont escaped to Montana.

The full-scale war which Riel had planned had never materialized. The English half-breeds, invited to join him at the beginning of the rebellion, had voiced their sympathy but had disapproved of resorting to arms. The great Blackfoot Confederacy in the south had also refused, partly because of the influence of Father Albert Lacombe, noted Roman Catholic missionary, and of Inspector Denny, who had retired and had become an Indian agent. Their refusal also came partly because the government, in alarmed haste, had sent huge supplies of food to them.

But W.G. Hardy's comment in *From Sea unto Sea* is perhaps the most illuminating: "What the Blackfeet noted most of all was the speed with which, by April 2, the CPR had deposited the Winnipeg militia at Qu'Appelle. They and all the Indians in the south realized what Riel had never understood—that in 1885 Canada had a transcontinental. That fact alone localized the insurrection." In any case Riel, who had hoped for a full-scale uprising of all the Métis, the English half-breeds and some 20,000 Indians, actually had under his command only about 500 Métis and 1,000 Indians.

From Batoche, Middleton's column marched west to Battleford, where Poundmaker gave himself up to prevent more bloodshed among the combatants. There at the Mounted Police barracks the British general, rotund and pompous, sat on a camp stool before the erect, dignified chief, esteemed by all who knew him as a particularly high principled human being. And there Middleton insulted Poundmaker and his followers throughout the question period, openly doubting Poundmaker's word and calling him a liar. At the end of what had actually been a trial, except for lack of legal procedure, Poundmaker was led away in handcuffs.

From Battleford, Middleton's column marched to Fort Pitt. There they met Major-General T.B. Strange and the Alberta Field Force which, advancing from Calgary and Edmonton, had been chiefly responsible for saving the western prairies from Indian war.

Inspector Steele's contingent in this field force was made up of the twenty-five Mounted Police who had served with him in the Rockies, part of a cavalry regiment, and a mounted corps known as Steele's Scouts. The Scouts, which Major-General Strange called the "eyes and ears" of his command, included about a hundred settlers and cowpunchers, a missionary, four Mountain Assiniboine Indians and other volunteers. Later in May a patrol party of Steele's Scouts found Cowan's mutilated body near Fort Pitt, with handcuffs which the Indians had found at the fort attached to his wrists, and part of his heart impaled on a stake nearby. A half-breed told later how, half an hour after Cowan was killed, three young Indians had cut out his heart, planning to eat a piece of it.

Inspector A. Bowen Perry's contingent in the Alberta Field Force contained twenty-four Mounted Police from Fort Macleod, an infantry unit and a transport section. When they reached the crossing point of the Red Deer River between Calgary and Edmonton, they found that the ferry had been smashed to bits by the spring floods. The river was in flood, 250 yards wide, with a strong current. The only visible means of crossing was a small skiff that would carry six persons.

Perry set fatigue parties to building a raft out of heavy square timbers they found on the river bank. Two hours later they began loading the nine-pounder gun they had brought with them, the gun carriage, ammunition and harness. They tied the horses' picket ropes together to make a 1,200-foot cable and fastened it to the raft. Then they took the other end of the rope across the river in the skiff, and twisted it around the trunk of a large tree.

The raft was then pushed into the river, with Perry and the gun detachment aboard, and it began to cross rapidly toward the north bank. But the rope frayed as it was paid off from the tree, and the slender cable parted. The raft was swept away downstream and back toward the south bank of the river. Inspector Perry and Constable Diamond dived into the icy water. Grabbing the rope they swam to shore with it and fastened it to a tree. But the momentum of the raft snapped the rope and again it drifted downstream until at last, about three miles farther down, the current drove it against the north shore.

The landing point, however, was under a cutbank thirty feet high. With great difficulty the men of the gun detachment hauled the gun, gun carriage, ammunition and harness up the almost perpendicular bank. Then, to get back to the crossing, they made a six-mile detour overland around a large swamp and cut more than a mile of new road through a heavy wood.

Wagons and carts were taken to pieces and ferried across the river, as were supplies. The horses swam over. The 150 men of the infantry unit crossed in the small skiff, six at a time, and stood guard in case of Indian attack. Last of all, the Mounted Police and teamsters crossed. Then the column proceeded to Edmonton, but only after Perry had thoughtfully obtained lumber from a nearby sawmill and had supervised the construction of a ferry for the use of other columns.

After Poundmaker's surrender the only important rebel still at large was Big Bear. But he had been pressed to the limit by Steele and his Scouts, and on July 2, famished and worn out, he was captured near Fort Carlton by three constables of Sergeant Smart's temporary detachment there. The militia went home and the North-West Mounted Police resumed full responsibility for maintaining law and order in the North-West Territories.

Later that year trials were held in Regina. Eight Indians, including

Wandering Spirit, were subsequently hanged at Battleford for various massacre murders. Poundmaker and Big Bear, both of whom were proved to have been overruled by younger Indians and had numerous other points in their favour, received three-year prison sentences at Stony Mountain Penitentiary in Manitoba. Poundmaker pleaded to be hanged instead. Although later their sentences were shortened, both chiefs emerged from prison as old and broken men, and died soon after. Eighteen Métis were imprisoned for terms of one to seven years, and two whites were tried but acquitted.

Louis Riel was found guilty of high treason and sentenced to death in spite of the jury's recommendation for mercy. This aroused great controversy. French-speaking Canadians, especially Roman Catholics, regarded him as a martyr, while English-speaking Canadians, especially Protestants, considered him a traitor. Experts at the trial had differed as to whether or not he was sane, and a jury in 1885 could make a decision only in accordance with the knowledge of the period.

On November 16, after many appeals and reprieves, Riel was hanged at the Mounted Police barracks at Regina. Engaged as hangman was an old freighter, Jack Henderson. Sixteen years earlier he had been seized by Riel's men and imprisoned at Fort Garry during the Red River insurrection, and he had not seen Riel since. After the execution false reports were circulated that Riel's body had been mutilated, so Commissioner Irvine had the coffin opened in the presence of the highly respected French-Canadian pioneer Treffle Bonneau before Bonneau took the body to St. Boniface, near Winnipeg, for burial.

For a while Mounted Policemen lacked due credit for their share in suppressing the uprising. Because they were not part of a military organization they received not one military award, although they had performed outstanding acts of heroism and, like the military, had suffered wounded and dead. The citizen-soldiers received medals and even land grants, but again the Mounted Policemen received nothing. Moreover, the government gave no recognition even for outstanding police services, such as when, at the end of hostilities, Inspector Steele saved the Indian Department thousands of dollars by preventing the looting of farm implements and stores from the Saddle Lake Indian reservation. It was not until many years later that an injustice was acknowledged and Mounted Policemen were presented with medals commemorating their part in the North-West Rebellion.

The duties of the Force after the Rebellion were more onerous than ever. First the men in scarlet had to gather evidence and witnesses for the trials of the rebel leaders. Later they furnished heavy guards for Riel and the eight Indians sentenced to be hanged, and for the other Indians sentenced to terms in prison. Then police in the north patrolled more intensively than before to guard against further Indian and half-breed disturbances. And police in the south had to instigate a new campaign against thriving whisky traders and smugglers who had taken advantage of the understaffed southern detachments to get back into business.

To handle this extra work and that arising from the rapidly growing population of the North-West Territories, Mounted Police strength was almost doubled. By the end of 1885 it stood at 1,039, with the police arranged in ten Divisions and stationed according to need in various sections of the Territories.

On March 31, 1886, Commissioner Irvine retired. Crozier, by then assistant commissioner, was also due to retire soon. So the government had to look elsewhere for the next Commissioner. They appointed forty-six-year-old Lawrence William Herchmer, English-born but with United Empire Loyalist ancestry, a brother of Superintendent W.M. Herchmer. His mother was a niece of J.M.W. Turner, the famous English painter.

Commissioner Herchmer, who took office on April 1, had no previous service with the Mounted Police, and only limited military association. But he had had experience in the North-West Territories as a commissariat officer of the Boundary Commission, as an inspector of Indian agencies, and as commissioner of the rebellion losses in 1885. His strength lay in being a strong disciplinarian with a genius for detail, both vital to a Force almost half composed of new recruits.

Herchmer was immediately and passionately devoted to the Force and determined to mold and improve it. He noted everything from the condition of the mess rooms to the fact that one inspector was "killing horses to see his wife regularly."

"Constable Hutchinson," Herchmer wrote to one officer, "states that he is liable to lose heavily through your ordering him away so suddenly, as he had bought a lot of pigs from you and the sows having just pigged. How did he manage those pigs on patrol?"

As Herchmer soon realized, the police were still an assorted lot greatly in need of specific instructions. So during his first year in office new standing orders were issued. These explained to every policeman his manifold duties and became the forerunner of the notable 'Rules and Regulations'. Other Herchmer reforms included authorization to establish a plainclothes detective section to make it easier to enforce the liquor laws, introduction of more efficient rifles, and inter-divisional shooting matches to promote greater interest in musketry. An indoor riding school was built at Regina, and more and better horses were purchased.

This fourth Commissioner regretted that his constables earned only fifty cents a day and that all ranks slept on lumber, and he worked indefatigably to improve their conditions. He could not persuade the government to increase pay and allowances, but he did secure pensions for NCOs and men, which encouraged them to stay with the Force rather than leave it after a few years' service, as many had done up to this time. He organized canteens that sold small supplies at cost, and he allowed the sale of beer in the canteens, aiming to keep the police out of liquor bars if possible. He instituted a system of compensation for kits so that care would be rewarded. He insisted on a better quality of buckboards for patrolling. He ordered telephones installed in southern detachments. And he persuaded the government to stop issuing "bell" tents in which bunks could not be used, so that the men had to lie constantly on the ground, thus contracting rheumatism. Instead he asked for oblong tents with three-foot walls. But even Herchmer could not obtain beds.

"The Indians at the Industrial School have beds!" he exclaimed. "Yet the police, the finest body of men in the country, still sleep on boards and trestles!"

The police meanwhile worked so hard that even on boards and trestles they slept soundly. In addition to their regular police duties, they still paid out Indian treaty money and helped poverty-stricken Indians and half-breeds. They constantly set a good example with their well-cultivated crops and vegetable gardens, which also helped to make official rations more enjoyable.

By 1890 the population of the North-West Territories was growing slowly: together with that of Manitoba it was well over 200,000. Small towns developed to serve the needs of farming communities with stores, mills, livery barns, schools and churches. The sod huts and log cabins of homesteaders and ranchers were being outclassed by frame buildings. Open areas were being fenced with barbed wire. And although most prairie roads were only trails, branch railways followed the settlements, which in turn pushed out again from the railways.

Checking the welfare of settlers continued to be an important duty, and in the post-rebellion period a patrol system was devised to protect every settler in every police district. Large districts, or Divisions, were split into detachment areas. Then the inhabitants of each detachment were listed on patrol sheets, which the settlers signed when the police called on them. Thus no settler was overlooked, no complaint uninvestigated.

During the same period Superintendent Steele introduced mileage returns of the distances travelled on duty, and the system was later adopted throughout the Force. In one year Mounted Police patrols out of Regina alone totalled 334,400 miles, or more than thirteen times the distance around the earth at the equator.

On the whole police work progressed favourably. But members of the Force encountered one obstacle almost impossible to overcome. All too frequently they found that certain criminals gained undue sympathy from local juries. Even in the face of overwhelming evidence against mail robbers and cattle thieves, juries said not guilty, or petitions were forwarded favouring a reduced penalty. Whisky peddlers in particular seemed to gain almost unanimous public support, for in spite of prohibition laws the settlers insisted on imbibing if they wished.

When the police persisted in enforcing the law, the settlers called "indignation meetings" to protest. T. Morris Longstreth wrote in *The Silent Force* of one called specifically to protest against the police "subpoenaing respectable and worthy citizens to give evidence as whisky sneaks, thus interfering with the liberty of free-born subjects."

"There seems to be an absurd idea," Superintendent Perry wrote in rebuttal, "that the dismissal of a charge means a snub to the Mounted Police, whereas it strikes home at the root of society and threatens the lives and property of the very men who jeer and flaunt."

In spite of difficulties, however, the Mounted Police gradually reestablished order over the North-West Territories. Ten years after the rebellion even the Indian problem seemed permanently settled, and most tribes had developed their reservations into productive farms with good herds of cattle. Some Indians increased their income by contracting for police hay or by delivering coal. Many lived in log houses, using carpets, washstands and, in contrast with the police, bedsteads. Also, schools were being established on Indian reserves and children were compelled to attend.

By 1895 the country's development had resulted in police operations extending to Fort Cumberland two hundred miles down the Saskatchewan River from Prince Albert in the east, to the Peace River district in the west, and to the Yukon in the north. Yet the government considered it safe to reduce the strength of the Force to 750. That reduction was a tribute to the Mounted Police, signifying that once again they had brought a difficult situation under control.

Chapter 8
To the Golden North
1894–1899

There is a small river not far from here that the Minister, the Rev. McDonald, saw so much gold on a year or two ago that he could have gathered it with a spoon. I have often wished to go but can never find the time."

This amazing letter, written at Fort Yukon in 1864 by an ex-Torontonian, seemed to imply an imminent gold rush. Instead, it was more than fifteen years before gold mining was even fairly well established.

The settlement of white people in the Yukon consisted chiefly of a few hundred easy-going gold miners. There were no telephones or telegraphs, and the only transportation was by flat-bottomed river steamer, scow, boat and canoe in summer, and by snowshoe and dog team in winter. Although in theory the district was governed from Ottawa, in practice it was controlled by miners' meetings, at which a majority vote settled even matters of life and death. In the early 1890s whisky traders appeared on the scene and trouble followed. Miners held their meetings in saloons, and important decisions made by men dulled with alcohol were less logical and fair than formerly. Also, the saloons attracted gamblers and card sharps. Quarrels and gunplay resulted.

The situation alarmed the Canadian government. It was irked by the fact that traders, going into the Yukon by the only possible route through Alaska, an American possession, evaded payment of Canadian customs duties. The government decided that the best solution would be to call in the North-West Mounted Police.

In 1894, Inspector Charles Constantine went to the Yukon to report on conditions there and, with the aid of a staff sergeant, to collect customs duties from established traders. Constantine was the right man for the job. Now approaching middle age, he had already served with the Force for eight years. Before that he had served with the Red River Expedition, in the North-West Rebellion, and as chief of the Manitoba Provincial Police.

He reported that order could be established in the Yukon by a Mounted Police detachment of two officers, a surgeon, six NCOs and at least thirty-five to forty men. Each member of the detachment, he warned, should be "of not less than two years' service, and from twenty-two to thirty years of age, of large and powerful build—men who do not drink." But the government was not willing to pay for a substantial body of police. When Constantine returned north in the summer of 1895, his detachment comprised only Inspector D.A.E. Strickland, an assistant surgeon, and seventeen NCOs and men.

The police party, accompanied by Mrs. Constantine, sailed up the Pacific coast to the mouth of the Yukon River in Alaska, then up the river for 1,500 miles. Late in July they disembarked at the mouth of Forty Mile Creek just inside Canadian territory, and began at once to build Fort Constantine.

Building what was then the most northerly police post in the British Empire was a laborious task. Summer temperatures stood at ninety degrees in the shade unless it rained, and then the mud was knee-deep. Logs had to be floated from the nearest forest sixty miles upstream, then carried by men whose shoulders grew raw and blistered. Before erecting any buildings the police had to clear the ground of a one-to-three foot layer of northern moss. The ground beneath was frozen solid. Nevertheless by November, when the sub-Arctic days averaged only four hours of daylight, Fort Constantine comprised nine substantial buildings, one of them seventy-five feet long.

Winter temperatures dropped to zero indoors, to seventy-seven degrees below outdoors. In the spring thaw the roof of the fort, hastily covered with earth the fall before, trickled streams of dirty water, and the bunk beds had to be covered with tarpaulins.

Yet Constantine often worked twenty hours a day, terming himself "Chief Magistrate, Commander-in-Chief, and Home and Foreign Secretary." He wrote that he "had three tables in my room, and a different kind of work on each. I walked from one to the other to rest." His men, meanwhile, checked river steamers and camping outfits for smuggled liquor; collected customs duties, gold royalties and miners' fees; and investigated innumerable cases of theft, cabins broken into, and claims jumped. Within a year the score of Mounted Police had established order and, through the same integrity they had exhibited on the prairies, had won the miners' friendly respect.

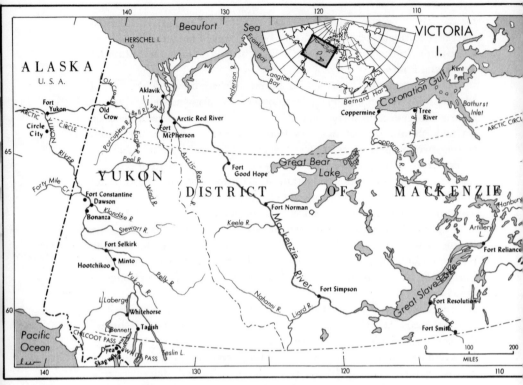

The Yukon, the Mackenzie Basin and the Western Arctic

Then in September, 1896, Constantine in his capacity of mining recorder signed three printed forms. They recorded the discovery of gold on Bonanza Creek, a tributary of the Klondike River, by George Carmack and his party. Soon hundreds of excited Yukon and Alaskan prospectors, learning of the fabulous quantities of gold on Carmack's claim, flocked to the Klondike. The great gold rush was on.

The police, underpaid and overworked, felt tempted to share in the strike. "It is pretty hard to hold the men," Constantine wrote to Commissioner Herchmer. Adding extra annoyance, their food ran low. They found they were short ten thousand pounds of flour, two thousand pounds of bacon, and all the dried apricots. Because there were no caribou that winter they had to endure the monotony of continuous pork and beans. And when Inspector Constantine asked for such supplies as a large coffee mill, a Maxim gun and four trolley wheels, he was sent by mistake about a ton of stationery. Yet all the Mounted Policemen remained loyal, and continued to maintain order among the swarm of fortune hunters.

But the police were too few, and in January, 1897, Constantine asked for reinforcements to increase his strength to at least eighty, all ranks. He also asked the government to authorize the investigation of the possibility of an inland, all-Canadian route to the Yukon. Even before Constantine's report reached Regina, Commissioner Herchmer had decided to send out a patrol to open up the Athabasca, Peace and Slave River districts and thus take one great inland stride into Canada's north country.

On January 4, 1897, Inspector A.M. "Buz" Jarvis, accompanied by a staff sergeant and two civilian drivers with dog teams, headed north from Fort Saskatchewan on a patrol that set a precedent for future inland winter patrols. Three long Indian toboggans held a tent, a camping outfit, sleeping bags, rifles, staple food supplies for the men, and dried fish for the dogs. Sometimes when the going was easy the men rode on the sleds, but usually they walked or ran behind. And when deep snow made the going hard they walked on snowshoes ahead of the dogs to break trail.

During the patrol the police visited traders, trappers, missionaries, half-breeds and Indians. They gathered information about the country, its inhabitants and its resources. They investigated minor crimes, took details of other offences for reporting to higher authority, and gave out handbills explaining game and fire laws.

By the middle of February they reached their destination, the fur-trading post Fort Resolution on Great Slave Lake, and two months later they were back at Fort Saskatchewan with two thousand dog-team-miles to their credit. In one great patrol the North-West Mounted Police had pushed halfway to the Polar Sea.

The gold rush continued. By fall, thousands of adventurers from all over the world—men, women, children, clerks, thieves, ministers, gamblers, carpenters, murderers—were streaming up the Pacific coast to Skagway and Dyea in Alaska, then trekking over the mountains into the Yukon.

Fortunately Constantine received reinforcements that fall. Inspector W.H. Scarth and twenty carefully chosen men, like the adventurers they came to police, took the short Skagway route. They packed their supplies on horseback over rain-drenched mountain trails to the head of navigation, then built boats and sailed down the Yukon River system to Fort Constantine.

Inspector Constantine immediately sent Scarth to Dawson to build Fort Herchmer, which later replaced Fort Constantine as North-West Mounted Police headquarters for the Klondike region. At Dawson, then a newly laid-out town at the mouth of the Klondike River, Scarth and his men found confusion everywhere. Shortage of supplies in the face of unusual demand had skyrocketed prices, with eggs costing $18 a dozen and sleigh dogs from $150 to $250 each, so the men who had not brought sufficient supplies with them soon were destitute. A seemingly inevitable epidemic of typhoid threatened the overcrowded, filthy, swampy town. And to make matters worse, ardent United States patriots insisted that the Klondike was American, and refused to obey Canadian laws.

Scarth dealt with all the problems. He made sure that the small supply of food was fairly distributed. He sent the destitute to the Lower Yukon, where prices were more reasonable, and from which point they could return to civilization. The Mounted Police surgeon tried to impress the Dawson townsfolk and campers with the dire need for sanitation. And the police reasoned, then if necessary dealt firmly, with over-zealous American patriots.

While the police in the Yukon grappled with the gold rush, the Canadian government decided to act on Constantine's suggestion that an inland, all-Canadian route be found to the back door of the Yukon. They instructed the Mounted Police to patrol from Edmonton via the Peace River to the Yukon, and to report on the practicability of such a route.

Inspector J.D. Moodie, who led the Edmonton-Peace-Yukon patrol which left Edmonton on September 4, 1897, realized that travelling more than a thousand miles through unknown wilderness would be a grim endurance test. His party, chosen with the utmost care, included keen young Constable F.J. Fitzgerald, who later became one of the Force's most daring northern travellers. The others were three special constables, a half-breed and an Indian guide. Special constables, incidentally, were engaged because of some special skill, as scouts, interpreters, guides, cooks, blacksmiths, and so on.

The patrol and their pack train of supplies plunged into the uncharted timber and muskeg. They chopped their way through three hundred miles of fallen timber, escaped a forest fire only by a last minute change of wind, and were constantly pestered by black flies and weakened by sickness. Ponies died from eating poisonous weeds. The guide went mad and disappeared into the wilds. At Fort St. John deep snow threatened to delay them till spring, but Moodie persuaded a local Indian to guide them through the mountain passes. Then, with hired dog teams and horse sleighs, the patrol fought its way through the passes and on north-westward.

But the pathfinder police had no way of reporting, either back to Regina headquarters or ahead to the Yukon. So in December, Commissioner Herchmer ordered three separate patrols to check on Moodie's progress. Each patrol helped further to open up the north country. The first patrol reached Fort Simpson, which was now the most northerly point reached east of the Rockies. The second patrol, which went by way of Lesser Slave Lake and the Peace River to Fort St. John, reported that the Moodie patrol had pushed on into the mountains.

Moodie and his men still pushed northward. By the beginning of October, 1898, they had been on patrol for thirteen months. Then the tattered, weather-beaten party, using hired pack horses after killing their own horses to feed dogs used earlier in the journey, reached the Pelly River, a tributary of the Yukon. Here they prepared to travel downstream to Fort Selkirk. They returned the horses to the Indian owner and dismissed him, cached pack saddles and other surplus goods, and set sail in a canvas canoe.

Floating ice, low water, rocks and rapids made the going perilous, and the canoe was frequently punctured. Moodie transferred two men and some supplies to a small raft to lighten the load, but the raft capsized. The men built a larger raft, but it was soon blocked in the ice channels. Moodie knew that they must have a sturdier canoe. After haggling a whole day he bought a Peterborough canoe from some chance-met prospectors, at the gold rush price of $450. Even then the awkward rafts had to be used for supplies, and this canoe in its turn was punctured. The patrol party spent precious time repairing it and portaging the canoe and rafts over ice-covered rocks.

Shortage of food weakened the men, and frozen clothes added to their discomfort. As they moved downstream the current grew so fierce that it almost sucked them under the floating ice, and canoeing became impossible. They cached their canoe and set out overland. For two days and nights with only occasional rest they plodded through the snow and stumbled over ice-glazed boulders.

On October 24 they reached Fort Selkirk, dazed with exhaustion. Since leaving Edmonton fourteen months earlier they had travelled 1,600 miles, including trips for supplies. Incidentally, the patrol's outstanding achievement marked the beginning of a great career for the almost fifty-year-old Moodie.

"I should say the overland route would never be used in the face of the quick and easy one via Skagway," Moodie reported of the Edmonton-Peace-Yukon route, and the government did not press the matter.

Meanwhile the North-West Mounted Police stationed in the Yukon still battled the disorder of the gold rush. Gradually they received reinforcements until, by the end of 1897, Mounted Police strength in the north stood at eight officers and eighty-eight other ranks.

One incoming party was led by Inspector Zachary Taylor Wood, the great-grandson of Zachary Taylor, twelfth president of the United States. He arrived at Skagway with police, dog drivers, stores and a hundred sleigh dogs. Wood himself stayed at Skagway, where he opened an office convenient for forwarding police reinforcements and supplies to the Yukon and for giving advice to travellers. There, too, he saw conditions which might well have developed in Canadian territory except for the Mounted Police.

Skagway's number one gangster terrorized the area. He was "Soapy" Smith, so named because of his ability to persuade people to pay ten dollars for cakes of soap wrapped in one dollar bills. Robbery and murder were routine. One Sunday morning Wood and another officer were awakened from their sleep on the office-cabin floor by a gang fight. Bullets whistled through the thin walls, but the affair was so commonplace that the men did not even get up.

During the winter of 1897 - 98 there was hunger in the Yukon for the second successive year. The daily ration at Fort Constantine fell to four ounces of bacon and eight ounces of flour for each man. Then the police heard of a raft load of meat frozen in thirty miles up river. The sleigh dogs sent with Inspector Wood had not yet arrived, so Inspector Scarth and seven men set out, hand-hauling four sleds. They paid $2,250 in gold dust for the 1,500 pounds of meat. Then they hand-hauled it thirty miles back to the fort, facing a bitter wind at thirty degrees below zero.

As winter continued, thousands more fortune hunters arrived at Skagway and Dyea. They climbed the Summit, crossed by the Chilcoot or the White Pass, and descended to Lake Bennett. There they planned to camp till spring and then sail downstream to the Klondike.

Obviously, spring would bring an even greater influx, so early in February, 1898, Commissioner Herchmer sent Superintendent Perry, a masterly organizer, to establish Mounted Police posts on the national boundary at those border passes. Perry organized and posted two strong police parties, one at the Chilcoot Pass under Inspector R. "Bobby" Belcher, and the other at the White Pass under Inspector Strickland. The posts were at first merely tents, but eventually they also included cabins.

Later in the month Superintendent Steele arrived from Fort Macleod to command the district, and Perry prepared to return to civilization. Trudging up the Chilcoot Pass, Steele's party faced a gale so cutting that the men often had to rush from the shelter of one tree to another, or huddle behind the heavily-laden transport company sleighs for a breathing spell. By noon progress was impossible, so they halted at the company's stables partway up the pass. The next day they passed

Sheep Camp, a tent town of many thousands of people, then overtook hundreds of over-burdened travellers staggering blindly through the storm. Many were floundering in drifts just off the trail and would have perished except for police assistance. The final incline was so steep that steps had been cut in the ice and a lifeline placed to mark the way, but the police could not find the lifeline in the storm, so they camped again till morning.

By the end of February, police posts at both passes were in operation, guarding the passes, collecting customs fees, inspecting prospectors' outfits to make sure they had enough food and equipment, and checking crime. Although violence and murder were prevalent in Alaska, men tucked their weapons in their packs on reaching Canadian soil, and the Summit detachments had little difficulty in that regard.

They encountered numerous other difficulties, however. At first Belcher's party had to pitch their tents on the ice of Crater Lake, just below the Chilcoot. One night in a below-zero blizzard the water in the lake suddenly rose six inches, soaking the bedding on the tent floor. For four days the blizzard prevented the men from removing the tents, so they took the sleds inside and slept on them to keep above the water at night.

Later a storm raged continuously for two months, till the snow on the level of the Summit was sixty feet deep. Then a further one-day snowfall of six feet completely buried the customs cabin and all the tents. During the height of the storm Belcher had to post a sentry to shovel away the snow and so prevent the sleeping men from smothering.

Firewood for the Chilcoot detachment had to be hauled seven miles by dog team. Various detailed records had to be kept, but often the necessary paper was snowed in somewhere along the trail from Skagway. The detachment had no safe, and the thousands of dollars collected in customs duties were kept in a bag in the office. Hence Belcher or his clerk must always be on guard in the flimsy cabin, which was grandly styled "the customs house and quarters for the officer in command," but which dripped like a shower bath, causing supplies, blankets and even papers to mildew.

Similar difficulties beset the White Pass detachment. Many men became ill, yet they remained on duty. Strickland himself worked on through a long siege of bronchitis till the doctor reported the matter to Superintendent Steele.

Steele, who had returned to Skagway, also had bronchitis, as the result of wading waist-deep in icy water then writing urgent dispatches for Perry before changing his clothes. He was under doctor's instructions not to return to the passes until cured. Nevertheless he climbed the

White Pass, ordered Strickland off duty, and installed another inspector in his place. But there was no one with enough authority to order Steele off duty, so he carried on.

From the White Pass he went on to Lake Bennett, where he found some seven thousand campers who spent every moment of the dim sub-Arctic days building boats for sailing to the Klondike in the spring. There he established headquarters for his own district which stretched north to Fort Selkirk. Then he settled down to an eighteen-hour work day and seven-day work week that included not only the usual police work, but also caring for the sick and burying the dead. During all that time the air for miles around rang incessantly with the sound of hammers, axes and whipsaws as more and more men arrived to prepare for the spring rush.

One of the first things Steele did at Bennett was order the painting of a number on every boat, canoe and scow. His men recorded those numbers together with the names and addresses of the occupants and their next of kin. Thus when the boats sailed north in the spring, police at Tagish and Selkirk could check the boats and their occupants against those records.

By May 29 the rotting ice had moved out of Lake Bennett and the great boat race to the Klondike began. A varied fleet set out. There were well-built skiffs; clumsy oblong tubs; scows with cattle, horses and dogs aboard; Peterborough canoes; and packing boxes with mackinaws for sails. "I went up the hill behind the office to see the start," Steele wrote later, "and at one time counted over eight hundred boats under sail on the eleven and a half miles of Lake Bennett."

In the afternoon he set out on the little iron steamer *Kilbourne*, planning to supervise their passage through the dangerous White Horse Rapids and the Miles Canyon. But after fifty miles, engine trouble forced the ship to turn back, and it was not until the next afternoon that Steele reached the canyon. There at the White Horse Rapids at the head of the canyon he found several thousand craft tied up.

In spite of the obvious danger, many boats had tried to run the dangerous rapids in the race to the goldfields. Corporal Dixon, a clever swift-water man, and his several constables from the detachment at the head of the canyon had risked their lives and saved a number of men, women and children from the swirling, rushing water. But 150 boats had been wrecked and ten men drowned.

Steele now assembled the thousands of travellers who had tied up their craft, afraid to sail further. "Many have said that the Mounted Police make the laws as they go along, and I am going to do so now for your own good," he announced. "No boat will be allowed to pass with human beings in it unless it is steered by competent men, and of that the corporal will be the judge."

Steele explained that the Mounted Police would list several of the experienced swift-water pilots already at the canyon for this work. They would serve in rotation at the reasonable fee of five dollars. Boat loads would be inspected. Women and children would have to walk the five miles around the rapids, under police protection. The travellers, apparently satisfied, obeyed his orders, and not one of the succeeding thousands of boats taken through the canyon was wrecked.

The day after the incident at the rapids, Steele returned to Lake Bennett. During the journey he met many more boats heading for the Klondike, but by the time he arrived at the lake it was almost empty of craft. The great rush along the "Trail of '98" was practically over.

In summing up Mounted Police work in the district to that time, Steele reported that his detachments had checked and advised more than 30,000 persons, and had checked and inspected more than 30,000,000 pounds of food. Also, at a time when total Mounted Police strength in the Yukon was less than two hundred, they had policed their territory so effectively that only three homicides, none preventable, were recorded. In addition they had collected $150,000 in customs duties and fees.

Their next task was to get that money, all in gold and notes, safely past the Skagway gangsters and on a boat bound for Victoria on Vancouver Island. By this time Inspector Wood had closed the Skagway office and moved to Bennett, so the police spread the rumour that "Zac" Wood was being transferred back to the prairies and was taking only his baggage and boatmen. Actually the Mounted Police kit bags carried gold and were so heavy that it took several "boatmen" to carry it all.

Perhaps news of the gold got out. In any case, when Wood reached Skagway he found "Soapy" Smith and his gang on the wharf. But the police had notified the captain of the CPR steamer *Tartar* of Wood's coming. As the inspector climbed onto the wharf he was relieved to see that the ship's hurricane deck was lined with sailors covering the pier with rifles. But perhaps "Soapy" had not seen what Wood had seen. He and his gang pushed their way through the crowd, closed in on Wood's escort, and began to jostle them. "Soapy" and Wood stood face to face, and gunplay seemed inevitable. But Wood refused to be panicked. "Soapy" decided not to attack, and changed his tactics.

"Why not hang around and visit Skagway for a day or two?" the gangster smilingly invited Wood.

Wood smiled back, refused politely, and walked up the *Tartar's* gangplank with his "boatmen" and his $150,000 "baggage." (Incidentally, "Soapy" Smith was killed about a month later, by a member of a newly formed citizens' committee in Skagway.)

By the end of June, 1898, the gold rush was over. Superintendent Constantine returned to the prairies and Inspector Cortlandt Starnes temporarily replaced him at Dawson. Now both police and government turned to the next task: to reorganize and clean up the Yukon. As of June 13, 1898, the Yukon Act severed the Yukon from the North-West Territories, and provided government of the region by a commissioner. The Yukon would have its own judicial institutions thereafter, and a legislative council, with Superintendent Steele appointed to the council.

The police in the meantime planned for greater efficiency in their own organization. Steele, who was now in command of all the Mounted Police in the Yukon, split his territory into northern "B" and southern "H" Divisions, with headquarters at Dawson and Tagish respectively. He decided to take personal command of the northern section.

Early in September, Steele arrived at Dawson, by then a town of five thousand inhabitants, but indescribably filthy and fever-ridden from the thousands of campers en route to the goldfields. Steele immediately ordered the building of thirty-four new prison cells, a hospital, quartermasters stores and offices. He also sent a party of police up the Yukon River to construct additional detachments every thirty miles, at points he had chosen on his way from Lake Bennett to Dawson.

Then the North-West Mounted Police set to work to clean up the Yukon, concentrating on Dawson. They patrolled everywhere, from the loneliest mining claims to the busiest street corners. They watched every saloon, every dance hall. A corps of detectives known only to Steele observed every proven or suspected criminal. The police undertook to enforce every law laid down in the Criminal Code and the ordinances of the Yukon council. They stopped the sale of liquor to children, insisted that gambling dens and dance halls be conducted honestly, and refused to permit obscenity and disloyal remarks in theatres. No liquor was to be sold without a permit and all public places must serve boiled water.

The Mounted Police arrested hundreds, taking the lesser cases before a Mounted Police officer as magistrate, the others before a higher court. Steele ingeniously made the offenders finance the Dawson Board of Health by ordering fines to be used for the hospitals, which were overcrowded with fever patients. He imposed staggering fines to help pay for milk at one dollar a tin, eggs at five dollars a dozen.

But the guilty preferred to pay up rather than face the alternative of working on the notorious Dawson woodpile. In one season police and government officials used almost one thousand cords of wood, equal to a pile a mile and a half long, four feet high and four feet wide. All of it was sawn into stove-lengths by prisoners working from dawn to dusk, even in forty below zero weather. Wife-beaters, disturbers of the peace, and numerous other offenders all took turns at the Dawson woodpile.

North-West Mounted Police work in the Yukon at this time included carrying and forwarding the mails, a public service the Force had rendered ever since it went north. As Christmas, 1898, approached and difficult winter travel made the police mail service more and more infrequent, some forty thousand people in the Yukon and adjacent Alaska mourned the fact that their mail was accumulating at Skagway. So Steele volunteered to establish a regular fortnightly service between Skagway and Dawson.

After the first trail-blazing trip, when river ice broke and two men were almost drowned, the service was a model of Mounted Police efficiency. Relay teams of men and dogs travelled night and day with over five hundred pounds of letters. Most teams were relieved every thirty miles—the distance between police posts—with the changeover taking less than twenty minutes, so that the six-hundred-mile trip was generally covered in seven days. During the winter of 1898–99, mail service patrols totalled a mileage equal to two and a half times around the world.

The police continued their other services with equal efficiency. Besides collecting the ten percent gold royalty due the government on mined gold, they escorted the gold from the Yukon banks to others at Seattle, Washington. According to Steele, the four men making the arduous eight-thousand-mile trip, with at least five tons of ingots each time, had more gold in their charge and under more difficult circumstances than any men who had performed such gold-escort duty anywhere in the world. Yet it was merely part of the work for which, including the extra pay allowed at that time for northern duty, they received $1.25 a day.

By the autumn of 1899 the Mounted Police in the north, numbering about 250 at their peak strength, had established order in the Yukon. "Those police fellers got a cinch on the country from the word go and they never let up," one old-timer said. "They ran the place like an all-fired day and night school. And it wasn't no picnic neither."

Superintendent Steele went back "outside" and Superintendent Perry went in to replace him. Going in via Skagway, Perry was struck by the complete change since he had established the Summit posts some eighteen months earlier. This time he travelled by railway almost as far as Whitehorse. Telegraph wire stretched almost to Dawson. Except in the outposts, civilians handled the mails. And the peaceful countryside was crossed with well-cut trails. Dawson itself was a well-drained city of substantial buildings, with sidewalks and electric lights.

Yet even as Perry noted these things, the Mounted Police were pushing farther north. In seeking three missing men during the fall and winter of 1899, Corporal G.M. Skirving patrolled from Dawson northeast to Fort McPherson, on the Peel River which flowed into the Mackenzie delta. He reached a new farthest-north point. Also, in making the first two-way patrol from Dawson to the Mackenzie River system, he had broken trail from the goldfields to a great all-Canadian waterway. That further advance to the north signified that the Force's successful policing of the gold rush was only the beginning of a great northern adventure.

Chapter 9
On the Northern Frontiers
1899–1904

Corporal Ryan of Hootchikoo, a small Mounted Police post on the Yukon River about fifty miles south of Fort Selkirk, was disappointed when his friend Ole Olsen failed to arrive for dinner on Christmas Day, 1899. But considering the heavy snowfall he was not surprised.

A week later, however, the corporal was alarmed to learn that the Norwegian telegraph linesman had set out from Fussal's Roadhouse at nearby Minto on Christmas morning as scheduled. Ryan learned, too, that Olsen had been accompanied by two young acquaintances from Dawson, Will Clayson, who had made a modest fortune in the goldfields and was carrying a large sum of money, and Linn Relfe.

As Corporal Ryan and a special constable searched the trail between Minto and Hootchikoo, they came to an unoccupied tent off in the bush. There they noticed several articles stamped with the name of an express company which had a cache nearby. Evidently the goods were stolen. Ryan knew that Constable A. Pennycuick at Fort Smith detachment had been looking for cache thieves. He notified that detachment and Pennycuick went down to investigate.

Ryan and Pennycuick found no trace of the missing men, and considered that they might have drowned in the Yukon River, which was still open in places. But when they searched the tent thoroughly on January 5, they found a pair of pliers like those used by Olsen on the Yukon Telegraph line, a rifle and a bag of cartridges. Then Pennycuick recognized the stove from a peculiar mark punched in it. He had seen it before, in the camp of two suspected cache thieves calling themselves Miller and Ross. The policemen now wired to Dawson and

Tagish, asking that descriptions of Miller and Ross be sent to all Yukon detachments, with orders for their arrest.

The day the wire reached Tagish, a staff sergeant there happened to see a Mounted Police wolf robe in a civilian's sleigh. The driver was George O'Brien, a well-known cache thief, on his way to the coast and "outside." He insisted that the Dawson police had given him the robe when they discharged him from jail several months earlier.

The staff sergeant wired Dawson and learned that the police actually had given the robe to the penniless O'Brien. But the Dawson police said they remembered O'Brien well enough to believe he was one of the cache thieves who called themselves Miller and Ross. So the Tagish police arrested him.

O'Brien, who now seemed remarkably prosperous with his striking black team and handsome yellow St. Bernard dog, had a suspicious amount of money, including two $100 bills in the soles of his shoes. His outfit contained field glasses, a carbine, two revolvers, ammunition, and two empty shells for a Winchester revolver. His sleigh was stained with what appeared to be blood, but a man cannot be charged with murder unless the fact of the murder is definitely established. So the police convicted O'Brien for the cache robberies, and continued to search for the three missing men.

With the tent as the focal point, Ryan and Pennycuick searched a strip of snow-covered country sixteen miles long and two-and-a-half miles wide. They found several trails leading from the tent to the Yukon River. One trail led to a clearing where a score of cottonwoods had been cut down to give a good view of the river trail from Dawson, as if someone wanted to watch gold-bearing travellers as they approached. In examining marks on the tree stumps the policemen saw that they had been chopped by an axe with several notches in the blade.

Near the tent the policemen swept away the snow. They found an axe with a notched blade, a double-bladed knife, the ashes of a fire, scraps of burnt clothing, and a roadhouse lodging receipt made out to Olsen. With renewed zeal they searched every inch of the woods and trails. After countless hours of kneeling and squinting along the surface of the snow, they saw two shallow impressions. There, digging down beneath the surface snow, they found huge patches of frozen blood, but no bodies. In the spring other police joined in the search. They found the fragment of a tooth, a belt, an oil bottle, and three bullets which had lodged in the earth or trees, but still no bodies.

Neither was there any link between O'Brien and the supposed murder until Pennycuick had a clever idea. He took O'Brien's dog to a trail near the tent and commanded him to "go home." The St.

Bernard obediently trotted to the tent and lay down at a spot where a dog might have been chained. He had linked his master with the crime.

Early in April the police and others sawed away long stretches of ice in the Yukon River. Then they dragged it, but without success. During the spring break-up, however, the Yukon River voluntarily gave up its dead. First came Clayson's body, riddled with bullet holes. Next came Relfe's, badly decomposed, but readily identifiable by the still-legible visiting cards in his pocket. His body, like Clayson's, contained bullet holes, and one bullet had broken a piece from a tooth. Olsen's body, discovered last, was also riddled with bullet holes.

The police spent the next year fitting together bits of evidence, locating and interviewing possible witnesses, and organizing their mass of information for presentation in court. Then in June, 1901, O'Brien was tried for murder.

The police produced eight witnesses, some of whom had travelled thousands of miles. Witness "Kid" West, who had worked with O'Brien on the Dawson woodpile, had come from Seattle to swear that the cache thief had talked to him of his plans for robbery and murder. When asked why he was willing to give evidence against a fellow criminal, the "Kid" explained that men like O'Brien were bad for the burglary business. "If this thing went on," he said, "the next time a little holdup is staged, a guy's liable to get forty years."

The axe and the tree stumps were exhibited in court. Then a Dawson sergeant testified he had given the axe with the notched blade to O'Brien on his release from jail. He remembered apologizing because the only axe the police could spare was such an imperfect one. Other witnesses identified the articles found near the tent. The knife, they swore, belonged to Clayson. The belt and the oil bottle were Olsen's, and the receipt for lodging had been made out to him at Fussal's Roadhouse. The bit of tooth fitted perfectly with Relfe's broken tooth.

Other significant details were disclosed. An unusual coin found on O'Brien belonged to Relfe. Shortly before his arrest O'Brien had tried to sell a strangely shaped gold nugget known to be Relfe's. By expert analysis the stain on O'Brien's sled was shown to be almost certainly human blood. The three bullets were from a rifle, a carbine and a Winchester revolver.

Gradually the crime unfolded. Early in December, 1899, O'Brien and his partner Graves, alias Miller and Ross, had robbed the express company's cache. Then they had set up their tent, cleared a lookout to the Dawson trail, made private trails to use for ambush, and kept watch with field glasses. On Christmas Day they shot Olsen and his companions. Then they stripped the bodies of certain articles; some they burned later, others they threw away. Finally they took the bleeding bodies down to the river on O'Brien's sled.

The judge and jury listened to the mass of evidence for eleven days. Then the jury pronounced O'Brien guilty, and the judge sentenced him to be hanged. Regarding the disappearance of Graves, the police reasoned that O'Brien had probably murdered him because he knew too much. Later a fourth body, decomposed beyond recognition, was washed ashore, substantiating their theory.

Ryan, Pennycuick and their co-workers won great praise for their persistence and their outstanding success in the case. The judge called the North-West Mounted Police "the pride of Canada and the envy of the world." The highest compliment, however, came from the murderer himself. As he walked to the gallows on August 23, 1901, he continuously cursed the Mounted Police.

One night in February of the following year three constables stepped out of character momentarily after a missionary from Alaska hurried excitedly to their border detachment at Wells. When he told Constable A.G. Leeson that a Chilcat Indian boy was being tortured to death for practising witchcraft, Leeson faced a dilemma. Canadian policemen had no authority on United States soil and, besides, he could not risk creating an awkward international situation. Yet he could not stand by while a boy was murdered.

Leeson solved the problem by protesting volubly that under no circumstances could the Mounted Police touch the case. However, as a private person armed with his own personal revolver he would be glad to help. He hurriedly changed from uniform to civilian clothes, and his two junior constables did likewise. Then the three private persons set out with their own revolvers, a pick, a shovel and an axe.

They followed the missionary to the Chilcat village and broke into the apparently empty house he indicated. Under the loose floor planking of an outer porch they found the scarcely conscious boy doubled up in an icy hole. They carried him to the missionary's house and revived him with food, heat and stimulants. Then he told them his story.

The Chilcat tribe believed that young Kodik was practising witchcraft and was thus responsible for the chief's illness. They decided that he must die. First they kicked his head to lessen his power. Then they starved and beat him, jabbed his chest with sharp sticks, tied him up and scalded him with steam from a boiling kettle. Finally they thrust him into the hole under the porch and left him to freeze to death in the forty-below-zero cold.

After hearing Kodik's story the three policemen remained at the mission till danger of reprisals seemed past. Then Leeson sent the other two back to the Wells detachment. Almost at once the Indians surrounded the mission and demanded that Kodik be returned to them. But the sight of Leeson holding a revolver kept them at bay, and at dawn they withdrew. Later in the day Constable Leeson smuggled the boy past the sleeping Indian camp to the police detachment across the border, where he stayed until he was granted permanent refuge at the Industrial School in Sitka, Alaska.

In July, 1902, the North-West Mounted Police, under the direction of Assistant Commissioner Wood at Dawson, began to investigate a much-publicized murder case. The only original clue was a key ring containing a name and address tag, found on a body decomposed beyond recognition.

After widespread and intensive work, the police located one of the two murderers through the boat numbering system established by Superintendent Steele during the gold rush. A detective in plain clothes followed clue after clue through the Yukon, Alaska and six of the United States, finally overtaking the other murderer in Nevada. Thus in less than seven weeks the Mounted Police tracked down two murderers, two thousand miles apart, through districts containing 2,500,000 people. And the only clue they had to start with was a key ring.

Other work of the Mounted Police in the Yukon during the early 1900s was less remarkable but no less important. They still made regular patrols, checked crime, mothered drunks, guarded long-term prisoners, and travelled thousands of miles to take lunatics "outside." They still aided other government departments by collecting various land and mine fees, issuing licences, collecting customs and taxes, taking census and guarding banks. For some of these extra duties they received compensation, but it was usually not commensurate with the work involved. For instance, extra remuneration for those handling mail at isolated posts in 1902 worked out to three cents a day.

In 1903 two outstanding patrols marked the further advance of the Mounted Police into the Canadian North. The first patrol penetrated still deeper into the western Arctic and sub-Arctic. The second opened up the eastern sub-Arctic and established Mounted Police authority in Hudson Bay.

The advance into the western Arctic, by way of the Mackenzie River system, was carried out by "G" Division which had headquarters at Fort Saskatchewan. Its aim was to occupy the Mackenzie River by placing a detachment at Fort McPherson and, if possible, another on Herschel Island. Superintendent Constantine of Yukon fame would lead the party from Fort Saskatchewan to Fort McPherson, then would return to Saskatchewan, leaving Sergeant F.J. Fitzgerald and four constables to carry on from there.

On leaving Fort Saskatchewan in May, Constantine and his men sailed up the Athabasca-Slave-Mackenzie River system. At first they used canoes, and at one point carried all their freight over a sixteen-mile portage. But from Fort Smith they travelled on the Mackenzie River steamer S.S. *Wrigley*.

About the middle of July they turned up the Peel River to Fort McPherson, a point 1,200 miles north of the nearest railway. Here they found the site of their new detachment a picture of desolation. There were only half a dozen buildings and a few native huts, and the land was swampy, cold and inhospitable. Superintendent Constantine sympathized with his men, but he could only rent an empty, well-constructed mission and leave them to establish themselves in the first Mounted Police detachment north of the Arctic Circle.

Before the superintendent returned to Fort Saskatchewan, he gave Sergeant Fitzgerald two important assignments. First, he was to patrol still farther north to Herschel Island, which was used as a whaling station, and if conditions justified the move he was to set up a detachment there. Second, he was to determine the easiest route between Fort McPherson and Dawson so that he could communicate with the outside world during the winter.

To Fitzgerald those assignments were a satisfaction and a challenge. They signified that he was attaining his ambitions, yet at the same time they presented him with more worlds to conquer. As a boy he had let an old sailor tattoo an emblem on the back of his right hand. He chose, not an anchor, but a star.

When he was only eighteen, his "blasted Irish assurance" helped him bluff his way into the North-West Mounted Police in spite of the requirement that a recruit had to be at least twenty-one. His splendid service with the Edmonton-Peace-Yukon patrol brought him promotion. To register for service in the Boer War he walked several miles carrying one boot because he had broken a toe the night before. Just before arriving he put his boot on and walked in without a limp. Outstanding service in that war brought another promotion. And now, aged thirty-three, engaged to be married to a charming girl, still ambitious and adventurous, he was in charge of Canada's most northerly police detachment, with two important assignments.

Two weeks after the police arrived at Fort McPherson, Sergeant Fitzgerald, Constable F.D. Sutherland and an interpreter set sail in a mission whale boat for Herschel Island at the mouth of the Mackenzie Delta. They found the rocky island, twelve miles long and from two-to-four miles wide, quite bare of trees and brush and even more desolate than Fort McPherson. By way of consolation, however, Fitzgerald and Sutherland were the first Mounted Police to make official contact with the Eskimos, and the first to enter a gateway of the famed North-West Passage.

A few days later the whaling fleet of the Pacific Steam Whaling Company arrived at Herschel. Its six ships were manned by about 250 powerful men who were not used to paying customs duties and who spent rowdy winters at the little island with plenty of liquor and native women. In spite of being overwhelmingly outnumbered, the scarlet-tunicked sergeant and his constable assistant met each captain as he stepped ashore. Fitzgerald issued blunt warnings that in future customs duties must be paid on all goods landed, and that liquor must not be supplied to the Eskimos.

Amazingly enough, the ships' officers accepted police authority with apparent goodwill, although an earlier report from a missionary had told how the natives used to get roaring drunk the moment the whalers arrived. They smuggled ashore a few bottles of liquor, but when Fitzgerald took one bottle from a native woman and broke it, then arrested the possessor of another bottle, debauchery ceased. Nevertheless Fitzgerald could see he would have to keep close check on the whalers, and he determined to establish a detachment on Herschel Island as soon as possible.

The return journey to Peel River showed what the police might expect from that merciless Arctic coast. While they camped on a sand spit a forty-eight-hour storm dashed their boat to pieces. The same storm ruined their provisions with salt spray, and as they travelled on in a hired Eskimo whale boat they had only a little flour, a few rabbits, and water from snow falling into the boat.

As for Fitzgerald's second assignment, he was unable to learn much that first winter about the route from McPherson southwest to Dawson, apart from the fact that there were three or four ranges of mountains between the two points. As late as March, 1904, no Indians had come from Dawson, so he could not get enough information to feel safe in setting out on a McPherson-to-Dawson patrol, and was even unable to send out a winter mail. Instead, the sergeant and his four constables made several shorter patrols out from Fort McPherson. And for the rest of the time the struggle for existence kept them almost fully occupied with fishing, hunting, and hauling firewood.

Meanwhile on August 22, 1903, a small police party had embarked from eastern Canada on the second great northern advance of that year. This advance, which established Mounted Police authority in Canada's eastern Arctic, was accomplished by fifty-four-year-old Superintendent J.D. Moodie, a staff sergeant and four constables.

Under the direction of Moodie, who a few years before had led the Edmonton-Peace-Yukon patrol, the police party sailed from Halifax on the S.S. *Neptune* with a government expedition bound for Hudson Bay. As they entered Hudson Strait, Moodie's party, like Fitzgerald and Sutherland, entered a gateway of the North-West Passage, but at the opposite, eastern extremity of the Passage. They called at coastal points on the mainland and on Baffin Island, interviewing missionaries regarding the condition of the natives, and informing whaling stations that in future customs duties must be paid.

On September 24 the police party reached Cape Fullerton, a whaling station and trading post in the best harbour on the western side of Hudson Bay. There they established a Mounted Police detachment of the newly created "M" Division of the eastern Arctic, for which later they would also establish headquarters at a point not yet chosen. As the Arctic winter of 1903-4 set in, however, Moodie and his men, like the Fitzgerald party in the western Arctic, had to content themselves for the time being with patrolling out from their detachment to learn something of their territory, and with fishing and hunting to provide themselves with food.

When the Commissioner reviewed the Force's northern work during this period, he remarked with satisfaction on the establishment of the detachments at Fort McPherson and at Fullerton. "They show," he said, "that no matter what the cost nor how remote the region, the laws of Canada will be enforced."

Chapter 10
Policing the Plains
1895–1904

While Mounted Police in the western Arctic and sub-Arctic grappled with the gold rush and then pushed farther north, and while others established themselves at Hudson Bay in the eastern sub-Arctic, the police on the prairies carried on as they had done in the post-rebellion decade of reconstruction. Their chief duties were still to patrol the plains, to maintain law and order, and to safeguard the welfare of the settlers.

Up to 1896 settlement was very slow in the region which would later become the Province of Saskatchewan and the Province of Alberta. Then in 1897 the federal minister of the Interior, Clifford Sifton, advertised in the United States and in Europe for potential settlers. Britishers, Americans, Scandinavians, Central Europeans and even many Canadians from Ontario eagerly flocked westward to take up free homesteads.

As early as 1896, efficient implements and machinery necessary to meet prairie conditions were available: the Oliver chilled-steel plough and the McCormick and Massey-Harris binders. There were also grain elevators for storage, and American experience in farming in regions with scant rainfall. But, as W.G. Hardy pointed out in *From Sea unto Sea*, "For Canada, the great and unrealized factor was the industrialization of much of Europe and the United States. Factory workers need bread and cities are parasites on the bounty of the soil." Canada's hard wheat was exactly what was needed for mixing with the softer wheat of Europe and the eastern United States. And more and more settlers migrated to the vast Canadian prairies to take up 160-acre homesteads and eventually to grow wheat.

A complaint of a settler to the police of the Duck Lake detachment in October, 1895, led to one of the most memorable manhunts in prairie history. After the settler's complaint that the Indian Almighty Voice had killed his cow, Sergeant C.C. Colebrook arrested the tall, distinguished-looking young Cree. He was sentenced to thirty days in the detachment cells. But that night he tricked the guard into opening the door, and escaped in the dark by swimming the icy Saskatchewan River. He called at the Cree reservation for provisions and his gun. Then, having persuaded an attractive young woman to go with him, Almighty Voice fled, well prepared for a long period of camping in the open.

A jealous brave informed the Mounted Police of Almighty Voice's plan. Sergeant Colebrook and a half-breed scout rode all night after the fugitives, and overtook them next morning. As Colebrook advanced to make the arrest, Almighty Voice warned the scout-interpreter that the policeman must stop or he would shoot. But Colebrook rode slowly forward, his right hand raised in a plea for peace. At ten yards the Indian shot Colebrook through the throat and he fell dead. The scout galloped back to the detachment, while Almighty Voice and the woman galloped away in the opposite direction.

For a year and a half the North-West Mounted Police tried in vain to locate the murderer. The government rejected Commissioner Herchmer's suggestion of a reward. Then indignant newspapers recalled a recent government reward of $500 for the apprehension of the person who had set fire to haystacks owned by an influential rancher. Eventually an equal reward was posted for Almighty Voice, but it accomplished nothing.

Then in May, 1897, the Cree suddenly appeared in the Minnichinas Hills about twenty miles from Duck Lake. He seriously wounded a police scout who happened to pass near him in the bush.

Inspector J.B. Allan, eleven men of "F" Division, and Postmaster Grundy of Duck Lake took up the chase, searching every gully and copse. They managed to drive Almighty Voice and two other braves who were with him into a large grove of poplars and willows. But they were too few to stand guard successfully. After trying in vain to set fire to the green underbrush, Allan led his party into the grove. The Indians opened fire, and Inspector Allan and Sergeant Raven staggered out, badly wounded. The police party withdrew.

By dusk the expected police reinforcements had not arrived. Corporal C.S. Hockin, now in command, feared that the Indians would escape. He and his men made a second attack. But again they failed to drive the Indians out, and this time their casualties were more severe. Corporal Hockin, Constable J.R. Kerr and Mr. Grundy lay dead. Again the diminished police party withdrew.

Reinforcements arrived from Prince Albert at sunset, with Superintendent S. Gagnon in charge of police, volunteers and a seven-pounder gun. Meanwhile Commissioner Herchmer had been informed of the situation by telegraph. He ordered his men to stop taking unnecessary risks, and sent Assistant Commissioner J.H. McIllree, two officers, twenty-four men and a nine-pounder gun by special train from Regina to Duck Lake.

On their arrival at the grove about 10:00 P.M., McIllree ordered the whole party to surround the wood in readiness for an attack at dawn. By this time settlers and Indians from miles around were there as spectators. But the only sign of life in the grove came at midnight when Almighty Voice called out in Cree.

"Send me food, for I am very hungry," he asked. "Tomorrow we will fight to the end." But the police made no reply, and he said no more.

At dawn Almighty Voice's mother seated herself on a knoll nearby and chanted her son's death song, praising his skill and daring, and pleading with him to be brave to the end. Simultaneously the police raked the grove with gunfire. Later they found Almighty Voice and one companion lying dead in a gun-pit the fugitives had dug. The third Indian lay nearby, also dead.

This same incident is described by Chief Buffalo Long Lance, the adopted son of Almighty Voice's mother, in the book *I Am an Indian*. His story depicts the "famous Indian outlaw" making "the greatest single-handed stand in all the history of the North American West," with "one thousand Mounties and volunteers standing by." In spite of a few inaccuracies of detail, it gives the underlying truth from the Indian point of view. It also indicates the tragic gulf between the whites and the Indians.

Another much publicized murder case during the same period was that of Charcoal, idol of the Blood Indians, admired and liked by the Macleod police. This incident was a tragedy from both police and Indian points of view since Charcoal—"the equal if not the superior in character and prowess of the ideal Indian of Fenimore Cooper's novels," according to Steele—had been provoked to murder.

Charcoal, like Almighty Voice, eluded the police successfully and could easily have escaped to Montana, but preferred not to do so. Eventually he was captured by his two brothers. He would probably have escaped the death penalty, except that he had also by then murdered Sergeant Wilde. He went to the scaffold singing his own death song, in one of the most regrettable executions in prairie history.

Other work of the time was varied. In 1897 Mounted Police under the command of Fort Macleod policed the Crow's Nest branch of the

CPR which was then being constructed from Lethbridge, through the Rocky Mountains, to Revelstoke on the main line. That same year a troop of North-West Mounted Police under Superintendent Perry went to London to join in Queen Victoria's Diamond Jubilee celebrations.

Some work resulted from cooperation with American authorities, an association that had continued since 1874, when Commissioner French led the Old Originals on that first mounted patrol of the Force in response to the American call for help. Now, on request, the Force tracked down American horse thieves and other criminals who crossed into Canada to avoid United States police.

The resourcefulness of the prairie police was well illustrated by Constable Clisby of the Saskatoon detachment on the Saskatchewan River. He received a wire notifying him that a prisoner en route to the Manitoba Penitentiary had escaped by jumping from a train as it passed through the detachment district. But the Saskatoon ferry was out of order, so the constable had to take his big bronco across the river by other means. Clisby considered crossing by the trestle bridge high above the swirling water, but he knew he could neither ride nor lead the half-wild animal across it. So he commandeered a railway handcar and built a platform on it. After coaxing the awkward bronco aboard, he hand-pumped the unique transport across the trestle bridge. He soon overtook the escaped prisoner at a farmhouse, where he found him filing off his leg irons, while the settler who had lent him the file looked on.

Later the police charged the settler with helping a fugitive from justice. But the two magistrates who tried their fellow citizen's case showed the same sympathy that local juries of the post-rebellion period had shown toward whisky peddlers, mail robbers and cattle thieves. They dismissed the charge.

Toward the end of the nineteenth century, when the South African Boer War attracted world-wide attention, hundreds of Mounted Police tried to join the Canadian expeditionary forces. At first the government said they were needed at home, but later the Second Canadian Mounted Rifles were recruited under Mounted Police supervision. These troops were placed under the command of Commissioner Herchmer, who had obtained Prime Minister Sir Wilfrid Laurier's permission for six months leave of absence from Canada, partly to compare his corps with other police corps of the British Empire. Herchmer and his contingent sailed from Halifax in January of 1900. Superintendent "Sam" Steele led a contingent too, Lord Strathcona's Horse, also recruited under Mounted Police supervision.

During the war an unfortunate thing happened to Commissioner Herchmer. It is impossible to judge it fairly without knowing all the details, including whether or not Herchmer's state of health made him unfit to continue in command, as a higher authority said it did. In any case, after his regiment was marched away without him he reasoned that if he could not serve at the front he would be more useful directing the Mounted Police at home. He returned to Canada.

Sir Wilfrid Laurier, however, regarded his unauthorized return as insubordination, and dismissed him. Herchmer, who in 1886 had taken over a Force crowded with hastily recruited, undisciplined men, and whose boundless energy and genius for detail had built up a splendidly disciplined organization of loyal members, considered his dismissal a bitter injustice. But his appeal for reconsideration was refused.

In August, 1900, Canadian-born Superintendent Aylesworth Bowen Perry became the fifth Commissioner of the North-West Mounted Police. Perry, not yet forty years old, was a graduate of the Royal Military College at Kingston and a lawyer. He had served with the Mounted Police for more than eighteen years, on the prairies, in the Yukon, and again on the prairies.

Commissioner Perry's first Annual Report summarized the Mounted Police situation as he saw it. The duties of the Force, he said, were increasing because of regular police work among a greatly increased population and also because policemen were giving more and more assistance to other government departments. For the Department of the Interior they protected timber lands. For the Department of Agriculture they served as cattle quarantine officers. For the Customs Department they collected duties. For the Indian Department they handled treaty payments. And for the Department of Justice they guarded prisoners and escorted them long distances to penitentiaries.

Also, Perry reported, the approximately five hundred police on the prairies plus two hundred and fifty in the Yukon were too few, particularly as ten percent of Mounted Policemen were replaced by new recruits every year. Considering only the organized part of the North-West Territories, there was an average of only one constable to every five hundred square miles.

In addition, weapons, equipment and uniforms were out of date. And most of the Force's best horses had been sent to South Africa, with resulting need for the acquiring of sturdy horses which, he suggested, might be bred to advantage in certain sections of the country.

Before long Perry had remedied the situation. Up-to-date weapons, lighter-weight saddles, and sturdier horses and transport wagons were authorized. Obsolete articles of uniform, including helmets, pill-box forage caps and white gloves and gauntlets, disappeared from everyday use. Wide-brimmed Stetson hats, which for several years men had bought for themselves, were now issued as part of the uniform. Breeches and jackets were of smarter cut. A practical brown canvas jacket was issued for certain duties, and winter clothing was especially designed to meet the needs in various parts of the country. Later Perry even managed to persuade the government to issue the police with beds. Also, to minimize the effect of the annual ten percent change in personnel, he arranged to keep a reserve of fifty recruits in training in Regina.

In 1901, Commissioner Perry reorganized the Mounted Police patrol system. He solved the problem of too few men for too many duties over too great an area by detailing a certain number to special patrol duty. Unlike the men at the stationary detachments, these special patrols kept constantly on the move, thus covering the greatest possible number of farms, ranches and settlements in the least possible time.

Perry's greatest innovation, however, was the crime report. He insisted that every member of the Force must report in detail on his patrols, investigations and other work. Detachments must send their reports to Divisional headquarters, which in turn must forward them to North-West Mounted Police Headquarters at Regina. There digests of the reports were card-indexed and kept in files, so that the Commissioner had at his fingertips specific information about any matter concerning any district.

Detailed information about the men also had to be reported. Every half-soled boot, every cold in the head, every case of frostbite was listed and filed. It was the beginning of the marvellous system of Mounted Police efficiency. It was also the beginning of many complaints from old-timers who resented having to transfer their riding breeches from the saddle to the desk stool.

"Six vouchers for a lunatic's expenses!" exclaimed Constantine. "Men should be available for duty, not tied down to a form-filling routine."

"Any prisoner in our guardroom for a week," reported another officer, "will, I can safely say, have twenty-five sheets of foolscap devoted to him." But Commissioner Perry persisted, knowing that the efficiency of the system would eventually justify the extra work it entailed.

In October, 1902, the Mounted Police began to scour the prairies in their third notable manhunt within a decade. This case, however, was characterized by painstaking detective work.

The Calgary city police had arrested Ernest Cashel, a Wyoming youth, on charges of forgery. Then he escaped and the Mounted Police were asked to assist in his recapture. For several months they followed various clues with no success. Then J.R. Belt, a rancher living east of Lacombe, disappeared, as did his horse, saddle, shotgun, clothes and a fifty-dollar gold certificate. A man resembling Cashel but calling himself Bert Elseworth had stayed at the Belt ranch for several days. Hence the police suspected that Belt had been murdered by Cashel, with robbery as the motive.

The case, now probably a murder case but lacking a body, began to resemble the O'Brien murders. Constable A. Pennycuick, who had worked successfully on the O'Brien case, was detailed to work on this one.

While Pennycuick concentrated on Belt's disappearance, other Mounted Police searched for Cashel. They heard how he had "borrowed" a horse then abandoned it, and how he later stole a diamond ring, then escaped by riding a freight train, on which he also stole clothing from the trainman's caboose. At last, in May, 1903, a constable at Anthracite arrested the fugitive. He was wearing corduroy trousers like Belt's, and he had the stolen ring in his possession. But there was no evidence to prove that he had murdered Belt, so he was charged only with stealing the diamond ring, and sentenced to three years in Stony Mountain Penitentiary.

Now Constable Pennycuick, who was still trying to link Cashel with Belt's murder, heard that the so-called Bert Elseworth had stayed at a half-breeds' camp near Calgary. Among clothing Elseworth had left there he found a corduroy coat that matched the trousers Cashel was wearing when arrested. From the description given by the half-breeds, who had seen Elseworth with Belt's gold certificate, Pennycuick believed he could prove that Elseworth and Cashel were the same man. The only missing link was Belt's body. Then in July a farmer found a body floating in the Red Deer River, and a deformity of the left foot proved it to be Belt. Significantly, bullet holes in the chest were of the same calibre as the rifle and revolver Cashel carried.

The Mounted Police charged Ernest Cashel with Belt's murder. He was tried, found guilty, and sentenced to be hanged on December 15. However, when Cashel's brother went from Wyoming to visit the condemned man, he slipped him two loaded revolvers. Later Cashel threatened to shoot the guards, and escaped. For several weeks the police continued to get reports of the dangerous, armed fugitive robbing ranches. But neither intensive police patrols nor a thousand dollar reward brought results.

Meanwhile Superintendent G.E. Sanders of the Mounted Police detachment at Calgary charted the times and places of the robberies. He reasoned that Cashel must be hiding in the Shepard district and that, since the robberies were committed at night, Cashel must sleep in the daytime. Sanders organized a gigantic search by police and volunteers. It began at 8:30 A.M. one Sunday in January, 1904, with five separate parties instructed to search every building, root house and haystack in the mapped-out area.

Three hours later Inspector A.W. Duffus's party was searching a shack on the Pitman ranch near Calgary when a bullet thudded into the wall beside a constable about to descend the cellar steps. The party immediately surrounded the shack. Duffus called for Cashel to surrender, but there was no reply. Duffus ordered his men to burn the shack, and soon Cashel staggered out through the flames. Choking with smoke, he surrendered without a struggle. Nine days later, having confessed his guilt, he was hanged.

By contrast with Cashel's peaceful surrender, a boisterous desperado at Weyburn in May of the previous year had put up such violent opposition that the townsfolk took cover rather than help a Mounted Policeman make the arrest. All afternoon the "Idaho Kid" had paraded the streets, taking pot shots at verandahs. When a citizen protested from a window, the "Kid" warned him to duck back or be made into a sieve. Another citizen protested, and the "Kid" shot his hat full of holes. The indignant Weyburnite threatened to have him arrested.

"There's no one in Canada big enough to arrest me," the "Kid" boasted. "What's more, if any Mounted Policeman comes butting into my game, I'll eat his liver cold."

Nevertheless someone wired the nearest detachment, and Constable L. Lett, who received the wire about 9:00 P.M., flagged a freight train and went to investigate. By that time the "Kid" and his wife had retired to their hotel room. Lett suggested that the angry citizens should help rout out the desperado, but no one was willing. Only the town's justice of the peace agreed to stand within calling distance of the "Kid's" room.

Lett bashed down the door and strode in. The desperado tried to pull a gun from his hip pocket, but the constable jumped at him. Then the two men fought it out, with "Idaho's" wife adding a jab from time to time. Before long the place was a wreck, and both men were badly banged up. But when they emerged from the room, Lett had the "Kid's" gun and the "Kid" was wearing handcuffs.

An equally spectacular arrest made near Leduc had an unexpected ending. Because no other policeman was available, the young and inexperienced Constable Forbes set out alone in a buggy in pursuit of a would-be murderer who had beaten up his family and several neighbours. At a point where the trail dwindled to a single track, Forbes stopped at an ex-policeman's house to leave the buggy. There, partly because Forbes had been warned that the fugitive might be accompanied by a second man, he persuaded ex-policeman Firth to go with him. The two rode on together.

After a time they saw two men riding ahead, and galloped to overtake them. Forbes arrested one man, who protested. The young constable pushed him into a mud hole, threatened to blow out his brains if necessary, and handcuffed him to a tree. Then he went to help Firth, who was struggling with his man in a grandstand-style exhibition of wrestling on horseback. Forbes kicked the man's horse from under him while Firth held him by the throat in midair.

Forbes' report, written later, finished the story. "I found I had arrested the wrong man," he explained. "But he was very peaceful."

Other Mounted Police experiences of the early 1900s, however, completely lacked humour. When Constable F.D. Sutherland went to arrest a lunatic thirty-five miles out of Fort Saskatchewan in 1902, the madman shot and killed a settler helping the constable, then turned on the policeman. In the ensuing struggle he bit a piece out of the back of Sutherland's scalp, and the policeman had to choke him to overcome him. With the help of several settlers, Sutherland made a strait jacket of potato sacks, strapped the lunatic to a mattress, and laid him in the police wagon. Then he drove back to Fort Saskatchewan, while the madman on the floor of the wagon strained at his bonds and cursed wildly every step of the way.

In April of the following year, when a terrible landslide buried part of the Rocky Mountain town of Frank a hundred feet deep in rocks and debris, the Mounted Police took a leading part in the rescue work.

There was little humour to be found in the tremendous amount of work necessary to check horse and cattle rustling in the foothills of the Rockies during that same period. Sergeant Egan worked for five months as a hired man on a ranch in order to get enough evidence to prove that the rancher was in reality an unscrupulous horse rustler.

Commissioner Perry spoke with pride of the organization he headed. King Edward VII, who succeeded Queen Victoria on the British throne, was also proud of it. He considered its thirty years of loyal service, beginning with the establishment of law and order in a land of whisky traders and Indians, and continuing without a break through periods of railway building, settlement, rebellion, reconstruction, a northern gold rush, and still further expansion to the North. In appreciation he proposed to dignify the Force with the prefix "Royal." By the beginning of 1904 it was an accepted fact both in England and in Canada that the Force's new name would be the Royal North-West Mounted Police.

**Royal
North-West
Mounted
Police
1904 – 1920**

Chapter 11
Northern Achievements
1904–1909

In the period following the elevation of the North-West Mounted Police to the Royal North-West Mounted Police in June, 1904, the work of the police on northern duty was varied and outstanding, beginning with a difficult murder case.

One day in September Indian Chief Moos Toos reported some suspicious circumstances to Staff Sergeant K.F. Anderson of Lesser Slave Lake detachment. Two white men had camped at Sucker Creek on his reservation a few days earlier, he said. Only one had left, and an Indian boy had noticed that his dog would not follow him. Then when the women went out to search for any useful odds and ends left at the campsite they noticed the remains of an unusually large campfire. Also, the leaves of an overhanging poplar tree were coated on the underside with a layer of fat which must have condensed on the cool leaves as dense smoke struck them.

"Someone burned flesh in that fire," Moos Toos said.

When Staff Sergeant Anderson and Constable Lowe sifted the campfire ashes they found bits of bone, buttons, and part of a large, coarse needle. Then in a hole under the ashes Anderson discovered bits of flesh, and what seemed to be a human heart. Meanwhile Moos Toos and his people waded about in a nearby slough. On the muddy bottom they found a camp kettle and a pair of boots stuffed with various articles, including rags and the remainder of the broken needle.

Anderson rode after the man who had left camp alone, and soon overtook him. Charles King explained that his companion, who he said was named Lyman, had left ahead of him. But Indian trackers could find no trace of the other man, so Anderson arrested King.

The staff sergeant realized that he did not have enough evidence to convict King of murder. However, the broken needle had already linked articles from the slough with the campfire and the suspected murderer. Perhaps the slough contained more clues. Anderson paid the Indians one hundred dollars to dig a half-mile ditch and so drain the slough into Sucker Creek. They found a little case of the type used for carrying English golden sovereigns.

The case proved to be a most important clue. Through the manufacturer's name on it the police traced it back to England. There they learned that a Mr. Hayward had bought it for his son Edward, who had taken it with him when he left for northern Canada. King had tried in vain to throw the police off the scent by saying that his partner was named Lyman.

In February, 1905, at Edmonton, Charles King stood trial for murder. Police witnesses proved that King and Edward Hayward had left Edmonton as partners, and that the camp kettle was their joint property. A pathologist from eastern Canada identified the charred bone, flesh and heart as human. Hayward's brother travelled all the way from England to identify the sovereign case as the property of his missing brother. King was found guilty and sentenced to death, and in spite of a second trial on a legal technicality, eventually he was hanged.

Probably the most disagreeable and nerve-racking experiences of Royal North-West Mounted Police in the North were lunatic patrols. Such patrols from Dawson and Whitehorse alone numbered as many as forty in one year, usually carried out by solitary policemen because no more could be spared from other duties.

In December, 1904, Constable A. Pedley, accompanied by an interpreter driving a second dog team, set out to escort an insane missionary about five hundred miles, from Fort Chipewyan to Fort Saskatchewan. Pedley bundled him in thick furs, put him in an Eskimo sleeping bag, and strapped him on a police dog sled. For five days the dogs struggled through the slush and water, while Pedley and the interpreter ran behind, wet to the knees. Yet when they reached Fort McKay, Pedley's first act was to purchase moccasins, not for himself, but as further protection for the missionary's frostbitten feet.

Out of Fort McKay temperatures dropped to fifty degrees below zero, and severe snowstorms made travel even more difficult. The madman caused extra trouble when he refused to eat. But when Pedley, earlier in the journey, had taken him off the sled for exercise periods to encourage his appetite, he had almost escaped. So now the constable undertook the unpleasant task of force-feeding him.

Then a terrible blizzard developed. Travel was impossible, and the flimsy tent useless. Pedley entrenched the dogs in the snow, with an upturned sled forming a windbreak. He lashed the mad missionary, still in his sleeping bag, to a tree. Then he and the interpreter climbed into their sleeping bags and lashed themselves to trees. And so they weathered the storm for forty-eight hours.

After the storm they pushed on south to the more sheltered, wooded country. But this area was infested with timber wolves. Each night Pedley had to light a huge fire to prevent the hungry creatures from attacking, then interrupt his sleep to wake and replenish the fire.

Meanwhile the madman raved incessantly, and again he refused to eat. As a last resort Pedley freed him for exercise. But the madman waited till the constable had his arms full of wood for the campfire, then bolted into the open. After a desperate chase for a quarter of a mile, Pedley overtook him. But to get him back to camp he had to tie his hands and feet, then carry him the quarter-mile, facing a bitter wind and numbing cold.

On January 7, 1905, Constable Pedley delivered his charge to Fort Saskatchewan, and the Mounted Police there relayed him to a hospital from which he was discharged as cured in less than two months. But Pedley himself was less fortunate. The great physical and mental strain had seriously affected him, and at Lac La Biche on the return journey he went violently insane. He in turn was taken to a mental hospital. Eventually, after six months hospitalization and three months leave, he returned to duty.

While Pedley was still in hospital, a police convoy set out from Fort Saskatchewan on a herculean assignment. In spite of Moodie's adverse report after his Edmonton-Peace-Yukon patrol in 1897–98, the government had instructed the Mounted Police to open an all-Canadian backdoor route to the Yukon. This Peace-Yukon trail, ordered from Fort St. John on the Peace River to Teslin Lake at the headwaters of the Yukon River, would thus have to be built over the most difficult 750 miles of mountain wilderness that Moodie had covered.

Furthermore, the government instructed, this Peace-Yukon trail must at first be suitable for pack animals, and so built that it could later be made into a wagon trail. It must be eight feet wide through the timber. Marshes and swamps must be overlaid with brush. Streams must be bridged. Rest houses must be built every thirty miles or so. Moreover, the whole trail must be so carefully marked and brushed that any traveller could follow it without a guide. Government officials at far-off Ottawa could not possibly realize the stupendous task they set. Commissioner Perry knew, but he could not oppose the government order.

So on March 17, 1905, the veteran pioneer Superintendent Constantine left Fort Saskatchewan in charge of a road-building convoy which included another officer, thirty NCOs and men, and a long procession of laden sleighs with sixty horses. During March, April and May they travelled north-west toward Fort St. John, while every warm spring day softened the river ice and made crossings more dangerous. At one crossing the cook wagon broke through the ice. Two men were almost drowned and a horse died from shock and exposure.

On June 1 the cavalcade pulled into Fort St. John. There, since that point would be a police headquarters for at least the first summer and the succeeding winter, Constantine and his men spent two weeks erecting suitable buildings and haying.

Then on June 15 they began to construct the Peace-Yukon trail. As they had no road-building machinery, they had to rely chiefly on axes for hewing through mile after mile of mountain wilderness. The work was exhausting. Yet they painstakingly followed the government's instructions, clearing away standing timber and windfalls, grading steep inclines, and bridging streams. By September 25, when they went into winter quarters, they had built ninety-four miles of trail, over mountain passes, down into valleys, across swampy lowlands, and up over more mountains.

Although winter at Fort St. John that first year was dreary, monotonous and bitterly cold, for the men of the advance section it was even more of a hardship. The supply steamer had arrived at the fort too late for supplies to be forwarded along the line of construction. Certain vital supplies were freighted by Mounted Policemen driving one-horse sleighs over the difficult mountain trail, but the horses became so exhausted that they had to be helped to their feet in the mornings. Under the circumstances new clothes and boots were not considered vital, and the men of the advance section had to replace their tattered clothing with moose hide and flour sacks.

The summer of 1906 saw a further 134 miles of trail completed, again under most difficult conditions. Such torrents of rain fell that Constantine could not even make an inspection of the complete route, and a hay crop put up with much labour was ruined. Some of the men were so fatigued that they had to be relieved, and thirteen horses died during the season.

Yet the spring of 1907 saw the trail-builders back at work. Again exhausted men had to be relieved, and twenty-six horses died. But by the end of that third season 357 miles of trail stretched out from Fort St. John, and the most difficult part of the road was completed.

Then the federal government decided that the venture was too much for them alone. They ordered Commissioner Perry to try to persuade the British Columbia government to share in certain expenses and work, but Perry could not persuade them. So the project was discontinued. Some of the ablest men of the Royal North-West Mounted Police had spent three exhausting years building a road to nowhere. Dozens of horses had died. Sickness and fatigue had injured the health of many men. Constantine, whose strength of character, sound judgement and physical strength had caused him to be chosen for much of the Force's pioneering, died about six years later from disease contracted during this and other strenuous northern work.

In the meantime, other northern police performed their manifold duties, achieving many "firsts." The most famous of all regular northern patrols, the Dawson-McPherson, was inaugurated in December, 1904, by Corporal H.G. Mapley. The assignment had been transferred from Fitzgerald at Fort McPherson, to Mapley starting at Dawson, because Indian and Eskimo guides were more easily obtained there.

In 1905, Assistant Commissioner Wood and his men, also at Dawson, were the first in the north to trace a criminal through fingerprints. Actually, Wood was far ahead of his time. For several years he had advocated that methods of crime detection currently used in Europe and the United States should be used in Canada. He not only advised the establishing of a criminal identification bureau at Ottawa (one was established years later), but he also suggested that such a bureau should include photographs, descriptions and fingerprints of everyone arrested.

The fingerprint case in 1905 supported Wood's recommendations. The prints, found on a candy box and a lamp chimney in a cabin from which a gold watch and other things had been stolen, were the only clues. Wood's next move forecast the modus operandi (mode of operation) method of tracing criminals, instituted by the Mounted Police about thirty years later. He reasoned that only thieves of a certain class would rob a cabin. Then he listed the five known criminals of that class in the district, and had all five fingerprinted. The prints of the man named John Mullen were identical with those on the candy box and the lamp chimney. Next the Dawson police searched Mullen's cabin, and found the stolen watch and other valuables. Hence they committed Mullen for trial and proved him guilty.

A few years later, Inspector A.M. Jarvis made the first police patrol of the western Arctic islands, cruising by whaler in search of a wanted man. That same cruise-patrol took him to a new Mounted Police farthest-north point, about 250 miles north of Herschel Island.

Another "first" occurred in the Yukon about this time, not only a northern but a Canadian "first." A group of revolutionaries, estimated at about two thousand, planned to overthrow all police authority in the Yukon and to establish a "liberty government." Then they would seize the banks and the mines, and before reinforcements could be brought in from outside they would flee from the country, taking every valuable they could carry. They had cached arms and ammunition at strategic points, and their plan of attack included maps showing the distribution of Mounted Police detachments and the number of men at each.

Superintendent A.E. Snyder at Whitehorse heard a rumour of the plot. When his men searched a stable loft where the principal revolutionaries reportedly held meetings, they found incriminating literature and even the seal of the "new republic." The leaders of the plot immediately left the country, and lesser party members either left or went into hiding. The Royal North-West Mounted Police had prevented Canada's first attempted revolution. But acting on government instructions, they did not press the matter further.

The police work of "M" Division in the Hudson Bay district progressed in the meantime, under the direction of Superintendent Moodie, who in the summer of 1904 had gone to Ottawa to report in person to the government. On his return to Fullerton he was accompanied by Inspector E.A. Pelletier, who had formerly served in the Yukon, and nine other ranks.

During the winter of 1904–5, as during the previous winter, Moodie and his men made many dog team patrols to learn more about the country, often building igloos for shelter en route. Their chief difficulty was to obtain enough healthy dogs to make the tiring journeys. Nevertheless, when an Eskimo brought a request for the police to send dogs to the Norwegian explorer Roald Amundsen, Moodie generously sent him ten. Although Moodie did not know it at the time, Amundsen and his ship *Gjoa* were in the process of making the first voyage through the North-West Passage, 1903–6.

During the late winter of 1904–5 the Fullerton police helped to establish a "first" for the Force. Corporal D. McArthur and a small party took the Mounted Police mail from Fullerton to Churchill, from which point it was relayed across country to Winnipeg. From there it went by train to Royal North-West Mounted Police headquarters in Regina. It was the first time Moodie and "M" Division had been able to communicate with Commissioner Perry at Regina by land.

There were other "M" Division achievements too. A constable travelled almost a thousand miles to collect customs duties from the captain of a whaling ship. Another constable covered a 1,350-mile patrol from Fullerton to Baker Lake and return.

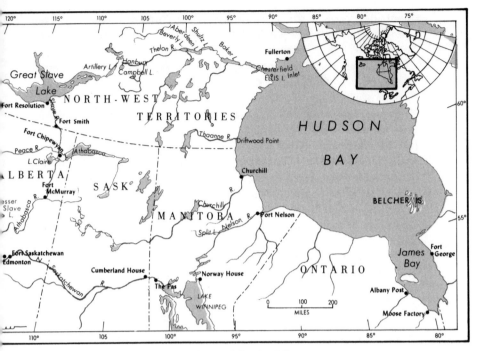

Hudson Bay and Region West

During the summer of 1905 the government ordered "M" Division headquarters moved from Fullerton to Churchill, because of Churchill's more favourable location on the inland water route and because of the projected Hudson Bay railway. This was accomplished the following summer, at which time Mrs. Moodie joined her husband.

The police of "M" Division found the winter of 1906–7 less unpleasant than the previous two. Moodie had persuaded the government of the need for supplying his men with caribou-skin clothing, with high-runnered Eskimo komatiks instead of low-slung toboggans, and with detachment buildings in which the walls had double air spaces for greater insulation against the penetrating Arctic cold.

That winter "M" Division opened up a new and important patrol route. Up to this time overland mail service between that Division and Regina had been in one direction only, from Fullerton via Churchill to Regina. Now Commissioner Perry decided to send winter mail and dispatches in the opposite direction, from Regina to Churchill. Inspector Pelletier, assisted by relays of other police and special constables en route, covered the most difficult part of the journey, from Mafeking, about fifty miles north of Swan River, via Norway House and Split Lake to Churchill. He left Mafeking on December 11, 1906, and on Sunday morning, January 20, 1907, arrived without mishap at Churchill, where he chanced on the pleasantly domestic scene of Superintendent and Mrs. Moodie coming out of church. On March 2 he was back at Mafeking with 1,400 dog team miles to his credit.

In the summer of 1908 Inspector Pelletier undertook the longest and most difficult of all Mounted Police patrols to that time. He aimed to link the Mackenzie River system with Hudson Bay, the western Arctic with the eastern Arctic. To do this he would have to cross the full length of the dangerous northern barren lands. And there his only possible route was by the chain of lakes and rivers from the eastern tip of Great Slave Lake via Artillery Lake, the Hanbury and Thelon Rivers, Beverly, Aberdeen, Schultz and Baker Lakes, to Chesterfield Inlet on Hudson Bay.

No white man, Indian or Eskimo had ever attempted that feat, and only a few outstanding explorers had travelled even part-way across the barrens. Yet Pelletier, on Commissioner Perry's instructions, planned not only to travel the complete route, but to extend the patrol still further. For before the Mounted Police party could even begin the patrol from Great Slave Lake, they would have to travel hundreds of miles to get to that point. Then finally, from the eastern extremity of the main patrol at Chesterfield Inlet, Pelletier intended to travel south by coast steamer to Churchill. From that point after freeze-up he would proceed by dog team along the now well-beaten route of the winter mails to Gimli railway station on Lake Winnipeg. Thus the scope of his patrol was amazing.

The reasons for the great patrol were fourfold. First, it would establish Canadian jurisdiction over the inland north country. Second, Pelletier would report on the country and the practicability of the route from the Mackenzie River system to Hudson Bay. Third, he would report on the number, location and condition of the natives. And fourth, he would report on the need to establish permanent Mounted Police detachments in that part of Canada.

Fort Saskatchewan was selected as the starting point of the gigantic patrol. Inspector Pelletier, Corporal M.A. Joyce, and Constables P.R. Conway and R.H. Walker, all experienced northern men, set out from that point on June 1 and sailed up the Athabasca River. Their two eighteen-foot canoes were fitted for sailing, rowing or paddling, and carried about a ton of supplies arranged in fifty-pound loads convenient for portaging.

From June 6 to June 26 they travelled from Athabasca Landing to

Fort Smith, not by canoe but by Hudson Bay scows, by river steamer, and in wagons. But at Fort Smith Pelletier decided that the summer was too short for him to wait for the river steamer originally scheduled to take his party to the real starting point at the eastern tip of Great Slave Lake. They must set out by canoe at once. So on June 26 he knelt with Joyce and Conway before a priest and received a blessing, just as La Vérendrye and Champlain had done centuries earlier. Then, with Walker, they took their places in the two canoes and shoved off for Hudson Bay.

The danger of crossing Great Slave Lake in canoes was heightened by a wind storm that marooned them on a rocky island for three days. They were delayed another four days by the portage at Artillery Lake. There they made nine trips of seven miles each to transport their numerous fifty-pound packages and their two canoes, pestered every foot of the way by clouds of black flies and mosquitoes.

For a time the four police met various Indian tribes travelling in boats and canoes toward Fort Resolution for their annual treaty payments. Then on July 23 they exchanged courtesies with a few Indians left behind to keep camp. Those were the last humans they saw till they neared Hudson Bay.

For about three weeks Pelletier and his comrades remained in the mossy barrens, sometimes enduring storms and making tiresome portages with their fifty-pound packages. But on the whole they were unusually lucky. Most of the time they paddled on without difficulty through the constant sunshine of the sub-Arctic summer, hearing only the splash of their paddles and the occasional whirr of a bird or the plop of a fish. Even their crossing of the height of land between the great Mackenzie basin and Hudson Bay was unspectacular: it was merely a three-hundred-yard portage with an almost imperceptible grade.

On August 12, having descended the Thelon River, they left the hazardous barrens behind and met their first Eskimos. Again the four canoeists pushed eastward, down Beverly, Aberdeen and Schultz Lakes, then down the Schultz River, shooting the rapids in one of the most exciting experiences of the whole expedition. Again they pushed eastward, down Baker Lake and Baker River.

On August 27 the four Mounted Policemen—Pelletier, Joyce, Conway, Walker—reached a point where the rocks bore indications of the tide from Hudson Bay. They had succeeded in linking the western Arctic with the eastern Arctic.

A few days later, according to a prearranged plan, they met a Mounted Police party which had sailed from Fullerton in the coast steamer *McTavish*. Pelletier sent his three companions north in a whale boat headed for Fullerton, where they would serve a term of northern duty. Then he boarded the *McTavish*, which was to take him south to Churchill, from which point he would make his way overland to Regina to report on his great patrol.

With Pelletier on the steamer were Corporal F.W. Reeves, two other police, Special Constable Interpreter Ford, and two natives. But the ship did not take them to Churchill. A severe storm wrecked it, fortunately in shallow water. Pelletier and the rest splashed through the icy water to an island, and later the inspector hired a whale boat which took them north to Fullerton. There he waited impatiently about seven weeks for the freeze-up that would allow him to travel to Churchill by dog team. It took several weeks more to persuade any of the necessary but reluctant Eskimo guides to go in that worst and darkest travelling season.

On the dark morning of November 30, Pelletier's little party set out. It included two Eskimos, Interpreter Ford, and two police chosen from the whole complement of eager volunteers, Sergeant D. McArthur and Corporal Reeves. Because Pelletier had feared to deplete Fullerton's scanty supplies seriously, his party took only two sleds and fewer supplies than were necessary, although they knew that if they could not shoot their own game en route they would perish. Also, they took only seventeen of Fullerton's precious sleigh dogs, whereas they should have had twenty-four.

Pelletier soon realized that his troubles were by no means ended. One dog vanished the first night out. Storms and rough going slowed progress. The cold was almost unbelievable. Game was scarce. At Christmas time the men's rations were cut to the minimum and the dogs travelled four days without food. On New Year's Day they had no heat, as they had used all their coal oil and were still travelling in the treeless coastal plain. Even when they reached the Driftwood Belt, wood was so scarce that they often had to eat fresh-killed meat raw. Perhaps most nerve-racking of all was the almost constant darkness of the sub-Arctic, winter-long night.

Nevertheless they arrived safely at Churchill on January 11. Here it took almost a month to assemble equipment and fresh dogs for the next stage of the journey, and here Constable C. Travers replaced Interpreter Ford.

The police and their two dog teams arrived at Gimli on March 18, 1909, and Pelletier's remarkable patrol was completed. It had included the first continuous journey across the entire northern barren lands and had set a new long distance record, 3,347 miles, for Mounted Police patrols.

At Gimli, Pelletier entrained for Regina. Three days later he arrived at Royal North-West Mounted Police headquarters, saluted Commissioner Perry, and gave a preliminary report of his nine-and-a-half month journey. Later he wrote a full report giving details of the route, the country and the population. Because of the scarcity of natives and the absence of whites along the hazardous barren lands route, he stated that there was no need just then to establish Mounted Police detachments there, nor even to make an annual patrol. In commenting on his own experiences he mentioned rapids, storms, shipwreck and scarcity of supplies with cool unconcern. "At no time on the journey were we in a precarious position," he declared.

Pelletier's attitude was characteristic of the Mounted Police on northern duty. "These strenuous men," Perry had called them, "who speak so modestly and yet so eloquently of difficulties encountered and hardships endured that I cannot but feel proud of being their comrade."

Chapter 12
Patrolling the Dangerous North
1910-1918

During the remainder of the period in which the Force was known as the Royal North-West Mounted Police, many of its members demonstrated that they shared Inspector Pelletier's attitude toward the difficulties and dangers of northern service. One of these was F.J. Fitzgerald who, after a well-earned leave "outside," returned to Fort McPherson in May, 1910, as a newly commissioned officer in charge of the Mackenzie River Sub-District in which he had formerly served as an NCO.

Fitzgerald had always regretted that the lack of guides at McPherson in 1904 had prevented him from inaugurating what had been planned as the McPherson-Dawson patrol. Instead it had become the Dawson-McPherson venture, skilfully led, originally by Mapley and later by Constable Forrest and Corporal Dempster, at first over Mapley's original route, and more recently over the new Blackstone River route. Now, as Inspector Fitzgerald, he had persuaded Commissioner Perry to reverse the direction of the 1910-11 annual patrol so that he himself could lead it from McPherson.

By 1910 the patrol was classified as an ordinary duty. Yet it was still extremely difficult with its intricate routing over almost five hundred miles of mountains and treeless plateaus, and with temperatures sometimes dropping to seventy below zero and causing dogs to bleed at the mouth. Thus the man who made the fastest time was recognized by his comrades as the unofficial champion of the North.

Inspector Fitzgerald determined to break the record set four years earlier by Forrest, but apart from that his northern experience convinced him that a patrol carrying fewer supplies and travelling at higher speeds would be more efficient. The three experienced northern men he chose to accompany him agreed. Two were constables of his sub-district, G.F. Kinney and R.O'H. Taylor. The third was the recently retired ex-Constable Samuel Carter, the only one of the party who had travelled, once and one-way only, Dawson to McPherson, over the new Blackstone route. Fitzgerald knew and admired Carter and his work. So he hired him as a special constable guide, partly to dispense with the notoriously slow native guide, and also to facilitate Carter's return to civilization. Fitzgerald himself had once covered the old Mapley route with Mapley. He was sure he would remember the part of that route which went from McPherson to the Little Wind River, where the new Blackstone route branched off.

The Fitzgerald patrol left Fort McPherson in the early morning of December 21, 1910. By the end of February, 1911, it was four weeks overdue at Dawson.

A search party of four went out into the dangerous, mountainous country, led by Corporal W.J.D. Dempster. On March 12 as they searched the Little Wind River they noticed a faint trail in the snow leading back toward McPherson. That evening they found old butter tins, corned beef tins, and a piece of a flour sack marked RNWM Police, Fort McPherson, left at a night camp. They knew then that they were on Fitzgerald's trail as he tried to return to his starting point.

The farther along the trail of retreat they went, the more uneasy the search party became. Several night camps were unusually close together. Then in a little cabin they found cached a toboggan, a wrapper and seven sets of dog harness. They also saw a dog's paws, and a shoulder blade which had been cooked and the flesh evidently eaten. At another cabin, only fifty miles from McPherson, they found cached away a RNWM Police dispatch bag and a bag of mail. Again dog bones were scattered about.

Next morning the search party pushed on through twenty-five below zero mist. Along the Peel River they found an abandoned tent, tent poles and a stove. That afternoon some ten miles still farther on, out on the river ice they found a toboggan and two sets of dog harness. All the moosehide ground lashings had been cut off.

A trail led from the toboggan to the river bank, where a fluttering blue handkerchief was tied to a willow, and then over the bank and into the timber beyond. There in an open camp they saw the frozen bodies of Constables Kinney and Taylor lying side by side. The dead men had an Alaska sleeping bag under them and two over them. A fire had been at their feet, and among the camping gear scattered about was a camp kettle half-full of strips of moosehide boiled into soup.

The story was apparent at a glance. Starvation had closed in on the retreating Fitzgerald patrol. Kinney and Taylor were unable to travel farther, so Fitzgerald and Carter had left them the bedding, most of the camping equipment, and all the food, such as it was. Then they had gone on, in a desperate attempt to reach McPherson and send back a search party. But the search party had not come. As they waited, Kinney and Taylor had shrunk to living skeletons, their flesh turned reddish black, their skin peeled off. At last the two men had died, Kinney of starvation. Taylor, also starving and probably delirious, had ended his misery with the rifle still grasped in his wizened hand.

Dempster and the others covered the bodies with brush, then camped nearby. The next morning, ten miles farther down the river and only twenty-five miles from Fort McPherson, they followed a second trail leading from the river to the woods along the bank. This time only snowshoes had been left at the foot of the bank. In a clearing in the woods above, amid a pitifully sparse litter of camping equipment, they saw the bodies of Fitzgerald and Carter. These two, like Kinney and Taylor, had become horribly emaciated, their bodies discoloured, their skin peeling, their extremities frozen and swollen. Evidently Carter had died first and Fitzgerald had ministered to him, for Carter was lying on his back, his hands crossed over his breast and his face covered with a handkerchief. Several yards away, on the spot where the fire had been burning and with two half blankets wrapped around him, lay Fitzgerald. His left hand rested on his breast but his right hand, the one with the star, was extended.

Later all four bodies were buried at Fort McPherson in separate coffins in a single grave. Still later an official inquiry into the tragedy was held, but it revealed little that was new. The causes were the small quantity of provisions taken, the lack of an efficient guide, and the delay caused by searching for the trail.

Excerpts from Fitzgerald's diary provided details. Until January 12, in spite of bitter cold, heavy going, open water and tired dogs, the party was not in too great difficulty. But that date found them at the end of the section of the route Fitzgerald knew, and Carter failed to remember the trail as he had expected. The next five days they spent searching for the trail, becoming hopelessly confused.

January 17: 23° below. Carter is completely lost and does not know one river from another. We have now only ten pounds of flour and eight pounds of bacon and some dried fish. My last hope is gone and the only thing I can do is return. I should not have taken Carter's word that he knew the way from Little Wind River.

January 18: 13° below. Killed the first dog tonight; hardly any of the dogs would eat him, and had to give them a little dried fish.

January 24: 56° below. Found the river open right across. Constable Taylor got in up to his waist and Carter went in up to his hips.

January 25: 53° below. Our food is now dog meat and tea.

January 30: 51° below. All hands feeling sick, supposed to be from eating dogs' livers.

January 31: 62° below. Skin peeling off our faces and parts of body, and lips all swollen and split. I suppose this is caused by feeding on dog meat.

February 3: 26° below. Men and dogs very thin and weak. We have travelled about 200 miles on dog meat, and have still about 100 miles to go, but I think we will make it all right.

February 5: 48° below. Just after noon I broke through the ice; found one foot slightly frozen. Killed another dog tonight; have only five dogs now, and can only go a few miles a day; everybody breaking out on the body and skin peeling off.

That was the last entry in Fitzgerald's diary. Probably his last act was to make the will found later in his pocket, written on a scrap of paper with a stick of charred wood. The last letters he wrote were, appropriately, the initials of the Force he served to the death.

All money in dispatch bag and bank, clothes, etc., I leave to my dearly beloved mother, Mrs. John Fitzgerald, Halifax. God bless all.

F.J. Fitzgerald,
RNWMP

A few years after the loss of the McPherson-Dawson patrol, investigations concerning two murder cases resulted in patrols equally dangerous and much more extended than the one undertaken by the Fitzgerald party. When Commissioner Perry heard the rumours of two murders, both implicating Eskimos of the Coronation Gulf district bordering the Arctic Ocean, he realized that the situation had changed since Pelletier had reported in 1909 that policing and patrolling of the barren lands were unnecessary. He ordered two separate investigation patrols. One would proceed from the Mackenzie River district toward Coronation Gulf; the other would go from eastern Canada toward the Gulf.

The case investigated from the Mackenzie River district concerned two missing priests, Fathers Rouvier and Leroux, stationed at Dease Bay at the northern extremity of Great Bear Lake.

Inspector C.D. LaNauze, one of the most noted of northern men, took charge of the case in the early summer of 1915. Assisted by others at various times, he spent that summer in the western Arctic and sub-Arctic questioning anyone who might have news of the priests. Then he and his small party wintered at Dease Bay in quarters they had built themselves, and in the spring they pushed north with dog teams over difficult, uncharted terrain to Coronation Gulf.

There LaNauze met Corporal W.V. Bruce, who had sailed partway from Herschel Island on the *Alaska*, a ship of the Canadian Arctic Expedition. Bruce by then had collected much of the priests' property during extensive patrols of the Gulf area, but had not yet discovered the murderers. Then one night as the two policemen sat in a foul-smelling, gloomy igloo questioning its occupants through their Eskimo interpreter Illvarnic who, incidentally, had spent four years with Vilhjalmur Stefansson, they learned the whole story. Eskimos Sinnisiak and Uluksak had coveted the priests' possessions. They had stabbed one priest and shot the other, and then had gone their separate ways.

Now Inspector LaNauze and Corporal Bruce each followed one murderer, in spite of the possible danger. On May 15, 1916, Sinnisiak was arrested on the southern part of Victoria Island by Bruce, who was thus the first Mounted Policeman to reach that great lonely island. And a week later LaNauze arrested Uluksak on an island in the Coronation Gulf. Neither Eskimo resisted arrest, and both confessed frankly.

The inspector and the corporal took their prisoners aboard the *Alaska* and sailed to Herschel Island. But communications between that remote island and Regina were slow. It was February, 1917, when the Dawson-McPherson patrol relayed instructions to Fort McPherson from Commissioner Perry that the Eskimos were to be taken to Edmonton for trial. After that the McPherson police had to patrol with the message to LaNauze at Herschel.

It was May 9 when Inspector LaNauze left the barren little island, in charge of a party that included Bruce, Illvarnic, the Eskimo prisoners Sinnisiak and Uluksak, and several native witnesses who would corroborate the murderers' confessions. And it was three months later when they reached Edmonton.

In August, 1917, Sinnisiak and Uluksak were tried, the first Canadian Eskimos to be tried on a charge of capital murder. The jury found them guilty, but because of their ignorance of the white man's law their death sentences were commuted to life imprisonment. Then, instead of being sent to a penitentiary, Sinnisiak and Uluksak were taken back north to be held as prisoners by the Mounted Police. As Commissioner Perry reported to the prime minister, his men had persevered with great tenacity for two years and four months to bring the case to a satisfactory conclusion.

The other murder investigation concerning Coronation Gulf Eskimos began after police of "M" Division heard that primitive Eskimos of Bathurst Inlet, just east of Coronation Gulf, had murdered the explorers Radford and Street. Commissioner Perry agreed that a special patrol party, strong enough to remain in the barrens for two years, should be sent to investigate.

Hence in July, 1914, Inspector W.J. Beyts, Sergeant-Major T.B. Caulkin, Corporal P.R. Conway and Constable E. Pasley sailed out of Halifax on the auxiliary schooner *Village Belle*, headed for Chesterfield Inlet in Hudson Bay. There they were to establish a base detachment and patrol north-west across the barrens till they contacted the Bathurst Inlet Eskimos and discovered the facts of the alleged murder.

For more than two years they battled the unfriendly sub-Arctic as they prepared for one final great patrol. They endured the intense cold of the first winter, 1914-15, living in a drafty, portable shelter, while they patrolled out, reconnoitering, planting food caches, and so on. The next summer the *Village Belle* was late in arriving with supplies. Early gales and blizzards beset the police as they continued preparations a little further into the barrens. On one occasion Beyts and his men chopped through six miles of solid ice to get a motorboat to shore.

During the next winter, 1915-16, when Beyts, Conway and three natives patrolled to plant a food cache along the Thelon River, their twenty-four ravenous huskies devoured parts of a dozen sets of harness. Then one of the huskies was attacked and eaten by the others. Later the exhausted, starving animals sickened and six died. Beyts knew he would have to wait till the following, third, winter to make the patrol with dogs to Bathurst Inlet.

But Inspector Beyts, too, was utterly exhausted and seriously ill. In September, 1916, Inspector F.H. French, nephew of the Force's first Commissioner and a man of considerable northern experience, arrived at Chesterfield Inlet aboard the *Nascopie* to relieve him. Beyts' only consolation was that he had broken the trail for his successor, especially by caching food supplies in the timber along the Thelon so that the returning Bathurst Inlet patrol could pick it up.

By the time Inspector French took over the investigation it had assumed a slightly different aspect. Because the information gathered by Beyts, Caulkin and the others indicated that the Eskimos had murdered Radford and Street under considerable provocation, the government had instructed the police that if such were indeed the case, they were to make no arrest. From this point, then, the Mounted Police continued their lengthy investigation of the tedious case, still under the most perilous circumstances.

With the approach of winter, 1916, Inspector French planned the Bathurst Inlet patrol. To accompany him he chose Sergeant-Major Caulkin, partly because he had learned to speak Eskimo. Then French, Caulkin and the others hunted and fished and made numerous patrols to cache meat, fish and other supplies along the first part of the route. Even so, it was possible to provide supplies for the out-going trip only: on the return trip the return party would have to depend chiefly on shooting game, a precarious situation.

On March 21, 1917, when lengthening days indicated the time opportune, French, Caulkin and three Eskimos set out on the hazardous Bathurst Inlet patrol. The Eskimos, as usual, knew only their own limited territory, but Caulkin believed he could find the necessary native guides en route.

After marching westward over frozen Baker, Schultz and Aberdeen lakes, the party turned and travelled north with migrating caribou, some of which they killed and used as food so as to conserve their supplies. Each morning disclosed five deerskin-clad figures and three heavily loaded sleds pushing into the great white northland. Each night found the party building snow igloos, unloading the sleds, feeding the twenty-five dogs, preparing the one good meal of the day, trying to thaw and dry their frozen clothes and travelling gear, then finally crawling naked into their sleeping bags.

There were the usual Arctic storms. The dazzling reflection of the sun on the snow turned the whole party snowblind for three painful weeks. One night a pack of wolves attacked the dogs. Yet the men persevered, and on May 7 Inspector French was able to make an important entry in his diary.

"Came within sight of Arctic Ocean at east side of Kent Peninsula at 6:30 P.M. and camped," he wrote. Then, almost as an afterthought: "Living on deer meat straight. All civilized grub gone. Oil out."

Now the little patrol party turned west, and a week later they reached the mouth of Bathurst Inlet. There they met Eskimos who knew the details of the Radford and Street murders and who with the usual Eskimo candour told the police all they knew. Several eyewitnesses gave clear, identical accounts corroborating earlier reports that Radford and Street had provoked the Eskimos to kill them. They also said that the three murderers had subsequently fled far away, no doubt warned by "Eskimo wireless" of how Sinnisiak and Uluksak had been arrested and taken away by Mounted Police the year before.

In view of Inspector French's instructions from the government it was now unnecessary for him to pursue the killers, so he made plans to return to Baker Lake. When the Eskimos told him of a trading post to westward, he decided to try to reach it to get supplies for the return patrol while travelling on the sea ice was still possible. After facing June snowstorms and occasionally falling through the opening ice, his little party reached the recently established Hudson's Bay Company post at Bernard Harbour on June 15. Up to that time the patrol had been on the trail for eighty-eight days and had covered more than two thousand miles on foot.

During the brief Arctic summer, French, Caulkin and their helpers waited at Bernard Harbour for the arrival of the expected Hudson's Bay Company supply ship, hoping to get passage to Herschel Island and so avoid the return patrol over the barren lands. But the ship failed to arrive so they prepared to return as they had come. They stocked up with supplies from the trading post, purchased a sled, and acquired several dogs to bring their total to thirty.

On September 1 they set sail in whale boats and headed for the mouth of the Coppermine River, making a 150-mile voyage that was the only water travel of the whole journey. Then at the Coppermine they made camp and settled down to fish and to await the freeze-up which would allow them to begin their return overland patrol.

When they left the Coppermine toward the end of October, the rapidly shortening days allowed only a few hours of daylight for travelling and hunting. Also, the caribou were so scarce that within a month, with only one-third of the journey accomplished, they were almost out of supplies.

By mid-December they were still in the barren lands and entirely out of dog food. Inspector French had to do what the ill-fated Fitzgerald patrol had done. First he abandoned a sled and divided the dogs among the three remaining sleds. A few days later he killed five dogs to feed the rest, and a day or two before Christmas he killed five more exhausted dogs. The men, too, were hungry and exhausted, and because no fuel oil could be spared they suffered the added discomfort of trying to dry their frozen clothing by sleeping with it next to their warm, naked bodies. By December 22 they were entirely out of food for themselves.

That same day, however, the party sighted a band of musk-ox. They temporarily held back disaster by killing the easily approachable animals, and celebrated Christmas, 1917, more as a season of Thanksgiving than of merriment. They spent the "holiday" at Musk-Ox Camp gathering firewood, repairing clothes and resting in preparation for the final lap of the patrol.

Then Caulkin, exploring south, found the Thelon River and the cache of supplies that Inspector Beyts had placed there in December, 1915. When the French party marched on early in January, 1918, they picked up that old cache. Part of the supplies had been destroyed by animals, but seventy pounds of flour, four tins of Oxo, and a few pounds of tobacco were still in good condition.

Yet even now French's difficulties had not ended, for his party must still follow the Thelon, then cross Beverly, Aberdeen and Schultz lakes before reaching Baker Lake. They could not afford to pause, even in blinding blizzards, and so went eighty miles off their course. Again food ran low and dogs weakened. Again French abandoned a sled and a tarpaulin. Again he killed dogs, three this time, to feed the others. Tak-Sak had pups: they, too, were killed and fed to the other animals.

By January 21 the patrol still had not reached familiar territory, and the disheartened Eskimos were suggesting that they were heading in the wrong direction. The men had no food but Oxo. The dogs were starving. In desperation the party cached everything but sleeping bags, rifles and ammunition, and whipped up the staggering dogs in a final effort. Later that day, although still in strange territory, they regained hope when they found caribou. They shot ten, feeling like men brought back from the edge of the grave. Then they came to familiar country, and on January 29, 1918, they arrived back at the Baker Lake detachment.

In making the Bathurst Inlet patrol French and Caulkin had been absent ten months, six of which were spent in travel. They had covered 5,153 miles—4,055 in actual patrol-miles, the rest in hunting, in seeking native camps and caches, and so on. Also, except for the 150 miles by whale boat, they had travelled those thousands of miles on foot, walking or running with the dogs rather than add to their load by riding, and all this through practically unknown Arctic territory. Unfortunately, the great patrol which had permanently weakened the constitution of Inspector Beyts, who had prepared the way for it, had also undermined the health of the officer who accomplished it, and several years later French was invalided from the Force.

The usually undemonstrative government lauded the two Mounted Policemen who had made the Force's longest patrol and, undoubtedly, the longest patrol of any police force in the world. Inspector French received the Imperial Service Order. Sergeant-Major Caulkin, who had been on the case since the beginning, received the King's Police Medal, often referred to as the policeman's Victoria Cross.

Yet for every dangerous northern patrol that brought recognition, scores of others went unnoticed. It is not possible to convey in words the characteristic courage and tenacity of the Royal North-West Mounted Police as they served in Canada's northland.

Chapter 13
The Prairie Provinces
1905–1919

In 1905, when the new Provinces of Alberta and Saskatchewan were formed, the responsibility for enforcing law and order there was transferred from the Dominion government to the provincial governments. These latter, however, acknowledged the work of the Mounted Police by arranging with the federal government for the Force to continue policing the area as before, but under time-limited contract agreements that could be renewed.

The federal government also acknowledged the value of the Mounted Police that same year by raising their pay. The Commissioner's salary jumped from $2,600 a year to $3,000. A constable's pay was sixty cents a day on engaging, but with annual increases could reach a maximum of $1.00, and other ranks received graded increases. Rations and quarters were still provided.

Increases in pay, however, could never adequately cover such services as Constable Conradi rendered one autumn day in 1905. He was having his noon meal with a rancher near Battleford, Saskatchewan, when they saw a raging prairie fire sweeping across the country from the south-east. The Young homestead, not far away, was in the path of the fire, but the rancher assured Conradi that he could not get there before the fire. But when the constable learned that the Young place was not fire-guarded, he dashed to the barn for his horse.

He reached the homestead ahead of the fire and helped the homesteader finish ploughing the fire guard, while Mrs. Young and the ten children set out pails and tubs of water, and soaked blankets and sacks. Then the men lit a backfire. But the prairie fire surged up and jumped the backfire at the spot where Conradi stood guard.

With the hot flames licking about him and the wind raging like a gale, the constable flailed the wet blankets against the burning grass and bushes. He fought until he was nearly suffocated, his hat burned off his head, his hair singed, and his shirt on fire. Then seeing the struggle was futile, he yelled to homesteader Young to collect his wife and children and follow him to the outhouses just out of the path of the fire. But Young was almost exhausted and Conradi had to drag him to safety.

By this time the smoke and flames were so dense that it was impossible to see more than a few yards. The women and children were not in sight. Conradi ran through the fire looking for them. He found them standing in the middle of a slough, choked by the heavy smoke, with the fire rapidly closing about them. He waded in, picked up the two youngest, and led them all out to safety just before the fire completely encircled the slough.

"My wife and family," the homesteader wrote later, "owe their lives to Constable Conradi, and I feel with them we shall never be able to repay him."

Other families in the Battleford area also had good reason to be grateful to the Mounted Police as they made patrols one severe winter providing relief for needy settlers. A police patrol found one family of three grown-ups and seven children starving, without food or firewood, and without even an axe to cut wood or a sled to haul it. They had given up hope and were huddled together in the centre of the floor, trying to keep one another warm. As in other such cases, the police provided food, clothing and other necessities, and hauled firewood from the bush.

In May, 1906, Mounted Police in Alberta were requested to cross into British Columbia to find and arrest three men who had held up and robbed a CPR passenger train near Kamloops. Although train robberies in the United States were commonplace, they were practically unknown in Canada, and the news that American bandits had held up a Canadian train caused great concern. So although British Columbia had its own provincial police, the Mounted Police were called in.

Sergeant J.J. Wilson and four other Mounted Policemen went by train from Calgary to Kamloops, where they learned that the bandits were heading south for the international border. The five policemen hired horses, rode through the driving rain until midnight, then camped at a ranch. At dawn they rode on, questioning ranchers and farmers. At noon an excited constable of the provincial police rode up saying he had sighted three strangers about seven miles away, carrying packs on their backs. He led the Mounted Police back to the place.

On seeing a wisp of smoke rising from a clump of bushes, the police dismounted and advanced stealthily into the bush. There they surprised three men eating a hurried meal around a campfire. The men, who later proved to be notorious American bandits named Bill Miner, William Dunn and Shorty Colquhoun, tried to appear unconcerned. But when Sergeant Wilson said he was placing them under arrest, Dunn began shooting and raced for the surrounding trees. Miner and Colquhoun also grabbed for their guns, but the police had them covered before they could shoot. Two policemen dashed into the bush after Dunn. In the following exchange of shots he was drilled through the leg, and before long he, too, was captured.

After taking a half-dozen revolvers and a rifle from the bandits, then dressing Dunn's wound, the Mounted Policemen took their prisoners to Kamloops, where subsequently they were given long prison sentences. After hearing his sentence pronounced, Dunn thanked Wilson for attending so carefully to his wound. "I guess it sounds funny coming from me," he remarked, "but I sure admire the way you boys work."

One of the most notable features of the Canadian prairies during this period was the continued influx of settlers. New railway lines spread farther into the developing west, and more and more immigrants took up free homesteads. By 1910 the white population, from the Red River to the Rockies, was about a million. Some immigrants went in to provide goods and services for the others: not only standard items of food, shelter and clothing, but also such new-fangled luxuries as fountain pens, alarm clocks, gramophones and "Model T" Fords.

Ralph Allen, in *Ordeal by Fire*, describes conditions in 1910: "The first gasoline tractors were already appearing, but the last teams of sturdy Doukhobor women, harnessed to a single-furrow plow, could still be seen on the wheat fields of Saskatchewan and Manitoba. In Winnipeg, Regina and Calgary the wooden mansions of the middle-men were multiplying fast, but in the intervening sub-continents of wheat and prairie grass there were more sod huts and poplar cabins."

Perhaps the most aggravating and embarrassing duties of the Royal North-West Mounted Police during the early 1900s concerned the Doukhobors, a Russian sect whose primitive religion and way of life had caused such conflict with Russian authorities that they had emigrated to Canada in the late 1890s.

With the help of the Canadian government, 7,500 Doukhobors had settled on land which became part of the Province of Saskatchewan in 1905. For some years they caused no serious disturbances, though they kept to themselves and made no effort to speak English. Furthermore, in Canada as in Russia, they refused to obey laws they did not like. Finally they so disturbed other Saskatchewan settlers that the police had to restrain them.

The Doukhobors, taking the Bible literally, decided no longer to take heed for their lives, their food or their clothing. They wandered about the country living like Adam and Eve. "Full band of fanatics perfectly nude marching on Hleboderno singing," one telegram advised Mounted Police headquarters, "wheeling dead woman in truck. Cannot persuade them to make a coffin."

On such occasions the police patiently rounded up the offenders and retrieved their clothing from along the line of march. Then they persuaded them to dress, or if necessary forcibly dressed them, and shepherded them back to their homes, protecting them meanwhile from angry settlers.

One chilly October day several hundred naked men and women marched across the prairie, looking for Christ. When the police intervened they agreed to go to the nearest village, but insisted that a policeman should ride in front. So when the psalm-singing, naked pilgrims arrived, attracting the curious attention of the whole community, the leader of the procession was a blushing young constable.

One of the worst experiences the Mounted Police had with the Doukhobors was in the spring of 1908, when seventy immigrants arrived in colonist cars at Yorkton. Immediately twenty of them, absolutely naked, dashed out into the streets. Inspector Christen Junget and his men herded them back into the railway cars, then hired the Yorkton Agricultural Hall while awaiting instructions from the Saskatchewan government. Because the government's answer was delayed, the police had to keep the Doukhobors in the hall for over a month while they raved constantly in religious mania. Then they moved them into tents in a fenced enclosure away from the town, but still the Doukhobors raved.

In mid-July the police were ordered to remove six men and six women to an insane asylum. The Doukhobors resisted, stoning the police and beating them with clubs, and it was only after a three-hour battle that the police could remove the twelve. Then the other adults went on a hunger strike and would not give any food to their children. Again the police entered the camp, this time to remove the children whom they took to Yorkton for proper care.

Toward the end of the month the adults were weak from starvation. The police fed the weakest forcibly, but several deaths seemed imminent. Just before tragedy struck, however, the police managed to persuade the Doukhobors to eat again. Their hunger strike collapsed and gradually they regained strength. By September most of them had lost their religious fervour and were sent to communal farms operated by other Doukhobors, and the remaining few were committed to lunatic asylums. But this was by no means the end of the trouble with the Doukhobors.

During the succeeding years the duties of the prairie police varied from breaking up gangs of horse thieves to sending a special contingent of nearly ninety Mounted Police, under Commissioner Perry himself, to represent the Force at the coronation of King George V in 1911.

The Commissioner's Annual Report for the following year commented that the population of the prairie provinces had doubled since the Force had adopted the prefix "Royal," and that police work had increased accordingly. Figures compiled from Perry's once-criticized files of detailed information showed that at the time he wrote the report Royal North-West Mounted Police strength stood at 654, all ranks. In the preceding twelve months the Force had dealt with 13,391 criminal cases and had secured 11,435 convictions.

Yet criminal cases were only a part of police duties. In June, 1914, after a mine disaster at Hillcrest, Alberta, Corporals F.J. Mead and A. Grant looked after 188 mutilated bodies as they were brought to the surface. Assisted by relays of miners the two corporals spent four sultry, noisome days and nights examining the grimy, bloody bodies, listing check numbers, making inventory of money and properties, washing mangled remains and wrapping them in sheets.

The next year, when Constable Rose was sent to Island Lake Reserve in Saskatchewan to enforce a quarantine for typhoid fever, he, too, performed a distasteful task. When a half-breed family near the reserve fell ill and the father died, the rest of the family grew hysterical so Rose took command. He dressed the body for burial and made a coffin, fastened with wooden pegs in the absence of nails. Because the flies were very bad, he stayed overnight in the same room with the corpse, while the almost delirious children of the family kept crying and clinging to him all night.

On another occasion Constable Moorehead risked his life trying to rescue four men from the reducing plant of the Natural Gas Company at Nanton, Alberta. Actually the men were already dead from the poisonous fumes, but Moorehead saw one body moving. In spite of the obvious danger he went in. He was struck by the same four-inch jet of escaping gas that was moving the body, and was blown to the opposite side of the high-pressure chamber. Fortunately another man had come by this time, and he reached in and pulled out the almost unconscious constable, who was groping in vain for the door.

As soon as Moorehead revived, he found a bar and pried off some of the corrugated iron near the bodies. He crawled in through the hole while the other man held his feet, and pulled out one of the dead men.

Then he went in and got another. He was so weak and exhausted by this time that he had not the strength to pull the third body out, but he crawled in and tied a rope to it. After it was pulled out he did the same with the fourth. Later the coroner sent Commissioner Perry a detailed account of the constable's conspicuous bravery, and he was promoted to Corporal Moorehead.

During the period the Force was known as the Royal North-West Mounted Police there was a definite trend toward modern police methods.

Mounted Police on the prairies changed their method of combatting a common practice of cattle rustlers, in which the rustlers used to re-brand cattle over the original brands and claim them as their own. During the first stage of their antirustling campaign the police shaved and photographed any questionable brand, so that the original brand was faintly revealed in the photograph. Then they decided that the killing of one animal would be insignificant if it led to the conviction of a gang of rustlers, and they adopted a new method. Now the police satisfied themselves as to the rightful owner of a stolen animal and then, with his permission, killed it. They skinned the part with the brand and soaked the skin in a chemical solution. Both brands were clearly visible on the underside.

Commissioner Perry also followed the modern trend. Although the eye-catching scarlet tunic had been replaced by a brown jacket for prairie duty, Perry knew that uniform of any kind attracted too much attention for certain investigations. As early as 1886 Commissioner Herchmer had authorized the establishment of a detective force, but although various policemen had worked as detectives, no definite part of the Force had formally been assigned to plainclothes work. Now Perry established the Detective Section. He also ordered the purchase of six motor cars.

No doubt the world war of 1914-18 partly accounted for these two innovations. Besides the routine police checking of 173,568 Germans and Austrians in Alberta and Saskatchewan, there was special need of plainclothes observation of undercover enemy agents. Also, until April, 1917, when the United States entered the war, there was need to patrol the international border in case American-based Germans tried to cross it to commit sabotage.

During the war years, in spite of police needs on the home front, Mounted Police strength dropped considerably. Men enlisted. Alberta and Saskatchewan formed their own provincial police forces in 1917, and Mounted Policemen went over to them. Later the Bolsheviks in Russia staged a revolution aimed at establishing communism. The

Allies offered to help the Russian government defend the country against this minority movement, and the Canadian government sent a Mounted Police cavalry unit to Siberia.

On November 17, 1918, as the cavalry unit embarked in Vancouver six days after the end of the war, Royal North-West Mounted Police in Canada numbered only 303, just three more than the authorized strength of the Old Originals. Rumours hinted that the organization would be disbanded.

The following month, however, the government ordered the Force recruited to a strength of 1,200. They recalled the Mounted Police stationed in France. Also, as the Allies decided that Russian political differences were no concern of theirs, Canada recalled the Mounted Police from Siberia.

Then the government announced that in future the Royal North-West Mounted Police would enforce all federal laws in the four western provinces—Manitoba, Saskatchewan, Alberta and British Columbia. Also, although each of these provinces would still enforce its own provincial laws, the Mounted Police would assist any provincial government on request, providing that the federal government agreed. The Mounted Police would, of course, continue to retain full police authority in the Yukon and the North-West Territories, including the districts of the Mackenzie River, Hudson Bay, and the Arctic islands.

To meet the expanded needs Commissioner Perry and the government planned a new distribution of the whole Force. Certain existing Divisions were rearranged and new ones created. Where necessary, new Divisional headquarters were established at vital points, although the Force's headquarters and training depot still remained in Regina. Then the organization was supplied with additional mechanized transport: two more passenger cars, ten trucks, fifteen motorcycles, and three sea-going motorboats—one for Hudson Bay, one for the Pacific coast, and one to be based at Herschel Island.

In June, 1919, however, during the Winnipeg strike, it was not the mechanization but the discipline of the Mounted Police that helped Canada through a critical period.

At that time many industrial workers in western Canada were rightly dissatisfied with poor working conditions, low wages and high postwar prices. This naturally led to organized agitation, and it was not only western Canadians who sympathized with the numerous strikes that broke out. But when extremists spoke openly of overthrowing the government of Canada, if necessary by force as the Bolsheviks had recently overthrown the Russian government, the situation became serious.

The key men advocating the revolutionary movement were members of the One Big Union or the Industrial Workers of the World, both of which sympathized with the Bolsheviks. They planned to paralyze important cities across the country by general strikes, and then take over the governments of those cities, with the ultimate aim of overthrowing the government of the whole of Canada.

Winnipeg by now was Canada's third-largest city. So when Winnipeg metal workers went on strike on May 1, 1919, it seemed logical to call a Winnipeg general strike. Sympathetic strikes spread to about 30,000 workers, including city firemen, light and power operators, telegraph and telephone operators, streetcar workers, garbage men, postal men, milk-and-bread delivery men, and newspaper workers (except those of the *Labour Journal*). Hence the city's services were seriously disrupted.

The Dominion government made no move to interfere. The affairs of Winnipeg were its own responsibility, with the Province of Manitoba also responsible to a certain extent. But because the Royal North-West Mounted Police now enforced the federal laws in Manitoba they had a detachment at Winnipeg, and Superintendent Cortlandt Starnes prepared to protect Dominion government property, including His Majesty's mails. Also, extra Mounted Police were sent to Winnipeg in case city or provincial officials asked the Dominion government for aid.

At first there was no violence. In spite of the inconvenience, many Winnipeg citizens still sympathized with the strikers. Then the strike committee began to allow some theatres to open and some companies to deliver milk and bread if they displayed prominently a sign reading "By permission of the Strike Committee." Now the ordinary citizens began to show resentment of the strikers' dictatorial control. They formed a citizens' committee for the protection of public rights, and soon thousands of citizens were acting as volunteer firemen, postal workers and so on.

The strikers in turn were annoyed and began to use violence. They hauled truck drivers from their trucks and beat them. A citizen who displayed the Union Jack was nearly murdered by a mob. The city police, in sympathy with the strikers, did nothing to maintain order. And the Mounted Police, still not asked to help, could only continue to guard Dominion government property and protect volunteer postal workers.

On June 9 the city authorities, realizing that they could not rely on the city police, dismissed them. Two thousand volunteers immediately took their places. The next day a young returned army sergeant, winner of the Victoria Cross, was on volunteer police duty. When strikers began to tie up traffic, he protested. They dragged him from his horse, then kicked him and jumped on him repeatedly. By the time onlookers rescued him his ribs were broken, his chest crushed, and one arm dangled helpless. Indignation swept the whole country, and the federal government passed a law providing for the arrest and possible deportation of persons trying to overthrow the government by force.

Meanwhile the Mounted Police had been investigating the true intentions of the strike leaders. They found evidence that instead of merely leading a legal labour movement, some of them were planning a revolution. Warrants were issued for the arrest of the leaders of the seditious conspiracy, and other warrants were issued to allow the Mounted Police to search their homes and offices for incriminating papers. At two o'clock on the morning of June 18 small squads of Mounted Police visited the bedsides of certain strike leaders, arrested them, and took them to Stony Mountain Penitentiary. Other squads gathered truckloads of incriminating documents from the prisoners' houses and the Labour Temple.

The arrest of these leaders prevented the revolutionary movement from developing further, but there was continuous danger of outbreaks by disgruntled strikers who still thronged the streets. In an effort to prevent possible violence, Winnipeg's Mayor Charles Gray temporarily forbade parades. The strikers planned one anyway, for the afternoon of Saturday, June 21. By noon of that day the heart of the city was crowded with tens of thousands of milling strikers, many of them armed.

At last the mayor appealed to the federal government for help. The government ordered the Mounted Police to prevent the parade that would obviously lead to bloodshed, and to restore order, using as little force as possible.

About fifty scarlet-tunicked mounted men trotted out of barracks after Inspectors W.C. Proby and F.J. Mead. Behind them came thirty-six others in motor trucks. A reserve of Mounted Police and a large contingent of militia remained on call, but neither was used. As the police neared Portage Avenue and Main Street, strikers crowding the streets and standing on roof-tops showered them with tin cans, bottles and bricks, stunning some of them. Then they closed in, jabbing the horses' flanks with pocket knives and broken glass, so that the riders were nearly thrown from the tortured animals. The police only parried the blows until Inspector Proby blew his whistle. Then they charged through the crowd, wheeled about and charged again, after which they once more merely parried blows according to their previous instructions to keep the use of force to a minimum.

Strikers carrying hidden revolvers now began to fire at the police.

Others beat them with sticks and rocks and tried to pull them from their horses. Men on roofs hurled down great chunks of cement. One striker hit Proby from behind, and a second aimed a revolver at him. A corporal probably saved his life by felling the second striker just as he prepared to pull the trigger. Then part of the mob turned on a stalled streetcar, rocking it and trying to upset it and the motorman along with it. Others produced papers and sticks and set it on fire. As Proby ordered his men forward the strikers managed to tear a piece from the side of the streetcar. They hurled it among the police horses and three fell.

"Kill the bloody yellow legs!" the mob shrieked and closed in.

"Draw pistols!" Proby ordered at last.

A first warning volley into the air had no effect. A striker dragged a constable from his horse and clubbed him. Several other policemen were likewise disabled. Mead's horse fell, throwing him, but he regained the saddle before the strikers got him. A corporal, struck on the head with a piece of steel and blinded by blood, escaped by holding the mob at bay with a drawn revolver while he felt his way along a wall until he reached a doorway.

By this time nearly every policeman was wounded. Now, still maintaining strict discipline, the battered police fired at the rioters in self-defence, aiming only to wound. Several men were wounded. One was killed. That was enough. The other strikers backed away.

Gradually the mob dispersed and the Mounted Police returned to barracks. Less than one hundred well-disciplined police had restored order in opposition to thousands of rioters, many of them armed. And the police had used their own weapons only as a last resort in self-defence.

Before Inspector Mead left the scene he called at an undertaking parlour to inquire after a wounded constable carried there for safety. In the room where the constable rested lay a body covered with a Union Jack. By strange coincidence it was that of Major-General Sir Samuel B. Steele (knighted for service in the First World War). The stalwart Old Original had been brought back for burial to the place where, some forty-five years earlier, he had begun his illustrious police career.

A few days after the Winnipeg riot, the general strike in that city was called off, and sympathetic strikes in other Canadian cities were cancelled simultaneously. The revolutionaries' plans to overthrow the Canadian government had been defeated.

The revolutionaries themselves were later tried in court on charges of seditious conspiracy. They made an incongruous outcry against such infringement of their civil liberties.

"Appeal is made by these men to British fair play," Commissioner

Perry remarked, "to protect them in their efforts to destroy British fair play."

The charges of seditious conspiracy were proved, thanks largely to the work of the plainclothes Mounted Policemen who had been checking the movements of aliens ever since the outbreak of war in 1914. When some of these aliens had threatened to turn legal labour organizations into tools of their revolutionary movement, young Constable F.W. Zaneth had managed to get himself hired incognito as secretary to the Industrial Workers of the World. From that vantage point he could see exactly what went on. Zaneth's testimony regarding the subversive principles advocated by the revolutionary conspirators helped to convict them, and they were sent to jail for terms varying from six months to two years.

Most of the western press spoke proudly of the Mounted Police, but the western labour press labelled them "strikebreakers." Yet they had only acted on government orders to prevent a forbidden parade and had gathered evidence against certain men, not because they were labour leaders but because they were plotting to overthrow the government, by force if necessary.

The Canadian government knew how vital a part the Mounted Police had played in averting a tragedy. Later that year it decided to enlarge the scope of the Force to include all federal police work in the whole Dominion. In November, 1919, an Act of Parliament made this possible. The Royal North-West Mounted Police would soon become the Royal Canadian Mounted Police.

**Royal
Canadian
Mounted
Police
1920 – 1973**

Chapter 14
Coast to Coast
1920–1930

T he Royal North-West Mounted Police became the Royal Canadian Mounted Police on February 1, 1920. The Force which had formerly enforced federal laws in the four western provinces would now enforce such laws in all nine provinces from coast to coast. It would also retain full police authority in the Yukon, the North-West Territories and the Arctic islands.

These new duties resulted in three important changes in organization. First, three new Mounted Police districts were formed: eastern Ontario, Quebec and the Maritime provinces. Second, the headquarters of the Force (but not the training depot) was transferred from Regina, Saskatchewan, to Ottawa, which was more central and, as the Dominion capital, would allow closer contact with other government departments. Third, the organizational work at headquarters was divided among four main branches: Criminal Investigation, Financial, Supply, and Adjutant's Departments.

The increase in duties led naturally to an increase in strength, so that by September, 1920, the Force had 1,671 members. One hundred and fifty-two of these were men who had transferred voluntarily from the Dominion police, which until February 1, 1920, had done the federal police work in eastern Canada.

Mounted Police expansion met with very little enthusiasm anywhere in the country. Western Canadians had regarded the Force as their own and were frankly disgruntled that it had gone east. Eastern Canadians were disappointed to see the "men in scarlet" wearing brown uniforms for ordinary drill parades and patrols. City folk regretted that the "Mounted" Police walked instead of riding prairie broncos on busy streets. Ottawans regarded the newcomers as just another group of civil servants, and confused them with the former Dominion police, whose more obvious duties in the capital had been chiefly to guard Dominion property and buildings.

As for the Mounted Police themselves, many of them too regretted the change. But they carried out their regular duties all across Canada, plus the many extras requested by provincial governments and federal departments. The country's needs had changed considerably from those of the early days, when the greatest demands were for policing the unsettled prairies, CPR construction and the gold rush. Yet the evolution of the Mounted Police from this point, as from the beginning, was still closely linked with the movement of Canadian history, with the development of the country, and with the needs of the time.

In Ontario, Manitoba and British Columbia, the Force helped the federal Department of the Interior and the various provincial governments by fighting forest fires. In several provinces they aided the Department of Agriculture by supervising the operation of pari-mutuel machines at race tracks. They assisted the Department of State by investigating and reporting on the newly formed Communist Party of Canada, which avowed a connection with the revolutionary Third International of Russian origin. For the same department they investigated the character and desirability of widely scattered non-Canadians, five thousand in one year alone, who were applying for naturalization. And all across Canada they provided guards for Dominion property, from the dockyards at Halifax, Nova Scotia, to those at Esquimalt, British Columbia.

When mail robberies occurred in Saskatchewan, the Royal Canadian Mounted Police solved the crimes. When bumper prairie wheat crops necessitated the sending of eastern harvesters, they provided guards for the special trains. When a ship arrived at Saint John, New Brunswick, with smallpox aboard, a sergeant and three constables guarded it, enforced the quarantine, and handled money and mail for the passengers and crew.

In 1921, at the request of the federal Department of Health, police detectives entered the anti-narcotic campaign. A case in Vancouver involved a Chinese merchant whose annual turnover in drugs smuggled from the Orient totalled almost a quarter of a million dollars. Drug cases were dealt with not under smuggling but under the Opium and Narcotic Act (later the Narcotic Drug Act). For several months plain-clothes officers worked on the case, planning carefully, watching patiently, and even getting the cooperation of RCAF planes which checked the movements of vessels in the Pacific Ocean. At last they arrested the Chinese in the act of smuggling cocaine ashore. But the law offered several loopholes, and although at his trial the Chinese pleaded guilty, his fine was a mere five hundred dollars. Commissioner Perry warned the government that it must provide stiffer legislation and higher penalties if it hoped to combat the drug traffic.

That same year Mounted Police maintained order without bloodshed during strikes in Ontario and Quebec. Others investigated illegal lobster fishing in Prince Edward Island, and protected vessels shipwrecked off Canada's east coast from fishermen plunderers. In Montreal and Quebec City, as at Halifax, the Force provided persons to meet incoming vessels, so as to protect young women from white slavers.

Yet in spite of the wide services rendered, the police encountered hostility, even from the House of Commons. The Liberals, who as the Opposition in 1919 had sharply criticized the government and consequently the Mounted Police for their handling of the Winnipeg strike, had succeeded the Conservatives in power, though without a majority, and they still showed a consistent antagonism. Moreover, they resented the fact that increased Mounted Police duties and additional strength now cost the unprecedented amount of $4,000,000 a year.

On April 4, 1922, the minister of Militia and Defence presented a resolution urging that for economy's sake the Royal Canadian Mounted Police be amalgamated with the regular defence forces and be sharply reduced. The spokesman for the recently formed Progressive Party, whose votes held the balance of power, suggested still further reduction and limiting of their work to the unorganized territories.

The Labour spokesman, J.S. Woodsworth, who represented Winnipeg Centre, pictured the Mounted Police as troublemakers whose presence in Winnipeg had caused the lawlessness during the general strike in 1919. "I submit," he concluded "that we should seriously consider whether we need to continue a Force of this character."

When the minister of Militia rose again, this time announcing Commissioner Perry's resignation, it seemed that the Royal Canadian Mounted Police was doomed. The government accepted Perry's resignation, since he requested it after forty years' service, including twenty-two as Commissioner.

Removing the Force was another matter, however. Members of Parliament who knew what the organization had done for the country spoke in its defence. When Woodsworth moved that the Royal Canadian Mounted Police be removed to Canada's outposts, and a new Dominion police force be organized, even the prime minister, W.L. Mackenzie King, reminded him that if the resolution carried as it stood, the very guards to the Parliament Buildings would have to be transferred to the Arctic Circle. Mr. Woodsworth's motion was defeated, 108 to 47. For the time being the Force was safe.

The former Assistant Commissioner Cortlandt Starnes followed Perry as Commissioner, although for the first year he was Acting Commissioner only, while Commissioner Perry had a year's leave of absence. Starnes, born and educated in Montreal, had first come in contact with the Force during the North-West Rebellion of 1885. Then a lieutenant of the Canadian militia, he had marched from Calgary to Edmonton in the same column as the youthful Inspector Bowen Perry of the North-West Mounted Police. Within a year Starnes joined the organization, and was appointed an inspector in March, 1886. During the next thirty-four years he served on the southern prairies, in the Yukon, at Hudson Bay, in Quebec and Manitoba. Then when the Force became the Royal Canadian Mounted Police, he went to Ottawa as assistant commissioner.

Starnes's experience and tact were invaluable during that period of the Force's uncertain tenure in 1922 and 1923. Although the police were flooded with requests to stop the smuggling of drugs on the Pacific coast and to check counterfeiting in the East, Starnes seriously considered even such requests as for someone to investigate the robbery of a wild duck's nest near Lake Superior.

"Good Lord!" he would exclaim to his departmental secretary. "Must I send out a constable every time a duck quacks?" But the Force's duties included helping the Department of the Interior enforce the Migratory Birds' Act. So if possible he would order his men to investigate.

In March, 1923, J.S. Woodsworth moved a motion to disband the Royal Canadian Mounted Police. George Black, the Conservative member for the Yukon, who for years had seen the Force in action, defended it at length. "The Mounted Police have been efficient in the West, and they are efficient today in other parts of Canada," he said. Then he listed the great variety of public services the Mounted Police rendered. He asked who would perform them if the Force did not. "The provincial and municipal forces are subject to local influence and pressure . . . [but] the Royal Canadian Mounted Police are above that sort of thing. They cannot be bribed, and they cannot be bluffed or intimidated. They are not now in politics and they never have been. . . . By comparison there is no police force like it in the world."

Woodsworth's motion to disband the Force was defeated, 156 to 23. Its members would continue to police all Canada. Also, significantly, the Force's claim to being non-political was even more firmly established. The Liberal Party had criticized it from the Opposition benches but now, as the government, supported it to the limit.

On April 1, 1923, Commissioner Perry retired to pension, having headed the North-West Mounted, the Royal North-West Mounted, and the Royal Canadian Mounted Police. He had also guided and developed the organization, which began as a simple body of prairie horsemen, toward a complex, modern, anti-criminal police force. Commissioner Cortlandt Starnes continued the development.

During the next few months the Mounted Police won favourable publicity, particularly for their campaign in eastern Canada against organized liquor smuggling which, like the narcotics in western Canada, had become a national problem.

One of the most dramatic of the four hundred liquor-smuggling cases they investigated over a one-year period took place in July, 1923, near Lahave, Nova Scotia. Detective Sergeant J.P. Blakeney, Corporal W.A. Caldwell and Constable F.P. Fahie, all dressed in plain clothes, set out in a motorboat to intercept the rum-running schooner *Veda M. McKeown*. They flashed a recognition signal to lull the suspicions of the captain and his crew of eight, and steered their boat near the anchored schooner. Then Blakeney, impersonating the expected buyer, climbed aboard.

After haggling with Blakeney over the price of the liquor, the captain ordered the crew to pass his ten-gallon kegs of rum to the two men in the motorboat below.

"Just a moment!" Blakeney snapped. "I'm a sergeant of the Royal Canadian Mounted Police and I'm also a Customs and Excise officer. In the name of the King I arrest you and your crew, and I'm seizing your ship and cargo."

Caldwell and Fahie leaped on board. For a moment no one spoke, and the nine rum-runners seemed to weigh their chances of overpowering the three police and escaping. But Blakeney warned them sharply that any attempt to escape would be dealt with severely. Then they merely cursed furiously and accepted the situation.

The next day the *Veda M. McKeown*, with its cargo of 1,700 gallons of rum, 190 cases of Scotch whisky and thirty-five cases of gin, sailed into port under Sergeant Blakeney's orders. Later the captain and the crew were prosecuted.

That same year Mounted Police in Montreal began to investigate the case of the Spanish consul. They suspected the consul, Don Miguel Maluquer y Salvador, of being involved in a ring of smugglers bringing illegal liquor and narcotic drugs from Spain to Canada, but they needed definite proof. They also suspected that corrupt customs officials in Montreal were allowing the illegal goods through customs.

Sergeant C.C. Brown posed as a rich American, Mr. Robino, and approached Don Miguel regarding the purchase of drugs. On August 9 the two men lunched together at the Ritz Carlton. Don Miguel promised to arrange for Mr. Robino to buy drugs through his friends in Barcelona. The drugs would be shipped to Montreal in small containers hidden in cases of olive oil.

Meanwhile, Don Miguel would introduce Mr. Robino to Raymon Tey de Torrents, who had an import-brokerage firm in Montreal. De Torrents in turn would arrange that some obliging customs officials would let the shipment of olive oil pass without inspection, for the small fee of four dollars a gallon.

A few days later, when Brown arranged details with de Torrents and Don Miguel, they pointed out that he must go to Spain himself to purchase the drugs. Brown, in his role of rich American smuggler, agreed nonchalantly. Fortunately the Mounted Police were able to persuade Ottawa that such an unprecedented expense would be worthwhile if it led to the rounding up of an international smuggling ring.

Soon the sergeant as Mr. Robino sailed for Spain. Staff Sergeant E.C.P. Salt also set sail, but on a different ship to avoid suspicion. He would be Brown's undercover assistant, and would later corroborate the sergeant's evidence. But a few weeks later, in Barcelona, Don Miguel's friend Felix Martorell refused to sell drugs to Mr. Robino. There had been a revolution in Spain, the country was under martial law, and he would not risk shipping drugs.

"What about alcohol then?" Robino-Brown asked. Martorell agreed to a first shipment of fifty cases of alcohol, to be labelled olive oil.

Sergeant Brown and Staff Sergeant Salt sailed back to Montreal, and at last the alcohol arrived. De Torrents needed $3,500 with which to bribe customs officials, and Brown and Salt planned to give him the money in the form of a cheque left for him in an envelope at a certain bank. They hoped he would immediately cash the cheque, for which the teller would give him marked bills. Other Mounted Police would shadow de Torrents and observe the transaction, an observation which would be admissible as evidence in court. Also, if de Torrents used the marked bills to pay the prearranged bribe to a customs official, the finding of the bills on that official would also implicate him in the crime.

On the day set for delivery of the alcohol, all but one of the cases marked olive oil passed through Montreal customs as de Torrents had promised. Then an honest customs official noticed that the last case was leaking—not olive oil but alcohol. De Torrents, whose import-brokerage firm had handled the deal, was notified.

"I know nothing of the affair! Even Mr. Robino I know only by name!" de Torrents protested volubly at the customs office. "Never again will I do a favour for such a customer," he added, with more truth than he realized.

Meanwhile Staff Sergeant Salt had arrested the Spanish consul. The court case that followed was a much-publicized victory for the Mounted Police. Don Miguel and Raymon Tey de Torrents went to prison, the latter being convicted of smuggling, rendering false invoices, forgery and perjury. De Torrents' import licence was cancelled, and in Barcelona Martorell was disqualified from exporting goods to Canada.

Even more important, however, was that Mounted Police evidence proved that certain customs officials were involved. As a result, a special parliamentary committee spent the next several years investigating the "degeneration" of the Customs and Excise Department. The committee recommended the dismissal of six Customs and Excise officials, the retirement of others, and the prosecution of twenty-five firms owing customs fees to the Crown. The committee also recommended the reorganization of the whole Preventive Service, with the Mounted Police to be used temporarily for such work at all important border points.

For the next few years the Mounted Police continued to battle smuggling, and to urge stiffer legislation and heavier sentences for smugglers. Then the case of Lim Jim showed that they were making headway.

The police had known for years that the rich Chinese was smuggling opium into Vancouver. But only in 1927 were they able to get the necessary evidence to charge the outwardly respectable merchant with the crime. Then he was fined heavily and sentenced to four years in jail. When his counsel appealed to a higher court, hoping for a reduction of the sentence, the Crown entered a counter appeal, asking for an even more severe sentence. The higher court staggered Pacific coast smugglers by increasing Lim Jim's term of imprisonment to seven years.

In 1928 the Province of Saskatchewan disbanded the provincial police force it had organized in 1917. Once more the province entrusted the enforcement of its provincial laws to the Mounted Police, setting the contract period at seven years with an option of renewal. Then the Mounted Police, who absorbed a large part of the provincial police they replaced, just as in 1920 they had absorbed members of the Dominion police, once again patrolled the Saskatchewan prairies. Again they enforced provincial statutes, apprehended cattle rustlers, solved murders and quelled riots of temporarily crazed Doukhobors. (The last three of these duties arise out of offences covered by the Criminal Code of

159

Canada, which is a federal statute, although the enforcement of the Code is a provincial responsibility.) They also continued to enforce all federal statutes in the province.

By the end of its first decade as the Royal Canadian Mounted Police, the duties of the Force in all parts of Canada had increased tremendously. According to Commissioner Starnes' Annual Report of September, 1930, his men, with a total strength of 1,245, conducted 72,007 investigations. Their amazing patrol mileage included patrols on horseback, by buckboard, car, motorcycle, dog team, canoe and motorboat. In the South Saskatchewan District alone it totalled almost a million miles.

During the same year Mounted Police had performed such miscellaneous duties as taking the census of waterfowl, and breeding sleigh dogs at Rockcliffe, near Ottawa. Also at Rockcliffe they were operating a secondary training depot to supplement the main training depot at Regina. They had collected the fur export tax, and had performed their famous Musical Ride in Canada and at the International Horse Show in London, England.

That 1930 report indicated some significant changes since the Royal North-West Mounted rode the plains. For instance, organized gangs of thieves in eastern Canada and of cattle rustlers in western Canada now used trucks and cars for speedier escapes. "City slickers" were not the only ones trying to evade court sentences by resorting to legal technicalities: the unsuccessful plea of one Indian fined for dangerous driving was that the corporal who overtook him must likewise be guilty of the same offence. A case in Ottawa arose from an aviator's flying dangerously low over the city.

But the Mounted Police, too, were progressing with the times. Increased mechanization; careful detective work; the keeping on file of detailed records of criminals; more intensive training in police work and in criminal law—all these helped them to outwit modern lawbreakers.

Also, the Force made more and more use of its Criminal Identification Branch. This was originally a department of the Dominion police taken over in 1920, and had been established at Ottawa some years earlier in accord with suggestions made by Assistant Commissioner Z.T. Wood and others. In the report year of 1929-30, the Mounted Police added an extra 34,056 fingerprints to the hundreds of thousands already on file in the Finger Print Section, and made more than 4,500 identifications through that section.

As Starnes' report indicated, there was now a definite trend toward modern police work.

NWMP

MAINTIENS LE DROIT

The badges and uniforms
of the Force
(drawings by
Sergeant Paul Cederberg)

RCMP to 1953

RNWMP

RCMP, 1973

RCMP 1953 to date

NWMP, 1873

NWMP, 1877

NWMP, 1901

RNWMP, 1905

1

Henri Julien, cartoonist, illustrator and artist, accompanied the march west on behalf of the Montreal periodical *Canadian Illustrated News.* This typical western thunderstorm was sketched by Julien on the night of August 3, 1873.

Officers and constables of the NWMP, 1874. Sub-Inspector Francis J. Dickens is second from the right.

Fort Macleod, 1874.

Indians trading at Fort Pitt, 1884. Big Bear is standing at centre.

Fort Walsh, 1878.

Members of the NWMP and scouts. Jerry Potts stands top right;
ex-Inspector Cecil Denny is in the middle row, extreme left.

Farwell Detachment, North-West Territories, 1888.
All buildings are constructed with local cottonwood logs.

Some Early Duties

A NWMP constable visits an Indian camp near Qu'Appelle,
North-West Territories, about 1883.

A symbolic "last spike" ceremony on the Canadian Pacific Railway line in 1885.
NWMP members in uniform stand at centre.

RNWMP constables at Yorkton, Saskatchewan, in 1907
during the Doukhobor land rush.

Louis Riel as he appeared about the time of the North-West Rebellion.

Gabriel Dumont,
commander-in-chief of Riel's forces.

Louis Riel in the prisoner's box
at Regina, 1885.

The NWMP guard room at Regina, 1885, in which Riel was imprisoned and hanged.

Gold-seekers climbing Chilcoot Summit, 1898.

NWMP and a U.S. customs officer
(extreme right) at the White Pass Summit
on the Yukon-Alaska border, 1899.

Revolver drill at Whitehorse, Yukon Territory, about 1900.

The Dawson police barracks, Yukon Territory, at midnight in June of 1899.
At the extreme left is Superintendent S. B. Steele; Inspector and Mrs. Cortlandt Starnes
are third and fourth from the left.

The NWMP band leads a parade at Dawson, 1902.

Northern Patrols

RNWMP patrol, Dawson to Herschel Island, 1910.

The Dempster patrol, ready to leave Dawson
in search of the Fitzgerald party of four,
who died tragically on patrol, 1911.

The trial of an Eskimo for theft,
at Port Harrison in northern Quebec, 1935.

A constable makes a call on a trapper in the remote eastern Arctic, 1957.

RCMP power toboggan patrol from Pond Inlet Detachment, NWT, down Bylot Inlet, 1970

The Force's most northerly detachment— Grise Fjord, NWT, 1973.

Transferring supplies from an RCMP plane to traditional northern transport, an RCMP dog team. By 1969 dog teams were replaced by power toboggans.

An RCMP Twin Otter, one of six providing main service in the North, 1972.

The Fourteen Commissioners of the Force

G. A. French (1873-1876)

Insignia of Commissioner's rank, 1973: crossed sword and baton surmounted by a crown.

J. F. Macleod (1876-1880)

A. G. Irvine (1880-1886)

L. W. Herchmer (1886-1900)

A. Bowen Perry (1900-1923)

Cortlandt Starnes (1923-1931)

James H. MacBrien (1931-1938)

S. T. Wood (1938-1951)

L. H. Nicholson (1951-1959)

C. Rivett-Carnac (1959-1960)

C. W. Harvison (1960-1963)

G. B. McClellan (1963-1967)

M. F. A. Lindsay (1967-1969)

W. L. Higgitt (1969-   )

By Air and Sea

Commissioner James H. MacBrien and crews take delivery at Toronto of four DeHavilland Dragonfly planes, the first aircraft of the RCMP Aviation Section, in 1937.

An RCMP power toboggan delivers an injured native to an airplane at Fort McPherson en route to hospital at Inuvik, NWT, 1969.

The first helicopter of the RCMP, acquired in 1972 and posted to Newfoundland for duty.

An RCMP single engine Beaver (left) and an RCMP Grumman Goose over Vancouver.

The RCMP patrol boat *Bylot* at Pond Inlet, NWT, 1970.

The *St. Roch* drifts in the ice pack in McClintock Channel, August 1942, en route eastward through the North-West Passage.

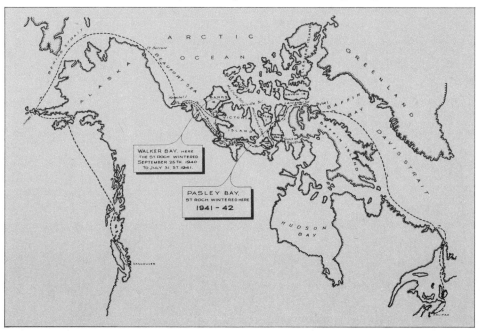

A sketch of the route travelled by the *St. Roch* from Vancouver over the top of North America via the North-West Passage.

The RCMP at Ottawa

"N" Division at Rockeliffe, Ontario, near Ottawa, 1920. The officers and men await more permanent quarters after their transfer from RNWMP headquarters at Regina.

The present-day headquarters of the RCMP at Ottawa.

A laboratory expert examines a counterfeit twenty-dollar bill.

A fingerprint expert at work in the Single Finger Print Section.

RCMP "Depot" Division, Regina, Saskatchewan.
Centre foreground is the barracks chapel on the south-west corner of the barracks square.

Foot drill in winter on the barracks square.

German shepherd police service dog "Sabre" with his dogmaster on tracking exercise.

Labrador police service dog "Jennie," who has just discovered 150 lbs. of hashish in the hems of a shipment of 400 fur coats.

An investigator at the scene of a safeblowing.

An RCMP expert removes skin from the finger of a cadaver for fingerprint identification.

An RCMP forensic science photographer photographs a physical match of two pieces of an automobile headlight, one found on the car and the other at the scene of a hit-and-run accident.

Comparison microscope to compare known with suspect items, in this case, two bullets.

A member of the Marine Section boarding a yacht to check life saving and other equipment.

On duty in a Divisional communications centre.

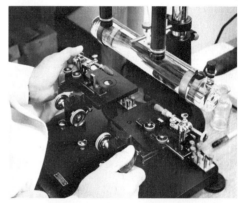

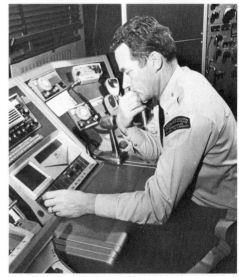

Selected Insignia

Deputy Commissioner
(worn on each shoulder)

Corps Sergeant Major
(worn on lower right sleeve)

Staff Sergeant Major
(worn on lower right sleeve)

RCMP Public Relations

A constable talks to children at an RCMP recruiting display.

The world famous Musical Ride in dome formation, Rockcliffe, Ontario, 1967.

The renowned RCMP band on Parliament Hill.

HRH Queen Elizabeth II, Honourary Commissioner of the Force,
talks to Staff Sergeant R. Cave of the Force on "Burmese"
(formerly the lead horse in the Musical Ride), after the mare
was presented to the Queen at Windsor Castle in 1969.

Chapter 15
The Land of the Eskimo
1920–1936

During the first few years after the Force became the Royal Canadian Mounted Police, the men in the far North were chiefly concerned with a wave of Eskimo murders. The first case centred on Ouangwak, a Paddlemuit of the Baker Lake district, who had murdered two brothers, also Paddlemuits, in a dispute over sleigh dogs.

In spite of Ouangwak's confession to Sergeant W.O. Douglas at Fullerton detachment, Canadian law demanded a full investigation to corroborate the confession and a trial in court. But transporting the many witnesses to a court in the south would be prohibitively difficult and expensive. So Commissioner Starnes proposed, and the Department of Justice approved, that in the summer of 1921 a court with all the necessary powers should sail to Chesterfield Inlet for the trial. However, in mid-winter of 1920–21, Ouangwak escaped from a makeshift detachment set up in the frozen wilderness near the scene of the murders. His remains were found the following winter.

In December, 1921, Staff Sergeant A.H. Joy began to investigate another notable murder case, which closed some twenty months later with a northern court like the one planned for Ouangwak's trial. Baffin Land Eskimos at Cape Crawford had killed Robert Janes, a trader from Newfoundland, and although Joy was the only Mounted Policeman in northern Baffin Land then he conducted the whole investigation.

The tall, broad-shouldered, thirty-three-year-old Joy had gone to Baffin Land with the annual supply steamer in the summer of 1921. In accord with government policy of sending the Force farther and farther north, he was to establish and take sole charge of a new detachment at Ponds Inlet (later called Pond Inlet). He was also to direct his

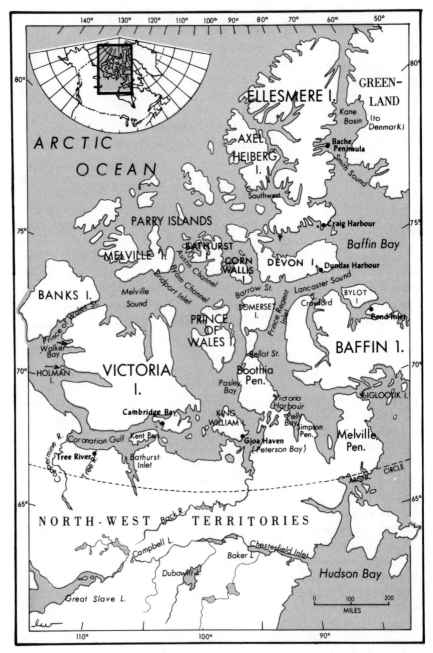

Canadian Arctic Islands

special attention to "an alleged murder of a Mr. Janes," and to this end had been appointed coroner and justice of the peace. He was well-fitted for the task, having spent many years in the western Arctic, where he had made a study of the Eskimos. Incidentally, while there he had ingeniously overcome his lack of a horse for his annual revolver test, mounted, by saddling a transport ox and using it for a mount.

As the first step in investigating the murder, Staff Sergeant Joy travelled by dog team from Ponds Inlet to Cape Crawford on the north coast of the western peninsula of Baffin Land. After mushing through the continuous gloom of the Arctic night for two weeks he arrived at the cape and questioned the Eskimos there. They showed him an icy mound. He opened it, and in the green flicker of the northern lights he saw the corpse of trader Robert Janes, in its frigid resting place of twenty months. When he examined the body in an igloo he found two bullet wounds.

But he could not take it for granted that murder had been committed: he must hold an inquest. Yet the Eskimos of the district did not know enough about the law to be able to serve on a jury. So the policeman packed the frozen remains on his sled and made the return trip of some two hundred miles through continuous night and dangerous storms back to Ponds Inlet. There he assembled a jury of three white traders. Then, in his capacity as coroner, he held an inquest at which he examined eight native witnesses who had travelled to Ponds Inlet for this purpose.

The witnesses told the same story that Joy had heard from other Eskimos: that the embittered trader had earned the fear and hatred of the natives, and had threatened to shoot their dogs and even some of themselves. In self-defence the Eskimos planned to kill Janes before he could carry out his threats. One native lured him from his tent. A second, Nookudlah, shot and wounded him. A third pushed him down. Then Nookudlah shot him again, this time killing him. The jury's verdict was that Robert Janes had been shot to death by Nookudlah, assisted by the other two Eskimos.

Now Joy, as justice of the peace, issued warrants for the arrest of the three Eskimos. He did not have to make a second trip to Cape Crawford to arrest them, however. "Eskimo wireless," effective as always, relayed news of the inquest to the Cape Crawford Eskimos. They persuaded Nookudlah and his two accomplices to go to Ponds Inlet and give themselves up. They did so the following summer, and Mounted Policeman Joy arrested them. Then he reassumed the role of justice of the peace, held the preliminary hearing of the Janes murder case, and on July 20 formally committed the prisoners for trial.

Later that year when the supply ship *Arctic* called at Ponds Inlet with supplies, it brought with it three Mounted Policemen as reinforcements for the former one-man detachment. Joy reported to the Mounted Police inspecting officer aboard that his case was ready for the court authorities. The officer, Inspector C.E. Wilcox, promised to relay that news to the Commissioner. Then Joy, assisted by the newly arrived policemen, guarded the Eskimo prisoners at Ponds Inlet until he received further instructions.

Meantime there had been other Eskimo murders in the Coronation Gulf district among the same tribe responsible a few years earlier for the killing of Radford and Street and of the missing priests, Father Rouvier and Father Leroux. Corporal W.A. Doak of Tree River detachment in that district tried to explain the murders to an official of the Hudson's Bay Company as they sat around a campfire in the winter of 1921.

"Ever since Sinnisiak and Uluksak were taken for the joy ride to Edmonton, shown the bright lights and given a couple of years imprisonment at Herschel, I've expected trouble," he said. He was referring to the two Eskimos who had been convicted of murdering the Roman Catholic priests and who had been sentenced to life imprisonment. After a few years of working for the Mounted Police in the North they had been allowed to go back among their own people in the hope that their experience would be a warning to other Eskimos. "They came back to their people with rifles, ammunition, trunks full of white man's clothing, and enough pale-faced cussedness to high-hat the rest of the tribe. Now they're big men among the natives, and some of the others think all they've got to do to have a good time is to stick a knife into someone."

A few months later Doak went to Kent Peninsula to investigate a series of cold-blooded murders. He arrested the only two murderers still alive, Alikomiak and Tatamigana, and escorted them to Tree River. There Doak in turn was murdered by Alikomiak, as was a Hudson's Bay Company factor.

In the summer of 1923, in accord with the policy previously established, the Canadian government sent two judicial parties, each of which included a judge, Crown counsel and defence counsel, to conduct trials in the North. The first party went from Edmonton to Herschel Island, gathering a jury from four H.B.C. posts en route. Alikomiak and Tatamigana were sentenced to death. An Eskimo in another murder case was found guilty of manslaughter and sentenced to one year imprisonment in the Herschel Island guardroom. Two others were acquitted.

The second judicial party sailed from Quebec on the S.S. *Arctic* early in July. Six weeks later they arrived at Ponds Inlet to hold what was probably the most northerly court in the world, and to try Nookudlah and his accomplices for the murder of trader Robert Janes.

With an August snow flurry beating against the window, court was opened in the double-walled, double-floored frame detachment of the Royal Canadian Mounted Police at Ponds Inlet. His Honour Judge L.A. Rivet of Montreal presided in his black robes while the lawyers for the Crown and the defence wore similar ceremonial attire. Inspector C.E. Wilcox, whom the *Arctic* had picked up en route, was there as officer commanding, wearing service blue uniform. Staff Sergeant Joy now acted as deputy sheriff, while one of the other three Ponds Inlet policemen acted as orderly to the judge, and the other two served as escorts for the prisoners. Their full-dress uniforms added brilliant touches of colour: scarlet tunics, yellow-striped breeches, gleaming Sam Brown belts, glistening buttons and spurs.

On one side of the courtroom sat the jury, the crew of the S.S. *Arctic*. On the other side sat the three Eskimo prisoners in clothing of skins. Eskimo witnesses sat near the front, ready to step forward when called. All the available space was crowded with natives taking advantage, though unknowingly, of their rights as Canadian citizens to attend this public trial. Gradually the odour of animal skins and human bodies wet with perspiration threatened to stifle the white men in the room.

The trial was conducted strictly in accord with all the decorum of a Supreme Court trial in civilization. Patient questioning through the interpreter induced the natives to retell the story of Janes' murder with simple honesty. The jury found Nookudlah guilty of manslaughter, and Judge Rivet sentenced him to ten years' imprisonment in Stony Mountain Penitentiary, Manitoba. The Eskimo who had lured Janes from his tent to his death was also found guilty of manslaughter, and was sentenced to two years' imprisonment with hard labour at Ponds Inlet. The third Eskimo was acquitted.

After complimenting the Mounted Police and Staff Sergeant Joy in particular on their efficiency, the judge addressed the Eskimos through the interpreter. If they behaved well they could expect kindness and protection from the police, he told them, just as the Mounted Police had told the prairie Indians fifty years earlier. But if they committed any crime they must expect to be punished. The Eskimos joined in three cheers for the judge.

Meanwhile, in 1922, Inspector Wilcox and several other policemen had established a detachment even farther north than Ponds Inlet. It was at Craig Harbour on Ellesmere Island, about 950 miles from the North Pole, and served as police detachment, customs house, and the world's most northerly post office. During their first winter there the men did not see the sun rise above the horizon from October 25 of one year to February 13 of the next. They endured intense cold and blizzards lasting twenty-one days at a stretch. Moreover, they had no dogs. Yet they set out on foot to make a number of patrols, some as long as seventy-five miles, and so obtained valuable information about the island and a collection of Eskimo relics.

A tragic incident in 1924 publicized the fact that not only the men on the mainly volunteer northern duty but their wives, too, faced hardship and danger. Margaret Clay, thirty-two-year-old wife of Staff Sergeant S.G. Clay in charge of Chesterfield Inlet in 1924, was such a woman. She had first gone north with her husband to the western Arctic, at which time her personal and household effects had been ruined in the sinking of an overloaded scow in the Athabasca River. Now the only white woman in the Chesterfield Inlet area, she spent much time alone while her husband made long patrols.

One September afternoon while Staff Sergeant Clay was away on a distant patrol to the Baker Lake–Thelon River district, Mrs. Clay took a walk. Later the two men remaining on duty at the detachment heard a dreadful clamour among the husky dogs. Corporal O.G. Petty and Constable H.W. Stallworthy rushed out and found a mass of yelping, snarling dogs worrying something on the ground. It was Mrs. Clay, her right leg below the knee almost completely devoid of flesh. The men beat off the dogs then carried her, still conscious, to the house.

They tended her as best they could, assisted by the other four whites of the little community, two Roman Catholic priests and two Hudson's Bay Company men. But in spite of injections of anaesthetics Mrs. Clay's pain became unbearable, and she begged repeatedly to have her leg amputated. Early next morning Father Duplain and Mr. Snow, as the most experienced, agreed to operate. While they studied a book on surgical work, Petty and Stallworthy prepared the instruments and dressings. Then Stallworthy administered the anaesthetic while the other two operated, assisted by a half-breed woman.

When Mrs. Clay recovered she was cheerful and thankful. Stall-worthy set out to get her husband, but an autumn gale forced him to turn back. Then the next day Mrs. Clay sank into a coma and died. For three days the men waited, hoping in vain that her husband would return, and then they buried her. It was weeks later that Staff Sergeant Clay returned and learned of his bereavement.

Yet in spite of tragic incidents the northern work of the Force went on. Patrols and investigations continued. Mounted Police administered relief to destitute Eskimos, helped natives suffering from tuberculosis, and rescued an Eskimo woman abducted by a native trader. And still they pushed on toward the Pole. Corporal Michelson achieved a new farthest-north patrol record in April, 1925, when he travelled from Craig Harbour, Ellesmere Island, to Kane Basin, about two hundred miles farther north on the same island.

The following year Staff Sergeant Joy established a detachment only about 650 miles from the Pole, at Bache Peninsula on Ellesmere Island, in the Kane Basin area. The detachment buildings, similar to others in the far North, consisted of living quarters, a store house, a blubber shed and two small but comfortable shacks for the three Eskimo families living there. Joy maintained the post for several years. But in some years the supply steamer could not get through the ice in Smith Sound to reach the detachment, so eventually it was closed.

Early in 1928 the Royal Canadian Mounted Police conquered the last stretches of Canada's mainland west of Hudson Bay when Inspector Wilcox, accompanied by three Eskimos, patrolled from Ponds Inlet south over Baffin Island to Melville Peninsula. When the patrol reached Igloolik Island the natives refused to go any farther into unknown territory. But even at that point the Mounted Police had broken the barrier of one of Canada's last northern frontiers.

While police in the eastern Arctic penetrated farther and farther into the frozen North, police in the western Arctic and sub-Arctic carried out assorted tasks, patrolling, investigating crime, checking the welfare of trappers and natives, and so on. During the early 1920s Mounted Police in the Mackenzie River district supervised and controlled an oil rush that followed an important discovery of oil there. Incidentally, when Sergeant H. Thorne returned to that district in March, 1921, after delivering a prisoner to Edmonton, he made part of the trip in an airplane belonging to the Imperial Oil Company, and was thus the first member of the Force to travel on duty by air.

In the winter of 1926–27, Inspector T.B. Caulkin organized the "Husky Express," a winter mail service and patrol along the thousand-mile coast between Cambridge Bay, Victoria Island, and Herschel Island. Two years later, although still a hazardous adventure, it had become recognized as a routine duty. One constable made such fast time over his stage that the native special constable declined to travel with him again, and gave up working for the police.

During the summer of 1928 men of the western Arctic Sub-District under Inspector V.A.M. Kemp as officer commanding, fought a terrible epidemic of influenza that attacked both whites and natives in the lower Mackenzie basin and along the Arctic coast. The natives succumbed by the hundreds, having no resistance to the white man's disease. Kemp himself took charge at Herschel Island, acting as doctor, undertaker and sexton, assisted by his own men and the few other white people on the island, including Mrs. Kemp.

Mounted Police at other detachments set up temporary hospitals and soup kitchens, dug scores of graves, and shot crazed and starving dogs which had not been fed or watered since their owners had died. At Fort McPherson, Corporal A.T. Belcher, himself only recently recovered, cooked soup and bread for two hundred patients, and had to shoot about fifty dogs and supervise the burial of thirty-one natives. Eventually, after the plague had caused seventy-four deaths—an alarming proportion of the native population—the handful of Mounted Police brought it under control, and no new cases developed.

That same summer Sergeant A.P. Colfer made the first patrol by air ever ordered specifically from headquarters, when he took an insane native from Fort Good Hope "outside" by airplane. The old "lunatic patrol" was thus modernized.

The most interesting event of the year, however, occurred on July 30. On that date the *St. Roch*, an eighty-ton power schooner built in Vancouver especially for Arctic travel, was delivered to the Mounted Police at Herschel Island to serve as a floating detachment. Members of the Force went aboard to act as crew as well as policemen, with Constable Henry A. Larsen as navigator, Constable M.F. Foster as engineer, and Sergeant F. Anderton in charge of the floating detachment. In summer the schooner would act as a patrol ship and supply transport for western Arctic detachments. In winter, frozen solid in ice, it would act as a stationary detachment.

During August, 1928, the *St. Roch* visited all western Arctic detachments. Inspector Kemp went with it, and thus inspected all those detachments in less than a month. In September the schooner made its way through early winter ice to Langton Bay at the foot of Franklin Bay, and soon was frozen in for the winter of 1928–29. During that time the police patrolled to locate other suitable winter harbours for the future. They also checked the welfare of trappers and Eskimos, and took the Eskimo census. The latter task was difficult, as usual. Many Eskimos still counted birthdays from "the year the three bears came down the river," and they exchanged wives at will, so that it was almost impossible to discover the parentage of various children.

Northern work during 1929 and 1930 was as varied as ever. Mounted Police in the western Arctic and sub-Arctic explained and enforced game laws, observed weather conditions for the Meteorological Bureau, and experimented with pack dogs instead of sleigh dogs. They rescued a trapper so painfully injured that he contemplated suicide, and they saved starving natives by directing them to more favourable hunting grounds. They searched for missing persons, with one search party patrolling from Fort Reliance deep into the heart of the barren lands along Pelletier's 1908 route to investigate the deaths of a prospecting party and to bury their remains.

The most remarkable northern achievement of the whole decade, however, was accomplished in the eastern Arctic. It was Inspector A.H. Joy's 1,700-mile, eighty-one-day patrol through the Parry Islands in 1929. It began at Dundas Harbour, Devon Island; proceeded west along the coasts of Devon, Cornwallis, Bathurst and Melville Islands to Bridport Inlet; headed north for about 150 miles; then angled northeast to Bache Peninsula.

Inspector Joy, Constable R.A. Taggart and an Eskimo set out from Dundas Harbour on March 12 with Constable R.W. Hamilton and a second Eskimo as temporary support. Almost immediately the patrol party encountered the usual hardships of winter travel in the far North. For miles at a stretch their only possible route lay through a narrow canyon with cliffs on one side and a hundred-foot wall of sea ice on the other. Sometimes that narrow canyon was blocked with huge cakes of ice broken from the wall of sea ice, and one of the men had to go ahead of the dog teams, chopping a passage. In other places severe winds had blown all the snow from the rocks, and the men had to help the dogs drag the sleds over miles of bare rocks.

Starving bears were an added danger. Once the patrol party, by now only Joy, Taggart and one Eskimo, was storm-bound in an igloo when a bear approached and began to tear food and clothing from a half-buried komatik. The police found to their dismay that the igloo doorway was blocked by a deep drift of hard snow, so they could not reach the rifle they had left conveniently loaded at the entrance. They added their shouts to the yelping of the dogs, hoping to frighten the animal away. Instead of leaving, however, the bear rushed at the igloo and tried to dig his way into the blocked entrance.

Fearful of being caught like rats in a trap, the policemen and the Eskimo hurriedly cut a hole in the igloo wall, intending to grab the rifle. The bear plunged for the hole, but the men beat him back. As the animal retreated, Taggart managed to seize the weapon. But with a sudden, swift motion the bear knocked it from his hand, then stood on it with both forepaws, snarling angrily through the hole in the wall.

A moment later the shaggy creature followed up his advantage by charging the igloo for a second time. With the strength of desperation one policeman struck him repeatedly with a stick, while the other stabbed at him with a butcher knife. Again the bear stepped back.

Again Taggart grabbed the rifle, and an instant later the bear fell, shot to death.

As the patrol proceeded, the men encountered still more difficulties and dangers. Wolves, exhausted dogs with bleeding feet, sleds with runners so split that only the heavy steel runners held them together, soft snow up among the mountains, all added to the worries of the little party. As many as seven mock suns at a time preceded dreadful blizzards. Meanwhile the men constantly suffered the usual discomfort of trying to dry perspiration-frozen clothing by the heat of the small primus lamps.

Yet Joy, Taggart and the Eskimo arrived safely at Bache Peninsula on May 31, having completed the patrol as scheduled. They had also conquered the last large group of Canadian Arctic islands, an achievement for which Joy and Taggart won international acclaim. Vilhjalmur Stefansson called it the "finest sledge journey ever made by the Royal North-West Mounted Police or the Royal Canadian Mounted Police."

A Mounted Police undertaking during the winter of 1931–32 also attracted much publicity, though of a different kind. This one was the manhunt for the "mad trapper," Albert Johnson.

Constables E. Millen and A.W. King, celebrating Christmas at the small detachment at Arctic Red River, North-West Territories, were interrupted by a group of indignant Indians complaining about a white man interfering with their trap lines. When Constable King went to the trapper's cabin on the Rat River to investigate, Johnson barred the door. When King returned with a search warrant plus armed reinforcements from Western Arctic Sub-Division headquarters at Aklavik, Johnson opened fire, seriously wounding the constable. King nearly died, but was rushed by dog team to hospital at Aklavik and survived.

Now an additional party of armed Mounted Police plus trapper-volunteers and special constables went to the Rat River cabin, with forty-two dogs and several sled-loads of provisions, dog food, flares and dynamite. But Johnson had fortified his cabin so well that even dynamite exploding against the cabin walls failed to rout him out. When the police-volunteer party's provisions gave out, they had to return to Aklavik.

When they once more went to the cabin, accompanied by a strong, well-equipped party, Johnson had fled. More volunteers joined in a great search, which later had the help of an airplane flown by the experienced northern pilot, Captain W.R. "Wop" May, and which lasted until toward the end of February, 1932. In shoot-outs with Johnson, Constable Millen was fatally shot. Staff Sergeant F.H. Hersey of the Royal Canadian Signals, a volunteer, was dangerously wounded through the lung, but survived, probably because Captain May rushed him to the Aklavik hospital.

At last, when the tracking party surrounded Johnson, he refused to give himself up. He scooped a trench in the deep snow and continued to fire until he was shot and killed. When Inspector A.N. Eames searched the body, he found nothing to identify the morose trapper who had apparently so dreaded investigation that he preferred violent death.

By 1933 northern Mounted Police were able to report that although lesser crimes were still being committed, the serious crime wave formerly so noticeable among Eskimos was well under control. Many of the Eskimos themselves expressed approval of the police efforts. The father of one boy sentenced to a prison term by Inspector A.E.O. Reames sent a letter written in Eskimo to thank the inspector.

"Thanks for helping us out last summer and may God bless you," runs a rough translation. "I was very pleased to know that my boy is well treated. It is far better for you to punish him than it would have been if God had done so. By next summer we will be getting short of clothing again and I was wondering if you could get some for us and send it to us by the policeman when he comes on the boat. . . . May God bless you."

"Not all the 'panhandlers' are to be found in large cities," Reames commented in his report to headquarters. "Note the technique of the touch."

In the summer of 1936, Commissioner Sir James MacBrien, in office since 1931, visited most of the remote detachments in the North-West Territories and the Yukon Territory by plane. It was not his first such inspection. In 1933 he had made a similar though more limited flight, after which he had reorganized all the North-West Territories and the eastern Arctic detachments. From that time on they comprised an enlarged "G" Division containing a million and a quarter square miles, with headquarters at Ottawa for greater administrative convenience.

MacBrien's tour of 1936, however, was particularly notable. His thirty-day, 11,000-mile flight was believed to be the longest single journey made by air in Canada to that time. By covering so great a part of the country in so brief a time and thus bringing even remote northern detachments into quicker, closer contact with Ottawa, the tour constituted another significant step in the conquest of the Canadian North.

Chapter 16
Modernizing the Force
1931–1938

In August, 1931, Major General James Howden MacBrien, former chief of staff of the Canadian militia, succeeded Commissioner Starnes, who retired with forty-five years' service. MacBrien, Canadian-born and educated, had served for one year in the North-West Mounted Police as a constable from 1900. His present aim was to speed the development of the Force into a well-equipped, highly trained organization capable of fighting modern criminals with modern methods.

Almost at once he began to regroup detachments and districts, and to establish each province or territory as a Division as far as geographically possible. The position of deputy commissioner was created, and the number of assistant commissioners increased from one to seven. The strength of 1,351 members in 1931 was increased to 2,348 the following year.

During 1932, MacBrien's scope became greater than he had anticipated. The Force then took over the provincial police work in Manitoba, the three Maritime provinces, and Alberta. It also absorbed and took over the duties of the Preventive Service of the Department of National Revenue. Thus, to avoid the corruption that had formerly permeated the Customs and Excise Department, the Force became responsible for that work, which until then it had done only on request.

Mounted Police of the Preventive Service from coast to coast now prevented persons from avoiding payment of customs and excise duties. Police at Nanaimo, British Columbia, found thirty-three large kegs of liquor hidden in a truckload of second-hand furniture. Police in Montreal arrested a man who manufactured cigars and packed them in cigar boxes whose excise stamps had been broken. He peddled them around to small shops, then got the boxes back to be refilled. Preventive Service men in Halifax found an ordinary-looking sink with a single faucet which at first gave ordinary water. On manipulation of a double set of pipes under the sink it gave rum instead.

The Marine Section of the Preventive Service exemplified the development of the period. Although its members were not classified as regular members of the Force until 1934, their qualifications were raised, and they were issued with faster boats, which they used in cooperation with RCAF aircraft. During their first seven months of working under the Mounted Police in Preventive Service duties, they seized the unusually large number of nineteen rum-running boats. They also prevented landings of liquor, aided distressed schooners, motorboats and fishing craft, and rescued shipwrecked fishermen.

Meanwhile some Mounted Police cases indicated the trend toward modern scientific methods. In December, 1931, a Saskatchewan farmer, Hans Pedersen, was found shot dead just outside his house. Constable R.M. Wood of Rosetown detachment saw that someone had tried to destroy the house: a coal-oil lamp lay in the middle of a partially burnt mattress. Wood took fingerprints from the lamp chimney. He then took the fingerprints of the dead man and learned that the prints on the lamp were not his.

Wood subsequently discovered that Pedersen's only known enemy, Paul Schudwitz, had borrowed a .22 rifle the day before Pedersen was shot. He also learned that Schudwitz had been seen firing a .22 rifle into the side of a grain elevator, so he dug the bullets from the building. Meanwhile an autopsy on Pedersen's body had disclosed the .22 bullet that had killed him. A ballistics expert now proved that all the bullets had been shot from the same rifle, indicating that Schudwitz had murdered Pedersen.

Two weeks later Schudwitz's shot and frozen body was found, a .22 rifle still clenched in his hands. The police shot bullets from that .22, and a ballistics expert proved, by the firing marks on them, that this was the rifle that had shot the other bullets. The police also found that Schudwitz's fingerprints were identical with those on the lamp chimney. Hence the coroner's jury stated that Pedersen had been murdered by Schudwitz, who later committed suicide.

In May, 1932, when Corporal Dickson of Truro, Nova Scotia, investigated a store robbery, he noticed fingerprints on three pieces of glass. He sent the glass to Ottawa headquarters. Fingerprint experts there discovered a print identical with the right thumb-print of a criminal named Hamilton, whose prints they had on file.

Later, in court, Staff Sergeant H.R. Butchers of the Finger Print Section produced photographic enlargements of Hamilton's right thumb-print and of the imprint on the glass. Then he explained the sixteen identical points of the enlarged photographs. Hamilton pleaded guilty. It was the first case in Nova Scotia in which a fingerprint expert's evidence resulted in a conviction.

In December, 1933, when two constables investigated a break-in in Manitoba, they collected a few green wool fibres they found clinging to the drilled portion of a vault, and others mixed with the steel drillings on the floor. Later they located three suspects, one of whom was wearing blue and green woollen mitts. The police sent the mitts, the fibres and some sample drillings from the vault to Dr. Glen Murphy, a Manitoba scientist. Dr. Murphy found that fibres from the mitts were identical with those from the vault door and from the drillings, and also that the mitts contained minute steel drillings. The three suspects were convicted, largely on the scientific evidence.

As Commissioner MacBrien's Annual Report for 1933–34 noted, the year 1933 commemorated the Diamond Jubilee of the Force. That report, for efficiency, covered eighteen months to March, 1934, so that succeeding reports could coincide with the government fiscal year ending March 31. It noted first publication of the official *RCMP Quarterly* magazine and the formation of a Mounted Police museum at Regina. Constables were now graded into first, second and third class, and paid according to training and experience. Also, continuous classes were being held as promotional or refresher courses for all ranks including officers.

Under MacBrien's direction the six months of training for recruits grew to include not only drills, equitation, musketry and lectures on the Criminal Code, on the Rules and Regulations of the Force and so on, but also jujitsu, study of federal and provincial statutes, typewriting, and care and operation of motor transport. Squads of recruits attended city police and assize courts, heard judges and magistrates lecture on criminal law, and cooperated with law students in mock trials. During the winter months, members of the Marine Section were trained in seamanship, signals, gunnery and engineering.

The standard for recruits had been raised during 1932, although for some time this had no effect on the number of applications. Between 1932 and 1936, a time of deep depression, about fifteen thousand men applied. Only 1,600 were accepted, including the men absorbed in 1932 from the five provincial forces and the Preventive Service. Applications, from all parts of the British Commonwealth, were almost as varied as those of the Old Originals of the 1870s: university graduates, farmers, aviators, divinity students, Royal Military College graduates, druggists and labourers applied.

One applicant wrote: "My age, twenty-three; occupation, relief work and ex-racketeer. I have spent three years in the penitentiary—no recommendation, but it could be made very useful." Another man admitted that he was applying by the same mail for a position as hangman.

In 1935, Commissioner MacBrien initiated the Force's sponsorship of some of its members as full-time university students. That first year seven students, six of whom were already university graduates, attended various universities all across Canada, all taking law. Six, including the original non-graduate, graduated with degrees. One of these was Constable M.F.A. Lindsay who some thirty years later became Commissioner. He attended classes at the University of Saskatchewan wearing uniform including breeches, high boots and spurs. Like the others, he worked at RCMP Town Station between classes and during holidays.

In 1935, MacBrien sent two senior officers to Europe for a three-months' course at Scotland Yard, and to study the police systems of England, France and Belgium. After their return he added nine subjects for recruits' training, including lectures on scientific aids to investigation, and portrait parlé (description of persons). To make time for this, and because more cars were being used, equitation was temporarily discontinued, although a Mounted Section kept up the Musical Ride.

Between March, 1935, and March, 1936, scientific aids gave successful results in at least six cases which would otherwise have been failures. Several were ballistics cases, including the notorious multiple murder Bannister case in New Brunswick.

In Manitoba a constable investigating a theft from a poultry farm noticed tire tracks about the premises. He telephoned the Criminal Investigation Branch at Winnipeg, and obtained the help of the C.I.B. photographer, who also knew how to make casts. After taking photographs the Winnipeg man built a low wall around the clearest tire tracks, then poured on them a mixture of melted beeswax, paraffin wax and resin. After the mixture hardened he removed it, thus having a permanent record of the tire marks of the thief's car. Later the photographs and the casts were used as evidence in court, and three men were convicted on several charges.

By 1935 the Single Finger Print Collection, begun in 1933 under the care of Corporal J.H. Barnett, totalled 35,000 cards. Each card displayed an impression of one of the ten digits of 3,500 known burglars and other criminals likely to repeat offences. A police investigator could now send any single fingerprint found at the scene of a burglary to this section, with a good chance that it would be identified as belonging to a known burglar. Single fingerprints not identified were filed in the Scenes of Crime exhibits for possible future identification.

During 1935 the Scenes of Crime collection filed three separate fingerprints from breaking, entering and theft scenes at Ottawa, at Hull, and at Jolliette. In January, 1936, the Single Finger Print Collection received the prints of a man named Gilmour, recently convicted at Toronto on four charges of housebreaking. On checking them against the Scenes of Crime exhibits, Corporal Barnett found that the three prints belonged to Gilmour. The police subsequently rounded up Gilmour and his gang, and they were convicted.

During 1936, "D" Division (Manitoba) kept a modus operandi record that listed crimes and criminals according to the way the crimes were committed. When a man named Patterson confessed to breaking and entering a store by drilling holes around the lock, a police check of modus operandi files showed that a store in another Manitoba town had been entered by the same method. The Mounted Police confronted Patterson with the earlier crime, and he confessed.

The crimes solved through modus operandi files attracted the favourable attention of Ottawa headquarters staff, including Assistant Commissioner S.T. Wood, one of the officers who had studied modern police methods in Europe. Wood, son of the Assistant Commissioner Z.T. Wood of Yukon fame who thirty years earlier had advocated modern methods of criminal identification, now suggested that modus operandi records be used on a national scale. Later this was done.

Firearms registration began in 1935 following an amendment to the Criminal Code. By March, 1937, Mounted Police across Canada had registered about 150,000 pistols and revolvers, and had filed records of them at Ottawa headquarters. The records were available to all Canadian police forces. Thus all police could identify stolen weapons and often could prove charges of housebreaking against thieves.

Credit for one innovation of the 1930s went not to Commissioner MacBrien but to Sergeant J.N. Cawsey of Bassano, Alberta. This was the introduction of specially trained police service dogs. Cawsey had bought for his family a specially trained German shepherd named Dale of Cawsalta (Caws for Cawsey, Alta for Alberta). The handsome, hundred-pound dog, a gentle companion for Cawsey's little daughter, also worked for the sergeant.

In November, 1933, Dale, wearing tracking harness with a forty-foot leash, guided his master and a constable through five miles of slushy snow and mud, from a stolen and abandoned car to a suspect asleep in an Indian cabin. This first case did not result in a conviction. Although police evidence included plaster casts of peculiar square-toed shoeprints along most of the trail, and of similarly square-toed shoes found beside the sleeping man, the judge refused to allow the evidence arising from the dog's tracking. Because the visible trail was broken in many places, the case was dismissed.

Cawsey continued to use the dog, however. Dale helped the sergeant to check freight trains for transients late at night. He found lost money on command, and once even without command. In 1934, in a blinding mid-winter blizzard at thirty-five degrees below zero, he saved the lives of his master and a constable by leading them from their car, stalled on the open prairie, to a tiny cabin. The following year Dale found a lost two-year-old girl for whom more than a hundred men had searched for sixteen hours. On the way to the area of search he had sniffed out, through rain and dark of night, two thieves hiding in a field, plus the stolen fountain pens they had thrown away.

Mounted Police officials had noted Dale's work since that first case in 1933. They now persuaded the reluctant sergeant to sell his dog to the Force. In October, 1935, Dale became an official member of the Royal Canadian Mounted Police, No. K470, and henceforth his work was recorded on his "personal" file.

Dale's successes led the Force to purchase his son, Black Lux, trained by the same Calgary trainer of Dale. Then they bought several more German shepherds and opened their own training kennels at Calgary (later moved to Regina). The Mounted Police dogs, unlike those of other police forces, were not trained to such specific purposes as tracking, searching or guarding, but received a wide variety of training over a nine- to twelve-month period. Thus they could adjust themselves to almost any emergency.

The police-trained German shepherds proved so useful in the prairie provinces and the Maritimes that in 1938 the Force opened a second training kennel at Rockcliffe and experimented with other breeds. Before long the dogs were working successfully on hundreds of cases including assault, theft, arson, murder, lost and missing persons, and finding illicit stills.

Regular work continued, as widespread and as varied as usual. In addition to the usual major cases there were lesser ones concerning the Schools Act, the Game and Fisheries Act, the Highway Act and the Minimum Wage Act. During the year 1933–34, members on duty travelled collectively 13,511,632 miles. In 1935, Mounted Police investigations of naturalized citizens' applications under the revised Old Age Pensions Act alone totaled 23,698.

In Alberta a constable arrested a Chinese for selling lemon extract, an intoxicant, to an Indian. Other police investigated a fraudulent scheme for selling Norwegian reindeer. A detective in Saskatchewan solved a number of depression-period cases in which persons using fictitious names wrote to mail-order houses for C.O.D. orders of clothing, then stole the parcels when they arrived at local post offices. Three Mounted Policemen, Sergeant S.T. Wallace, Constable G.C. Harrison and Constable J.G. Shaw, were shot to death while chasing Doukhobor bandits.

Almost the whole Force did Preventive Service work. Policemen found bootleg liquor in a baby's crib, in an old lady's hot-water bottle, and in a milk wagon whose driver provided his customers with "white" or "dark," that is, milk or rum. Other police found illicit stills in a chocolate factory, in a lumberyard, and in a former bake shop that still advertised "Mother's Tasty Pies." Others tracked down the source of marijuana cigarettes sold in a large eastern city. Mounted Police in the Montreal district set a new record when they seized a large still even before it began to operate.

The most adventurous work of the Preventive Service, however, was done by the Marine Section. Smugglers used fewer sailing vessels and more fast motorboats equipped with high-frequency wireless sets that picked up orders from illegal high-powered stations on shore. But the police also had fast motorboats, and gradually captured those of the smugglers.

Merely capturing the rum-running boats was not enough, however. The liquor smuggling was usually organized by "higher-ups" who escaped punishment because they did not actually handle the liquor. So senior police officials decided to bring those key men into the picture by charging them with conspiracy.

In this way they broke up a liquor-smuggling ring in Quebec. The planning was done in Montreal by Superintendent F.J. Mead, and in Quebec City by Inspector H.A.R. Gagnon, son of Superintendent Sévère Gagnon, one of the Force's Old Originals. The case involved months of investigation, the synchronization of arrests in widely scattered towns and villages, and the painstaking, detailed organization of evidence. Then forty-seven persons were convicted, including the three heads of the smuggling ring who were sentenced to from two to four years in jail. Seven vessels were seized. For months afterwards there was practically no smuggling in that area.

One famous case of the period demonstrated the dual capabilities of the Preventive Service, on the high seas and in the courts of law. It began eight miles off the coast of Cape Breton, Nova Scotia, when

Preventive Service men aboard the RCMP patrol cruiser *No. 4* located the auxiliary schooner *Kromhout* one windy day in December, 1933. *No. 4* ordered the ice-coated schooner to stop, but instead it nosed through the choppy waves out to sea. The small patrol boat followed. After a twenty-two-mile race, the ship's master, Ross Mason, at last ordered his men to heave to.

The Preventive Service men climbed aboard, and discovered that the *Kromhout* was carrying five thousand gallons of contraband liquor. First Officer MacKenzie and three others remained on board as a prize crew. Then, with the little patrol boat towing the big schooner, they headed for North Sydney. Late that night, however, the crew of the *Kromhout* overpowered the prize crew. They cut the tow line, doused all lights, and made away in the darkness. By the time the crew of *No. 4* had hauled in the ninety-fathom tow line, the schooner had such a head start that it got away.

Almost immediately Mounted Police wireless reported the escape to authorities in Newfoundland and St. Pierre. So when the schooner entered St. Pierre the next morning, French officials seized it, arrested Ross Mason and his crew, and notified the Mounted Police at Halifax. Mason and the others felt sure that a skilful lawyer could prevent their conviction, especially as the *Kromhout* was first seized outside Canadian territorial waters. They waived extradition, and willingly accompanied the police back to Halifax.

Later Mason stood trial on three counts. One, theft of the *Kromhout*, since according to the legal definition his taking the ship after police seizure was theft. Two, similarly, theft of the cargo. Three, obstructing a public officer in the discharge of his duties. Mason's lawyer fiercely contested every legal point, but eventually his client was convicted on all three charges and went to jail for three years.

Preventive Service experience in such cases led the Force to recommend changes in weak laws. As a result, new regulations forced masters of certain vessels to report to Customs as to their ports of call, cargo, and so on, or incur penalties of $400 or forfeiture of their ships. The Customs Act was amended to provide for "continuous pursuit" of a vessel refusing to halt when challenged beyond Canadian territorial limits, a point contested bitterly in the *Kromhout* case. Also, to cover a point vital in conspiracy charges, the Customs Act was amended and a penalty set to provide for the production of all papers, books and invoices on reasonable suspicion of a violation of that Act.

Meanwhile the Mounted Police conducted a successful campaign under the Opium and Narcotic Drug Act. In this field, too, the government adopted the changes in legislation recommended by the Force.

But the police sometimes met insurmountable difficulties. For example, three members of the Montreal drug squad worked long and hard to get evidence against Frenette, a man they believed to be one of the most important illicit narcotics dealers there. They watched while a buyer sitting in Frenette's car paid the dealer with marked money, which they later recovered from the car. The same police, in a police car, chased Frenette in his car immediately after the transaction, but he crashed his car and escaped. During the chase he had tried in vain to throw out of the window a bottle of drugs, and the police found this with the marked money in the car immediately after the crash. They thought they had enough evidence to convict him, if not of trafficking in narcotics, at least of possession. But when they took the case to court Frenette swore that the articles found in the car were not his, and he was acquitted.

In a disappointing Liquor Act case a witness committed proved perjury. But when he was charged the jury deliberated only ten minutes and declared him not guilty. The judge's rebuke to the jury probably voiced the thoughts of the police: "Don't be aghast if the laws are broken when, in the face of strong evidence on a serious charge, a jury can come to so easy a decision."

Many Mounted Police duties of the 1930s arose directly out of the depression. For instance, the police enforced the Railway Act to prevent transients taking free rides on freight trains. They also kept the peace at strikes which developed across the country. Both duties caused transients, unemployed, strikers and labour groups to accuse the Mounted Police of prejudice against labour, although they merely enforced the law.

The most important duty arising out of the depression concerned the Communists, who took advantage of disgruntled labour to foment strikes and other disturbances by which they planned eventually to overthrow the Canadian system of democratic government. For ten years the Mounted Police, the Ontario Provincial Police and various city police forces had made a sustained investigation of Communist activities and this culminated in a noted trial at Toronto in November, 1931. The Province of Ontario charged eight Communist leaders, including the Party leader, Tim Buck, and Sam Cohen (alias Sam Carr), with being members and officers of an unlawful association. This came under Section 98 of the Criminal Code, which was later repealed. The eight were also charged with seditious conspiracy. Men of many police forces gave evidence, but the most valuable came from a Mounted Policeman.

In 1921, Constable J. Leopold had joined the Communist party under an assumed name and had remained a member for about seven years, until he was expelled. His testimony, together with pamphlets, membership cards and other items seized from Communist party offices, wove an inescapable web about the accused. They were proved to be members and officers of the "Communist Party of Canada, Section Communist International," directed from Russia and aimed at the overthrow by force of every existing non-Communist government in the world.

"This conquest does not mean peacefully capturing the ready-made bourgeois State Machinery by means of a parliamentary majority," stated a document of the Communist International seized by the police. "[It means] the violent overthrow of bourgeois power, the destruction of the Capitalist State apparatus, bourgeois armies, police and judiciary, parliaments. . . . [to be achieved by] strikes and demonstrations, a combination of strikes and armed demonstrations and, finally, the general strike co-jointly with armed insurrection against the State Power."

The jury pronounced the eight accused guilty as charged. The judge sentenced them to prison terms: seven men, including Tim Buck and Sam Cohen, to five years, and the other man to two. The judge also ordered the deportation of the foreign-born, but the Ontario Court of Appeal allowed an appeal against this.

Overt Communist party activity was now disorganized. But individual Communists infiltrated key positions in legal labour unions and in relief camps. Then, to embarrass the authorities, they fomented labour and relief-camp strikes. The party claimed responsibility for ninety percent of all strikes in Canada between 1933 and 1935, many of which the Mounted Police had to oversee.

Miscellaneous police duties through the busy 1930s included guarding such prominent visitors as U.S. President Franklin Delano Roosevelt, and policing public functions like the Fishermen's Exhibition at Lunenburg, Nova Scotia. Assistant Commissioner S.T. Wood headed a contingent of the Mounted Section at the coronation of George VI in May, 1937. While abroad the assistant commissioner made a further study of Scotland Yard and other European police systems.

The Mounted Section performed the Musical Ride in various parts of Canada. The horses came to know the routine as well as did their riders. Once when a stunting airplane swooped directly over the troop, causing one horse to throw its rider, the animal did not pause for the constable to remount. Instead it continued, riderless, in perfect formation to the last of the intricate figures.

As for the public's opinion of the Mounted Police during the 1930s, two points are indicative. One, all six provinces whose provincial police work was done by the Force—three prairie and three Maritime—renewed their agreements. Two, some small western towns asked the Force to take over their municipal police work. At first the Mounted Police merely helped several municipalities to reorganize their own forces. But in 1935 they began to police Flin Flon, Manitoba, and in 1937 Melville, Saskatchewan.

The Annual Report of March, 1938, listed several points of progress. A scientific laboratory had been established at Regina the year before, under Dr. Maurice Powers, a specialist in forensic medicine. He and other Mounted Police had taken extensive courses in Canada and the United States, in order to work in the laboratory and teach in training classes. A Photographic Section and a Crime Index based on the modus operandi system had been established. The *RCMP Gazette*, first published in 1937, was being distributed all over Canada with information about persons wanted, important arrests, stolen cars, and so on. In 1937 the Force had purchased four DeHavilland "Dragonflies" and established its own Aviation Section. The Marine Section was now using two new speedboats specially designed by a famous racing-craft designer.

That Annual Report indicated that Commissioner Sir James Howden MacBrien (he was knighted in 1935) had done what he had set out to do. The Force was well on its way toward being a well-equipped, highly trained organization capable of fighting modern criminals with modern methods.

Chapter 17
An Officer's Son Takes Command
1938-1939

Ironically, the Annual Report for the year ending March 31, 1938, which indicated how well Commissioner MacBrien had accomplished his aim of speeding the Force's modernization, was not written by Sir James MacBrien himself. He died on March 5, after a serious operation, and was succeeded by the former Acting Deputy Commissioner Stuart Taylor Wood.

Canadian-born, Commissioner Wood, son of the former Assistant Commissioner Z.T. Wood, had from childhood in Dawson City become imbued with the spirit and traditions of the Force. After attending Upper Canada College he went to the Royal Military College to prepare himself to follow in his father's footsteps through service with the Royal North-West Mounted Police. After graduation he was appointed an inspector of the Force in 1912. His varied experiences included duty at Herschel Island and in the four western provinces. He had also taken a course at Scotland Yard, had studied European and American police methods, and had spent about two years at Ottawa headquarters as director of Criminal Investigation for the entire Force.

Commissioner Wood, like his predecessor, believed that modern methods would lead to a more efficient Force. During his first year in office the Police College at Regina, by then recognized as the National Training Centre, was attended not only by Mounted Police but also by policemen from other Canadian forces. Also, for the first time, it was attended by members of the Marine Section.

Divisional headquarters across the country gradually established their own Photographic and Finger Print Sections. They also set up small laboratories for teaching the making of casts, the raising of filed-off automobile serial numbers, the observation of glass fractures and so on. Before long, Mounted Police everywhere were taking photographs, drawing plans of highway accidents, and taking plaster and moulage casts of shoeprints, overshoe prints and tire tracks.

Constable Wickstrom of "K" Division (Alberta), while investigating the shooting of a horse, took casts of a hoof print and a hoof. Working under difficulties without plaster or wax, he ingeniously melted the brown wax cover from some old "B" batteries he found nearby and used this for making the cast. His results caused the suspect to confess to having shot the horse in mistake for a moose.

In Prince Edward Island a man stole non-negotiable securities and then phoned the owner, offering to return them if he would drop fifty dollars in bills while walking along a certain street. The Mounted Police sprinkled the money with malachite green, a powder scarcely visible when dry, but which shows plainly when wet. The thief escaped arrest as he picked up the bills. But later when the police located him they asked him to wash his hands, which turned a vivid green. A jury found him guilty of theft.

Meanwhile some of the staff of the scientific laboratory at Regina earned notable honours. When Dr. Maurice Powers received his degree of Doctor of Medical Science at New York University, his was the first such degree issued in North America to one who had specialized in forensic medicine and toxicology. Sergeant J.A. Churchman, a ballistics expert, became a Fellow of the Royal Microscopical Society of London, England. Corporal J.I. Mallow was admitted as a member of the Royal Photographic Society of London, England.

Laboratory men also won recognition from other Mounted Policemen. During the year ending March, 1939, policemen from all parts of the Force, including those in the Yukon, sent exhibits from 297 cases to the Regina laboratory. Experts performed autopsies; others examined blood, bullets, fingernail scrapings, hairs, documents and burnt paper; and others made more than four thousand photographic negatives, prints and enlargements.

The testimony of the laboratory experts was invaluable at the conclusion of a murder case. The investigation began in November, 1938, when Mounted Police at Regina learned that a car belonging to J.A. Kaeser of Moosomin, Saskatchewan, had been abandoned in Winnipeg. The upholstery of the car was covered with blood.

The police soon discovered that Kaeser had not returned home from a visit to Regina in early November. From Regina headquarters they broadcast, over a commercial station, a description of the missing man and his gray Chrysler coupé. A farmer's wife near Sintaluta, Saskatchewan, remembered seeing a similar car in a nearby field. She searched and found Kaeser's body at the edge of a slough. Mounted Police who claimed the body saw that he had been shot several times through the back and through the back of the head. They also found five .38 calibre cartridge cases nearby.

Now Mounted Police and city police at Winnipeg investigated further. They learned that the Chrysler coupé had been driven from the West by Harry Heipel, who had rented a room in Winnipeg for a few days from November 9. Moreover, Heipel had left a bloodstained raincoat behind. And he had disposed of the dead man's suitcases by checking them in the baggage room at the CNR station.

The police in Winnipeg also learned that Heipel had worked as caretaker of a farm in Arcola, Saskatchewan, until the first week of November. Now the Arcola Mounted Police searched the farm, and found several .38 calibre cartridge cases. A boy told them that he had seen Heipel with a loaded revolver and extra shells, and he gave the police one of the shells.

Later the testimony of the experts convicted Heipel of murder. Corporal Mallow produced enlarged photographs of the body and of other items. Dr. Powers testified that the stains on the car's upholstery were human blood stains, as were those on the raincoat, which was identified as belonging to Heipel.

Sergeant Churchman's evidence, however, was probably even more important. He had examined not only the bullets, but also the cartridges, both those found near the body and those found on the Arcola farm where Heipel had worked. First he testified that the bullets had been shot from a .38 calibre revolver. Then he produced greatly magnified photographs of the two sets of cartridge cases. Even to untrained eyes the similarity was damning. "I believe," Churchman concluded, "that the two sets of cartridges were fired from the same revolver, a .38 calibre revolver with a slightly damaged firing pin."

Harry Heipel was found guilty and hanged at Regina in April of the next year. Later the murder weapon was discovered. It was a .38 calibre revolver with a slightly damaged firing pin.

Laboratory work not only proved guilt, but also cleared innocent persons of suspicion, as when an Indian baby died suddenly in April, 1939, and its mother was suspected by neighbours of having poisoned the child. Dr. Powers tested various poisonous and nonpoisonous roots used by the Indians, including one that the mother had given her baby. He concluded that the infant had died of natural causes.

Because the National Training Centre and the Crime Detection Laboratory at Regina proved so useful, buildings for a similar police college and laboratory were erected at Rockcliffe. Other modern developments were continued or introduced.

The Aviation Section not only flew its "Dragonflies" (reduced to three by March, 1939) in cooperation with the Marine Section, but also housed one of them at Regina to take members of the laboratory to give court evidence throughout the country and to transport Dr. Powers to distant points to perform autopsies. A Noorduyn "Norseman" seaplane equipped with floats, skis, wheels and two-way radio equipment was purchased, and stationed in the Mackenzie River district in 1939, the first police airplane ever operated in the far North.

Mounted Police at Regina used a commercial radio station there to broadcast information about stolen property, escaped criminals and mental patients, confidence men and so on. "L" Division headquarters in Prince Edward Island was equipped with radio to contact Mounted Police stations, airplanes, boats and automobiles.

The *RCMP Gazette* doubled its content and trebled its circulation. The Photography Section experimented with movies, then with colour movies. The *Quarterly* included such articles as "The Identification of Hair according to Black, Yellow or White Race" and "Mechanics of Motion as Applied to Highway Accidents." From June 1, 1938, all reports on Criminal Code investigations were read by experienced crime readers at Ottawa. This ensured that no investigation would be abandoned until every possible avenue of inquiry had been exhausted.

Regular policework during the same period went on as usual. The Preventive Service in eastern Canada practically put the rum-runners out of business, so that rum was sold in some government stores for the first time. Moreover, successful conspiracy cases, in which the Mounted Police obtained convictions for offences committed some three years earlier, frightened the rum-runners. They were afraid to enter port in ballast for fear that their past activities would result in the forfeiture of their vessels.

However, the scarcity of smuggled liquor resulted in more illicit stills, so the Preventive Service continued to have plenty of work to do. They found stills in swamps, in garages, in a cheese factory, and in an eight-room house built so that the condensing coils of the still ran through the ceilings and floors. In these excise cases as in customs cases which involved smuggling, the police learned that the surest way of bringing organized gangs to justice was to charge them with conspiracy.

Prairie police still carried on their depression-time duties, taking applications for relief, registering recipients, and actually handling the relief itself. Also, they concentrated on both day and night patrols in an effort to apprehend criminals and prevent crime.

In "F" Division (Saskatchewan), where harvest time meant that storekeepers in small towns without banks held unusually large sums of money to cash grain cheques, constant patrols helped to ward off professional safeblowers. In "D" Division (Manitoba) two constables making a night patrol arrested two men who aroused their suspicions when they tried to avoid stopping to have their car checked and thus became involved in an accident. While the first patrol party was waiting for assistance to pull the car out of the ditch, another patrol arrived and reported a holdup. The two men admitted their guilt and later were convicted in court.

In Vancouver the Mounted Police were, as usual, chiefly concerned with drug cases and smuggling. Their prolonged vigilance secured the conviction of a Chinese labour contractor whom they had suspected ever since 1925 of dealing in narcotics, but only now were able to prove guilty. In the same province they also continued to escort registered mail, to guard the Bank of Canada, and occasionally to apprehend Japanese living in the country illegally.

Police from coast to coast still performed miscellaneous duties ranging from delivering mail to a lightship to arresting counterfeiters, to seizing abandoned decoy ducks under the Migratory Birds Convention Act.

Mounted Police in most settled areas were on the lookout for the plant known to drug users as marijuana, and to farmers as a quick-growing plant that made a splendid windbreak. During April, 1938, the Opium and Narcotic Drug Act was amended to make cultivation of *Cannabis sativa* illegal except by permit. Enforcing the amendment meant much extra work, particularly as newspapers publicized the newly revealed narcotic qualities of the weed-like plant.

The North, like the rest of Canada, experienced the progress of civilization. Although Corporal E.A. Kirk was absent from his detachment at Old Crow, Yukon Territory, for twelve days at a time, he contacted the detachment every evening with his homemade portable radio, even in forty-eight below zero weather. In his absence Mrs. Kirk sent telegraphic messages from the home transmitter. Incidentally, a new duty in the Yukon at that time was to check and register planes at Dawson and Whitehorse, thus recalling the gold rush days when the North-West Mounted Police checked boats.

Progress in the eastern Arctic included experiments with electric lights, even at remote Craig Harbour. The post office at that detachment still retained the distinction of being the most northerly post office in the world, and for years the annual supply ship had carried several bags of mail sent by philatelists and addressed to themselves. The

Mounted Police postmarked the mail and the philatelists thus obtained stamps with rare cancellations. During this period all northern areas— formerly "B" and "G" Divisions—were amalgamated into "G" Division for greater efficiency.

During the early months of 1939 the Force prepared for the visit of King George VI and Queen Elizabeth to Canada by setting up elaborate security systems. Then Commissioner Wood and several other Mounted Police accompanied the party across Canada during their visit in May. Even police service dog Dale took part by searching all box cars and buildings near the station at Unity before Their Majesties arrived at that small Saskatchewan town.

At Regina, the Royal couple toured the Mounted Police barracks, of especial interest since King George was, as Queen Elizabeth II became later, the Force's Honourary Commissioner. The band which welcomed them with the national anthem was formed of thirty-four trained musicians, a far cry from bands of the early days when a man might be given a French horn because it seemed the right size for his figure.

Their Majesties saw the buffalo head in the billiard room, inspected the scientific laboratory, and signed the visitor's book which held such famous signatures as Sir Wilfrid Laurier, Winston Churchill, Vilhjalmur Stefansson and John McCormack, the operatic tenor. They also visited the chapel, which was originally a canteen built in eastern Canada and transported in sections to its present site by steamer and ox team in 1885, and converted to a chapel in 1894. As Their Majesties looked at the memorials to the men of the 1874 march, the 1885 rebellion, and others, the King asked about the Fitzgerald patrol.

Such duties as those connected with the Royal Visit gave the Mounted Police much publicity, so perhaps they were not surprised when a Saskatchewan woman wrote to ask the prices on private armed guards. But when Lance Corporal S.J. Leach—this rank has since been discontinued—escorted eight Indians to the Australian Royal Easter Show he was surprised, when he reached Honolulu, to see how far the fame of the Force had spread. The patriotic parade there to celebrate George Washington's birthday included a float carrying six make-believe "Mounted Policemen."

During the first eighteen months Commissioner Wood held office it must have seemed to any casual observer that the organization carried on much as usual. Actually, however, there was one notable difference. The Mounted Police realized the probability of war and prepared accordingly. As early as April, 1938, Mounted Policemen were engaged in work classified as public security. They surveyed railway bridges, canals and dockyards, and interviewed the staffs of large public-utility corporations to advise on how to protect their plants. They also undertook secret-service work, investigating a large number of persons likely to be considered enemy aliens in the event of war.

As a further pre-war measure, Commissioner Wood authorized a radical change in the Royal Canadian Mounted Police Reserve. The section had been organized in 1937 to train suitable young men annually so that they might join the Force later if they wished, and to maintain a reserve strength for emergency. About three hundred such young men had been recruited at various points from coast to coast and given short training courses. As war appeared to be inevitable, the Mounted Police realized that instead of having to call a large number of individuals from scattered points, they should be able to get assistance more quickly. So they centred Reserve activities in larger cities, beginning with Toronto and Winnipeg, and accepted men other than merely the young ones who might eventually join the Force.

Bank managers, printers, mechanics, doctors, truck drivers, chemists, lawyers, clerks and others volunteered their services and their cars. Then they devoted evenings and holidays to drill and training, until several substantial Reserve units had been developed at strategic points.

By the late summer of 1939, war seemed imminent. In any event, the Royal Canadian Mounted Police had laid the groundwork for Canada's security.

Chapter 18
During World War II
1939 – 1945

When Canada entered World War II in September, 1939, the Royal Canadian Mounted Police were ready for the emergency, chiefly because of their preliminary surveys and investigations of the previous eighteen months. Within a few hours of the declaration of war they made simultaneous arrests all across the country of known Nazi sympathizers, and they posted guards at vital points, thus preventing possible sabotage.

The thirty or so vessels of the Marine Section, except for a few fast motorboats, were turned over to the Department of National Defence, as were the radio stations and all equipment for the directing of patrol boats from shore. More than two hundred Marine Section men volunteered for the Royal Canadian Naval Reserves and the Marine Auxiliary Branch of the Royal Canadian Air Force. All nine members of the Aviation Section and their three "Dragonfly" planes went over to the RCAF, leaving only the "Norseman" for police use. Also, a limited number of men were allowed to form the No. 1 Provost Company, Royal Canadian Mounted Police, for service with the First Canadian Division overseas.

Other than these, the government decreed, no Mounted Policemen would be released from their vital home duties. Then, to prepare for the anticipated extra work, the Force replaced uniformed clerical workers with women, re-engaged ex-members and pensioners, and hired about twelve hundred special constable guards. Even so, by March, 1940, regular strength was fifty men fewer than pre-war strength.

Soon extra work almost swamped the police. They maintained guards at canals, bridges, dockyards, armouries, RCAF stations, wireless and radio stations, large grain elevators, and public utilities in cities. They helped to guard war factories and to check their security. They established new detachments, including one in Ontario at Camp Borden, with one constable in sole charge to check the petty thievery and bootlegging at the military and air training centres.

Across the country Mounted Police registered enemy aliens, then had them report regularly to police detachments. When Italy entered the war in June, 1940, they arrested possibly dangerous Italians, and registered more enemy aliens. But once again there was no sabotage in Canada.

As the war progressed, unanticipated duties appeared. When an excise tax was imposed on raw tobacco, Mounted Police patrolled the tobacco-growing provinces of Quebec and Ontario, at first to make the regulations known, and later to ensure tax payment. In connection with the new Defence of Canada Regulations they registered over 1,700,000 rifles and shotguns and they re-registered all revolvers and pistols. They assisted in censorship. For instance, they checked war plants' reports from insurance company inspectors to head offices outside Canada, in case they contained information of value to the enemy.

Meanwhile many former duties were intensified. The Central Finger Print Section had to keep records of enemy aliens and of all prisoners of war brought to Canada. That Section also had to check the finger-prints of all persons employed in essential war industries, of prospective entrants for the RCAF, and so on. The Intelligence Section had to investigate more and more potential and actual enemies.

The Communists tried to undermine government authority by calling its internment policy "unconstitutional" and by accusing the Mounted Police of "witch-hunting." The police were not surprised, since the Russian government had concluded a non-aggression friendship pact with Germany in August, 1939. But many loyal Canadians, knowing nothing of these Communist tactics, echoed their embarrassing accusations, and agitated for the restoration of civil liberties and the repeal of the Defence of Canada Regulations. They, too, decried the "Gestapo methods" of the Mounted Police and refrained from cooperating with them, thus hindering investigations.

In 1940 the Communist party was declared illegal and some of its leaders were interned. But other leaders went underground and remained active. The Young Communist Party distributed leaflets in schools and universities, urging students not to volunteer for service in a "capitalistic and imperialistic war." Others distributed similar leaflets among military trainees. Older Communists engaged in subversive radio broadcasting from illegal transmitters.

191

In December, 1940, during the Battle of Britain, Torontonians trying to tune in to the BBC on shortwave radio heard instead a local propaganda broadcast. The Mounted Police, alerted, also listened in. "This is the voice of free Canada," a man's voice announced, followed by the Communist *Internationale*. "Workers of the world, unite!" the voice resumed. Then, in the name of the Communist Party of Canada, the speaker urged Canadians to quit the war effort and make possible a speedier union of workers everywhere.

Investigation was difficult because the transmitter was installed in an automobile that roamed the snow-covered countryside. The police suspected a Toronto man who was a known Communist sympathizer, a radio mechanic and a devotee of skiing. When Constable D.W. Mascall arrested Allan Beswick Parsons on January 15, 1941, Parsons had on him the script of a talk which had been broadcast five days earlier, and a driver's permit for a Chrysler sedan. Later the police found the sedan, which contained a complete radio transmitter with a range of two thousand miles.

Parsons had been driving to the country, ostensibly to go skiing. There he would erect an aerial and broadcast his propaganda. Later he was convicted on several charges, including three under the Defence of Canada Regulations which the Communists were striving to have repealed, and was sentenced to jail.

Mounted Police in the armed forces, meanwhile, served in other ways. The Provost Company in Europe worked on special investigations, trained other provost companies, and supplied control and other services for the Canadian army. Men of the former Marine Section helped build up the Canadian navy, which was pitifully small in 1939. They formed a nucleus of instructors for other seamen. They helped organize port defences and examination stations, coastal and sea-going patrols. They helped formulate shipping controls, supervised the construction of new types of ships, and later they held key positions in convoy duties.

"Seamen?" one naval official remarked early in the war. "I have no seamen except the 'Mounties' and the 'Rummies' they used to chase."

Mounted Police war work on the home front reached staggering proportions. In one year on the Welland Canal alone, police inspected 6,721 vessels and crews totalling 137,073 persons. The Central Finger Print Section received 250,825 sets of fingerprints that year, nearly double the number the preceding year, many of them of persons engaged in war industries. At Japan's entry into the war in December, 1941, Mounted Policemen again made simultaneous arrests. And again there was no sabotage in Canada.

When Wartime Prices and Trade Board regulations ordered the conservation of foodstuff, rubber and gasoline, the Mounted Police enforced them. They also helped the Foreign Exchange Control Board to prevent the illegal export and import of stocks and bonds, the illegal removal of valuable foreign exchange currency from Canada, and the illegal export of high-grade gold to the United States. Both the theft and the illegal export of gold hindered Canada's war effort. The stolen gold lessened the government tax on mine profits. Its export reduced the amount of gold the Canadian government could sell to the United States for American dollars which in turn would buy vital American-made war supplies.

One of the most important wartime cases began in July, 1941, when Mounted Police working with the Foreign Exchange Control Board in Toronto heard of a gang smuggling high-grade gold from northern Ontario mines to the United States. Detective Corporal W.H. Kelly, Constable W.E. McElhone, and two men from the Board investigated full-time for several months, sometimes assisted by other Mounted Police, the Ontario Provincial Police, the Toronto, Kirkland Lake and Timmins city police, and regular mine investigators.

Kelly and McElhone spent many days and nights shadowing several points, including a gold assay office in Toronto. In this way they learned the identity of some of the high-graders and their modus operandi. They noticed that although many persons brought gold from the north to the assay office, in general they belonged to one of two groups and were all residents of the Timmins district. They discovered, too, that when a runner arrived in Toronto with a load of gold, he would pass it to a Toronto woman named Newman. If Mrs. Newman knew and trusted the runner, she would accept his assay figures, pay him, and resell the gold to a man named Sidney Faibish. But if she doubted him, she would send sample drillings of each gold button to the assay office to check before paying for the metal.

After two months the Mounted Police knew the movement of high-grade gold in Canada. But they needed evidence of its export before they could charge the high-graders under the Foreign Exchange Control Board regulations. Then in mid-September, 1941, they followed a car bearing a New York State licence from the Faibish home in Toronto to Buffalo, New York. There they learned that the car belonged to a Buffalo man named Abrahams. They gave their information to the United States Treasury officials in Buffalo, and from that time on the movement of the gold was covered on both sides of the border.

Next, Kelly and McElhone learned that for over a year the Abrahams car had been making almost weekly trips from Buffalo into

Canada. They had other indications that the car was being used to export the gold, and decided that on the next trip they would try to seize the gold in transit.

On Saturday, October 4, the Abrahams car made its next trip to Toronto. When it returned that evening to re-enter the United States at Buffalo, United States customs officials searched the car and the men in it. One passenger was wearing, under his shirt, a specially made canvas vest. Its several oversized pockets bulged with large buttons and bars of gold worth $10,000.

Early the next morning more than sixty policemen took part in pre-planned simultaneous searches at Toronto, Timmins and Kirkland Lake in Ontario, and at Val D'Or and Perron in Quebec. At the Faibish house the police found over $8,000, a gold button worth approximately $1,500, and scales, weights, acids and drills used in the handling of gold. There they also found notebooks which contained figures pertaining to weights, measures, assays and values of gold. The same notebooks listed telephone numbers that linked Faibish with other persons involved. Smaller seizures were made at the homes of Mrs. Newman and others of the gang.

The trial that followed lasted five weeks, with eighty witnesses for the Crown producing some 150 exhibits. On convictions of conspiracy, Faibish was sentenced to four years' imprisonment and a $7,000 fine, Mrs. Newman to three years and a $5,000 fine, and three others to lesser terms and amounts. Others were convicted of other charges in Canada or the United States.

Some war cases that same year were concerned with the illegal possession of codeine (a drug vital to the war effort), with persons making statements likely to prejudice the safety of the state, and with the attempted smuggling of diamonds in defiance of the Foreign Exchange Control Act. A corporal at Old Crow, Yukon Territory, found one war duty pleasing—the forwarding of $432.30 donated voluntarily by the none-too-wealthy Indians there, and intended for homeless or orphaned children in bombed London.

The only work that decreased notably during this period concerned the Communists. They completely reversed their policy in the summer of 1941, when Russia was attacked by Germany and hence joined forces with the Allies. The Canadian Communists immediately supported the war effort, joining in patriotic rallies and Victory Loan drives. The Canadian government lifted the ban on the Communist party, and the Intelligence Section turned its attention elsewhere.

Two years later the Russian government announced the dissolution of the Comintern, its international coordinating agency. The Communist Party of Canada then renounced its affiliation with Russia, and re-formed as the Labour Progressive Party. The new political party ostensibly supported Canada's war effort, but as later events proved, key party members were actually engaged in espionage for the Soviet government.

Meanwhile, the Force expanded as best it could to meet its widening responsibilities. By March, 1942, it reached a total strength of 4,743, including 1,506 special constable guards. But by March, 1945, regular strength was again down almost to the pre-war level.

As the workload increased, Mounted Policemen worked day and night. They did strike duty at steel plants and other vital war industries. They policed such important defence projects as the Canol Oil Pipeline Road, several airports in the eastern Arctic, and the Canadian section of the Alaska Highway, part of which was built on Constantine's Peace - Yukon Trail of 1905 - 7. They checked night clubs and theatres to ensure that the new amusement tax was collected and recorded. They traced persons who failed to file income tax returns.

One case of tax money not paid to the government concerned Caledonia Farms Limited, a large company of wholesale and retail butchers in southern Ontario, which Mounted Police and excise tax auditors began to investigate during the summer of 1943. A tax auditor's checking of the firm's books had aroused his suspicion that the company had evaded payment of thousands of dollars in sales tax due on cooked meat. Then employees admitted that the assistant manager, Stanley Goldstein, had sold considerable meat, both cooked and fresh, "through the back door," and that the sales had never been recorded.

Scientific laboratory examination of invoice slips disclosed that items of fresh meat had been added to the slips after they had been receipted by the customers—that is, after the customers had accepted their orders and paid for them. A handwriting expert proved that many of the fraudulent entries were made by Stanley Goldstein. Obviously he wanted to indicate that the company had sold the meat when it was fresh, and not taxable, to avoid sales tax on the cooked meats.

The owner and manager, Morris Goldstein, came under suspicion because he had never asked to examine any production record from the cooked-meat department until after the tax auditor's visit. His company employed salesmen who handled cooked meats with no firm brand name on the casing.

Finally it was proved that Caledonia Farms Limited owed $40,000 to the Department of National Revenue. The government ordered prosecution of the two men chiefly responsible for the company's affairs, the owner-manager and the assistant manager. When Morris and

Stanley Goldstein were tried, however, only the latter was convicted, and his fine was a mere $1,000 or one year in jail. But the Mounted Police could only investigate and present their findings in court.

Much extra work during the latter part of the war came from such black-market offences as the counterfeiting of gasoline and food ration coupons, the trafficking of loose gasoline coupons, and the theft of ration coupons and books. In eastern Canada counterfeiting of coupons became so common that the Crime Detection Laboratory at Rockcliffe set up a central filing system for the classification and origin of each type as it appeared in circulation.

In Edmonton the janitor of the building containing the regional oil controller's office got genuine coupons by salvaging "over-issue" coupons from the incinerator. Members of the oil controller's staff themselves threw them in and waited for them to burn up, but at the same time the janitor would toss in large strips of heavy paper, ostensibly to cause a blaze. The paper acted as a damper and prevented the coupons that landed between the layers from being burned or scorched. Later the janitor recovered the undamaged coupons. He tried to avoid suspicion by selling them, not directly to garage men and car owners, but to a "middle man." But the Mounted Police apprehended the janitor, his "middle man," and a car owner who had used the stolen coupons. All three were convicted and fined.

The overworked black-market squad in Toronto began to suspect every stranger. Two of the squad overheard Joe, the proprietor of a greasy little restaurant, making a deal with a tough-looking man called Charlie. The deal involved "ten A's, ten B's and five C's," which were the classifications of gasoline ration books. When Charlie went around to the back door to make his delivery the Mounted Police followed to make the arrest. Charlie proved to be a baker delivering pies lettered A for apple, B for blueberry and C for cherry. Nevertheless the policemen inspected the gasoline ration books of both the baker and the restaurant owner. There they found, between the pages of genuine coupons, several pages of counterfeit coupons. It was Charlie's and Joe's turn to look sheepish.

From coast to coast black-market squads campaigned against the illegal sale of textiles, the sale of goods above the ceiling price, and so on. In eastern Canada they proved a tire-ration official of the Wartime Prices and Trade Board guilty of conspiring to submit falsified applications for rationed tires. In western Canada they proved a used-car dealer guilty of seventy charges under the price ceiling regulations.

In Prince Edward Island, when Summerside detachment police arrested four men making illicit liquor in two huge stills, they found five hundred pounds of sugar and a lot of molasses. They not only proved that the four men had conspired to defeat the revenue laws of Canada, thus securing the first conviction for such conspiracy in that province, but they also obtained the conviction of three of the men on charges of hoarding sugar and molasses.

Prisoners of war entailed a great deal of extra work. In the year ending March, 1945, the Photographic Section made 29,000 photographs, and clerical workers typed as many descriptive forms. The investigation of 171 escapes that year kept some policemen from their regular work for days at a time.

Escaped prisoners of war came to dread the use of police service dogs. Four who escaped from an internment camp near Magrath, Alberta, in August, 1944, drove in a stolen car to within four miles of the American border. Before abandoning it they sprinkled pepper in and about it to foul the trail. But the Mounted Police gave their dog Smoky the scent from a pair of socks they had obtained in the camp, and let him sniff about an old well where the escapees had been seen. Smoky led the police several miles away from the car and directly to the four men crouching in bushes on a hillside.

Right up to the end of the war in August, 1945, the Mounted Police handled a tremendous number of investigations. In January alone they tried to locate 18,000 army deserters and absentees. As the end of the war approached they arranged for the exchange of interned civilians between Canada and other countries. They also investigated Canadian personnel for the United Nations and its agencies, and refugees to Canada from foreign countries.

During the whole war period the RCMP Reserves had helped substantially, beginning with the earliest surprise arrests of German aliens in September, 1939. Men of the Reserve units at Halifax, Montreal, Ottawa, Toronto, Winnipeg, Calgary and Edmonton worked with black-market squads. They helped to guard the British prime minister, Winston Churchill, and the American president, Franklin D. Roosevelt, at the Quebec Conference. They checked vessels at ports, investigated subversive activities, and tested the security of war plants by trying to get past the guards without passes. When enemy submarines penetrated the Gulf of St. Lawrence, they sacrificed their vacations to help patrol that area. When the police of one of Canada's largest cities went on strike, brokers, truck drivers, insurance men and doctors paired with regular Mounted Policemen for patrol duties, while a lawyer operated the police radio.

Many of the Mounted Police who served with the armed forces won honours. Those who had remained on the home front, however, came under neither military nor civilian classification. In the King's Honour Birthday List of 1943, Commissioner Wood had become a Companion of the Order of St. Michael and St. George (C.M.G.). Otherwise Mounted Police serving on the home front received neither wartime honours nor the gratuities paid to the armed forces doing clerical work in Canada. Nor did these Mounted Police receive the wartime cost-of-living bonus received by other government employees. But they, too, had done important war work, and it was largely to their credit that Commissioner Wood could report, year after year, "No sabotage."

On June 21, 1940, the 104-foot schooner *St. Roch* sailed north from Vancouver, ostensibly to deliver 151 tons of coal, fuel oil and general supplies to western Arctic detachments. Actually the skipper, Sergeant Henry A. Larsen, had secret orders from Commissioner Wood to sail through the famed North-West Passage and continue on to Halifax.

Only the sailing sloop *Gjoa*, skippered by Roald Amundsen, had conquered the dangerous passage, from east to west via the southern route in 1903-6. But the time had come for Canada to reinforce its claim to the Canadian Arctic, a point of significance in war and peace. So the Royal Canadian Mounted Police were given the task.

Norwegian-born Larsen, with navy, navigation, trans-Atlantic and Arctic experience, for years had longed for such a challenge. As the *St. Roch* rounded the Alaskan peninsula and headed east into gales, the crew of eight made frequent dashes to the rails, but the ship's roll merely exhilarated Larsen. Occasionally they stopped to barter with the Eskimos for fur clothing, to discharge their cargo at the police detachments, to take on sleigh dogs, and so on. Then by late July the voyage became an almost constant struggle with the elements.

By day heavy ice threatened to crush the ship. At night young ice froze the ship to the floes, so that the men had to use blasting powder then ram their way out. Tempers frayed with the constant fight against wind, ice and fog. Sometimes Chief Engineer Corporal M.F. Foster stopped the engines and they drifted with the ice. Sometimes they moored to a huge ice floe while Larsen snatched a little sleep. Sometimes they faced about and sailed west. One constable, prone to seasickness, had to be left at a northern detachment. But gradually they inched eastward.

By September 25 they had sailed 5,220 miles. Because it was too late that year to go farther, they anchored in Walker Bay, about three hundred yards offshore of Victoria Island. Larsen and his crew, now only seven, unloaded all fuel oil, coal and boats on the beach. Thus the lightened ship would ride higher and be less embedded in the winter's ice. Next the sailor-police rigged a canvas cover over the whole ship and erected radio aerials. Later they trained the sleigh dogs, caught and stacked fish for dog food. And by the end of October, when the *St. Roch* was completely frozen in, they were ready for winter.

During that winter of 1940–41 they kept in touch with Ottawa headquarters by two-way radio. They also patrolled by dog team to the Arctic islands, one patrol of six hundred miles lasting six weeks. They took the census, visited Eskimos, and issued destitute rations where necessary. As spring approached and geese honked overhead, they scraped and painted the ship and overhauled its engines.

At last, on July 31, 1941, the warmth of the Arctic summer slackened the ice pressure enough for them to ram and blast their way out and continue their eastward voyage. About two weeks later they sailed into the uncharted part of the North-West Passage to face more formidable difficulties than ever. On September 3, to avoid a violent storm and incoming ice, they were forced to enter Pasley Bay on Boothia Peninsula. The ice closed in and carried the helpless ship about for several days. On September 11 the whole inlet froze over solid. After only six weeks of summer suitable for sailing, the *St. Roch* was in its winter quarters for 1941–42.

The second winter went much as the first, except that the weather was even more severe, the patrols even longer. Also, tragedy struck when Constable A.J. Chartrand, the only French Canadian among the crew, died from a sudden heart attack. The others, unable to dig a grave in the frozen earth, placed their comrade's body in a hillock on shore and built a rock cairn over it.

The next summer, on August 3, after eleven months of winter at Pasley Bay, the crew blasted the ship free and sailed eastward again. Larsen reported that the next part of the journey was the worst of all. On August 12 one cylinder head broke down, and from then on the *St. Roch* operated on only five cylinders. Later they barely managed to skirt a whirlpool that sucked a huge narwhale under like a bit of driftwood. Now the fiercest gales of the voyage and the most massive ice floes suggested a third ice-bound winter. But somehow they got through to Baffin Bay, and so passed out of the North-West Passage proper.

By October 11, 1942, when they entered Halifax harbour, they had battled the stark forces of nature for twenty-eight months and had sailed almost ten thousand miles. They had also become the first to sail the North-West Passage, via the southern route, from west to east. For this feat the Polar Medal was awarded to Sergeant Henry Larsen, Corporal M.F. Foster, and Constables W.J. Parry, A.J. Chartrand (posthumous), F.S. Farrar, G.W. Peters, P.G. Hunt and E.D. Hadley.

Two years later Staff Sergeant Larsen skippered the *St. Roch* back through the North-West Passage, with a different crew except for Corporals Peters and Hunt. Again the schooner and the crew battled gales, fog, snow, ice floes and icebergs. This time they sailed the northern route in one season, leaving Halifax on July 22, 1944, and arriving in Vancouver on October 16.

They were thus the first ever to sail that route, and the first to sail either way through the Passage in one season. Also, the *St. Roch* was the only ship to have sailed through the North-West Passage in both directions. Even more important however, was that the Royal Canadian Mounted Police had reinforced Canada's claim to the Canadian Arctic.

Meanwhile during the war years, the Force's regular work went on across Canada as usual. In the Maritimes, although annual pre-war seizures of ten thousand gallons of rum had dropped in 1940–41 to seventy-five gallons, illicit stills continued to flourish. Most of the seventy-nine cases worked on during the year by the dog Prince were excise tax cases. Prince helped the police to get so many convictions that one Nova Scotian appealed to a higher court against the admissibility of evidence resulting from the dog's work. When the conviction was upheld it established an important precedent. (The first case in which evidence produced by a dog was accepted in a Canadian court occurred in February, 1940, and concerned Black Lux, son of Dale.)

In Quebec and Ontario, where the Mounted Police enforced only federal statutes, they continued to aid other police forces. For instance, the *RCMP Gazette* published the photographs of a man named Wood, plus a list of his known offences and his modus operandi. City police who saw the item collected more information, and Wood was later convicted of forty offences in eleven towns in the two provinces.

One man, charged by the Ottawa city police with breaking and entering, changed his "not guilty" plea to "guilty" when he saw a member of the Finger Print Section in court. "Even if I have a million excuses, he has my fingerprints," a guard overheard him explain later.

The various identification sections at Ottawa headquarters grew more and more important. For efficiency a new Criminal Identification Branch (Ident) was set up in January, 1944. It had six sections: Central Finger Print; Central Modus Operandi; Central Photographic; Ticket of Leave (relating to paroled persons); Firearms Registration; and *RCMP Gazette*. Meanwhile the Police College and Laboratory had been in operation at Rockcliffe since 1939.

When Manitoba renewed its agreement with the Royal Canadian Mounted Police for a period of ten years from April, 1940, the Force could undertake greater expenditures than were possible on short-term agreements. They installed a modern radio system. It included a specially built transmitting station, VY8T, about seven miles west of "D" Division headquarters, Winnipeg; receiving sets in twenty-three detachments; nine cars equipped with two-way radios; and two one-way equipped cars. Some equipment at the station sent and received messages within the Force, other equipment kept in constant touch with the Winnipeg city police, and an electrically-controlled illuminated map showed immediately the position of every Mounted Police radio car in service.

The Musical Ride had been discontinued, but now the police purchased the site of old Fort Walsh in Saskatchewan and the surrounding land as a police farm for breeding horses. Before that they had merely owned the handsome black stallion King and had raised a few colts each year.

Also in Saskatchewan the Scientific Crime Detection Laboratory at Regina was extraordinarily helpful. Experts there proved who slashed the oil paintings in the Manitoba Legislature, who had stolen a mile of wire from the fence of an Alberta ranch, and that a suspected safe-cracker had hidden nitroglycerin in the wagon of a Saskatchewan farmer. Laboratory work continued under Dr. Frances McGill of Regina after Dr. Powers was killed in 1943, in a plane crash while on duty. Dr. McGill was the only woman, other than the Queen, to be given honourary membership in the Force.

In Alberta, as elsewhere, "work as usual" often meant a very crowded day. One July day Constable D.F. Von Blarcom of Brooks detachment, accompanied by a police magistrate, drove fifty miles to set up a temporary court in the community hall at Cessford and thus save the accused, who was penniless, the expense of travelling to court at Brooks. Then he drove another ten miles to bring the accused to court. On the way home through the rough badlands, the constable and the magistrate met a truck with outdated licence plates. The constable laid a charge and handed a summons to the truck driver, who asked to be tried at once. The constable opened court in the name of the King. The truck driver pleaded "guilty" and paid his fine, then the "court" moved on. By then it was 9:30 P.M. but someone stopped them in Patricia and asked the tired men to settle a disorderly conduct charge. They held court in the hotel lobby. At last the constable took the magistrate home, then drove to his own home, to supper and to bed.

Mounted Police on the Pacific coast during the war years still campaigned against the drug traffic. The irregularity and secrecy regarding shipping had made it difficult to smuggle drugs from the Orient. But that merely led to more breaking and entering of drug stores and to more theft of drugs from doctors' bags and hospitals. The police made so many arrests that illicit drugs became scarce, and the price of a five-tael can of opium that formerly sold for $55 rose to $500.

The public made various requests for personal service. A young lady asked the police to find a man to whom she had been strangely attracted. He was about five feet, six-to-eight inches tall, about a hundred and seventy pounds, with fine features. The two had not spoken but they had looked intently at each other as the girl had left a certain train. She was willing to pay three dollars if necessary.

Regular work in the North continued but with improved facilities. In 1941, religious frenzy and murder reminiscent of the early 1920s broke out among Eskimos on Belcher Island, Hudson Bay. But now, in addition to the older means—"moccasin telegraph," dog team, canoe, railway gasoline speeder, train and steamer—the police used the "Norseman" sea plane and contacted Ottawa by radio. Again a judicial party from Ontario held northern court, but this time the whole case was concluded in about five months. Over the next few years police in the western Arctic and sub-Arctic built up a widely scattered "fleet" of one passenger car, twelve trucks and four jeeps.

Perhaps the most notable development of the period occurred in 1944, with the creation of a Personnel Department of specially trained officers and NCOs. The suitability of a recruit would in future be judged not only by his physique and formal education but also according to his personality and mentality. Also, as the Force acknowledged that policemen like others suffered from frailties, fears, setbacks and frustrations, it provided a department whose chief concern was the welfare of the men.

As for the status of the Force by the end of the war, three facts were indicative of its new importance. All six provinces with provincial policing agreements renewed them—Alberta for five years, the Maritime provinces for seven, and Manitoba and Saskatchewan for ten. By 1945, ten years after the Force's first such agreement with Flin Flon, they were policing by request fifty-six cities and towns in the three prairie provinces. Foreign countries were now sending representatives to study the Force's famous organization, administration and training methods. The worth of the Force was recognized by this time, not only at home but also abroad.

Chapter 19
Soviet Espionage
1945–1949

Probably the most important investigation in the history of the Force, and consequently in the history of Canada, began in Ottawa on September 7, 1945, about a month after the end of World War II. That morning Igor Gouzenko, a cipher clerk of the USSR Embassy, defected to Canada and disclosed to the Mounted Police existence of a Communist espionage system which threatened the security of the country.

For some years the Force had known of Soviet Embassy espionage and its recruiting of agents. They had been well aware that when Russia announced dissolution of the Comintern in 1943 it did not mean that there were any real changes in Soviet policy of eventual world domination, through espionage and any other means deemed necessary. Mounted Police officials had warned the government of the situation and that some of the government's own departments were probably penetrated. But the documents Gouzenko had removed from the Embassy files and turned over to the police disclosed an espionage network far more insidious than the police had suspected.

Gouzenko's exposé came as the result of his two years in Canada as a cipher clerk on the USSR Embassy staff in Ottawa. During that time he had been amazed at the complete freedom of Canadians, particularly during elections, a freedom which belied propaganda spread in Russia to the contrary. He and his wife were also amazed at the quantity and the quality of goods available, also contrary to propaganda, to any would-be purchaser regardless of class or occupation. At first they did not believe that they were allowed to buy the fruit, bacon and other foodstuff set out so lavishly, even in wartime, in the big chain grocery stores. Furthermore, Gouzenko had grown to despise the two-faced way in which the USSR professed to be a friendly ally of Canada, yet had set up an espionage system through which the Russians were obtaining secret information.

In August, 1945, when Igor Gouzenko was told that he must soon return to Russia, he decided instead to reveal the situation to the Canadian authorities and to ask for their protection. During the rest of the month and the early part of September the code clerk earmarked scores of key documents in the Embassy files.

On the night of September 5 he took the documents to his apartment on Somerset Street, having left the Russian Embassy forever, he hoped. But later that night an Ottawa newspaper refused to take him seriously. The next day when he went to one high government office after another, then back to the newspaper, still no one would help or advise him. Gouzenko feared that the Russians would probably kill him if possible, not only to get rid of the strongest evidence against their espionage system, but also to intimidate other possible defectors. All day Gouzenko, his wife and child stayed away from home. That night they took refuge in a neighbour's apartment. The neighbour, a member of the RCAF, asked the Ottawa city police to send protection, which they did.

Meanwhile the USSR Embassy realized that Gouzenko was missing. That same night four Embassy men went to Gouzenko's empty apartment, broke the Yale lock, and ransacked the place. When city police arrived they found Vitali Pavlov, second secretary and consul of the Embassy proper, in a clothescloset. Pavlov's other, secret position in Canada was as head of the NKVD, the Russian secret police, forerunner of the KGB. Lieutenant-Colonel Rogov, assistant military attaché, was in another closet, ransacking it as the police entered. Pavlov told the police that the rented apartment was Embassy property and so they could do what they liked with it. Then they invoked their diplomatic immunity and refused to stay to discuss the matter.

The next morning the city police took Gouzenko to Mounted Police headquarters, where Gouzenko turned over his documents and told his story. He asked that he and his family be placed in protective custody as he feared for their safety, and this was done at once.

Several months later, while Gouzenko was being cross-examined in court by a lawyer who was trying to discredit his testimony, he was asked why he had not gone to the police in the first place. "I thought there might be spies in the Mounted Police," he said. Then, after being ridiculed for such a notion, he continued, "Why not? There was one in Parliament."

As soon as the Mounted Police were convinced that Gouzenko was telling the truth, they began to ferret out details from the mass of documents he had given them. Up to this time they had had no experience in investigating specific cases of espionage, but their previous experience in investigating large criminal conspiracies proved invaluable.

The espionage case was directed by Assistant Commissioner H.A.R. Gagnon, director of Criminal Investigation, with Inspector J. Leopold of the Intelligence Section (later the Special Section) in immediate control. It involved a stupendous amount of work. In most instances Gouzenko knew only the code names of the non-Embassy members of the espionage system, and had never seen any of them. So after the Mounted Police translated, sorted and checked the documents, they had to follow even the most minute clues to identify those members. Then they had to try to learn the espionage activities of each spy, and again follow every possible clue toward proof and corroboration of such activities. Not only was this necessary so that the police themselves could piece together the whole truth, but also so that if the spies were later charged in court the police could present evidence strong enough to convict them.

A vital step in the investigation was to establish the connection between the non-Embassy spies and the Embassy itself. The Mounted Police accomplished this through the dozens of papers which Gouzenko claimed had been written by Colonel Zabotin, the military attaché, by Lieutenant Colonel Motinov, the assistant military attaché, and by Lieutenant Rogov, another assistant military attaché.

After the experts at the Rockcliffe laboratory gave the papers the routine treatment accorded questioned documents, investigators checked the various places at which Canadian friends had entertained the three Soviet officers. At a hunting lodge they obtained a guest book containing the signatures of all three. They were gratified to see that Rogov and Motinov, in addition to signing their names, had written briefly to express appreciation of their friend's hospitality. A handwriting expert compared the entries in the guest book with the writing on the papers, and stated definitely that Gouzenko had brought the genuine writing of the three Soviet attachés.

During the investigation, the police found proof of something they had already suspected—that members of the Soviet Embassy staff were not always used solely in the occupations for which the Embassy requested their entry into Canada. For instance, one man whose entry was requested as "chauffeur to Soviet Military Attaché," was actually a captain and a member of the espionage ring with the cover name of "Chester." Another, whose entry the Canadian government had allowed as "doorman attached to Soviet Military Attaché's staff," was also an espionage worker with the cover name of "Henry."

In all, Mounted Police discovered that forty-two persons in the espionage system were designated by cover names, and they established the identity of most of them. Thirteen of those identified were members of the Soviet Embassy staff in Ottawa, and included Colonel Nicolai Zabotin, his assistant and his cipher clerk (not Gouzenko); a commercial attaché and one of his staff; a colonel of Red Army Intelligence; and the *Tass* newspaper correspondent.

Several others identified by name spied for the Soviets in the United States including an American scientist and an official of the Soviet consulate in New York. Among those identified by code name only were two Canadian Army colonels, three Soviet agents in Montreal, one in the United States and four in Switzerland.

Two weeks after the spy investigation began, Commissioner Wood informed Prime Minister Mackenzie King that the Mounted Police were ready to present him with a brief of the salient facts. As the prime minister and a few other government officials heard the briefing officer's explanation of the charts and diagrams which the Mounted Police had prepared, they stood aghast at the magnitude of the espionage system and at its success in obtaining secret information for Russia.

As the briefing officer pointed out, the information fell into three distinct categories—military, economic and political. It concerned many research developments which would play an important part in the post-war defences not only of Canada but also of the United Kingdom and the United States. Military information included data on atomic energy, radar, Asdic (anti-submarine devices), explosives and propellants. In addition to espionage agents furnishing the Russians with such military information, they had provided them with a sample of Uranium-235 which was used in the production of the atomic bomb. Economic information included details of industrial production, location of industries, transportation and planning. Political information related to the policies of the Canadian, British and American governments.

Mounted Police work on the investigation up to the briefing of the prime minister, however, was only the beginning. Next came the tedious business of tracing the identity of the spies named in the Embassy documents by code names only.

"Alek," for instance, the Mounted Police knew from the documents to be the man who had given Colonel Zabotin information about the atomic bomb and had supplied the sample of uranium. Thus they also knew he must be a scientist. They had learned, too, from the copy of a report sent by Zabotin to Moscow, that early in September "Alek" would leave Canada and fly to London, where he would work at King's College.

When Prime Minister King went to England in October to confer with the British prime minister, Clement Attlee, about the espionage case, he also conferred with officials of Scotland Yard. Before long the Yard had identified "Alek" as Dr. Allan Nunn May, a British nuclear physicist who had recently been working with the Atomic Energy Project in Montreal. Now Scotland Yard kept Dr. May under close observation, while the Mounted Police across the Atlantic gathered more evidence against him.

During the next few months the police learned that at least twelve of the code names belonged to persons in important positions in Canada. They were: David Gordon Lunan, editor of *Canadian Affairs*; Israel Halperin, professor at Queen's University and formerly major, Directorate of Artillery, Canadian Army; Raymond Boyer, professor at McGill University and a specialist in explosives; Squadron Leader M.S. Nightingale, RCAF; Lieutenant David Shugar, formerly RCN; P. Durnford Smith and Edward Mazerall, employees of the National Research Council; James Scotland Benning and Harold Samuel Gerson, employees of the Department of Munitions and Supply; Eric Adams, employee of the Bank of Canada; Emma Woikin, cipher clerk in the Department of External Affairs; and Kathleen Willsher, assistant registrar, Office of the United Kingdom High Commissioner, Ottawa.

Up to this time the Mounted Police had carried out the investigation in secret. But as it progressed there were several indications that the Soviet government knew that the investigation was under way. For one thing the Russians had been unable to locate Gouzenko since he had disappeared from the Embassy in September. Military Attaché Zabotin, responsible for the success of espionage operations in Canada, probably feared for his own safety if the truth behind Gouzenko's disappearance became known. In any case, at first he merely reported that Gouzenko had stolen Embassy funds. Nevertheless, the Russians must have learned that their cipher clerk's disappearance carried a more important significance. Zabotin was recalled to Russia in December, 1945, and departed in notable haste without notifying the Canadian authorities. A few days later Soviet Ambassador Zarubin also returned to Moscow.

During the whole investigation Gouzenko and his family remained in protective custody, their whereabouts kept secret. But the fact that Mrs. Gouzenko was expecting a baby complicated the situation.

A member of the Force who spoke Russian posed as her husband, and the two of them were given National Registration Certificates under assumed names. At the appointed time the "father" took his wife to a small, well-equipped hospital in northern Ontario. To avoid embarrassing questions the Mounted Policeman took on the role of the nervous and excited expectant father, shouting in a heavy Russian accent at the admitting nurse, and appearing not to understand her. Finally he flourished a big roll of banknotes and threw a handful on the counter.

"I pay now," he declared. "No more talk. You put wife in bed for get baby."

The stratagem worked well. After the baby was born the Mounted Policeman called at his headquarters in Toronto and passed out cigars.

Early in 1946 the Canadian government realized that the existence of the espionage investigation could not remain secret much longer. Yet they still seemed reluctant to make the matter public, considering it politically dangerous and personally embarrassing. According to *The Horsemen*, by C.W. Harvison, then a superintendent working on the case and later Commissioner of the Force, the prime minister's first reaction had been "on being told of the defection, and of the contents of the documents . . . to urge that Gouzenko be taken back to the Embassy, together with the papers he had removed." Even now that the investigation had proved the seriousness of the affair, Mackenzie King, always noted for his caution, still hesitated.

Nevertheless, as a preparatory move toward bringing the espionage investigation out into the open, on February 5, 1946, the government granted authority for the setting up of a Royal Commission which would probe more thoroughly the circumstances reported to them by the Mounted Police. For the next few days the Commission's two members, Mr. Justice Robert Taachereau and Mr. Justice R.L. Kellock, both of the Supreme Court of Canada, considered evidence given by the police and by Gouzenko.

Nine days later the Royal Commission recommended the detention and interrogation of the twelve persons the Mounted Police could prove were linked with the code names, also of Squadron Leader F.W. Poland, an intelligence officer of the RCAF. Several other persons who were likewise involved in espionage but were not public officials were not recommended for detention then, but would be dealt with later. It was not possible to detain or interrogate any of the thirteen members of the Soviet Embassy identified as part of the spy system. Those with diplomatic standing had diplomatic immunity, and the others merely remained inside the Embassy until they were recalled to Russia.

On February 15 the Mounted Police effected the detentions. They did so under authority of an order-in-council dated October 6, 1945, which had been prepared for just such an eventuality, but which had been kept secret as a security measure. In making the detentions, the police attracted the attention of newspaper reporters, and thus news of the espionage case reached the public.

When the Mounted Police detained the thirteen as recommended by the Commission, they took them to the barracks at Rockcliffe. There they were placed under close guard pending their appearance before the Royal Commission. Dr. May, meantime, was being interrogated by Scotland Yard.

The Communist press and Communist-inspired speakers immediately made a great outcry about the Mounted Police abusing the civil liberties of the detainees by holding them incommunicado. There were also charges of "police brutality" and "Gestapo tactics." However, as the Royal Commission pointed out, the detained persons themselves made no complaints about their treatment, about their living quarters set up in the rooms normally occupied by visiting NCOs and officers on classes, or about their food, which was the same as that eaten by the police at the Rockcliffe barracks.

As the Commission continued its inquiry it learned that, with the possible exception of Emma Woikin, every member of the spy ring was a member of or a sympathizer with the Communist party. Furthermore, the two main cogs in Zabotin's spy ring were Fred Rose, Labour-Progressive member of Parliament, and Sam Carr, an organizer for the same party.

Polish-born Fred Rose, the Commissioners learned, had taken an important part in the activities of the party's Communist International section since 1925, at which time he joined the Young Communist League. In 1931-32, soon after returning from Russia and a six-month course of Communist instruction, he was convicted of sedition and served one year in jail.

During the early part of World War II he wrote anti-British pamphlets which were published in English and French. In June, 1940, when the Communist Party of Canada was banned, Rose went underground but continued to write such pamphlets. After his arrest by Mounted Police in September, 1942, he promised an Advisory Committee on Internment not to participate in Communist party activities, and hence was released from custody. Later, on formation of the Labour-Progressive Party, Rose was elected federal member of Parliament for a Montreal riding. A party magazine exhibited before the Royal Commission discussed the formation of the party thus: "The Communist party being outlawed by the King Government we established the Labour-Progressive Party with a Marxist program, and utilized the possibilities and the wide-spread progressive sentiment to strengthen our Party and extend its influence."

Other documents which the Mounted Police presented to the Royal Commission proved that Fred Rose had offered his services to Zabotin in 1942, just prior to his signed promise not to participate in Communist activity. Since that time, working under the code name "Debouz," Rose had played a key role in organizing a group of agents in the National Research Council. The documents proved further that he was linked to at least ten other Soviet agents in Canada and the United States. Also, he had reported to Zabotin various secret information, part of which he had obtained from army officers and part from secret sessions of Parliament.

On the instructions of the Canadian government the Mounted Police arrested Rose on March 14, 1946, charging him with violation of the Official Secrets Act. When summoned before the Royal Commission on April 18, however, he refused to testify on the grounds that he had already been committed for trial on the Official Secrets Act charges.

The background of Fred Rose, the Mounted Police pointed out to the Royal Commission, was closely paralleled by that of Sam Carr. Carr, whose proper name was Schmil Kogan, and who had used several aliases including Sam Cohen, was born in the Ukraine and had emigrated to Canada in 1924. Like Rose he joined the Young Communist League in 1925, and four years later he went to Russia for a course in Communist instruction. In 1931, using the name Sam Cohen, he was appointed secretary of the Communist Party of Canada. Later that year he became a naturalized Canadian, and still later in the same year was convicted of being a member and an officer of an unlawful association and was sentenced to five years' imprisonment.

After his release from jail he continued, like Rose, to be an active party worker. Also like Rose, he went underground in 1940 and remained in hiding until he was arrested by the Mounted Police in September, 1942. He, too, signed a pledge promising to refrain from participating in Communist party activity and accordingly was released from custody. Later, on formation of the Labour-Progressive Party, Sam Carr became its national organizer.

Documents which the Mounted Police presented to the Royal Commission indicated that in spite of Carr's promise to the contrary, he had taken part in subversive activities on behalf of the Soviet government. A notebook entry showed that, under the code name "Frank," he had been assigned "the task of developing our work in the Ministry of National Defence, the Ministry for Air, Ministry of the Navy, and the military staffs." Other documents showed that Carr had accepted money for performing such tasks. Still others showed that he was the head of an Ottawa-Toronto group of agents, that he was active in recruiting additional agents, and that he undertook to facilitate the illegal entry of Soviet agents into Canada.

Members of the Force went to Carr's home to serve him with a notice to appear before the Royal Commission, but they were unable to find him. Later they had good reason to believe that he had fled the country and had gone to Central America.

When the Royal Commissioners made their final report on these espionage activities in June, 1946, they stated that Rose, Carr, Lunan, Halperin, Boyer and others had communicated secret information to the agents of a foreign power. They also stated that Rose and Carr had recruited other agents for the same organization. They thanked the Mounted Police for work on the investigation, commenting that such work was "up to its usual extremely high standard," and mentioning special appreciation of Inspector Leopold's "particularly valuable service."

In the meantime several persons involved in the espionage activities had been charged under the Official Secrets Act and had been taken before the regular criminal courts. This procedure was necessary since under Canadian law the findings of a Royal Commission are not legal and conclusive proof of guilt. The purpose of this, as of any Royal Commission, was not to prove guilt, but to discover the full facts of the matter under scrutiny.

Within a year of the establishing of the Royal Commission, eighteen persons appeared before the courts of law, with Gouzenko personally testifying against each accused person in compliance with the ordinary rules of evidence, and with the Mounted Police testifying regarding their part in the investigation. The hearings of the cases and the subsequent appeals lasted over a period of thirty-two months.

Unfortunately, Deputy Commissioner Gagnon never knew the complete results of the investigation he had directed so zealously. He died in December, 1947. Ironically, his death occurred only a few weeks after an Ottawa newspaper had reported that he would succeed Commissioner Wood early in 1948, when Wood was due to retire at the completion of thirty-five years of service. As it happened, Commissioner Wood was still well below the sixty-two-year age-limit set by statute, and he agreed to continue in office.

By December, 1948, convictions were registered against Fred Rose, David Gordon Lunan, P. Durnford Smith, Edward Mazerall, James Scotland Benning, Emma Woikin and Kathleen Willsher, and they received various terms of imprisonment up to six years. In addition John

Soboloff, a doctor, was convicted of being implicated in a false passport application and was sentenced to a fine of $500 or three months' imprisonment. Henry Harris, another man involved in a false passport application, was also found guilty, as was Harold Samuel Gerson, but on appeal both decisions were reversed. Dr. Alan Nunn May was convicted in London and was sentenced to ten years' imprisonment.

Warrants for the arrest of Sam Carr and Freda Linton, who had worked at the National Film Board, remained unexecuted at the end of 1948. Linton, like Carr, had considered it wise to leave Canada. In January, 1949, however, Sam Carr was arrested in New York by the Federal Bureau of Investigation and was turned over to the Mounted Police. In April he was convicted of conspiring with USSR Embassy officials to utter a forged passport for a Russian agent, and was sentenced to six years in prison. His appeal later that year was dismissed. Shortly after Carr's conviction, Freda Linton surrendered voluntarily to Mounted Police in Montreal, but charges against her were withdrawn, because of lack of sufficient evidence to prosecute the case in court.

The final count was ten persons convicted, nine acquitted, one convicted in England, and the charges against one withdrawn. Explanation for the high acquittal rate lies in the fact that the rules of evidence in trial courts are much stricter than those of a Royal Commission. Thus not all the evidence produced before and accepted by the two Supreme Court judges comprising the Royal Commission was allowed as evidence in the trial courts.

Igor Gouzenko and his family became wards of the government. They lived in obscurity, and although Gouzenko later published books and articles, even during personal appearances he did not show his face in case the Russians might track him down and retaliate against him. The government granted him a life-long pension in gratitude for his invaluable service to Canada and to our allies in disclosing the huge espionage system which involved not only numerous Canadians and other nationals but also, most significantly, about one-third of the Soviet Embassy staff in Ottawa.

Chapter 20
The Post-War Period
1945 – 1950

A number of cases after the ending of World War II in August, 1945, concerned prisoners of war interned in Canada. One gruesome case had begun earlier, at Internment Camp 132, which held twelve thousand prisoners at Medicine Hat, Alberta. Prisoner-of-war Sergeant Karl Lehmann was brutally beaten and strangled in September, 1944, and the scene had been set up to resemble suicide by hanging. The Mounted Police suspected that Nazi extremists had formed a camp Gestapo and had murdered Lehmann because they believed he was anti-Nazi. But fellow prisoners, threatened with a similar fate to Lehmann's, insisted that the murder was suicide.

After V-E Day those prisoners felt free to talk. Thus the Mounted Police uncovered documentary evidence that German prisoner-of-war activities in Canada were controlled, through a secret system of communication, by the highest-ranking German officer interned in the country. They also discovered the identity of leaders of the Gestapo group at Internment Camp 132, and obtained proof as to which four men had murdered Lehmann. The following year they were charged with murder, found guilty, and hanged at Lethbridge.

Other post-war cases arose from the continued rationing of such foods as butter and sugar. In the spring of 1946, men of the black-market squad in Montreal found sheets of counterfeit butter-ration coupons among a grocer's sheets of genuine coupons. On tracing them they discovered that more than 125,000 similar coupons had been used or distributed by two milkmen, a dairy employee, a restaurant operator, a commercial traveller and several other men. They finally traced the coupons to a home on Seymour Street where J.B. Boissonnault, his wife and a printer operated a complete printing press and turned out coupons by the thousand.

During the previous summer Boissonnault and his brother-in-law had been responsible for the circulation of half a million counterfeit sugar-ration coupons, for which offence Boissonnault had paid a $2,000 fine. Apparently he had manufactured the butter coupons to reimburse himself for the fine on the sugar coupons offence. This time, however, his penalty was $5,000 or two years in prison. He decided to serve the prison term.

The scarcity of textiles led to some of the largest black market operations ever. Early in 1946 the Toronto black-market squad learned that a tailor named Morganstern was selling suits above the ceiling price. He said that he had to, because his wholesale supplier, Shiffer Lightman Woollens, demanded a "bonus" when selling yard goods to the tailors of the district. A second local tailor confirmed Morganstern's story: paying a "bonus" was the only way he could get enough cloth to stay in business.

In May the black-market squad searched the Shiffer Lightman premises. They seized ledgers and documents and two small notebooks which listed the names of retail clothiers and tailors, with figures which seemed to represent amounts of money. The notebooks were the key to the whole investigation. One name listed was that of the second tailor. Eight of the eleven entries by his name matched the records he had kept of his "bonus" payments.

Abraham Shiffer insisted that the entries in his notebooks represented legitimate sales, but the firm's account books showed no corresponding entries. Then the Mounted Police interviewed other retailers named in the notebooks. Twelve of them admitted paying black-market prices to Shiffer Lightman Woollens. One had had to forfeit $2,100 in war savings certificates as security before the Shiffers would do business with him. In all, according to the notebooks, the Shiffers had received about $60,000 in "bonuses."

As the Mounted Police knew, Lightman had sold his interest to Abraham Shiffer, who in turn had sold the whole business to his son, Joseph Jack Shiffer. In February, 1947, the two Shiffers were tried, each on twelve charges of selling cloth at prices in excess of the ceiling and on twelve charges of issuing false invoices. Both father and son pleaded guilty and paid fines of $350 on each charge, a total of $16,800. After further investigation they were fined an additional $40,000 for having violated the Income War Tax Act and the Excess Profits Tax Act. They also had to pay about $30,000 in income tax on earnings they had failed to disclose.

Later that month thirty-nine tailors were charged with purchasing cloth above the ceiling price. Ten paid fines ranging from $100 to $200 each. Two who had purchased cloth at black-market prices and then had re-sold it at still higher prices were convicted of selling goods above the ceiling price. One was fined $100, the other $1,000.

Thus the work of the Toronto black-market squad resulted in the collection of about $90,000 from this one group of textile black marketeers alone. In addition the Shiffers paid undisclosed penalties of thousands of dollars to the Department of National Revenue on the taxes they had attempted to evade.

The Force by this time was engaged in post-war reorganization of the Marine Section. Its pre-war strength had been almost halved by war, casualties, invaliding and so on. But those former members who could do so returned to duty, a nucleus to train newcomers.

By June, 1945, Commissioner Wood had arranged with the War Assets Corporation to augment the few remaining serviceable vessels with a balanced fleet of modern ships. Four (originally eight) former minesweepers became "Commissioner"-class vessels: *French*, *Macleod*, *Irvine* and *MacBrien*. Four "Fairmile"-class motor launches became the middle-sized "Fort" class: *Forts Pitt*, *Walsh*, *Selkirk* and *Steele*. Thirteen forty-eight foot harbour defence patrol craft became the "Detachment"-class boats: *Aklavik*, *Chilcoot*, *Cutknife* and so on. By March, 1947, the Marine Section had become a Division of 195 members, with headquarters in Halifax. Post-war duties, like pre-war, consisted chiefly of combatting smuggling and rescuing distressed vessels, but on one occasion Marine members fought a forest fire.

In mid-December, 1946, the *Irvine* went to the aid of the Dutch freighter S.S. *Marleen*, in distress off the Gaspé coast in the Gulf of St. Lawrence. The Mounted Police ship was commanded by Sub-Inspector R.J. Herman, O.B.E., who had received one of the fifty-two armed services decorations and honours awarded Mounted Policemen.

The *Irvine*, which had been working off Sydney, Nova Scotia, rounded Cape North and steamed into the Gulf. But wintry gales and heavy seas forced it to take shelter in Souris, Prince Edward Island. The weather grew worse, with the wind reaching force nine on Beaufort's scale, which lists the highest wind force, a hurricane, as twelve. When the ship left Souris it was impossible for it to round East Point to proceed across the open Gulf. Herman awaited favourable tide conditions, then ordered a quick run through the Northumberland Strait. Meanwhile, heavy sleet coated the vessel with ice. Hour after hour in flailing wind and bitter cold, the crew, backs aching and faces freezing, chopped constantly to remove the ice from the decks and gear.

215

After three days the Mounted Police sighted the freighter *Marleen*, which was flying distress signals indicating that the ship's boilers were completely broken down and that it was entirely out of fresh water and supplies. The *Irvine*'s crew used a Coston gun to shoot a towline aboard the freighter. But it was almost impossible to manoeuvre the vessel under tow, because of bad weather conditions and also because the *Marleen*, having no power, could only be steered by the almost useless hand-steering gears.

Later that day, when the Mounted Police ship dropped anchor in the lee of Sandy Beach Point, the police were able to board the Dutch vessel. They transferred the sailors, pitiably weakened by cold and exposure, to the *Irvine*. Then some of the police put in five more hours of backbreaking work to loosen the *Marleen*'s frozen gear.

The next day they made necessary repairs on the freighter, helped the revived crew back aboard and arranged for a tug to attend the *Marleen*. Then at last Sub-Inspector Herman skippered his own ship back toward the Nova Scotia coast.

The Aviation Section, too, was reorganized. By March, 1950, personnel reached twenty, exclusive of office staff. Their seven planes were two twin-engined Beechcraft, one Grumman "Goose" amphibian, a "Norseman," one Cornell, one small Stinson ("hedgehopper," the men called it), and one "Beaver" (bush-type) which operated on wheels, skis or floats. The officer commanding "B" Division (Newfoundland) requested but did not receive a helicopter.

Headquarters of the Aviation Section was at Rockcliffe, with detachments at Regina, Edmonton, Vancouver (mobile), and Winnipeg. The police used the planes for transporting officers, men, laboratory experts and police service dogs, for customs and excise work, and for rescue work in mountains and bushland. During the disastrous Red River floods in the spring of 1950, the "Beaver" made innumerable trips to Morris and district, where twenty-five feet of water covered part of the town. Again and again the Mounted Police pilot skilfully used as a landing strip a mile and a half of No. 75 Highway which had not been flooded.

The Force as a whole gradually readjusted to peacetime conditions. It retained the wartime practice of using civil servants for office work, thus leaving uniformed members free for police duties. Special constable guards were discharged when no longer needed. But the particularly useful RCMP Reserve continued, with 410 members in March, 1947.

A Reserve constable from Montreal who happened to be in Rivière-du-Loup, Quebec, effected the arrest of cigarette-smuggler Lucain Dumont and his agent Bouchard. For three years the Mounted

Police had been unable to catch Dumont in the act of smuggling, as the Reserve constable knew well, since he had relieved at Rivière-du-Loup detachment during the previous summer. So one evening in mid-February, 1949, when he happened to be driving about the town and recognized Dumont's car, he followed it. He saw Dumont and a passenger getting out of the car periodically, carrying well-filled shopping bags. He tried to get in touch with the Mounted Police but he learned they were out on patrol.

So the Reserve constable drew up to the car and identified himself. On seeing cartons of American cigarettes in the car, he detained Dumont and Bouchard and sent two passers-by to get help from the municipal police. After the Mounted Police arrived back in town, both men admitted they were guilty of possessing smuggled cigarettes.

Police college classes for experienced policemen had continued throughout the war, but were now expanded, and once again attracted members of other police forces. Recruiting, which had been discontinued, was resumed. Recruits were given a more vigorous and varied course of academic and practical studies than previously, with swimming, lifesaving and equitation back in the curriculum.

The Musical Ride, like recruiting, had been suspended, but the Mounted Police received so many post-war requests for performances that it was revived in 1948. Ever since Commissioner Wood was a young officer he had dreamed of black horses as a perfect contrast for scarlet tunics. Now he instructed the riding staff to choose some blacks from its own horses and to purchase others if necessary, thirty-five in all and matched for size. Thus the famous all-black troop came into being, trained, as were the specially chosen ride-recruits, under the direction of riding master Staff Sergeant C. Walker. The troop made its first appearance in the fall of 1948.

The Mounted Police band had continued to function at Ottawa headquarters during the war, with members doing clerical work by day and performing at Victory Loan Drives and patriotic parades at night and on weekends. After the war Commissioner Wood sent the band on a major tour, its first. The chief aim was to stimulate recruiting, but the tour was also the achievement of another of Wood's dreams.

In the summer of 1948, with Inspector J.T. Brown as director of music, the forty-one musicians flew in an RCAF "North Star" from Rockcliffe to Edmonton. Then they toured by bus, giving concerts from Edmonton to Winnipeg and going in reverse over part of the route of the Old Originals in the great march of 1874. In Edmonton they played under the hospital window of an elderly ex-sergeant, only a few days from death, who longed to hear the band before he died. The next day they had morning coffee with ex-Assistant Commissioner C.D. LaNauze of northern renown. Again and again they performed at places familiar through the history of the Force: Calgary, Macleod, Lethbridge, Maple Creek, Regina, Prince Albert and so on. At Macleod they met old-timers as low in regimental numbers as 1,233. The regimental numbers of some of the bandsmen were in the 13,000's.

The tour accomplished its chief aim. "For the first time since the beginning of the Second World War," Wood wrote in the 1949 Annual Report, "we are in sight of some relief from the heavy burden borne by this Force due to the lack of recruits. At last we have been able to secure several hundred men. . . . We are still looking for five hundred more."

One notable development of the post-war period was the great use of radio. All planes of the Aviation Section and all vessels of the Marine Division were now equipped with two-way radio, as were Marine Division headquarters at Halifax and the detachment at Saint John, New Brunswick. Radio-equipped cars operated at various points across Canada, working through city police systems in Ottawa and Vancouver. At Montreal the Force took over the frequency modulation equipment which it had used during the war while cooperating with the armed services.

In the summer of 1946, Mounted Police at Dundas Harbour, Devon Island, established one of the most northerly radio stations in North America. Although the men had had no previous experience in radio, they installed the apparatus from written instructions and soon became proficient operators.

The greatest development in radio communications, however, took place in the prairie provinces, where the "D" Division (Manitoba) radio system established in 1940 had proved invaluable. FM base stations were now set up in Manitoba, Saskatchewan and Alberta. Detachments were fitted for two-way communication with the nearest base station by FM radio-telephone. By early 1949 the prairie network system included eight control stations, sixty-two two-way patrol cars, 154 patrol cars with receivers only and 143 detachments with receivers only. Under ideal conditions prairie FM transmissions have sometimes been received, loud and clear, at Dundas Harbour.

Successful cases soon proved the worth of radio communication. Saskatchewan radio linked a Mounted Police plane, police cars, searchers using walkie-talkies, and police service dogs Pal and Silver, in a successful manhunt for two armed bank robbers en route from Quebec to British Columbia. At Amherst, Nova Scotia, four men were back in custody seven hours after breaking out of jail. Credit in that case was due not only to the newly installed radio system but also to the wives of the detachment men. The women operated the radio to maintain contact with their husbands and the other searchers.

Although there was a slight decrease in the Force's workload immediately after the war, it soon rose to the wartime peak when total strength, including civil servants, was approximately 5,500. The total strength in March, 1949, was slightly less than 4,000. And of these, more than two hundred police were occupied full-time with such new duties as those under the Combines Investigations Act, the War Services Grants Act, the Unemployment Insurance Act and the Dependents Allowance Act.

Even so, the Force had voluntarily undertaken, in the fall of 1945, the "Youth and the Police" movement. Individual members devoted themselves, also voluntarily, on duty and off, to the unspectacular undertaking which was, nevertheless, one of the most notable in the Force's history. The aim was simply to make friends with young Canadians, to reduce juvenile delinquency and eventually to reduce the number of adult criminals, simultaneously augmenting the number of good Canadian citizens.

Even before operation "Youth and the Police" began, individual Mounted Policemen had voluntarily organized recreation for young people in their own detachment areas and had held sports days and Mounted Police band concerts at industrial schools. The young people had responded with such enthusiasm that Deputy Commissioner F.J. Mead planned an operation in which Mounted Policemen would address groups of young people. Departments of education welcomed the plan and the prairie provinces became testing grounds.

At the invitation of school boards, smartly uniformed young policemen gave talks in schools, beginning with exciting topics like "Policing the Far North." By the time they reached "The Duties of the Public toward the Police," "police" meant the friendly speaker, and "public" included the youngsters who listened. By the end of the school year in June, 1946, the Mounted Police had spoken to audiences totalling 123,000 in all provinces.

With the re-opening of school that fall, other groups requested the talks. The program was expanded to include public and separate schools, high schools, junior church groups, Junior Red Cross, YMCA groups, Kiwanis and other clubs, district Youth Councils, industrial schools and children at Saturday morning movies. Most talks were in English but in Quebec bilingual Mounted Policemen spoke in French if requested.

The program also expanded in other directions. All across Canada

219

members of the Force reacted to the friendly response of the young people and recognized this opportunity for service, especially among underprivileged boys and girls. Men now voluntarily gave up their free evenings, Saturday afternoons and Sundays for youth work. They coached hockey and ball teams, organized Boy Scouts, taught first aid classes, and refereed boxing. A constable in Cape Breton organized soft-ball teams in five fishing villages so isolated that he found he had also to teach the youngsters how to play the game. Another, in Saskatchewan, taught boys and girls to curl, then arranged a bonspiel.

News of the successful program spread to other countries. Officials in the United States, Australia, New Zealand and Malaya advocated similar youth programs. By special request Sub-Inspector W.H. Kelly spoke on "Youth and the Police" to the Federal Congress of Correction at Boston, Massachusetts.

By the end of 1948, in schools alone, members of the Force had given about twelve thousand talks to almost a million youngsters. In all parts of Canada youngsters asked for autographs. In Nova Scotia children greeted Mounted Policemen on the street, and the younger ones waved each time a police car passed. A constable who spoke to about five hundred Grade IX and X students at a Toronto collegiate was so hemmed in by admirers that the school authorities had to rescue him. Three boys who had broken into a store and headed out of town returned and told the constable what they had done. "You told us at school we should come to you if ever we're in trouble," they explained.

Incidents all across Canada indicated to the Mounted Police that all their efforts, both on duty and off, plus all the extra organization and report-writing involved, were worthwhile. They continued for several years, but eventually the pressure of other duties forced them to cut back drastically on their "Youth and the Police" work.

Duties in the North increased after the war. The revival of gold-mining operations attracted thousands of prospectors and mine workers. This plus other population expansion led to a great increase of Criminal Code cases, in one year alone by more than forty percent. Increased traffic on the Northwest (formerly Alaska) Highway system led to more accidents, hence the need for more highway patrols and stricter enforcement of traffic laws. Infractions of the Indian Act also increased greatly. Almost all of them were related to intoxicating liquor, and they included not only the manufacture, sale or possession of liquor, but also assault, breaking and entering, and theft.

The Yellowknife detachment was experiencing one of its usual busy days when the officer commanding made his inspection. He found a vigorous court battle taking place in the detachment office, while a mental patient screamed interminably in the one and only cell. Seven prisoners sat outside the cell, having been moved out to make way for the mental patient. The bodies of four persons accidentally drowned lay in the police warehouse. And a dozen Indians banged on the back door of the detachment to request that they be issued with destitute rations.

The granting of family allowances meant that the police had to register all Eskimo families entitled to them. But before the police at Aklavik could complete the forms, which listed ninety-five children of the nomadic natives, they first had to register the births of forty-seven of them, some of whom were more than ten years old.

The northern police also had to issue allowance credit slips to the parents, and to ensure that they received full value when they "spent" the slips at the trading posts. To do this the Pond Inlet detachment men had to make a round trip of nine hundred miles to Somerset Island. Later they were relieved of that duty when the managers of the very remote posts were appointed as sub-registrars.

On April 8, 1950, the northern patrol schooner *St. Roch* headed not north but south from Esquimault. It sailed to Halifax by way of the Panama Canal, under the command of Inspector K.W.N. Hall. Arriving there on May 29, the ship which during the war had made two voyages through the North-West Passage was thus the first vessel to have circumnavigated the North American continent.

Sergeant F.S. Farrar, third mate and photographer, was the only one of the North-West Passage crews to make the trip. Pestered by reporters wanting to know how he felt, he shrugged off any credit. "Had I done it alone by canoe," he wrote later, "I might have boasted a little."

By the time the *St. Roch* made its southern voyage, Inspector Henry Larsen had become the officer commanding "G" Division (Yukon and the Northwest Territories but with headquarters in Ottawa). Beginning in early June, 1950, and accompanied by a staff sergeant, he established a different kind of record. Travelling 17,328 miles by plane, boat and police car, he inspected detachments in all sub-divisions and the eastern Arctic in the same year.

Other Mounted Police had, as usual, been employed on a great variety of work. During the Canadian Seaman's Union strike along the Great Lakes waterways in 1948, 150 Mounted Policemen spent three months there, protecting federal government property, enforcing the Criminal Code, and helping other police forces to keep order. Later, other members of the Force collaborated with an eminent legal authority in writing the book *Law and Order in Canadian Democracy*. One of its uses was as the basis of a night course given by the University of Ottawa, at which officers of the Force lectured.

When a CNR transcontinental train and a Labour Day holiday train collided at Dugald, Manitoba, on September 1, 1947, in the worst collision to that time in western Canadian railroading history, the first persons to be notified from Dugald were the members of the nearby Transcona detachment. Soon all available men from Divisional headquarters at Winnipeg arrived. Somehow they brought order out of the horrible confusion of the dead and the dying, the strewn and flaming wreckage of the holiday train's wooden coaches, and the possible explosion of a nearby gas and oil storage warehouse. Skilfully they controlled the huge traffic tangle as ambulances, police cars, taxis, curious passers-by, frantic relatives and even men on tractors headed for the scene.

For several days they supervised searches of the wreckage and debris for even minute scraps of clothing and jewellery. Then they meticulously conserved and tabulated their findings to help identify bodies burned beyond recognition. Later they arranged a mass burial of unidentified victims and acted as pall-bearers.

Still later, for the information of the coroner and the Crown attorney, Mounted Policemen prepared a brief. It gave full data concerning identification of the dead, the structural details of both trains involved, descriptions of exhibits, and particulars of evidence to be given by fifty-six witnesses. With the brief were a set of twenty-seven photographs and a scale plan of the Dugald station area with a representation of every railway car superimposed on it in its after-wreck position. This pictorial record, all done by the "D" Division photographer, also indicated factors which might have an important bearing on the accident.

For its work in connection with the disaster, the Force received letters of praise from bereaved relatives, church and civic officials, the coroner, the chief commissioner of the commission hearing, and the counsel representing the CNR and railway brotherhoods.

During the post-war period, as throughout the Force's history, men lost their lives while serving, both on and off duty. One of the latter was Constable A. Gamman, who on May 25, 1950, was walking to his Montreal home for lunch when a bank manager outside a bank shouted that there had just been a hold-up. At that moment a shot rang out and the bank manager fell to the sidewalk. Constable Gamman, in uniform but unarmed, dashed forward and grappled with the gunman, and was fatally wounded by one of three shots fired at point-blank range.

There probably would have been a death on duty in Saskatchewan in September, 1948, except for the intervention of a corporal's wife. A murderer who was being held overnight in the Balcarres detachment near Regina at first seemed a model prisoner. But late that night, on being given permission to go to the bathroom, Frank Catalack suddenly grabbed a chair and struck Corporal P. Beach over the head. Pat Beach, knocked almost unconscious, was alone in the detachment office and unable to defend himself as the murderer battered him again and again. The details of the next few minutes were written later by the corporal's wife Muriel, one of the many "wives of the Force" who are truly its unsung heroines.

"I was in bed upstairs reading when close to midnight I heard a crash and a groan. I ran downstairs in my pajamas and into the office. My husband was lying on the floor covered with blood. Catalack was in the act of raising a broken chair to hit him again when I rushed him and got the chair away and was able to hold him off until my husband got to his feet. He was reeling but hung on to Catalack.

"I ran into the living room and picked up a large ginger ale bottle and rushed back into the office and hit Catalack over the head. That slowed him down and I got to the phone and rang it but the central did not answer. I tried to shout into it as we fought around the office.

"My husband and I were able to push and pull Catalack into the cell. My husband was struggling with him in there but I couldn't close the door as Catalack had an arm through the opening. He tore my pajamas off and was getting away. I got to the phone and central answered and I told her to get help.

"Catalack made for the outside door and my husband, groggy from the blows, followed him. I watched to see what direction they took as they fought down the street. I ran upstairs, threw on a housecoat, picked up our three-year-old son, ran down again and out the back door. I could hear my husband's voice in the darkness. I called to him, then there was silence. I stayed on the sidewalk shouting for help, then someone came and told me they had him."

Neighbours had heard Mrs. Beach's cries for help. Two men quickly helped the corporal subdue the criminal, who by this time was bleeding profusely from wounds in the head. Catalack eventually cheated the hangman by killing himself in the Regina jail. For several weeks he hoarded pills prescribed for his sleeplessness, and then he took a lethal overdose.

Much regular post-war work was a continuation from earlier years. In the Criminal Investigation Department, all sections of the Identification Branch accumulated more data, which helped to solve more crimes and more mysteries. One involved the identification of a badly decomposed, headless body of which Ident men established the time of death by the presence of fly chrysalids in the body cavities.

By March, 1947, the Central Finger Print Section had almost a million prints on file, and by the following March had grown so large that the Single Finger Print Section was established as a distinct unit. By March, 1950, the expanded Modus Operandi Section had become the Crime Index Section.

The Preventive Service was fully occupied. Once sugar and molasses were readily available again, illicit stills flourished, especially in the Province of Quebec. On the other hand, post-war scarcities resulted in the smuggling from the United States of such goods as nylon hose, electrical wiring and cartons of cigarettes. Not only professional smugglers, but ordinary "good citizens" took part.

"My mother says you can bring anything back from the States as long as you sit on it," a six-year-old girl told the five-year-old son of a Mounted Policeman.

As shipping returned to pre-war conditions, so did trafficking in narcotics. During the fall of 1947, drug-squad men in Vancouver seized a huge cache of opium from a Dutch freighter in a North Vancouver dry dock. The seizure, reported by newspapers as the largest ever made to that time, had a black-market value of $4,648,000.

The most notable development during the whole post-war period, however, was the appearance of organized crime—and the Force's immediate efforts to combat it.

The 1949 Annual Report told of two cases involving large illicit distillery plants, both in the Winnipeg area. In both cases the Force invoked conspiracy charges, which allow different rules of evidence from those of ordinary criminal law. This gives the police more chance to prove the guilt of those involved in what is sometimes a very intricate web of crime. In one case twelve persons were convicted; and in the other, five.

In the 1950 Annual Report, the biggest organized crime case concerned "a narcotic conspiracy on the part of a syndicate organized to transport drugs from Ontario for distribution on the west coast. . . . We were successful in convicting two of the principals and three other members of the syndicate."

The 1951 report gave details of "one of the most insidious cases" of international organized crime conspiracy. American criminals in Buffalo had manufactured counterfeit ten-dollar Canadian notes, which were then smuggled into Canada. A crime syndicate in Toronto controlled their distribution to all the provinces. Then members of an organized narcotics syndicate and other criminals "pushed" the counterfeit bills, beginning simultaneously on Labour Day weekend, 1949.

After the Force's close liaison with the FBI, a Mounted Policeman posed as an out-of-town criminal and negotiated with the Toronto syndicate for the purchase of $25,000 in counterfeit bills. Subsequently, all members of the Toronto syndicate and many of the narcotics syndicate were convicted of trafficking in counterfeit money.

Meanwhile, beginning on April 1, 1949, both the duties and the scope of the Force were expanded. On that date Newfoundland entered Confederation, and thus the Royal Canadian Mounted Police became responsible for enforcing federal laws there. Sixteen months later, by agreement of the provincial government and the federal government, the Force also took over the provincial policing there, absorbing the Newfoundland Rangers in the process.

On August 15, 1950, at the request of the British Columbia provincial government, the Force took over the policing of that province and absorbed its provincial police.

Even before that time, however, the Mounted Police had taken on responsibilities farther afield than most of its own officers realized. Commissioner Wood's report of 1948 had mentioned one specific subject so casually that few if any except the persons directly concerned paid any attention to it. "Our new duties in connection with visa control in Europe are important and by no means easy," the Commissioner had written.

The Force was no longer based only in Canada. Without fanfare, without a whisper of publicity, it had expanded to Europe.

Chapter 21
Further Development and Expansion
1950–1960

The Force entered the 1950s with Commissioner Wood still in command, but on April 30, 1951, after nearly forty years of service, he retired. Typically, he worked overtime on his last day of service. He was succeeded by Leonard Hanson Nicholson, who was forty-six, and formerly an assistant commissioner.

Nicholson had originally joined the Force in 1923 and served for three years. Then he joined the provincial police of his native New Brunswick, and later the Nova Scotia Provincial Police. He returned to the fold as an inspector when the Force absorbed the provincial police of the Maritimes in 1932, then spent several years in charge of the Criminal Investigation Branch, first in Nova Scotia and later in Saskatchewan. In 1941 he joined the Canadian Army, and eventually became Colonel Nicholson, provost marshal. Back in the Force in 1946, he was appointed an assistant commissioner, and became director of Criminal Investigation at Ottawa.

Commissioner Nicholson's term of office was marked by increased police duties, expansion in several areas, increase in personnel, higher pay, better living and working conditions, and several significant changes in the structures of the Force.

Year after year duties increased in all departments, in Criminal Code cases as much as 37.6% in one year. In the early 1950s this was partly due to the advent of Newfoundland into Confederation and the provincial policing of that province and of British Columbia. But in succeeding years the pressure continued.

There was more general crime, more juvenile crime and, for a time, more organized crime. More Canadians tried to evade the Customs Act and to defraud the government through the Income Tax Act. More Indians committed infractions of the Indian Act. When the Wheat Board Act was passed, aimed at more stable farm incomes through more equitable sales, farmers disregarded that Act and sold their wheat to suit themselves. Canadians set up more illicit stills, smuggled more American cigarettes, passed more fraudulent cheques, trafficked in more narcotics, committed more robbery with violence, and more frequently drove their cars while intoxicated.

Some increased duties, like those concerning the Doukhobors, were beyond the capacity of the Force. From March, 1952, to March, 1953, Doukhobor settlements in British Columbia experienced more than sixty separate acts of incendiarism and dynamiting of power lines and railroad tracks. Mounted Police supervised additional railway guards, and the Force supplied an extra twenty of its own men for the danger spots. But, Nicholson reported, it was "a physical impossibility for a police force, however augmented, to patrol every bridge, underpass and culvert, and every mile of track through the region."

Also in the early fifties, the police faced increasing traffic in narcotic drugs. During 1952–53, the total number of arrests for violations of the Opium and Narcotic Drug Act was the highest it had been for years. In 1954, for the first time, a few teenagers were found using narcotics. Nicholson wrote: "Drug addiction is the outward manifestation of social and medical conditions which enforcement authorities alone are not competent to cope with."

By 1956, with bulk seizures of heroin greatly increased and marijuana coming into prominence, it became more and more apparent that enforcement alone would never provide a satisfactory remedy. "While there is an addict market there will be criminals to supply it," the Commissioner wrote. By 1959, police were seizing larger amounts of heroin and marijuana, organized drug syndicates were swinging into action and more persons in the entertainment field, particularly in Montreal, were known to be using marijuana.

Other work also increased throughout the Force during the 1950s, partly because of the normal population increase in the post-war period and partly because of the influx of thousands of immigrants from war-torn Europe.

Post-war prosperity meant that more Canadian families had cars and many had two. In Alberta alone in the year ending March, 1954, sixteen patrol cars were used full-time on traffic duty, travelling nearly a million miles. More Canadians had pleasure boats, too. Hence the Mounted Police had first to draft for the government and then enforce new boating regulations to ensure the safety and the proper operation of boats. From March, 1959, to March, 1960, they inspected 41,000 boats. The government sought to bring even destitute Eskimos into the affluent society. So Mounted Police had to compile questionnaires on all male Eskimos between the ages of ten and thirty suitable for vocational training.

The Force expanded as much as possible to meet the need, and by March, 1954, had reached maximum authorized strength: 4,420 regular uniformed members, plus special constables, civilians and civil servants, making a total of 6,222. "I feel sure that the pay increase authorized December 1 had much to do with the satisfactory condition," Nicholson wrote.

Even so, the workload increased. During the five years from 1953 to 1958, the number of federal statutes, Criminal Code and provincial statutes cases increased by 73.7%, while the strength of the regular uniformed members increased by only 15.3%. Men who through the war years and the immediate post-war period had dreamed of a normal family life in the foreseeable future, still worked eighteen hours a day on investigations, or took briefcases of work home for evenings, weekends and holidays.

In an effort to prevent crime the Force published, in English and French, an illustrated booklet *Crime in Your Community*, and distributed it widely across Canada. It invited the cooperation of merchants, businessmen and householders in crime prevention, and suggested security measures that they could take. The demand so far exceeded the supply that a second booklet was published: *Beware of Bad Cheques*. Also distributed to business establishments was a printed card to be hung near a telephone, advising the merchant how to assist police if the premises were attacked. The card came with a descriptive chart which could be filled in while the event was fresh in the merchant's memory.

The Force attacked the problem of scarcity of manpower by making the most effective use of what manpower it had. For a time the Musical Ride was discontinued. Wherever possible, Mounted Police on security guard duty of federal government buildings were replaced by men of the Corps of Commissionaires. This continued the trend begun in 1945, although it was still the responsibility of the Force to supervise the commissionaires' work.

During the early fifties the Mounted Police set up, for the first time, an inspection team. Its function was to visit all Division and Sub-Division headquarters and a few representative detachments once a year, and to examine all phases of administration and operation. Soon the team grew to two teams. Each was made up of an inspector, a senior NCO, and a constable-clerk, with an additional senior officer in charge.

The teams alternated between work at headquarters for about six months of the year and inspectional duties the other six. The inspection teams proved their worth by enabling the Force to cut down on certain clerical work and to improve efficiency in the field, and the teams became a regular part of the organization.

The most important innovation of the whole decade, however, was the setting up of establishment tables covering all regular positions in the Force by rank and duty. That is, an analysis was made of the workload and the responsibilities of every man in every part of every Division to discover whether there were enough Mounted Police, on the basis of a reasonable day's work from each, to handle the total work of the Force.

The survey proved unmistakably that the Force was understaffed. It also proved that many men were doing work beyond the ranks they actually held. As a result, the financial watchdogs of the federal government, the Treasury Board, not only authorized additional manpower but also authorized the cost of additional promotions. By March, 1960, total strength was 7,558, and many men had been promoted to ranks commensurate with the work they did.

For years efficiency had suffered through lack of working space at Ottawa headquarters in the Justice Building near the Houses of Parliament. In January, 1953, headquarters moved to what was then the edge of the city into a great seminary building. This the government first rented, then purchased, together with about 140 acres of splendid building land, approximately ten of which were retained by the Mounted Police for additional headquarters buildings and such things as possible crime detection laboratories. Over the next few years the interior of the seminary with its classrooms, private chapels and dozens of living units with private baths and toilets was rebuilt to fit specific police needs. During the same period, across the country, standardized detachment buildings were designed and built according to police specifications.

In November, 1954, Marine Division headquarters was moved from Halifax to Ottawa. This meant more centralized and efficient control of the watercraft now in use not only on the east coast but also off the west coast and on many inland waters. Gradually a modern fleet was constructed specifically for Mounted Police needs. By March, 1960, it included three "Commissioner"-class ships, three "fort"-class ships, twenty-two "detachment"-class ships and five motorboats. Other boats used for the enforcement of the small-vessel regulations were the responsibility of land Divisions.

The Air Division was also modernized and expanded, until fifteen operational craft and one training craft operated out of twelve bases across the country. More cars and motorcycles were purchased, and vehicles replaced earlier to maintain a higher standard. Even old type-writers, nearly 1,700 of them, twenty to thirty years old, were replaced over a five-year period.

Existing radio networks were extended and new ones set up. More two-way radio cars were used, and patrol boats on the Great Lakes were also fitted with two-way radios. Several radio-telephone sets were installed in the far North, so that even detachments at Spence Bay, Craig Harbour, Chesterfield Inlet and Port Harrison could readily communicate with more central points. Ten portaphones allotted to Air Division planes enabled them to communicate directly with all radio-equipped detachments, cars and search parties in their respective Divisions.

During the late 1950s the Mounted Police installed a Telex system at all main points from coast to coast. This toll tele-printer network allowed any station to make direct printed contact with any other by dialing the appropriate Telex number. This practically eliminated the need for relaying messages.

Notable developments also occurred in other areas during the fifties. For instance, the Crime Detection Laboratories developed new tech-niques. During one year alone these related to the examination of oils, blood groupings, the scale that measures the oxidation of alcohol in the body, to the construction of an indented writing box for use by docu-ment examiners, and to a refinement of the methods of determining factors involving auto accidents.

The Identification Branch installed new machinery in the Name Index System, and made use of the "Soundex" system to speed the searching of index cards. The same Branch established a Fraudulent Cheque Section for more efficient examination of questioned cheques, which by the end of the decade reached a total annual value of nearly $900,000.

Radar speed meters and breathalyzer units enabled the Force to be more effective in gathering evidence to place before the courts in cases of speeding and of impaired and drunken driving.

During this decade the Force stressed training and education as never before. For example, the Annual Report of 1956 listed the follow-ing as having received regular training: recruits, in-service members, Canadian Police College graduates, Marine refresher class members and equitation class members. Training at the Divisional level covered twenty-five subjects: from motorcycle training to Identification Branch training; from traffic control to senior administration courses; and from a personnel officers' indoctrination course to a counter-sabotage course.

During one typical year, 1956, eight members of the Force attended university full-time, working toward degrees in law, commerce and science. Seven took night classes in scientific disciplines. Seven others, members of the Force's training staff, enrolled in the RCAF's School of Instructional Techniques. Even bandsmen followed the trend: three of them attended a seven-month course at the Toronto Conservatory of Music.

The Annual Report of 1960 announced that Headquarters Division, which had operated as a Division since 1952, had been reorganized. It would be headed as before by the Commissioner, but with two deputy commissioners, one for Operations and one for Administration. Six directorates now included: "C"—Operations and Criminal Investigation; "I"—Security and Intelligence; "A"—Administration and Organization; "M"—Marine Services; "T"—Telecommunications; and "S"—Services and Supply. Thus was laid the basis for the present-day organization of the Force.

In March, 1959, events in Newfoundland proved what the Mounted Police have always known but what many Canadians have never fully accepted. That is, although the Force has a duty to enforce the laws in areas in which it is the police authority, it is not an autonomous organization. For instance, Mounted Police contracts with provincial governments must be approved by the federal government. Although the contracts state that in an emergency, on request of a provincial attorney general, the Force may provide him with extra Mounted Police, this is in fact possible only if the federal government agrees. Thus if the federal government believes, or professes to believe, that policing in the provinces from which the extra manpower is temporarily provided will suffer, that government can refuse to allow the Force to provide it.

This became the focal point of friction between the Conservatives in Ottawa and the provincial Liberals in St. John's during the "woods labour war" in Newfoundland in early 1959. The Mounted Police were caught between the two opposing parties.

The trouble began when the International Woodworkers of America tried to unionize loggers and other woodworkers. Employees of two of the largest companies in the province went on strike, hoping to force management to recognize the union. Premier Joseph ("Joey") Smallwood's government opposed the IWA, fearing that the province's economy would be ruined if mainland hours and wages were imposed. Smallwood tried to eliminate that danger by organizing a rival union, the Newfoundland Brotherhood of Wood Workers.

Violence broke out between strikers and non-strikers, resulting in property damage and injury. The Mounted Police, even with reinforcements from the Newfoundland Constabulary, could not keep the peace. On March 8, at the request of Superintendent A.W. Parsons, officer commanding "B" Division, the Newfoundland attorney general asked the federal minister of Justice and attorney general of Canada, E. Davie Fulton, for fifty Mounted Police as reinforcements "under the terms of the contract." Instead of complying, however, Fulton merely instructed Commissioner Nicholson to "watch the situation closely."

Nicholson realized the inherent danger. He assembled fifty men from nearby provinces and had them ready, with aircraft, waiting for the order to go. Then violence increased. Union offices were wrecked, several men were seriously injured, and one of the Constabulary died after receiving a skull fracture which resulted in severe brain damage.

Three days after the initial request for reinforcements, Fulton informed Nicholson that the cabinet had decided it was impossible to supply fifty extra police "without prejudicing the other responsibilities of the Force."

The next morning Commissioner Nicholson resigned in protest. He had insisted from the beginning that sending fifty men from the Force's uniformed strength of about 5,300 would not in any way disrupt policing elsewhere. He took the cabinet's decision as a breach of faith since the federal government would not allow the Force to live up to its contract with a provincial government.

Another officer of the Force, however, had been reasonably sure, from March 8, that no reinforcements would be sent. The same day as the Newfoundland request reached the federal government a senior cabinet minister had said to him: "I'm damned if we'll pull their political chestnuts out of the fire."

Nicholson's letter of resignation indicated that he was well aware of the political aspects of the situation and that he realized the same thing might happen again. "Bearing in mind that we have similar contracts with seven other provinces the decision of this government has a peculiar significance," he wrote. "I have no option but to ask you to accept my resignation." It was the second time in the Force's history that a Commissioner had resigned over what he considered improper interference from the federal government. The other man so to protest was George A. French, the first Commissioner. The strife in Newfoundland was not resolved in Ottawa but in St. John's when the provincial government passed legislation making the IWA illegal.

On April 1, 1959, English-born Charles E. Rivett-Carnac, former deputy commissioner on leave pending pension, became the tenth Commissioner. He had joined the Mounted Police as a constable in

1923, and had moved with more than usual speed up the promotional ladder. His loyalty to the Force probably influenced him to return temporarily after Nicholson's resignation. But one year later, because of ill health and after serving nearly thirty-seven years, he retired. He was succeeded by Commissioner C.W. Harvison.

Expanded duties of the Force had entailed sending Mounted Police to Europe to handle security duties related to immigration processing there. During the immediate post-war period there had been great pressure on Canada, as also on Australia and the United States, to take large numbers of immigrants wishing to leave Europe for the Western Hemisphere. These would-be immigrants included persons living in refugee camps after fleeing areas controlled by the Nazis, the Soviet government, or Soviet satellites. Canada not only felt it a duty to relieve the pressure on the European countries but also welcomed immigrants. However, Canadian authorities knew that there were not only desirable applicants but also undesirable ones, criminal and political. For example, they knew that many immigrants were lying about their backgrounds, and that Soviet-bloc countries were using the movement of refugees to plant spies abroad.

As the security service of Canada, the Force had a vital interest in the screening of immigrants. Hence Mounted Police had been sent to Europe to interview all applicants.

They tried to keep criminals out of Canada, and to ensure that each applicant was honestly concerned with emigrating and was not directed to Canada for subversive purposes. They also tried to prevent the entry of German or Austrian immigrants who belonged to such organizations as the Gestapo which were responsible for war-time atrocities, as well as any who had been employed in secret intelligence work. However, they could only report on the facts they found. The final decision regarding admission of immigrants was and has always been that of the minister of Immigration.

Mounted Police visa control operations in Europe began with the stationing of one man in London in 1946. By 1951, Mounted Police at various Canadian immigration posts in Europe, assisted by such employed civilians as ex-Scotland Yard officers, operated with loose supervision from the London office. A senior NCO was in charge in London, with ex-Superintendent James Wright, who lived there after retirement, as an adviser. The whole operation was supervised at long distance from Ottawa headquarters. However, Mounted Police work needed closer control and direction so that it would not be submerged in immigration organization.

In July, 1951, Inspector W.H. Kelly began a three-year term abroad by settling into a top-floor office in Canada House, Trafalgar Square, London. As visa control officer, Europe, he visited regularly all Mounted Police offices on the continent and ensured that each became and then remained a Mounted Police entity. By July, 1954, sixteen offices had been located in Great Britain, Germany, Austria, Italy, Greece, France, Sweden, Denmark, The Netherlands, Belgium and Finland.

Kelly was also liaison officer with various police forces and security and intelligence organizations throughout Europe, and with the drug authorities and the criminal laboratories of the British Home Office in London. Thus the Mounted Police came into close contact with Scotland Yard, the British Security Service MI5, the French *Sûreté*, the West German Federal Police, and other police forces in all the countries in which they had offices. During the Interpol (International Criminal Police Organization) Conferences of 1952 and 1953, held at Stockholm and Oslo respectively, Canada's delegate was the RCMP liaison officer, Europe. Also, he was on the spot to organize the visit to London of the Force's Mounted Contingent for the coronation of Queen Elizabeth II, in June, 1953.

The international activities of the Mounted Police during the fifties were not limited to European functions, however. By 1957 the Force's membership in the constantly growing Interpol brought it in contact with about sixty other member nations around the world.

The Force also maintained membership in the International Association of Chiefs of Police, which united law-enforcement bodies in the United States. It continued its close liaison with the Federal Bureau of Investigation, with the Federal Narcotics Bureau, and with U.S. customs, secret service and immigration departments. This liaison with the United States, begun in a formal way in the early 1940s, was mainly carried out through a Mounted Police officer and staff stationed in Washington, D.C., and an FBI agent and staff stationed in Ottawa.

By 1959 the European operation had grown to the point where the Mounted Police officer in London was a liaison officer only. A second officer was stationed at Cologne, Germany, as visa control officer, with operational control transferred back to Ottawa. Also by this time the Force had an office in Tel Aviv. The Israeli office was part of an expansion which would eventually lead to the establishing of Mounted Police offices around the world.

Chapter 22
The Attack on Organized Crime
1960–1963

Canada is presenting an increasingly attractive target for organized crime," Commissioner Clifford Walter Harvison wrote in the 1960 Annual Report.

Montreal-born Harvison, the tall, slim officer who succeeded Commissioner Rivett-Carnac on April 1 that year, knew this from personal experience. He joined the Royal North-West Mounted in 1919, served three years with the newly designated Royal Canadian Mounted Police, and served with the Force continuously from 1932. After gaining wide experience in criminal investigation in Quebec, he was commissioned in 1938. Later he took charge of Criminal Investigation Branches in Quebec, Manitoba and British Columbia. Still later, at Ottawa headquarters, he was director of Operations and Criminal Investigation and then director of Security and Intelligence, after which he became officer commanding "E" Division (British Columbia), the largest Division in the Force. For one year he went back to Ottawa as deputy commissioner, Operations. Then, at age fifty-eight, he became the Force's eleventh Commissioner.

Harvison knew that for more than a decade highly organized crime systems had operated in Canada. He feared that the criminals would become so entrenched as to pose an almost insurmountable problem to the police, as the Mafia had done in the United States. He was well aware that when the American authorities had at last made a great drive against their organized criminals, they had flocked to eastern Canada, particularly Montreal.

It was true that since the late 1940s the Mounted Police had successfully used conspiracy charges in several organized crime cases involving

illicit distilleries, narcotics and counterfeit banknotes, and that some of
the principals had received prison sentences. But as usual, other organized criminals stepped forward, and the crime rate continued to rise.

Harvison's work in criminal investigation led him to recognize not
only the national danger from organized criminals, but also the main
problems in dealing with them. He decided to attack this form of crime
by first attacking the problems hampering his own men.

The main problem, he could see, arose from the fact that organized
crime differed greatly from ordinary crime. For one thing, the police
had difficulty in identifying the guilty organizations. Also, the leaders
were practically immune to prosecution because they took no overt part
in the crimes they had planned. Even those who actually committed the
crimes were less likely to be identified than ordinary criminals. For
instance, in ordinary crime a complainant and other witnesses will
usually assist the police in identifying a suspect. But organized criminals
intimidate potential witnesses by threatening and, if necessary, instigat-
ing torture, murder and bombings, so usually no one will testify against
them.

Commissioner Harvison attacked the problem of organized crime's
"difference" by establishing National Crime Intelligence Units at seven
major centres from Montreal to Vancouver and staffing them with
twenty-one men. They became fully operational in 1961, gathering
information for a national central repository at Ottawa.

The new National Crime Intelligence Units began to ascertain the
memberships of organized criminal groups, their specialties and their
characteristic methods. Harvison grew more concerned about the hold
organized crime was gaining in Canada. In November, 1961, when he
addressed the Canadian Club in Toronto, he ignored the tradition of
the Force to be silent on potentially controversial matters and spoke out
publicly on syndicated crime.

The syndicates, he said then, and repeated later in his book *The
Horsemen*, were tightly organized, multi-million-dollar organizations
headed by hoodlums, thugs and murderers who had clawed their way
to power and amassed huge personal fortunes by ruthlessly eliminating
their competitors. Goon squads on their payrolls enforced rigid discipline within the syndicates and terrorized outsiders. The syndicates
bribed and corrupted the police and government officials, and bought
off, ruined or murdered others inclined to oppose them. In case of
trouble they were defended by their own highly paid lawyers, and
supported by other syndicates.

Harvison told his Canadian Club audience that some of the huge
illicit stills set up by Canadian criminal organizations a few years earlier

had used engineers and construction crews provided by the notorious "Legs" Diamond mob and, later, the Purple Gang. Big American crime syndicates, he said, were active here in narcotics trafficking, in counterfeiting and in the protection racket.

That Canadian Club speech had several notable effects. The first was a meeting attended by Harvison and the highest police officials of Ontario and Quebec—the only provinces in which the Mounted Police were not engaged in provincial policing. These leaders of the Mounted Police, the Ontario Provincial Police, the Quebec Provincial Police, the Metropolitan Toronto and the Montreal City Police discussed methods of improving the exchange of criminal information. This was of vital importance, as up to this time most police forces, except the Mounted Police, were working on an individual-case basis, with little effort to correlate information coming in from all sources. The representatives of the five main forces of Canada agreed to pool information regarding travelling criminals, suspected organized crime offences, and so on. This would be added to the Canadian and United States information the Mounted Police already possessed. Thus any contributing force interested in any particular criminal could readily obtain all the available information on him, his associates and their activities.

Harvison's speech aroused much controversy, especially in Ontario. Some critics professed not to believe his charges. Others wanted to know how such a situation had been allowed to develop. The leader of the Opposition in the legislature, John Wintermeyer, made embarrassing charges against the provincial government. Then came the discovery by officers of the Ontario Provincial Police of corruption in their own anti-gambling squad. As a result, the government established the Ontario Police Commission. It would have continuing responsibility to inquire into all matters affecting the maintenance of law and order in the province, and to exercise supervisory powers with respect to provincial and municipal police forces.

A little more than a month after Harvison's speech, the Ontario government established a Royal Commission on Crime, headed by Mr. Justice W.D. Roach of the Ontario Supreme Court. It would inquire into specific matters referred to by John Wintermeyer, including the existence of so-called organized crime.

Commissioner Harvison submitted a brief to that Royal Commission in November, 1962. He now gave specific details of organized criminal activities over the preceding ten years, and named the organized criminals involved. He also informed Judge Roach of specific links between the Mafia in the United States and organized criminals in Canada. He referred especially to the Apalachin meeting in New York

State five years earlier which was attended by sixty-three notorious and suspected racketeers, many of them members of the Mafia. Then he linked Canadian residents to the Apalachin meeting.

One Apalachin attendant, for instance, had financial interests in horse racing and a racing farm in Ontario. Another attendant had a commuter's permit for several years, allowing him to visit Ontario points frequently, allegedly visiting friends and attending to financial interests there. Still another had financially backed several large-scale stock-fraud operations in Canada. Many other Apalachin attendants maintained contact with various persons in Canada over the years.

Harvison also told the Royal Commission about a well-known American associator with criminals, a suspected drug trafficker whom the Mounted Police and the Department of Immigration were at that time trying to deport from Canada. The man had previously been deported from the United States to Cuba. But there he had obtained an entry permit from the Canadian Embassy in Havana and "now resides in Ontario." The man had been convicted in absentia in Italy, in 1925 of premeditated murder, in 1927 of armed robbery, and in 1932 of attempted robbery, armed robbery and attempted murder. Yet Canadian authorities were having great difficulties in deporting him "because of certain technicalities."

Several of Harvison's examples of narcotics cases proved that international organized crime had taken hold in Canada. One concerned a narcotics ring which transported heroin from laboratories in France to Italy and there hid the drugs in the false bottoms of trunks. Members of the crime ring then distributed the trunks among the possessions of Italians emigrating to the United States, where other members would recover them.

In May, 1961, twenty-four members of that narcotics ring had been charged in New York City, including criminals from the United States and Italy, and four residents of the Toronto area. In November, while twelve persons were before the courts, one man had been murdered and four others, including Alberto Agueci, one of the Canadians, had skipped bail. Soon afterwards, Agueci was found murdered, gangland fashion, near Rochester, New York, his body burned and mutilated, identifiable only through fingerprints. The three others who skipped bail were later arrested in Spain, travelling on Canadian passports fraudulently obtained.

Commissioner Harvison ended his brief to the Ontario Royal Commission by giving two examples of interprovincial organized crime, both "highly lucrative rackets." The first example was counterfeiting activity which was centred in the Montreal area, although the notes were distributed all across Canada. Organized counterfeiting was on the increase, he declared. In 1960 the Mounted Police recovered about $192,000 in spurious notes; in 1961, about $264,000; and in the first eight months of 1962, more than $765,000.

The second example of "highly lucrative" interprovincial organized crime was the manufacture and distribution of illicit spirits. This, too, was centred in the Province of Quebec. From April, 1961, the Royal Canadian Mounted Police had seized twenty-nine commercial-type stills (as distinct from the more than three hundred small, non-commercial type seized in the same period). All except one operated in Quebec. Spirits from these twenty-nine stills were seized in the Ontario cities of Toronto, Brockville and Sudbury, and also in Prince Edward Island. The Mounted Police estimated that three-quarters of the quality spirits seized in Ontario originated in Quebec. This required a criminal organization operating in both provinces.

Mr. Justice Roach presented his Royal Commission Report to the Ontario government in mid-March, 1963. He stated that organized gambling had reached a "staggering" volume, one organization taking in an estimated ten million dollars a year. Referring to organized crime in general, he confined his remarks chiefly to the Mafia. "There is no evidence before me that it [the Mafia] does subsist in organized crime or that any of the activities of those engaged in organized crime were in any way associated with the Mafia," he reported.

Commissioner Harvison must have been shocked, but he could not publicly criticize the report of an eminent judge. However, his Crime Intelligence Units had continued to gather intelligence on organized crime, and this was supplemented since his Canadian Club speech by information gathered by the police forces of Ontario and Quebec. He knew beyond any doubt that organized crime continued to spread insidiously throughout Canada.

On August 16, 1963, Harvison repeated his warning, again in public. This time he gave a news conference at the Canadian National Exhibition in Toronto. Whether or not the American crime syndicates which were increasing their operations in Canada were actually members of the Mafia, he could not say. But they certainly were Mafia-like. And again he gave details.

The news media played up Harvison's warning. As a result, at the end of the month the Ontario Police Commission recommended to their attorney general that the Commission itself should make an intensive and continuous inquiry into the extent of foreign-controlled and other large-scale organized crime in the province. The attorney general agreed. Soon the Ontario Police Commission began an inquiry of a scope never before undertaken by any Canadian law-enforcement supervisory body.

In early September the Ontario Police Commission on Organized Crime questioned Commissioner Harvison at length. He told them about the almost fatal beating of one criminal; the disappearance and suspected murder of another; small-loan money-lending at twenty percent a week or 1,040% per annum; and recent Toronto cases involving half a million dollars worth of stolen furs and jewellery, all traced to one man in New York. Profits from money-lending, successful thefts, gambling establishments and so on were enormous. The profits were put back into criminal operations which made more profit. Syndicates not only employed the most expensive lawyers but even paid pensions to the wives of the convicted.

Later, members of the Commission, which included a Mounted Police staff sergeant, interviewed Ontario police officials and visited law-enforcement agencies in the United States, gathering detailed information about organized crime there. In Washington they attended the public questioning of Joseph Valachi, an admitted member of the Mafia or Cosa Nostra.

Valachi was the first member of that organization ever willing to violate the solemn oath of secrecy by testifying publicly. He also was a self-admitted peddlar of narcotics, a hoodlum, a racketeer and a murderer, and was serving a long term of imprisonment. He described in detail the organization and the operations of the infamous Vito Genovese syndicate and its typical methods of enforcement of discipline. His testimony corroborated what the police had already learned.

At one point Valachi referred to Canada and to Vito Agueci, one of the four Torontonians in the international narcotics ring which had smuggled heroin into the United States in immigrants' trunks, and a member of the same family as Alberto Agueci.

"He knew I belonged to Vito Genovese because Vito Agueci himself is a member from Canada."

"From Canada?"

"Yes."

"He is a member of another family, though?"

"In Canada."

"The Buffalo family?"

"Buffalo and Canada is all one. When I say Canada, I mean Toronto."

The Ontario Police Commission knew that they were establishing the truth about the state of organized crime in Ontario. Harvison, on receiving reports of the Valachi testimony, knew that they were also breaking trail for the rest of Canada toward public knowledge about organized crime in other parts of the country.

Commissioner Clifford W. Harvison retired on October 31, 1963, after only three and a half years in office. But he had served approximately thirty-six years with the Force, mostly in the direct fight against crime. This experience had given him the background to initiate during his brief term as Commissioner what only he was capable of initiating then: the attack on organized crime.

Chapter 23
Day In and Day Out
1951 – 1967

All three Commissioners who served in office long enough during the period from 1951 to 1967 to analyze the situation stressed to the federal government that the Force was overworked. Even in 1954, when Commissioner Nicholson reported with satisfaction that at last the Force was up to authorized strength, there still were not enough police to do, without undue strain, the increased work demanded of them.

"Our members during the year under review have worked longer hours than ever before in the history of the Force," Commissioner Harvison reported in 1961. And he repeated the message in 1962.

On November 1, 1963, the fifty-five-year-old, Saskatchewan-born George Brinton McClellan succeeded Harvison to become the Force's twelfth Commissioner. He had attended Royal Military College for a time before joining the Mounted Police in 1932, and after seven years was commissioned. He, like Harvison, had had wide experience in police work, from Nova Scotia to British Columbia. He, too, had experience in Intelligence work, both in the field and as the officer in charge of the Intelligence Branch (later the Security and Intelligence Directorate) at Ottawa headquarters. Later, after three years as officer commanding "K" Division (Alberta), he became deputy commissioner, Administration, in 1959, and still later, senior deputy commissioner, Operations.

"I am concerned by the long hours of work which are being put in by members on police duty," Commissioner McClellan reported in 1963. "Long hours have been traditionally a part of service in the Force ... in recent years, however, the average working day has been increasing in man-hours considerably beyond the national trend and there is no compensation for overtime." Like Harvison, he echoed the same sentiment each year he was in office.

Although the government, through Treasury Board, allowed repeated increases in both pay and personnel, these were never enough to compensate for the constant increase in duties. Moreover, the men most affected had no spokesman of their own. As the whole Force was uncomfortably aware, when the Commissioner spoke to Treasury Board he represented both men and management. No matter how dissatisfied the men themselves might be, they had no way of bringing pressure on the government to correct the situation. Unlike other police forces they had no police association, no public spokesman, and no means of arbitration.

By 1967 salaries had reached a reasonable level, which the government had ordered to be worked out by averaging the pay of a number of leading police forces, so that the Mounted Police would be neither the highest-paid police in the country nor the lowest. Also, it allowed the Force gradually to cut its work-week to five days. Office staff benefited, but Mounted Police on operations cannot work to an eight-hour day or a five-day week. Free overtime remained a feature of the Force's service, amounting to millions of man-hours every year. Meanwhile it continued to do all the federal policing in Canada, all the provincial policing except in Ontario and Quebec, and all police work in the Yukon and the Northwest Territories, plus, by 1967, municipal policing in about 125 towns and villages. Regular uniform strength, which in March, 1952, had stood at 4,517, had increased by March, 1967, to 8,041.

Whether or not the members on operations resented the overtime about which they had no choice, they worked as necessary, at any hour and under any conditions. It was half-past one in the morning when, on April 23, 1960, the Vancouver-based Marine Division patrol boat *Little Bow II* answered a request for help. The thirty-six-foot tugboat *Westminster Chief* had been stolen from New Westminster. When the patrol boat approached the tug, the stolen vessel manoeuvred at full speed, and tried three times to ram the police boat. The NCO's report concluded: "As all attempts to halt this tug met with negative results, the NCO in charge finally ordered the ship's rifle broken out and warning shots were fired, at which time the tug halted. When finally boarded, the two youths, aged seventeen and nineteen, were taken into custody and turned over to the New Westminster City Police."

The overtime service of a group of Mounted Policemen and of two in particular, in the Province of Quebec in December, 1961, paid off particularly well.

For some time the police had believed that Fernand Gendron of Roxton Falls was the financial backer of an organized bootlegging operation. But he operated a garage and also dealt in used cars. Whenever the police checked one of his vehicles it disappeared from the highways, and they had no way of knowing what replacement vehicle he was using next. Early in December, however, they received information that Gendron had set up a cache of yeast, molasses, sugar, malt and gallon cans on the farm of Joseph Dufault of Ste. Hélène, about fifty miles east of Montreal.

Mounted Police from Sherbrooke, from Montreal Sub-Division Headquarters and from the Montreal Preventive Service were detailed as "stakeouts" on a twenty-four-hour basis in the vicinity of the cache. A light aircraft from Air Division also joined in the daytime watching.

For more than two weeks poor weather conditions by day and darkness by night made watching difficult. Then on December 20, some of the hidden watchers saw a pick-up truck leaving the cache. They followed it through a heavy snowstorm to the outskirts of Quebec City. There, far enough away from the cache so as not to arouse his suspicion, they stopped the driver, Henri Galipeau, whom they knew. They seized the 213 gallons of alcohol they found in the truck and the truck itself, which was fictitiously registered.

The police expected that this would alert Gendron, and so end any activity around the cache. But they continued their round-the-clock watching, even over Christmas Day. At 3:30 P.M. on December 28, another truck arrived loaded with ingredients. All police vehicles, unmarked of course, took up key positions controlling exit highways from the cache. When the truck left some police cars followed, unobserved, to St. Hyacinthe.

There the truck paused momentarily for a traffic light. Constable J.C.A. Dufresne jumped out of one police car and clambered into the back of the truck. The police vehicles still followed but at a considerable distance. At Richelieu the truck's driver left it parked for the night behind a restaurant, then left on foot. As soon as it grew dark Corporal J.E.G. Noiseux climbed into the back of the truck to join Constable Dufresne. All night the two men shivered in the bitter mid-winter cold.

The next day, when the loaded truck left Richelieu, the Air Division plane shadowed it until it parked behind a barn near Bedford. By this time Dufresne and Noiseux were frigid and cramped. But just as they considered leaving the truck, a second driver took over. So they stayed with it until nine-thirty that night, when at last it stopped at what they presumed to be a farm. They did not know where they were, or how many persons might confront them when they got out, or if the other police had successfully followed them in the dark.

Nevertheless the corporal and the constable emerged. They immediately arrested the five men they saw: Fernand Gendron, the financier of the organization; Laurent and Normand Gagnon, the operators of the still; and Armand and Yvon Gaouette. Then, almost at once, police reinforcements drove up. They seized a great commercial still capable of producing 200 gallons a day, 196 gallons of illicit alcohol, 1,000 gallons of mash, forty gallons of first-run alcohol, fifty-seven hundred-pound bags of white sugar and 459 gallon cans. They also seized the delivery truck in which the corporal and the constable had hidden. Later, at the Dufault farm, the police seized fifteen barrels of malt syrup, 51 hundred-pound bags of white sugar, 1,534 empty gallon cans, several empty barrels and a few gallons of illicit alcohol. Their overtime had paid off in the largest seizure of the year under the Excise Act.

Nine months later, members of the counterfeiting squad of the C.I.B in Montreal worked around the clock for seventy-two hours investigating the source of four counterfeit five-dollar bills. By the end of that time they had set a record by completing the whole complicated investigation. They had found the entire stock of counterfeit bills, $40,000 worth in three separate caches. They had also found and seized the offset printing press and all other paraphernalia, and had located and arrested the three men involved.

By contrast, however, men of the Portage la Prairie detachment, Manitoba, put in eighteen hours a day for three successive days with no success. Neither they nor the Indians and other volunteers who worked with them in late July, 1954, could find the body of an Indian boy who had drowned in the Assiniboine River. After three days one of the Indians, with police approval, went to another reserve for the help of the noted Indian "witch-doctor" Louie Prince. Prince gave a remarkable exhibition of his craft. Without going near the place himself he successfully directed the police to where the child's body lay far downstream, just beneath the surface of the water, caught on some branches and out of sight.

While the Portage la Prairie men were dragging the Assiniboine River, other members of the Force were setting out from Halifax aboard the *St. Roch* for a final epic voyage, through the Panama Canal, back to Vancouver. On arriving there in October, 1954, after eighty-one days, the schooner established the record of two complete sailings around North America. Superintendent Larsen went out to meet his former ship and skippered it for the last few miles home to North Vancouver where it had been designed and built in 1928. The next day Assistant Commissioner Charles E. Rivett-Carnac, who later became Commissioner but at that time was officer commanding "E" Division (British Columbia), presented the *St. Roch* to the city of Vancouver, to be maintained as part of a maritime museum.

In the summer of 1959 an off-duty constable stationed at Bell Island detachment, Conception Bay, Newfoundland, made a most unusual arrest. He and another constable, one hot Saturday afternoon, had taken their wives down to "the beach," one of the only two places on the island where dips in the great cliffs allow access to the water. While one of the policemen was away from the beach for a short time, the other one noticed a small boat some distance off shore. It sat unusually deep in the water as if it contained something very heavy. The two persons in the boat tried to manoeuvre it out of sight of the beach to the comparative security of an overhanging deep-water cavern. The constable's suspicions were aroused. The Dominion Steel and Coal Corporation of Canada (DOSCO) at that time operated, at Bell Island, the world's largest subterranean hematite iron-ore mine. It experienced many thefts, including expensive items offered as scrap metal to dealers on the island.

As the boat moved out of sight the constable decided he must investigate. But there was no boat available. Because of the great cliffs all around the coastline, he would have to swim. He had perfected his swimming as a recruit, but he was not necessarily prepared to swim three hundred yards of deep ocean water, flanked by overhanging cliffs with no foothold. Nevertheless he plunged into the bitterly cold water and swam to the cavern.

Negotiating a final bend, he came upon the boat and its two occupants. They not only offered no resistance, but seemed too dazed to realize that the great copper-wire cable coiled at their feet, worth $1,200 and taken from the Dominion pier, was irrefutable evidence against them. By this time the second constable was swimming for the cave. But he was not needed. A boat soon came into view, with the two culprits in custody and the first constable as navigator.

Some of the extra volume of work during the 1950s and 1960s, as throughout the Force's history, resulted from the strange behaviour of certain members of the public. For instance, some businessmen are so easily duped that they will even cash receipts and photostatic copies of cheques. This probably explains why the booklet *Bad Paper*, Number 6 of the "Crime in Your Community" series and published in the early sixties, proved the most popular of the series to date.

In North Sydney, Cape Breton Island, a retired boat captain who kept a small tobacco and confectionery shop gave the police double trouble by keeping his life savings of $15,000 in cash. He was robbed of $12,000, which was recovered. After that he kept the whole $15,000 on his person, and his son and two accomplices robbed him with violence. It took several Mounted Police, several North Sydney town police, and a dog with a dogmaster to catch the thieves and recover most of the money. It also took many hours of police time later, when they successfully took the case to court.

One difficulty the police frequently faced during this as during every period was that many confirmed criminals did not receive sentences that would deter them from committing similar crime in the future. Part of this difficulty stems from the law itself. That is, if an accused is found guilty of more than one offence, the presiding magistrate or judge can, and usually does, specify that he is to serve any jail terms not consecutively but concurrently.

In April, 1958, near Port Hawkesbury, Cape Breton Island, a masked man using a sawed-off shotgun robbed a mail train. He escaped with $10,000 in stamps, five hundred morphine sulphate tablets, and some diamond rings and wrist watches. From 6:45 A.M. when Sydney detachment received word of the robbery, members of the Force painstakingly searched most of the island and the mainland of Nova Scotia. At 5:30 A.M. the next day they arrested the man, Russell Francis Ross, and lodged him in Inverness County jail (not a Mounted Police responsibility) to await trial. Then both the Force and the Postal Department conducted tedious investigations to recover the mail, to direct it to its original destination, and so on.

A few days later Ross broke out of jail, and again all detachments in the area were alerted. After an intensive search the police recaptured him, this time in seventeen hours. In July a judge sentenced Ross to four years in the Dorchester Penitentiary for the armed postal robbery. The judge also sentenced him to an additional one year for the prison break, but this was to run concurrently, and to an additional six months regarding the drugs, also to run concurrently. In retrospect it seems that Ross lost nothing by attempting his jailbreak.

Perhaps the most depressing aspect of the sentencing of criminals occurs in Mounted Police prosecutions under the Excise Act in the Province of Quebec. Judges there, almost without exception, give surprisingly light sentences in this area of crime, especially for offences involving illicit stills. Usually fines are assessed on first offences, with jail terms in default. Usually the fines are so small (the minimum) in comparison with the profits made from the offence that the criminals can easily pay their fines and still be far ahead financially. On second offences the mandatory jail term is usually kept to the minimum.

Sentences meted out in the Gendron case must have been particularly depressing to the constable and the corporal who rode in the back of the truck, nearly freezing. Estimating that the two hundred gallons produced daily by the illicit still sold for a minimum of ten dollars each, one day's production was worth $2,000, of which approximately two-thirds, or $1,333, would be profit. Thus every thirty-day run-off would give profits of about $40,000. The judge sitting on the case in the Sweetsburg court fined Gendron, the financial backer, $2,000 and costs, and the two still operators and the other two workers $1,300 each and costs. Dufault, on whose farm Gendron had the cache of ingredients, was fined $100 and costs at St. Hyacinthe. Gallipeau, the first truck driver, was fined $200 and costs at Quebec City. All were given the option of short jail terms, but all paid the fines.

The probable explanation for the light sentences in Quebec lies in the fact that the Excise Act is a federal statute, and also that the large tax at time of manufacture on alcohol legally manufactured in Canada goes to the federal government. The same situation exists in other provinces. But the Quebec courts are the only ones to give the impression that they believe the violation of certain federal statutes is not as important as the violation of other statutes.

Although large stills are also found in Ontario and Manitoba, Quebec usually holds the annual Canadian record of seizures related to illicit stills. In 1956, total excise seizures made in Quebec were 205; the next highest number, in Manitoba, 88. In 1963 and 1964, the majority of illicit commercial stills were seized in Quebec. In 1967, of the 6,014 gallons of illicit spirits seized, 4,943 were produced in Quebec. Such factors make "C" Division one of the most overworked in all Canada.

Canada's centenary of Confederation in 1967 greatly increased the demands on the Mounted Police. They participated in celebrations all over the country, and were responsible for the security of the more than sixty members of visiting royalty and heads of state. They also accompanied and guarded the Confederation trains and caravans. They, like other police, had to contend with an influx of such petty criminals as pickpockets, who came to Canada from all over the world to take advantage of the crowds attending festivities across the country.

Even the permanent Centennial flame lit on Parliament Hill added a small responsibility. When coins thrown into the water were designated for a retarded children's fund, Mounted Police kept pilferers from what the local press called "the best-guarded wishing well in the world." Other duties on the Hill continued as usual—protection of government property, traffic control and so on. Tourists from all over the world took innumerable snapshots and asked innumerable questions, especially the classic: "Where's your horse?" One satisfied tourist exclaimed, "You Mounties sure are more helpful than real policemen!"

Expo 67 brought many thousands of foreign visitors to Montreal during Centennial year. The international exposition also placed an added burden on the Mounted Police. "C" Division had the main responsibility, although men from Ontario and the Marine Division shared the work. They protected the Canadian government pavilion, made Marine patrols of the Expo site, and so on.

When Charles de Gaulle visited Expo 67, Mounted Policemen in charge of his security wore civilian clothes and mingled with the crowds swarming about him. In order to stay as close to the general as possible yet appear natural, they would rush forward, shouting "Vive de Gaulle!" and leading the cheers and applause. When the general shook hands with one or two of his more obvious admirers at each public performance, it was often a Mounted Policeman on security duty who received the first handshake.

All the extra duties were fulfilled, as usual, through unpaid overtime. Mounted Police at Expo 67, serving side-by-side with Quebec Provincial Police and Montreal city policemen, must have been uncomfortably aware of the fact. The other policemen openly discussed the trips to Florida and the fur coats for their wives they planned with their overtime pay, which could be $5,000 over the six-month period.

In spite of no overtime pay, however, the Mounted Police evidently gave satisfactory service. In 1966 all eight provinces in which they did the provincial police work renewed their contracts, each for a ten-year period. It was the first time renewals were made simultaneously, and the first time such long contract periods were negotiated. It not only assured the provinces of continuous service, but it allowed the Mounted Police to plan for their own needs until 1976.

On the credit side of the ledger during the 1950s and 1960s the Force noted continued public cooperation. This they have always classified as "the greatest single factor in the detection and apprehension of crime."

Alert citizens averted bank robberies. In Kamloops, British Columbia, a radio station and cooperative citizens helped to rescue an abducted man. Four observant Boy Scouts at summer camp at Châteauguay, Quebec, alerted the police to cattle smugglers, then helped to catch them. Information from the despondent husband of a pathetic drug addict led not only to her rehabilitation but to the arrest of six organized drug traffickers. But it seemed more than the police had a right to expect when a bootlegger cooperated by trying to peddle his wares at the home of a Mounted Policeman, and when a smuggler by mistake loaded an unmarked police car with contraband beer.

Along with the work and overwork, the debits and credits of the period, went the risks involved in the duties of the Force, and the extra voluntary risks taken by individual members. Almost every Annual Report and every *RCMP Quarterly* announced awards and commendations for bravery to men who were wounded by armed bandits or mentally disturbed persons, or who showed bravery during rescue from drowning, floods, burning buildings, gas-filled wells and so on.

When the superintendent of a gypsum quarry at Windermere, British Columbia, was buried under six feet of frozen gypsum rock in a cave-in, the surrounding rock wall threatened to collapse and bury the man and his four rescuers. Constable H.D. Bowyer, although coatless, threw himself spread-eagled against the frozen gypsum wall and stayed there for an hour and a half. Then, with the help of Corporal K.M. McHale and one of the other men, the superintendent was freed. Constable Bowyer later became seriously ill with pneumonia, but recovered.

Constable H.M.C. Johnstone of Maillardville detachment, British Columbia, sped to the scene of a bank robbery in response to an alarm given by the bank manager. As he entered the door he was felled by a bullet from the revolver of one of the three bandits in the bank. A second bandit immediately opened sustained fire at Johnstone as he lay on the floor. The constable returned the fire from where he lay. Then a third bandit ran from the back of the bank toward the front door, and fired several shots point-blank at the constable as he passed him.

Johnstone by now was suffering wounds in his right side, right chest, right forearm, left hip, left shoulder, left palm and left little finger. He had fired all his ammunition. Nevertheless he struggled to his feet and staggered after the two bandits who had fled outside. Then he collapsed on the pavement. They in turn collapsed on the pavement, one dead and one wounded from the shots the constable had fired while in the bank. Johnstone managed to sit up, and he covered them with his empty revolver. The third bandit now came out of the bank and meekly surrendered to the constable. The next day Johnstone was promoted to corporal. Eventually he returned to duty, but he never completely recovered from his wounds.

Two Mounted Policemen, one in Cape Breton and one in British Columbia, survived murder attempts by intoxicated Indians using axes. A third policeman on another reserve in British Columbia was shot through the heart by an Indian. His life was saved by an Indian youth, John Robertson, who, in spite of not being familiar with the operation of a car, drove the constable at high speed to New Westminster Hospital just in time for an emergency operation.

Other Mounted Policemen lost their lives on duty, thirty-three during the ten-year period from 1953-1963. Most of them were constables, but the group also included two corporals, a sergeant, a staff sergeant and an inspector. Causes of death varied: from the crash of an Air Division plane while searching in the mountains to drowning when a patrol boat capsized; from a private airplane striking a patrol car to "shot and killed by an Eskimo"; from "died of exposure when car became stuck in snowbank" in mid-winter on the Saskatchewan prairie to "died from carbon-monoxide poisoning on board boat" in the far North.

In November, 1966, Constable G.D. Pearson of Edmonton detachment, twenty-three years old and married less than three months, was shot and killed when he answered a call to stop a fight in a highway cafe.

In June the following year two corporals, also in Alberta, responded to a telephone call from a man in Grande Prairie who said he had just murdered his common-law wife and wanted to give himself up. As the two policemen entered the yard, a shot rang out. Corporal D.A. Harvey dropped dead, shot through the chest by a man hidden at an upstairs window.

The risk of death, like the probability of overwork, is not uncommon in the service of the Royal Canadian Mounted Police.

Chapter 24
The Problem of Drugs
1959–1966

Year after year throughout the 1950s Commissioner Nicholson had reported a serious increase in drug trafficking. The drug trade continued into the 1960s. The Mafia and other organized criminals in Canada and abroad were still deeply involved, although the Mafia was reportedly withdrawing since the United States in 1956 made jail sentences mandatory for trafficking in narcotics.

In spite of Mafia agreement at the Apalachin meeting in 1957 that they would withdraw, the enormous profits and quick turnover tempted the younger men to continue to deal in narcotics, not only at home but also in Canada and elsewhere. They limited their activity to the whole-sale level so as to keep away from the risky business of selling locally in sub-wholesale or lesser lots. But in any case, where one trafficker withdrew, others moved forward to fill the gap. In 1966 the illicit drug trade was still flourishing.

The Mounted Police, like all other police, have difficulty investigating drug trafficking. For one thing, few if any persons involved, not even defrauded buyers, ever make complaints to the police. Also, even when the police have a "lead," scarcely anyone will cooperate by giving further information. Hence the only way the police can investigate successfully is through the use of informants (most of them paid), or by the police themselves acting as undercover agents.

In his *RCMP Quarterly* article "Undercover Agent," Constable J.C. Hunt from the Kootenay area of British Columbia explained how he carried out a special assignment from March to July, 1962. Incognito, from a downtown hotel in Vancouver, he was to gather information and make purchases of drugs in connection with the Food and Drugs Act and the Narcotic Control Act.

Hunt learned the methods and the jargon of the underworld. He no longer shaved or had his hair cut. He stooped slightly, walked with a limp, dressed in shabby clothes, and tried to look "as forlorn as the lowest element on Skid Row." He adopted the role of "goof-ball" and heroin addict, fresh from the east coast, and completely "wired up" (addicted). Rumours soon spread that he was a "goner."

"Goof-balls" or "bombers," incidentally, like amphetamines, barbiturates and their derivatives, are controlled drugs. Not only can they induce intoxication and erratic behaviour, but according to the records of the Vancouver coroner's office, thirty-one deaths in 1962 were attributed to barbiturates alone.

Constable Hunt gradually wormed his way into drug circles in the east end of Vancouver, and eventually a "pusher" sold him two bombers for a dollar. Now the pushers referred to him as "the fellow wired up on goof-balls," and he found it easier to purchase drugs. Sometimes he took a bus from his flophouse to Skid Row, mingled with heroin pushers and addicts, made unsuspecting "friends," and learned the latest events about traffickers and the flow of heroin. At other times he revisited the east end, lolling around beer parlours and restaurants with his original drug circle "friends," and buying "goof-balls" from time to time.

After several months the Force decided that Hunt should try to purchase heroin from the Skid Row traffickers. He tried to live the part of a heroin addict, adopting the characteristic "nervous hands and shifty, suspicious outlook," always looking as miserable, ill and dejected as possible. The traffickers would not sell heroin unless the buyers were well known to them. But Hunt was able to obtain "character references" from his east end goof-ball friends who were known to the traffickers on Skid Row. He made purchases of heroin till the end of July.

Early in August the Vancouver drug squad, which had supervised Hunt during the whole period, moved in to arrest forty-two persons. They were charged with violations under the Food and Drugs Act and the Narcotic Control Act. Twenty traffickers were convicted and sentenced to long prison terms.

Not only the sentences testified that Constable Hunt had done a good job. During the trials one of his "friends" pleaded not guilty; then on hearing Crown evidence he changed his mind. Staring at the undercover agent he said, "Anyone would have taken pity on Hunt. The way he looked, I thought he was a sick, sick addict."

No matter what methods the Mounted Police used to combat the drug traffic, they had neither the manpower nor the resources to halt it. Even so, they kept trying.

In 1959 the Mounted Police and the U.S. Bureau of Narcotics put the main supplier of narcotics to eastern Canada and the United States, Giuseppe Cotroni of Montreal, out of business through a ten-year jail term. In 1960 the Force seized ninety-one ounces of heroin, the largest amount taken to that date by the police of western Canada, from Edward Sawicki, a major trafficker in the Vancouver area. He was sentenced to fourteen years in the penitentiary. In 1961, with a member of the U.S. Bureau of Narcotics acting as undercover agent and with Windsor city police cooperating, the Force led another successful investigation. It removed Nicholas Cicchini, a major Canadian trafficker and organization man, from both drug trafficking and counterfeiting.

Usually the trafficking in heroin took place in large cities. But as the police arrested more and more principals there, others tried to avoid arrest by making their deliveries in rural areas.

One afternoon in June, 1962, a farmer and his fifteen-year-old son were repairing fences along a side road in West Flamborough township near Hamilton, Ontario. About three o'clock a car drove up. It stopped in line with a large pine tree, and the driver got out and threw something in the ditch. The farmer remonstrated about his throwing garbage along the road, but the man merely drove away. Half an hour later the boy was driving his father's tractor past the same place. Curious, he stopped to look in the ditch. There he found a cellophane package of eight small envelopes, each containing an ounce of white powder.

Later that afternoon the package was turned over to an Ontario Provincial Police constable from nearby Waterdown. He telephoned the Mounted Police detachment at Hamilton. By 6:30 P.M., two members of the Narcotic Squad were in the Waterdown office, making a field test of the powder. It proved to be heroin, the eight ounces worth thousands of dollars on the illegal market.

Now the three police drove to the farm, hoping to replace the important cache before anyone arrived to pick it up. With the boy directing them, at 8:40 P.M. they returned the package to its original position in front of the pine tree. By this time more Mounted Police had arrived from Hamilton with binoculars and other equipment. Two constables hid themselves in a swamp across the road, while two other policemen concealed their radio car in a nearby farmyard. Two others drove away to get more men and cars to cover the area.

At 9:01 P.M. a 1961 Cadillac with American licence plates drove up and stopped abruptly between the concealed policemen and the cache. The policemen heard the car door open and close, then footsteps receded across the road. After about twenty seconds they moved toward the car, where one man sat in the driver's seat. Another man was crossing the highway, carrying the package of heroin. The police arrested both men.

Joseph Augello and Michael Tascarella, both of Buffalo, claimed that they were only out driving. Answering a "call of nature," they had turned into the side road, and Tascarella had accidentally found the package. However, as the Mounted Police learned by phoning the American authorities, Tascarella was suspected of activity in the illicit drug traffic in Buffalo, and he had a long criminal record.

Later, during the trial, the Crown presented evidence that the seized heroin was seventy-eight percent pure. The eight ounces could easily be adulterated to twenty-four ounces, which could fill 10,000 capsules worth six dollars each, for a total value of $60,000. The two traffickers pleaded not guilty, but the jury found them guilty. The judge called them "merchants of misery," and sentenced each to fifteen years in jail.

Successful drug investigations continued year after year. In 1963 the Force broke up a heroin syndicate of five persons headed by Charles Cipolla of Guelph, Ontario, which supplied the Toronto and Hamilton market. Cipolla was sentenced to twenty years' imprisonment, three others to fifteen years each, and the other member to five. In 1964, after Cipolla's imprisonment had disrupted Toronto's supply of heroin, a licenced pharmacist with part-ownership in four prosperous discount drug stores helped fill the gap. He and his wife diverted heroin and morphine from legal sources. The Toronto drug squad got them, too.

Also in 1964, the Montreal drug squad arrested the men who supplied Vancouver with its best-quality white heroin, completely cutting off Vancouver's supply. Chinese in Vancouver offered poorer quality heroin from Hong Kong as a substitute, and the Vancouver drug squad put them out of business.

But always other traffickers kept the lucrative business going. This created more heroin addicts, which in turn made the illicit enterprise still more profitable. Police records indicated the alarming rate of increase by the number of new heroin addicts they detected each year. The known increase climbed from thirty in 1962, through 56, 70, 197, to 203 in 1966, and still the police did not know of all the addicts. The number of known criminal addicts rose from 2,792 in 1957 to 3,182 in 1966. The occurrence of these addicts in Canada in 1966 was about sixteen per 100,000 of population. But Vancouver had about half the known addicts, hence the ratio there was much higher.

It seemed that anyone who wanted to make a quick and substantial profit could join the narcotic trafficking. The enterprising assortment included a Uruguayan diplomat, several members of the Greek community in Montreal, and a Belgian citizen attending a chiropractic college in Toronto. Police believed the Belgian was the major distributor

255

of narcotics to Toronto's Yorkville Village. Crew members of Air France carried sixty-two pounds of heroin to Montreal. But none of these managed to evade arrest.

Neither did the west coast criminal addict who swallowed his complete "outfit"—glass eyedropper barrel, hypodermic needle and rubber bulb— in an attempt to outwit the police. An x-ray showed the eyedropper barrel in his stomach, and the other articles in his lower bowel. Authorities at the Okalla Prison Farm in British Columbia stated later that he had "successfully passed the articles without injurious effect."

Some cases indicated to what lengths organized criminals would go to keep others from testifying against them. In December, 1965, drug squad men in Vancouver arrested a retired doctor, his common-law wife and a second man for trafficking in heroin. The following March while Dr. R.H. MacLaughlin and Margaret Ann Cunningham awaited trial, they were murdered. Investigators reported that the murders had the appearance of gangland slayings that were carried out to prevent the victims from testifying against other principals in a well-organized crime syndicate. Police learned later that MacLaughlin had travelled to the Near and Far East as a courier for the syndicate.

By the end of 1965 the most serious problem of the police was no longer the use of such "hard" drugs as heroin but the use of so-called "soft" drugs. In fact, the increasing use of marijuana by young persons constituted the greatest law-enforcement problem in the history of the Force. The police had no choice but to enforce the law by arresting users and traffickers. But when they did so, they were bitterly accused of lack of understanding and of "police brutality" by the involved young people, by parents, and by others who refused to believe that there was anything wrong with the use of soft drugs. Moreover, the police were blamed because their prosecutions under the Narcotic Control Act of young people found in possession of marijuana resulted in those young people acquiring criminal records. As the critics pointed out, marijuana was not a narcotic.

The police knew this. But it had never been removed from the drug schedule of the Act which Canada had passed in accord with an international convention signed many years earlier. As long as the law existed the police had no choice but to enforce it. Yet the Force had never in all its history been so criticized for enforcing an unpopular law. Press and television coverage distorted the police role by playing up only the sensational aspects of the news they covered. The federal government grew so disturbed at the situation that the minister of Justice authorized the courts to disregard the punishment in the Act and to impose small fines and suspended sentences on charges of mere posses-sion. Nevertheless, any conviction established a criminal record, and criticism continued.

The use of LSD (Lysergic Acid Diethylamide) increased without hindrance. In the absence at that time of any law regarding its use, the police could only observe and report its use to the Food and Drug Directorate. Paradoxically, they could arrest sellers, as the uncontrolled sale of the drug was illegal.

As young persons disregarded the law related to the use of marijuana, they simultaneously promoted among themselves an illegal traffic in drugs. This traffic was then exploited by criminal traffickers whose principal motive was profit, and drug usage increased. During 1966, 398 persons were charged for offences relating to marijuana, as compared with seventy-eight in 1964. One of these was Paul Bois, a medical student who had nine pounds of marijuana and seventy-five capsules of LSD hidden in the garage in which police found him and four other young persons smoking marijuana. Two men deeply involved in the international trafficking of marijuana were Siddique Ashraf and Mahammed Ashraf, Pakistani nationals living in Toronto. They smuggled hashish (a concentrated drug from the marijuana plant) from tribal territory adjoining Pakistan into Canada in the form of "plates" stitched inside polo saddles. These two men admitted that they had complete control of the illicit marijuana traffic in the British Isles and Europe. They said that their aim was to gain control of the hashish and heroin traffic in Canada and the United States.

The abuse of soft drugs became so widespread that the Mounted Police encountered a new problem. Up to this time, drug work in places other than Canada's largest cities had been done by plainclothes men of the regular Criminal Investigation squads. Now the police had to begin establishing, in smaller cities, special drug squads similar to those already working in Vancouver, Edmonton, Calgary, Winnipeg, Toronto and Montreal. This removed men from other types of criminal investigation, so that other work now suffered. Similarly, the "soft" drug work took policemen from "hard" drug work, and trafficking in heroin increased.

On the whole the Force controlled trafficking in hard drugs reason-ably well, but the abuse of soft drugs ran wild. Even when other police forces became alarmed and undertook to increase their assistance to the Mounted Police in the enforcement of the drug laws, which was solely a federal responsibility, their combined efforts could not prevent increased trafficking in and use of illicit soft drugs.

Commissioner McClellan appealed to society in general. "The

epidemic increase in the use of marijuana and LSD indicates that their control cannot be left to the police alone ... but calls for the earnest attention of government at every level, social workers, the medical profession, the educators and the Canadian community as a whole."

But the uncoordinated efforts of various groups had little effect on the deeply entrenched drug problem. The abuse of drugs, both soft and hard, increased. More soft-drug users tried to escape from reality and some of them turned to hard drugs in the process. More addicts needed more drugs to sustain the habit. More traffickers pushed more drugs as they sought exorbitant profits. And more people criticized the Royal Canadian Mounted Police for its enforcement of the drug laws. As for the police themselves, they had every indication that the situation would grow worse before it would grow better.

Chapter 25
Uniting against Organized Crime
1959–1966

O ne aspect of organized crime which was in no way connected with drugs or with the criminal gangsters in Canada or the United States came to the attention of the Royal Canadian Mounted Police toward the end of 1959. It concerned illegal immigrants from China, coming to Canada by way of Hong Kong.

As the Mounted Police had pointed out for years, the Canadian government's immigration policy was lax in many ways. For instance, no system of visa control under Mounted Police supervision was maintained in the Far East and in South East Asia because the government paid less attention to the danger of undesirable immigration from those areas than from Europe. The time came when the Department of Citizenship and Immigration suspected that many Chinese immigrants were fraudulently entering the country. They asked the Force to investigate.

The Mounted Police set up a special team, later known as the Passport and Visa Fraud Section, to study immigration files in Ottawa. From files selected at random this team found evidence of misrepresentation on the part of hundreds of Chinese persons who had entered Canada. Their estimate for the past ten years was about 11,000.

This revelation disturbed the Force, and the Security and Intelligence Directorate in particular. They realized that the laxity of government policy was an open invitation to Communist Chinese intelligence agencies to mingle their own agents with the ordinary Chinese who entered Canada illegally. These spies could then settle down and apparently become good citizens. Later, if Canada recognized China and the Chinese established an embassy here, Chinese intelligence agents would already be in the country to form the basis of an intelligence network.

A further possibility disturbed the police. They knew that once Chinese intelligence agents got into Canada, they could cross the border and similarly infiltrate the United States. They would not have to wait for the establishing of diplomatic relations with the United States before setting up an espionage system there. As soon as the United Nations accepted China as a member, the Chinese intelligence service could use the United Nations headquarters in New York as a base from which to direct their agents already in the United States.

The Mounted Police hoped that the Canadian government would adopt a policy aimed at deporting the illegal Chinese immigrants. Instead, the government set up an adjustment statement program. This allowed the illegal entrants voluntarily to admit their offences without penalty, and to remain in Canada if they then applied in the normal way for immigrant status.

Since it was obviously futile for the Mounted Police to make an all-out drive against potential spies, they now tried to stem the flow of illegal immigrants. With the cooperation of the Department of Citizenship and Immigration, the Fraud Section concentrated on exposing the leaders who were assisting the illegal immigrants. During the first year of investigation, members of the Fraud Section arrested sixteen principal agents on the west coast and charged them with a total of seventy-nine offences ranging from forgery, uttering, aiding and abetting, and perjury to conspiracy. In the same period they also located several hundred illegal immigrants and referred them to Citizenship and Immigration for adjustment of status.

Other members of the Force went to Hong Kong to investigate the flow of illegal immigration from its Asian source. Of course they had no jurisdiction there, but they received assistance from the Hong Kong police. Later the Force arranged for the Hong Kong police to send to Canada a group of their own men, bilingual in Chinese and English. The Mounted Police swore them in as special constables engaged as translators and interpreters. This cooperation to combat what by this time had become the "Chinese immigration scandal" resulted in the laying of charges against an additional thirty principal agents in Canada. It also led to the discovery of many instances of income tax evasion, fraudulent passport applications, and other related offences.

By March, 1963, the police had the situation sufficiently under control to allow the Chinese special constables to return to Hong Kong. But fraudulent entries of Chinese immigrants remained a problem. By now the Force also had a new crime to investigate. In spite of the adjustment statement program, some Chinese already in Canada persisted in supplying false statements to the Department of Citizenship and Immigration. During the year ending March, 1963, the Mounted Police had prosecuted twenty-three such cases, and still the offences continued.

The illegal entry of persons of ethnic groups other than Chinese also posed a problem, although no other group had as well-organized a system as the Chinese. Some travel agents in Canada and some organizations in Italy conspired to allow an unknown number of illegal Italian immigrants into Canada. In addition, ships' deserters entered the country illegally, although these entries were unorganized.

Also during this period, the illegal entry of organized criminals from the United States and Europe continued to be a serious problem in spite of Mounted Police cooperation with foreign law-enforcement agencies. These and other organized criminal activities kept the police busy investigating many kinds of crimes.

In 1959 a large theft-ring was stealing late-model cars in the eastern United States and smuggling them into Ontario. Sometimes the criminals rented Cadillacs and other expensive cars from U-Drive companies in the United States and drove them across the border. There other members of the ring stole bills-of-sale from legitimate firms, and the bills were completed to fit the stolen cars. Then the criminals registered the stolen cars as if they were their rightful property, and were all set to make what seemed legitimate sales. In 1962 the Mounted Police put out of operation a large car-theft and car-smuggling ring operating between the eastern United States and Quebec, and, in 1964, one operating between the northwestern United States and Alberta.

Other organized criminals preferred to traffic in jewellery, watches and furs. The Force's Preventive Service in Toronto and the Metropolitan Toronto police cooperated during 1963 on a big investigation that culminated in the seizure of uncut diamonds and jewellery worth half a million dollars, some of which had been stolen from Quebec and some from New York and Antwerp. This huge seizure led to the break-up of a Toronto ring of organized criminals handling and disposing of stolen valuables.

In a separate investigation in Toronto the same year, Mounted Police arrested an American citizen in possession of more than $72,000 worth of stolen diamonds and jewellery. Later they also seized an additional $35,000 of stolen jewellery and furs which the same man had brought into Canada. Also during 1963 the Force entered an investigation already begun by the Toronto police. This led to the break-up of a jewellery theft-disposal-fraud ring in which the value of the stolen goods was estimated to be as high as $7,000,000.

Two men and a woman organized a system of travelling from Australia to Asia and then to Europe, where they purchased watches and jewellery which they subsequently smuggled into Canada for resale. But in 1964 members of the Mounted Police Preventive Service in Winnipeg seized about $10,000 worth of both these items, and later the Preventive Service in Montreal seized jewellery worth about $60,000. The three criminals were fined a total of $1,100, which might or might not have been enough to dissuade them from similar schemes in the future. No doubt the judge took into account the fact that the seized goods, smuggled commercially, were also forfeit.

In 1965 two orientals set themselves up as partners in a newly formed import company in Vancouver. Then they smuggled in jade figurines, statues and snuff bottles. Information from the Vancouver city police alerted the Force, and its Vancouver Preventive Service seized the jade goods valued at $13,000. The Mounted Police in turn alerted the United States Treasury Department, after which customs agents in New York and Los Angeles seized similar items valued at $15,000. Another organized crime business was inoperable, at least temporarily.

One American case during the sixties led to the harshest criticism ever aimed at the Force. In October, 1963, American authorities notified the Mounted Police that they had arrested Joseph Michel Caron in Laredo, Texas, and had seized seventy-six pounds of heroin which he was bringing in from Mexico. Caron, a Canadian, was acting as a courier for the notorious Quebec criminal, Lucien Rivard. The United States laid charges of importing narcotics against Rivard and asked the Canadian government to extradite him. The Mounted Police arrested him in mid-June, 1964, and he was held in Bordeaux Jail, Montreal, awaiting extradition proceedings through the Quebec courts.

The United States government engaged the Montreal lawyer Pierre Lamontagne, who also acted as Crown prosecutor for the Mounted Police drug cases, to represent them. Rivard applied for bail. Lamontagne protested that Rivard would break his bail bond and flee. So Rivard was refused bail.

About a month later Lamontagne was offered a bribe of $20,000 if he would stop objecting to Rivard's application for bail. The actual offer was made by Raymond Denis, executive assistant to the minister of Citizenship and Immigration in the Liberal government. But Denis was acting on behalf of Guy Masson, a political organizer of the Liberal party, who had been told that if Rivard was not extradited the Liberal party chest would be given $60,000. Masson in turn was acting for other persons, including Mrs. Rivard, in whose Royal Trust account the $60,000 lay waiting.

Lamontagne did not accept the bribe. But he did not immediately report the attempt to the police either. During the next few weeks Denis and others pestered him to withdraw his objections to bail for Rivard. Three of them were, like Denis, Liberal party men: Guy Rouleau, Liberal member of Parliament and parliamentary assistant to Prime Minister Lester B. Pearson; André Letendre, executive assistant to the minister of Justice; and Guy Lord, special assistant to the minister of Justice. At last Lamontagne found the pressure too great. On August 10, twenty-six days after the first approach, he reported the events to the Mounted Police in Montreal who reported it to headquarters at Ottawa.

The Force began at once to investigate the allegations of attempted bribery. But they were not able to ascertain all the facts because the only person involved who was willing to tell them the truth was Lamontagne. By September 18 they had not been able to obtain corroborating evidence of Lamontagne's accusation against Denis. So the minister of Justice, Guy Favreau, who had personally read the police file, told Commissioner McClellan that he believed there were no grounds for a criminal charge against Denis. On Favreau's instructions, the police closed the file.

That would probably have been the end of the affair, except that some Opposition members learned about it. In the House of Commons on November 23 they questioned the minister of Justice about the Lamontagne affair and its implications of corruption in government. Erik Nielsen charged specifically that Raymond Denis, while executive assistant to the minister of Citizenship and Immigration, had offered Pierre Lamontagne a bribe of $20,000 for his cooperation in not opposing bail for Rivard. Two days later the harried minority Liberal government appointed a Royal Commission of Inquiry, headed by Chief Justice Frédéric Dorion of the Supreme Court of Quebec.

Before the report was published, the Force received bitter but unjust criticism. They were blamed because Rivard had escaped from Bordeaux Jail on March 2, 1965. He had scaled the prison wall by throwing a water hose over it after being given permission to flood an outdoor skating rink—in forty-degree weather. Critics of the Force overlooked the fact that Quebec's jails are a provincial responsibility, and that the Mounted Police have nothing to do with their security.

Then the Dorion report, published in late June, harshly criticized both the minister of Justice and the Mounted Police. Chief Justice Dorion wrote that he had no doubt that Denis had offered Lamontagne a bribe, and that Favreau should not have ordered the case closed without obtaining the usual legal advice from his own department. He stated that the Mounted Police had mismanaged the investigation, had prolonged it so unnecessarily that the witnesses had been able to confer with one another, and had placed restrictions on the work of the investigating officer.

It was true that the investigation had not been conducted with the usual Mounted Police efficiency. But that was because this investigation was unique. It involved the office of the minister of Justice, and so it was not directed and controlled at field level but from Ottawa headquarters. This restricted the freedom of the investigators, and created delay in receiving reports and issuing further instructions.

The chief justice also blamed the police for concluding the investigation prematurely. But Commissioner McClellan's advice to the minister on September 18 was sound, for at that time there was no corroborating evidence of Lamontagne's accusation. Furthermore, his delay of twenty-six days in reporting the matter to the police, in McClellan's opinion, "destroyed his credibility as a witness."

The most regrettable feature of the Dorion report, from the police point of view, was Dorion's assumption that police investigators could have discovered the truth as exactly as he did. Many of the persons involved had lied to the police or had refused to talk to them, and nothing in Canadian law prohibits this. But Chief Justice Dorion interviewed those same persons under oath, and had the help of twenty-five lawyers to cross-examine them. And even so, several were convicted later of perjuring themselves during his Royal Commission of Inquiry.

The chief justice's most severe criticism concerned the Force's lack of fluency in French. It was not justified. The investigation was directed by a French-speaking member, Deputy Commissioner J.R. Lemieux, who dealt with the French Canadian minister of Justice. The officer in charge of the investigation was French-speaking Inspector J.P. Drapeau, and three of the other four investigators were also French Canadians. It is true that the reports written by the French Canadians were in English and were processed by English-speaking members at Ottawa headquarters. But this was the routine of a Force doing eighty-five percent of its work in English-speaking areas of Canada and using a single language for rapid communication.

In any event, Chief Justice Dorion's criticism concerned only the manner in which the Force had handled this one case. Although he said the police were "human beings who cannot claim to be infallible and who sometimes commit errors," he also described the Mounted Police as "this police force whose efficiency is beyond question."

The Rivard and Lamontagne affairs and the Dorion Report were an important lesson to the Force. In the future the police would investigate cases that involved politicians and persons with political connections exactly as they would any other cases. No politician, any more than any ordinary citizen, would be allowed to know details of an investigation until it was completed. Even then, the decision about prosecution would be made by the departmental officials who normally held that responsibility.

A few weeks after publication of the Dorion report, the Mounted Police recaptured Rivard in a summer cottage near Montreal. Later, in Texas, he was sentenced to twenty years' imprisonment plus a fine of $20,000. Thereafter Montreal ceased to be the North American centre for the supply of heroin.

Raymond Denis was found guilty of having offered a bribe and of conspiracy, and was sentenced to two years in jail. André Letendre automatically lost his government position when Favreau resigned. Guy Lord had already left the government before the Dorion inquiry. Guy Rouleau resigned, first his government position and then his seat in Parliament. Guy Favreau, because of extenuating circumstances, became president of the Privy Council one week after his resignation as minister of Justice. And the system of fund-raising for the Liberal party, basically the cause of the whole trouble, was changed.

About the same time as the Rivard-Denis scandal, several other Mounted Police cases were made public. These too linked politicians and criminals, and they heaped more embarrassment on the minority Liberal government. One concerned Onofrio Minaudo of Windsor, Ontario, a suspected member of the Mafia. He had been ordered deported in February, 1961, because of convictions in Italy for murder, armed robbery and double murder. His departure had been delayed until March, 1964, mainly because three politicians had pleaded for him over the years. Two were D.F. Brown, Liberal member of Parliament for Windsor, and Richard Thrasher, one-time Conservative member in the Windsor area. The third was Paul Martin, a Liberal cabinet minister and Secretary of State for External Affairs.

Another case linked Yvon Dupuis, Liberal minister without portfolio, with an alleged gift of $10,000 to help a racetrack syndicate obtain an operating licence. Dupuis resigned under great pressure from Prime Minister Pearson. Later he was prosecuted and convicted, although on appeal the conviction was quashed.

A third case concerned Harry Stonehill, a wealthy businessman who had been deported from the Philippines and later ordered out of Mexico. In June, 1963, from British Columbia where he had invested some money, Stonehill applied for landed immigrant status, but his background was against him. He sent a man to Ottawa to appeal. When this man met Raymond Denis, executive assistant to the minister of Citizenship and Immigration, Denis asked him if Stonehill had thought of investing $25,000 or $30,000 in "us." At the Dorion inquiry Denis explained that he had been joking. But the records of Citizenship and Immigration showed that the Liberal party treasurer wished to be kept advised of the outcome of Stonehill's appeal. In any case, Stonehill left Canada in January, 1965.

Later that year Commissioner McClellan told the government that only immediate coordinated police action would prevent organized crime from becoming as entrenched in Canada as it was in the United States. He pointed out that experience across the border had shown that corruption of politicians was a prerequisite for the success of that type of crime. Prime Minister Pearson was in a very receptive mood.

In January, 1966, at McClellan's suggestion, the Liberal government called a federal-provincial conference of attorneys general on organized crime. The delegates agreed that the five point program presented by the Force should be implemented as soon as possible. The Force itself would implement the four principal points. One, they would expand their Crime Intelligence Service. Two, they would improve the National Police Services by such things as the introduction of wire-photo services and a stolen automobile bureau, and by more modern and bilingual data-handling methods. Three, they would extend and improve their national telecommunications network. Four, they undertook to train experienced officers of any Canadian police force in fighting organized crime, and to establish and administer a new bilingual Canadian Police College for senior federal, provincial and municipal policemen.

Other important achievements grew out of that January conference. The Special Investigation Branch of the Department of Citizenship and Immigration was expanded to help prevent the admission of alien criminals into Canada. And Solicitor General Lawrence Pennell, whose ministry had succeeded the ministry of Justice in direct supervision of the Force, announced the federal government's authorization of $40,000,000 for a national crime computer as an extension of the National Police Services.

During the summer of 1966 the Mounted Police and others attended a second federal-provincial conference. This one aimed to combat financial crimes, especially frauds involving securities which caused the loss of millions of dollars by persons who had believed they were dealing with sound institutions. Now the Force agreed to set up a special national repository of information on securities frauds, to be available to all police and to provincial securities commissions. The Force also agreed to establish, in all major cities from Halifax to Vancouver, securities fraud squads made up of its own lawyers, accountants, and experienced criminal investigators. From their inception in 1966 these squads worked to coordinate the investigations of securities crimes in all parts of Canada and in other countries when necessary.

At last law-enforcement bodies could attack all facets of organized crime in a concerted way, not as independent organizations concerned with local problems but as a united national front.

Chapter 26
Spies, Politics and Security
1952 – 1969

During 1966, while Commissioner McClellan was still in office, the federal government appointed three Royal Commissions, all dealing with security. Two of the three cases dealt with individuals whose illegal activities the Royal Canadian Mounted Police had observed for several years. The third placed the Force itself on trial.

The first Royal Commission was appointed, ironically, to look into complaints made by George Victor Spencer, whom men of the Security and Intelligence Directorate had consistently observed spying for the Soviet Union. Spencer, an employee of the post office in Vancouver, had subsequently been dismissed. He was not prosecuted, mainly because the information he sold to the Russians was not secret. But the government would not allow him to receive a pension, and instead returned what he had paid into the fund. Spencer protested this as very unfair.

Prime Minister Pearson pointed out to the House of Commons that two of the Soviet Embassy staff had been expelled from Canada for espionage (one of these concerned another case) and that an unnamed Canadian civil servant, although guilty, was gravely ill and would not be prosecuted. But in November, 1965, Spencer, who had been treated for lung cancer, and who was obviously sick and weary, identified himself to a Vancouver reporter.

Now both the minority Liberal government and the police were bitterly attacked in the House of Commons, in the press, and by civil-rights organizations. Various critics demanded a full inquiry into the case of this seriously ill man who had been denied his pension and also the right to clear himself of the charge of spying. The Mounted Police were indignantly accused of having "grilled" him during the period in which he had had an operation and cobalt treatments for cancer.

In the middle of a heated debate in Parliament on Friday, March 4, 1966, Prime Minister Pearson suddenly announced that he himself would telephone Spencer to ask if he would like an inquiry into the manner of his dismissal. On Monday, March 7, Pearson told the House of Commons that he had telephoned Spencer, and that as a result he had appointed a Royal Commission of Inquiry into Spencer's complaint.

The facts revealed before Commissioner Mr. Justice D.C. Wells and covered in his report dated July, 1966, indicated, among other things, that Spencer had been fairly treated and that his activities on behalf of the Soviet Union were a classic example of Russian espionage at work.

George Victor Spencer, born in England but living in British Columbia since the age of three, had become a member of the Communist party during the depression years. After the war he was expelled from the party, which was then known as the Labour-Progressive Party, because of arguments with other members. His repeated attempts to rejoin were rejected, but he became a member of the Canadian-Soviet Friendship Society. Meanwhile he became a part-time worker with the post office. In July, 1949, he became a permanent member of the staff at the Vancouver city post office. As a civil servant he then signed the oath of allegiance and oath of office and secrecy.

In 1956, when Russian freighters went to Vancouver to load wheat, the Canadian-Soviet Friendship Society was invited to visit the ships. In this way Spencer met Youri S. Afanasiev, then commercial attaché of the Soviet Embassy in Ottawa. They met several times and discussed Spencer's long-standing urge to visit the Soviet Union.

For several years Spencer heard nothing from the Russians. Then, according to his statement, which he gave in Vancouver to Sergeant Maurice Low and Constable K. Dane, and which was entered as an exhibit at the Royal Commission, he received an anonymous telephone call. As a result he went to the corner of Main and Broadway and was met by a man who said he was from the Russian Embassy in Ottawa. Without giving his name, the man asked Spencer to fly to Ottawa "to discuss exchanges of a cultural nature." Spencer agreed and soon afterwards did so, using his mother's maiden name, MacNiel (sometimes spelled MacNeil).

This first meeting took place on Saturday, October 8, 1960, in Spencer's motel room in Ottawa, with the man from the corner of Main and Broadway present, still unnamed. A second unnamed man was also there. Spencer said later that he looked like a photo which the Mounted Police identified as one of Lev Burdiukov, an intelligence agent.

At this first meeting, according to Spencer's statement, the Russians asked him for all possible detailed information on ethnic groups and their members, and general information about British Columbia. The Russians set a date for the next meeting, and a plan for all future meetings. Each would be on a Saturday, at 7:00 P.M., in a motel on the outskirts of Ottawa. They also set up a code for writing letters about future meetings. Burdiukov would write that "there will be a film available to show" on a certain date. Spencer would reply that "we can" or "we cannot" show it. Letters to Spencer would carry his own name and his actual address, but would contain only the bare message. Spencer would reply to "The Film Editor of the Soviet Embassy," but would not include his own name or any return address.

At this point in his statement Spencer explained that all he wanted was a free trip to Russia. But, as Mr. Justice Wells said later, the system of signals indicated that he knew that he was doing or would in future do something wrong.

The police knew that Spencer was in contact with Russian intelligence. As the director of Security and Intelligence, Assistant Commissioner W.H. Kelly, told Mr. Wells, the police saw him contact Afanasiev while the Russian ships visited Vancouver. But they didn't pay much attention to the meeting on that festive occasion. Four years later, however, in Ottawa in October, 1960, they saw Spencer meet two other Russian intelligence officers, Lev Burdiukov and Rem Krassilnikov.

After that, the Security and Intelligence men kept Spencer under surveillance. They saw him meet Burdiukov for a second meeting on March 4, 1961, when, as he admitted later, he gave the Russians the requested information about ethnic groups, including Russian, Ukrainian, German and Chinese. As Kelly explained, Soviet intelligence wants information about the Russian and Ukrainian groups in this country because these are often anti-Soviet. Soviet intelligence agents then try to discredit them through character assassination, or to disrupt their meetings, or to blackmail individuals into working as spies by threatening to harm their relatives still living in "the old country."

Later the police observed Spencer meet Burdiukov for five other meetings, from August, 1961 to February, 1963. They also watched him perform various tasks for the Russians. They did not arrest him, however. For one thing, they knew he had no access to secret information. Also, by watching, they learned the Russian technique of handling agents. Perhaps most important, Spencer led the police directly to members of the Soviet Embassy who were in reality KGB men, and at the same time his actions gave the police exact knowledge of some of the Soviet "targets" in Canada. In effect, the Russians were unknowingly presenting the Security and Intelligence Directorate with such details of their espionage methods as could form the basis of a handbook on how to trap Soviet spies in the future.

The Mounted Police watched Spencer for about two years after his final Ottawa meeting, but apparently he was no longer keeping in touch with the Russians. So, early in 1965, they confronted the postal clerk with the facts of his espionage. He freely admitted what he had done and gave them a lengthy statement.

It was lucky for the police that they acted then. Although Spencer had been in good health during his espionage period, he now had an advanced case of lung cancer, and he died a month after the Royal Commission was appointed. As Mr. Justice Wells conducted the inquiry, Spencer's own statement of more than forty pages not only admitted what the police already knew but supplied many further details.

Some of Spencer's activities for the Russians seemed, on the surface, to be harmless. For instance, from tombstones in local cemeteries he collected names of the dead, each with birthdate and deathdate. He collected information about schools and apartment houses that had been burned or torn down, and about businesses, logging camps and machinery repair shops which had been discontinued or had gone bankrupt. He also gave the Russians pictures of clothing worn at different seasons in the Vancouver area, and descriptions of local customs.

Harry Rankin, the lawyer representing Spencer's interests, protested that Spencer had not broken any law, so these activities should not be held against him. But Kelly, who had been associated with Security and Intelligence work for more than ten years, disagreed.

Kelly explained how the Russians work. Before they smuggle their own men into another country, they set them up as "illegals" with complete biographies to allow them to pose as nationals of that country. Russian "illegals" smuggled into Canada are set up with false information: date of birth, schools they have attended in Canada, places where they have worked, apartments they have lived in, and so on. A name from a tombstone, with a suitable birthdate to tally with the approximate age of the "illegal," would allow that Russian to obtain from the provincial statistics department a duplicate birth certificate. This the "illegal" could then use as authentic. If the real person named had died, preferably at an early age, then there was almost no chance that the certificate would ever be questioned. And if the schools, places of employment and apartment houses named by the "illegal" no longer existed, authorities had no way of checking the authenticity of the "illegal's" documentation. Prior knowledge of Canadian clothing and customs would prevent the "illegal" from looking and behaving like the alien he actually was.

"Indeed," as Mr. Wells pointed out, "many of the Russian requests of Spencer could be used for documenting a foreign person as a Canadian for espionage purposes anywhere in the world."

Spencer did a very thorough job. He supplied a list of motels and hotels in British Columbia and also, he seemed to remember, a copy of a tourist accommodation book issued by the tourist board. For full information about schools before 1941, he secured details from the Vancouver school board. He gave Burdiukov his own driver's licence and got a duplicate for himself. He tried, on request, to get names of "card-carrying" railroad employees and of a reliable ex-party member who would presumably befriend any "illegals."

Spencer made, at his own suggestion, a trip along the Trans-Mountain Pipeline during his summer holiday of 1961. He drove from Vancouver to Prince George to Dawson Creek, then returned by a different route, taking pictures and movies along the way. He photographed oil refineries, something he thought was a pumping station, valleys, mountains, oil tanks, towns, bridges, highway scenes, hydro transformers, and so on. Later he gave the prints and negatives to the Russians.

Security and Intelligence men were not far behind Spencer on his pipeline trip. They tried to duplicate his pictures for possible use later as evidence against him. As Corporal K.E. Hollas told Mr. Justice Wells, information about the Trans-Mountain Pipeline, which supplies the west coast with oil and gasoline, would be invaluable to an enemy in wartime.

"In addition to the above," Spencer's statement continued, "I supplied general films of Vancouver . . . city road maps of Vancouver and district . . . five or six maps of the lower mainland as far as Chilliwack. These maps contained everything, showing boundaries, railways, harbours, airports, bridges, highways . . . the water system for Vancouver. . . . He [Spencer's Ottawa contact] was interested in the procedure for crossing the U.S.-Canada border and the forms required for emigrating to the U.S.A. I got some U.S. immigration forms at the U.S. Consulate. . . . "

Two of Spencer's assignments were to give the Russians information about service stations for sale in the Vancouver area, and of farms for sale in the southern part of British Columbia. The service stations, the Mounted Police believed, could be bought by "illegals" and used as bases for espionage. Farms close to the American border would be ideal "illegal residences" for the establishment of an espionage network covering the west coast of both Canada and the United States. As Mr. Wells commented, if the Russians themselves had tried to get the information which Spencer gathered for them, they would have been so conspicuous as to be immediately suspect.

Spencer's statement stressed that he thought he was not doing anything wrong, not even when he gave post office security information to "the man I think is Burdiukov in Ottawa." Yet as a civil servant he had sworn not to "disclose, or make known any matter or thing which comes to my knowledge by reason of that employment." He had, in fact, told the Russian all he knew about the inner workings of the post office: how inspectors checked for suspected "dope," stolen goods, raffle tickets, or sweepstake tickets; how fast the mail travelled; how the post office could check on any person's mail, but that no mail bag was ever checked without a definite order.

After this the two men agreed to test the post office. Spencer assured Burdiukov that a letter would not be stopped because a little corner was torn off a stamp, or because of any markings on the envelope flap. So the Russian sent test letters, which the postal clerk sent back unopened with special blots of ink on them or with a corner cut off a stamp. Nothing happened to the letters, so the Russians took Spencer's word that the postal system was safe for their purposes.

Toward the end of Spencer's statement he explained that after his seventh trip to Ottawa he had felt he would never be offered a free trip to Russia. He did not answer the Russians' next request for a meeting, and he heard no more from them. He declared that he had not accepted money from them, except for his actual expenses. But after disclosing his identity to the Vancouver reporter, he was interviewed on a television program which revealed pertinent facts. Mr. Wells examined the transcript and commented: "The truth probably is that he received somewhere between $3,200 and $6,800."

In early April, 1966, George Victor Spencer died "as a result of pulmonary thrombosis secondary to resection of the left lung." His lawyer insisted to the end of the inquiry that Spencer had done nothing wrong.

In the Royal Commission report dated July, 1966, Mr. Wells disagreed, on the grounds that a civil servant is in a special position. Not only should he observe his oath of allegiance and his oath of secrecy, but he could be expected to be more loyal and responsible than an ordinary citizen. Mr. Wells said that although he had the gravest doubts whether Spencer could have been successfully prosecuted for his offences "that does not mean that Spencer was not guilty of the grossest misconduct in his office." He reported that he believed that Spencer had been well aware that he was doing wrong, that during most of his dealings with the Russians he was perfectly healthy, and that although his subsequent lung cancer was a "pitiful condition," the government of Canada had treated him with "forbearance and fairness."

As for Spencer's treatment by the Mounted Police, Mr. Wells included in his report a letter which Spencer of his own accord had written and delivered to the Force's office in Vancouver in mid-January, 1966. It repeatedly denied any charges of "grilling" or "third-degree methods." Spencer concluded with this tribute: "The officers who spoke to me would qualify as nurses. If they had more schooling, they could be doctors, and contrary to what we often see on the TV they did not grill, shout or get mad, but treated me as a human being whose first job is to get well."

The second Royal Commission of 1966 was appointed after a battle of nerves in the House of Commons. This caused Lucien Cardin, the minister of Justice, to strike back at the Opposition leader John Diefenbaker. Cardin threatened to disclose a security scandal which had occurred while Diefenbaker was prime minister. So on March 14, exactly one week after the Spencer inquiry was set, Mr. Justice Wishart F. Spence was commissioned to inquire into "matters relating to one Gerda Munsinger."

Mr. Spence's report, made public about six months later, revealed sensational facts about Mrs. Munsinger and her associations a few years earlier with members of the Conservative government of that time. The German woman was a self-admitted espionage agent who had carried out several missions in Europe under the direction of a major in the Russian intelligence service. She also had a record of convictions as a prostitute, a petty thief and a smuggler. Yet she had been acquainted with several Cabinet ministers, and had even met Prime Minister Diefenbaker. The most significant fact, however, was that she had become involved in an intimate relationship with Pierre Sévigny a few weeks after his appointment as associate minister of Defence.

The Mounted Police had known of Mrs. Munsinger's background since 1952, through their visa control, whose European investigations had resulted in the government refusing Mrs. Munsinger's application for a visa. So in 1960, when the police were instructed to investigate her application for citizenship, they were surprised to learn that she was even in the country. What disturbed them most, however, was that their investigation disclosed Mrs. Munsinger's intimacy with the associate minister of Defence. Also, as the Spence report indicated later, Sévigny was trying to facilitate Mrs. Munsinger's citizenship application in spite of police information against her.

Commissioner Harvison and Deputy Commissioner McClellan briefed the minister of Justice, Davie Fulton, on the possible danger of the situation. Mrs. Munsinger, they explained, might still be working for the Russians. In any case, she was a likely subject for re-recruitment. Also, her known association with Sévigny in Montreal made both of them vulnerable to blackmail by the Montreal underworld.

Fulton in turn alerted Prime Minister Diefenbaker, who told Fulton later that no breach of security had yet occurred and that he had ordered Sévigny to stop associating with Mrs. Munsinger. And that, from Diefenbaker's point of view, seemed to be the end of the matter. Actually, however, the relationship between the cabinet minister and the former spy continued, and so did the danger.

The Force continued to investigate and to report back to their minister of Justice until Mrs. Munsinger left Canada for Germany in February, 1961. The danger remained that Sévigny might be black-mailed, but the police had no power to investigate his activities further without definite instructions from their minister or his department. Fulton never gave those instructions. Neither did his successor Donald Fleming, whom Harvison and McClellan also briefed about the affair. So Sévigny remained associate minister, and acting minister of Defence in the absence of the minister, until February, 1963, when he resigned.

The Munsinger-Sévigny affair, like most security investigations, would normally never have come to the public's attention. Even Lucien Cardin, minister of Justice in another government several years later, would probably never have known about it. Security files, like those of other investigations, are held by the Mounted Police, not by the Department of Justice. They can be seen, on request, but they are not automatically shown to a succeeding government.

After the Liberal embarrassment over the Rivard-Denis affair, however, Prime Minister Pearson had asked Commissioner McClellan if he had any files indicating anything scandalous about any member of any political party over the past ten years. McClellan had mentioned the Munsinger file. Mr. Pearson read it, and apparently some other Liberals had also learned of its contents.

Mr. Justice Spence's report stressed that although no actual breach of security had occurred in the Munsinger case, the risk was very real. He found it "startling" that Diefenbaker had made the personal and private decision to leave Sévigny in his "dangerous cabinet position," and had not even told the minister of National Defence of the security risk in his own, most vulnerable department. As for the police, he reported: "I can find no criticism whatsoever of the Royal Canadian Mounted Police. The action of the Force was efficient, prompt and discreet."

Not all opinions of the Force were as favourable at that time, however, and neither had they been in the past. For many years individuals and organizations had criticized various governments for their policies in connection with the country's security screening program, and the Mounted Police for their methods of implementing them. Members of the New Democratic Party and of its predecessor, the Canadian Commonwealth Federation, had always believed that the Force did not know the difference between socialists and Communists, and hence discriminated against them. Civil-rights groups consistently complained about the manner in which the Mounted Police investigated persons regarding security screening for classified employment in the civil service. Other groups complained about alleged Mounted Police undercover work on university campuses.

During the turmoil in the House of Commons in early March, 1966, Opposition criticism of the minority Liberal government and of police action reached a peak over the alleged injustice to Spencer. It seemed that the government might be overthrown. In any case, when the prime minister voluntarily telephoned a person he knew to be a spy to determine whether the spy wanted an inquiry, it indicated to knowledgeable persons how anxious the government was to appease the Opposition.

That same weekend the Munsinger case became public, and it seemed certain that the Opposition would retaliate with the strongest possible assault on the government. But the NDP held the balance of power. If the Liberals could appease them, the government would be safe, at least temporarily. On the afternoon of March 7, fifteen minutes after Pearson had announced the Spencer inquiry, he suddenly announced another. This one would inquire into the general field of security. In effect, the Force and its methods would be on trial.

The Royal Commission on Security was appointed later, on November 16, 1966, with Mr. Maxwell Weir Mackenzie, a former deputy minister of the federal government, as chairman. Its other two members were the Quebec lawyer Yves Pratte and M.J. Coldwell, former leader of the CCF, long time member of Parliament and critic of the Mounted Police. It would inquire into security methods and procedures; it would consider the rights and responsibilities of individuals; and it would advise on "what security methods and procedures are most effective and how they can best be implemented." During the next two years the commission heard 250 witnesses in 175 sittings. It had access to all pertinent government departments, including the Mounted

Police, and their files. It visited the United States, Great Britain, France, Holland, Hong Kong and Australia to study security policies and procedures.

The commission report of September 23, 1968, completely supported the views of the Mounted Police. "The main current threats to Canada are posed by International Communism and Communist powers . . . the most important Communist activities in Canada are largely directed from abroad. . . . As far as espionage is concerned . . . military information appears to remain of considerable importance . . . [but there may be] a somewhat higher priority upon the acquisition of scientific, technical, economic and political information including unclassified information of seeming technical or strategic value." The Force found great satisfaction in the fact that all three members of the commission, including Coldwell, recommended not more individual freedom but stricter regulations in all areas of security.

"Few errors of fact or mistakes have come to light," the commission reported. "Most of the apparent contentious cases . . . have arisen from misunderstandings." In fact, the Force had handled an average of 150,000 security cases a year for the previous ten years. There were only ten contentious cases in that period, and the Force was in error in only three of them.

The only apprehension the Mounted Police felt followed the recommendation that the Force's Security and Intelligence Directorate should be replaced by a civilian security service. This was something that others had suggested in the past. But the Force had always contended that its unique and widespread organization was best suited to maintain national security.

By the time the Royal Commission report on security reached the House of Commons on June 27, 1969, Canada had a new prime minister and a majority Liberal government. As Prime Minister Pierre Elliott Trudeau tabled the report he emphasized that the Force would remain as Canada's security service.

"We are keenly aware that the Royal Canadian Mounted Police is one of the most honoured and respected of Canadian institutions," he declared, "one of the world's finest."

Chapter 27
Front de Libération du Québec
1963 – 1972

During the fall of 1970, the Front de Libération du Québec (the Quebec Liberation Front) drew Canada into the "October Crisis." Since 1963 the Royal Canadian Mounted Police had been concerned with the activities of this subversive organization.

The FLQ was an offshoot of the legitimate Quebec separatist movement. But it was classified as subversive because it aimed to turn the province into a socialist and separatist state not by lawful means but by force. The FLQ planned to separate Quebec from the other nine provinces of Confederation, without the approval of the majority of the inhabitants of Quebec and without the agreement of the other provinces or of the federal government. Early in the life of the organization its members stole weapons from armouries, stole explosives from wherever they could get them, and stole equipment from broadcasting stations. They robbed banks to finance their movement.

Although the Mounted Police as the federal police were responsible for investigating the subversive aspects of the movement, they do no provincial or municipal police work in Quebec. Hence the Quebec provincial and municipal police were responsible for investigating the crimes committed by the FLQ and its sympathizers. However, the Mounted Police had a particular responsibility to assist the Quebec police in investigating crimes against federal government property, and because of the Force's methods of gathering intelligence it was able to help the local police in pinpointing FLQ members responsible for other crimes.

The FLQ realized that the Mounted Police were a dangerous hindrance to its movement. On the night of April 20, 1963, they threw a bomb through the window of "C" Division headquarters in Montreal, damaging the building. That same night a watchman at an army recruiting centre died when a bomb exploded in a garbage container. During the following months police and army experts dismantled numerous bombs which had been placed in mailboxes. One army expert was almost killed but survived, maimed for life.

During 1963, through the combined efforts of the Mounted Police and the Quebec police, eighteen persons were charged with 165 crimes. Sixteen were convicted, and most of them received long prison sentences. But other FLQ members continued to commit crimes to further their revolutionary independence movement.

In January and February of 1964, members of the FLQ and similar groups broke into two armouries and stole $41,000 worth of rifles, machine guns, grenades and ammunition. From February to April they robbed three banks of about $17,000. In October, when Queen Elizabeth visited Quebec City, she did so under threat of assassination. Meanwhile, the Mounted Police had learned that the FLQ was receiving help from Cuba and Algeria, and also that the movement contained persons advocating Communism Chinese-style. Bombing, other crimes and violence continued.

Early in 1965 a bomb threat against the Statue of Liberty and other American monuments led the New York police to report to the Force that there was a connection between the FLQ and the Black Power movement. Also during 1965, the police learned that the FLQ was disseminating extreme separatist propaganda. It advocated rebellion and gave details of how to make bombs, how to conduct armed holdups, and how to conduct guerrilla warfare. That same year a secret training camp was discovered.

During the following year FLQ members stole large quantities of dynamite from construction firms, more rifles and ammunition from armouries, and uniforms from a college cadet unit. Bombings killed several persons. Six members were charged with non-capital murder but were convicted of manslaughter after pleading guilty to that lesser crime.

Although the Mounted Police were still investigating the subversive movement, they did so only as a federal force, in the interests of national security. Not only do such crimes as theft and bombing come under the Criminal Code, enforceable by the provinces, but so does advocating the overthrow of a provincial government by force, which is sedition. Thus if any authority prosecuted FLQ members for sedition, it would have to be the Quebec authorities. And they held to their earlier decision to try to control the situation by charging individuals with the crimes of theft, robbery, bombings and so on, although in this way they were obviously unable to halt FLQ activity. In any case, the Mounted Police could only report to its own authority, the federal government, all the facts of the matter.

During Expo 67 the FLQ remained underground. But in Montreal the following year the group emerged on St. Jean Baptiste Day, June 24, to fight pitched battles with the police. They attacked Prime Minister Trudeau as he sat on the reviewing stand, throwing bottles and other missiles at him while he shook his fist at them.

Later in 1968 they resumed their bombings, first attacking liquor stores in support of striking employees, as if hoping in this way to get reciprocal support. In October they stole 7,300 sticks of dynamite from a construction company. For the next five months they bombed ferociously: political clubs, industrial and mining companies, company union offices, the T. Eaton Company and many mailboxes. They also bombed the Montreal Stock Exchange (twenty-seven wounded), and many other organizations they considered to be prospering financially at the expense of the Quebecois. When the city of Montreal offered a $10,000 reward for information about the bombings and the Province of Quebec matched it, the FLQ bombed city hall. One twenty-four-year-old self-admitted revolutionary pleaded guilty to 124 criminal counts related to the long series of bombings. But after he was sentenced to life imprisonment, others carried on.

Raids on FLQ headquarters during 1969 by the combined forces of the Mounted Police, the Quebec Provincial Police and the Montreal city police uncovered information that certain members of leftist groups aimed to join the FLQ in a planned armed insurrection. Some of the persons involved were members of the Company of Young Canadians, an organization sponsored by the federal government. Bombings continued, and the home of Jean Drapeau, mayor of Montreal, was virtually demolished.

In February, 1970, when police stopped a panel truck in the east end of Montreal they found a sawed-off shotgun, a man-sized wicker basket, and a document announcing the abduction of the Israeli consul in Montreal. In June, in a Laurentian village, police found six FLQ members with a cache of stolen firearms and explosives, and also the draft of a ransom note for the planned kidnapping of the U.S. consul in Montreal. The police thwarted both these planned kidnappings. But the second plan was almost identical to a third, unknown to the police in advance, and destined for success a few months later.

Three days after the raid on the Laurentian village hideout, a bomb exploded at Defence Headquarters, Ottawa, killing a woman and inju-

280

ring two other persons. The FLQ by this time was comparing its liberation movement with those in Palestine and Vietnam, and with Black Power in the United States. CBC interviews and news photos showed FLQ members being trained for guerrilla warfare in Palestine.

Police now reported reliable rumours of a planned "big autumn offensive." This, plus information gathered by the Force over the seven-year period since 1963, plus seized lists of persons designated for assassination, finally allowed the police to convince the federal authorities that the situation was serious. But still the Quebec authorities kept to their policy of refusing to prosecute such acts as seditious. Perhaps this was partly because sedition is one of the most difficult offences to prosecute successfully, as was proved later in FLQ court cases.

On the morning of October 5, 1970, four members of the FLQ kidnapped James Cross, the British trade commissioner, at gunpoint from his home in Montreal. The ransom note made seven basic demands on the "ruling authorities" which must be met in order to preserve the life of "the representative of the old, racist and colonialist British system." The authorities must call off the police. They must publish the FLQ manifesto in newspapers and on television. They must liberate twenty-three "political" prisoners (they were actually convicted criminals). The authorities must also provide plane transportation for all freed prisoners and their wives and families who wished it to Cuba or Algeria. They must reinstate the "Lapalme boys," the postal drivers who had lost their jobs with the federal government when their contract expired. They must pay a ransom of $500,000 in gold bars. And finally, they must identify the informant who had helped the police to establish the identity of an FLQ cell.

The kidnapping of a British diplomat undoubtedly concerned the federal government, but it was politically expedient to move only with the approval of the Quebec government. Moreover, the Trudeau government refused to be pressured into paying the ransom, believing that this would only invite other kidnappings. Premier Robert Bourassa played down the kidnapping and made his scheduled trip to New York to encourage investment in Quebec. Communiqués went out from both sides but with no results, and the life of James Cross continued to be threatened.

On the evening of October 10, four men with guns snatched the Quebec minister of Labour and Immigration, Pierre Laporte, from the street in front of his own house. That same evening an anonymous phone call to the house where Bourassa was staying said that the FLQ would get him too.

Meanwhile the full resources of the Mounted Police, the Quebec

Provincial Police and the Montreal city police came into play. Within a few days of each kidnapping the police knew the identity of the kidnappers, but were unable to locate them.

The Quebec provincial government refused to ransom Laporte, just as the federal government had refused to ransom James Cross. But a surprising number of students and political activists praised the FLQ and its objectives. So now the Quebec government called on the federal government for the army to help the overworked police in fending off what seemed like a move toward anarchy. Troops immediately took up defensive positions in Montreal, Quebec City and elsewhere, and students and activists immediately demonstrated their opposition.

On Saturday night, October 17, the police received a warning note, and a little after midnight they found the body of Pierre Laporte in the trunk of a green Chevrolet left at the St. Hubert Air Base. About twenty-four hours later, after a phone tip to the police by a woman, they found the house where he had been held and murdered.

The Quebec government now asked the federal government to invoke the War Measures Act, which can be used in time of war or other emergency. Regulations under this Act would allow the prohibition of membership in the FLQ. They would also give the police extraordinary powers, mostly for the detention of persons and for the searching of persons and places.

On Monday, October 19, one hundred and ninety members of the House of Commons voted approval of invoking the War Measures Act. Sixteen members of the NDP voted against what they considered a too severe restriction of civil liberties. Other groups and individuals all across Canada also immediately protested such "curtailment of civil liberties." This was in spite of the fact that the regulations did not apply to the whole of Canada, or even to all persons in Quebec, but only to the subversive section of the separatist movement in Quebec.

At about the same time, the attorney general of Quebec ordered the director of the Quebec Provincial Police to assume authority over all municipal police forces in Quebec, including the Montreal city police. But he was not in control of the Mounted Police, who continued to cooperate as before. By early November the police, all three forces working together, had arrested 439 persons under the War Measures Act. Only sixty were detained, most of whom were charged with sedition. When they appeared before Quebec juries during 1971, however, not one was convicted.

Also by early November the federal and provincial governments had offered a reward of $150,000, believed to be the largest ever in Canada, for information leading to the arrest and conviction of the kidnappers of Cross and Laporte. The Mounted Police believed that if a reward had been offered earlier it would probably have resulted in an earlier capture. But in this inflammatory political situation the federal government would not make even this move alone, without Quebec's approval.

The police have never revealed, and probably never will, whether or not the posting of the reward had anything to do with their almost immediate success. But soon afterwards, on November 6, Montreal city police arrested Bernard Lortie in a Montreal apartment. He confessed to his part in the kidnapping of Laporte and gave the police information on the three others involved, Paul and Jacques Rose and Francis Simard, for whom the police continued to search.

The Mounted Police believed that they had located the apartment in a north Montreal triplex where James Cross was hidden. On November 30 they moved a corporal and his wife into the apartment above it. The corporal spent hours on the floor, listening, and what he heard indicated that Cross was indeed there. The Mounted Police alerted all other police forces, and the combined police plus the army surrounded the place. But the police were afraid to make any sudden move in case the kidnappers murdered Cross.

At 2:00 A.M. on December 3 they cut off the electricity to the triplex and settled themselves to wait until the criminals were forced out. An hour later an FLQ man threw the police a note in a piece of pipe, asking to negotiate. Later that day Cross was released. He was, in the words of one popular magazine, "the first victim of a political kidnapping ever to be rescued by police action." Simultaneously, in accord with earlier government promises, the three kidnappers and a few other persons boarded an RCAF plane and were immediately flown to Cuba, whose government had agreed to accept them.

Now the three police forces concentrated all efforts on finding the murderers of Pierre Laporte. Again it was Mounted Police work that led to success. On December 22, on the basis of information accumulated by the Mounted Police about persons who had associated with Lortie, the Rose brothers and Simard, the Quebec Provincial Police arrested eleven men. The Mounted Police had been particularly interested in one of them, Michel Viger, who for no apparent good reason had rented an old farm house near St. Luc, twenty miles southeast of Montreal. On December 28 Viger led the provincial police into the farmhouse basement. There the intensive manhunt came to an end when the police found Paul and Jacques Rose and Francis Simard in a tunnel off the basement.

These three, plus Bernard Lortie, were later charged with kidnapping and murder. Paul Rose and Francis Simard were subsequently sentenced to life imprisonment for manslaughter. Bernard Lortie was sentenced to twenty years and six months for kidnapping and contempt of court. In December, 1972, Jacques Rose was acquitted of the charge of kidnapping, and in February, 1973, of the charge of murder. In July, 1973, he was found guilty of being an accessory after the fact of kidnapping. He was sentenced to eight years' imprisonment, but released on bail pending his appeal. Nine other persons were convicted of being accessories and received jail terms.

Although the Force had no authority in the criminal aspects of the FLQ situation, it was criticized for not having done more. When Commissioner W.L. Higgitt appeared before a House of Commons Justice Committee in March, 1971, some questions, especially those from David Orlikow, NDP member for North Winnipeg, implied that the Force's lack of French-speaking members adversely affected its ability to infiltrate terrorist groups. Higgitt pointed out that the Mounted Police staff in Montreal is bilingual, more than ninety-eight percent French-speaking, and that they were investigating in cooperation with other police forces whose members were French-speaking. Then Orlikow, a frequent critic of the Force, suggested that the Force's number of French-speaking Mounted Police must have been inadequate since it was standard procedure, or so he believed, for security forces to prevent such activities as those of the FLQ.

As Commissioner Higgitt explained, the Force knew what was going on, but under the circumstances no given number of Mounted Police could have prevented it. And although Higgitt did not say so, apparently Orlikow, like many other Canadians, either did not know or refused to acknowledge three unique political facts of our national life. One, the Force is subject to federal authority. Two, the federal-provincial-municipal division of authority over enforcing Canadian law limits Mounted Police activity. Three, our highly controversial federal-provincial relations, especially those between Ottawa and Quebec, influence the federal government as to what actions are politically feasible for the Force to take.

Even so, the two kidnappings and murder—according to Higgitt "probably the most vicious and complicated crimes ever committed in Canada"—were completely solved in sixty-two days. As he said to the Justice Committee, "From a police point of view that's a pretty good record."

Chapter 28
Toward a New Era
1966-1973

As the Force neared the end of its first century it continued to serve Canada as it had done from the beginning—that is, according to the needs of the people and the social and technological conditions of the period. This, from the mid-1960s onward, meant not only stepping up its efforts against long-standing categories of crime that continued to increase, but also constantly adapting itself as new needs, new types of crime and new criminal methods developed.

The work of the Commercial Fraud Sections, set up across the country from 1966 to fight securities and other financial frauds, illustrates the Force's present-day methods.

The career of Inspector H. Jensen, in charge from Ottawa of all sections from their inception, indicates Mounted Police reaction to present-day problems, the educational opportunities it provides for a considerable number of members, and the response of those members to such opportunities. Jensen was a constable with eight years of general police service when in 1960 the Force chose him from its regular members and sponsored him at the University of British Columbia for a one year non-degree course with commercial subjects predominating. He did so well that from 1962 to 1964 the Force sent him to the University of Alberta for his Bachelor of Commerce. By 1966 he had been promoted to sub-inspector, transferred to Ottawa, and put in charge of the new Commercial Fraud Sections. Then on his own initiative he took night courses on his own time, and in 1970 graduated from Carleton University with an M.A. in Public Administration.

Under Inspector Jensen's supervision the Commercial Fraud Sections investigate criminal aspects of securities and bankruptcy frauds, and although municipal police have the power to handle these matters, they cooperate with the Mounted Police. The sections investigate about 250 cases of criminal bankruptcy and about 300 commercial frauds each year. The Securities Frauds National Information Centre handles about five thousand inquiries annually from the various Mounted Police sections, from provincial securities commissions and from other police forces. Investigations have taken members of the sections to the United States, to many countries of Europe and to South America. By 1972 the Commercial Fraud Sections contained 128 men, about one-third of them with university degrees in commerce, law, economics, or business administration, or with professional accountants' certificates. The others were taking at that time, or would in future be taking, specialized courses at various universities.

A typical Commercial Frauds case began in November, 1968. The three principals, Duncan Crux, Gerardius Polvliet and Margaret Harling, set up a number of public savings and investment companies in Vancouver and in other cities in western Canada. After persuading the public to invest about $90,000,000, they then used their personal skill in bookkeeping to defraud the investors.

They were able to do this because in addition to their Commonwealth Group of public companies, which included such ones as Commonwealth Savings Plan and Commonwealth Investors' Syndicate, they also set up several private companies for themselves, some in Canada and some in Switzerland. Then Crux, Polvliet and Harling illegally transferred funds from the public companies to their private Canadian companies. Next they transferred the private Canadian company money to their private Swiss companies. They hoped to hide the money in the Swiss companies, but even if their thefts were discovered, they had reason to believe that they would be able to keep the money, as only they knew where it was deposited.

Their bookkeeping knowledge enabled them to confuse provincial and federal authorities by organizing the Canadian companies through different legal firms, and by having the fiscal years of the companies end at different times. But when the superintendent of insurance in British Columbia examined their books, they aroused his suspicions. Income tax investigators also had difficulty in checking the Commonwealth Group books because their warrants were quashed by the courts. Suspicion increased, and at last orders were taken out under the B.C. Securities Act which allowed the Force's Commercial Fraud Section to examine the books.

As accountant investigators, all of them regular Mounted Police members of the section, analyzed the account books of all the Commonwealth companies in Canada, they gradually understood the nature of the operation and also the extent of the frauds. Meanwhile the records led the investigators to Switzerland, where they located the Swiss companies set up by Crux, Polvliet and Harling.

In late 1969 the Mounted Police laid charges against all three swindlers. Duncan Crux was charged with fraud, theft and issuing false prospectuses when certain Commonwealth companies were formed. But because it was impossible to keep such an investigation secret, Crux had fled to the Bahamas before the charges were laid. It took the police eighteen months to obtain his extradition, but at last he was returned to Canada in the summer of 1971. The same charges were laid against Gerardius Polvliet. Margaret Harling was charged with theft, but died before the case was concluded.

In the fall of 1971 Crux and Polvliet were found guilty. Crux, the master-mind, was sentenced to seven years in prison, and Polvliet to three; $70,000,000 was eventually returned to the investors who had been defrauded. Even so, $20,000,000 was still outstanding, a loss to the investors and a gain for the criminals. Incidentally, the estimated cost to Canadian taxpayers for the two-year investigation and prosecution was another $1,000,000.

"The old type of bold and unsophisticated criminal has been replaced by sophisticated businessmen who, with the necessary assistance of lawyers and accountants, have succeeded in setting up various corporations which they, the businessmen, use as a shield to obscure their criminal activities," the Commissioner of the Force commented to a Canadian Club audience in April, 1971. He estimated that a billion dollars had been bilked in Canada over the previous two decades.

Unfortunately for the record of the Mounted Police, a member of the Toronto commercial fraud squad succumbed to the temptation always present in handling large amounts of cash. In January, 1970, Eldon D. Davie, a well-respected corporal with ten years' service, was entrusted with $36,420 seized at Toronto Island Airport from a couple who were later charged with conspiring to commit fraud by disposing of stolen securities in the Bahamas. Between January and December, Corporal Davie helped himself to more than half the money from the safety-deposit box where it was stored, and used it to cover his losses on the stock market. In December, when the case was heard in court, the theft came to light. The Force immediately dismissed Davie and laid criminal charges. By the time his case came to trial he had made full restitution, but he was sentenced to a jail term of eighteen months definite and nine months indefinite.

An investigation which was underway when the first Commercial

Fraud Sections were organized proved that there was a need for the Force to continue its anti-espionage work. The case, like that of George Victor Spencer, is a classic, textbook example of how the Russians conduct their espionage in Canada.

The investigation began in Ottawa at nine-thirty on the cold, quiet Sunday morning of February 13, 1966. When two Security and Intelligence Directorate men happened to see the Soviet Attaché Eugeni Ivanovitch Kourianov driving on Highway 15 just west of Ottawa, their car followed his. Soon several other Mounted Police, also in plainclothes and in unmarked cars, joined the surveillance. The police discreetly followed Kourianov as he drove an unusually roundabout route to an Ottawa westend shopping centre where he parked his car behind a high snowbank. Then he took a bus to central Ottawa. There the police watched him as he walked for miles up and down and across various streets in the centre of town, then took a bus to the eastend Elmvale Shopping Centre. There the police observed him slowly stroll about for nearly an hour, as if taking a leisurely Sunday morning walk.

At 11:30 A.M. a bus arrived at the shopping centre, and the police, still hidden, saw Kourianov meet a man who got off it. Now the two men walked slowly along nearby residential streets, talking together for forty minutes. Two of the police saw Kourianov give the other man a "white paper-like object" which he put in his wallet before they parted and went in opposite directions. The "S and I" men followed the unknown contact as he hitchhiked his way home. Later they learned that he was Bower Edward Featherstone, who operated a printing press in the government department that printed maps.

Security and Intelligence men investigated for eight months. Then in late October, 1966, they raided the employees' lockers at the surveys and mapping branches of the Department of Energy, Mines and Resources. In Featherstone's two lockers, Corporal Paul D. Wendt found, among other things, two identical marine charts of the sea bottom fifty miles southeast of Cape Race, Newfoundland, both marked confidential, and a non-classified geo-chemical map of the Keno Hills area of the Yukon.

The lockers also yielded two envelopes postmarked early in March, 1966, each with the name and address heavily penned out, and each containing a letter referring to "your check" and "your order," but written so that a casual reader could not grasp the meaning. Wendt also found a plastic jar containing a handwritten note which read: "Take a bus to corner of Brookfield and Riverside Drive. Hydro post at corner Metcalfe and Gilmour. Next date March 27 at 9:00 P.M. on Shillington Street."

A few weeks later Bower Edward Featherstone, twenty-seven, who had worked on the printing of maps for the Mines Department for ten years, was charged with obtaining and retaining confidential documents for a purpose prejudicial to the safety of the state. The USSR was named as a possible beneficiary.

During the court hearings a naval expert explained that he had ordered the confidential marine charts to pinpoint shipwrecks off the east coast. Navy defence ships would be able to tell from the charts, plus their sonar readings, which objects on the ocean floor were old wrecks and which were probably submarines. But if these confidential charts ever got into foreign hands, the submarines of other governments would also know the exact location of the wrecks and could hide next to them, so that the navy would have no way of knowing the foreign submarines were there.

As for Featherstone, the Mounted Police had gathered evidence indicating that he had been friendly with a Soviet Embassy official who had lived in the same apartment building a few years earlier. An Embassy employee had soon given him the chance to make some extra money by becoming a "live letter drop." So, for a fee of thirty-five dollars each time, Featherstone had received and passed on to certain persons any letters mailed to him and specially marked with the "Ottawa, Ontario" designation underlined in red. On each occasion Featherstone had received a telephone call telling him to deliver the letter to someone who would meet him at the Elmvale Shopping Centre.

As the Crown prosecutor stated, the fact that Featherstone had obtained and retained the confidential marine charts indicated that the Russians now considered he was trained well enough to do more important jobs for them. It also indicated to the police, although the point was not made in court, that by first involving Featherstone as a "live letter drop" the Russians later were in a position to blackmail him into doing what they demanded. This is a well-known Russian tactic for recruitment of espionage agents.

On April 24, 1967, as Featherstone cradled his head in his hands and his wife sobbed audibly, he was sentenced to two and a half years in Kingston Penitentiary for violating the Official Secrets Act. In the meantime, Kourianov had returned to Russia and, as is customary in such cases, another Soviet attaché subsequently replaced him without restriction.

On August 15, 1967, the federal government appointed the Force's thirteenth Commissioner, fifty-eight-year-old Ontario-born Malcolm Francis Aylesworth Lindsay, former senior deputy commissioner. Lindsay, like Inspector Jensen, was a product of the Force's university training program. But the new Commissioner had the unique distinction of having been one of the first group of university students ever sponsored by the Mounted Police.

He had joined the Force at Regina in June, 1934. But in that year of depression many recruits held qualifications far beyond the minimum, and Lindsay held a Bachelor of Arts degree and had done one year toward a law degree. This led to his inclusion in that first group which Commissioner MacBrien chose in his drive toward efficiency through higher education. Constable Lindsay returned to the University of Saskatchewan, and in 1937 he graduated with a Bachelor of Law degree.

He gained wide experience over the years. After being commissioned in 1943 he served in New Brunswick and Manitoba, and later attended the National Defence College at Kingston, Ontario. In 1955 he became adjutant of the Force and, simultaneously, commanding officer of "H.Q." Division, Ottawa. Then, still at "H.Q.," he became, in turn, officer in charge of Administration and Organization, deputy commissioner in charge of Administration, and then senior deputy commissioner in charge of Operations.

During Commissioner Lindsay's two-year term of office the Force greatly increased its contact with Interpol. In addition to frequent direct radio contact between the Mounted Police and Interpol's head office at Paris, there was more frequent communication between Canada and the other 103 member countries. During 1968 there were 6,722 exchanges of correspondence, circulars, radio communications and so on.

One international investigation, mainly of concern to Japan, was begun by the Vancouver Preventive Service in 1967. Three men—one believed to be from Toronto, one from Cologne, and one Canadian from California—had formed a company which exported tin pails of grease, presumably for cooking, from Vancouver to Japan. Obviously their legitimate profits were not enough to cover their large expenses. The Japanese police, alerted by the Force, discovered that the Japanese office of the Canadian firm was operated by a French national, an American and an Israeli. They, too, had expenses too high to be covered by their legitimate profits.

Eventually the Mounted Police proved that the tin pails had false bottoms which were being used to smuggle millions of dollars worth of gold into Japan, where its importation was illegal. But the criminals were never charged with their crimes. It is not illegal to export gold from Canada. And although Interpol linked the Canadian-Japanese operation with a well-known international organized crime syndicate, for various reasons police in other countries were unable to get enough evidence to obtain convictions.

Also during Lindsay's term of office the Mounted Police conducted, on behalf of the United States government, an investigation which evoked for them the most heartfelt gratitude of any during the Force's entire history. The work of Mounted Policemen during April and May, 1968, enabled the FBI to find the assassin of the Reverend Martin Luther King.

The Negro-rights leader had been shot and killed by a sniper in Memphis, Tennessee, on April 4. After an extremely difficult investigation the FBI suspected that James Earl Ray, who had escaped from a United States prison about a year earlier, was somehow involved. But even by late April they still lacked evidence to indicate that he was actually the murderer. Rumours were circulating in the United States that the FBI was not trying to find King's murderer, allegedly because that organization, and Director J. Edgar Hoover in particular, had little sympathy for King or his cause.

As a high-ranking FBI official explained later to a senior Mounted Police officer, "We suspected Ray. We had followed him. And we had lost him. We were absolutely stymied."

On April 20 the FBI sent the Mounted Police a wanted notice, with photographs, for the arrest of James Earl Ray, listed as dangerous and considered armed. Members of the Force reasoned that even if Ray had come to Canada, he might also have left. If so, he would need a Canadian passport. So, in addition to the usual methods of seeking a wanted person, five Mounted Policemen were detailed to check files of passport applications. Instead of combing only the files of the present period, they checked from April 23, 1967, the date on which Ray, using the alias Eric Starvo Galt, had escaped from the United States jail.

On May 23, 1968, after the five-man team had checked about 250,000 applications, Constable J.R. Murray found an application in the name of Ramon George Sneyd, dated April 18, 1968, at Toronto. Although the accompanying photograph was a poor likeness of Ray, Murray recognized him. An immediate check in Toronto indicated that the information contained in the application was false, and that the travel agency which had assisted Ray to obtain the passport had booked his air passage to Europe a day or two after he had received it.

The Mounted Police promptly notified the FBI which in turn alerted all European police forces. On June 8, 1968, Ray was arrested at London Airport as he arrived from Portugal. He was armed at the time, as the FBI had suspected. Later he was convicted of the murder of Martin Luther King.

An indication of the FBI's appreciation of Mounted Police cooperation in solving a case of world-wide significance came soon after Ray's capture. In addition to the usual letter of thanks from the director of the FBI to the Commissioner of the Force, J. Edgar Hoover wrote a rare personal letter to Constable Murray thanking him for his invaluable assistance.

By the time Commissioner Lindsay retired on September 30, 1969, he had completed the normal maximum of thirty-five years of service. He also had the satisfaction, on looking back over the past few years, of perceiving that during his term of office and the preceding year, the Force had made strides toward still greater efficiency.

In the notable year of 1966, the Force's telecommunications network, already the largest of its kind in the world, added a colour-sensitive wire photo service. This transmits photographs of documents and fingerprints with true fidelity over a distance of four thousand miles. During that same year, a National Auto Bureau was opened at H.Q., Ottawa, and later it was linked with the National Crime Center at Washington, D.C. Also in 1966, the National Police Services in the French language had its inception. As a first move, twelve bilingual members of the staff worked full-time preparing, translating, checking and typing criminal records for French-language police forces.

A major change in recruit training began in 1967–68, when formal centralized training at Regina was cut to six months. This was followed by a further six months of on-the-job training under the guidance of specially trained NCOs, at selected detachments in provinces under contract with the Force. Equitation had already been dropped from recruit training, and was continued on a voluntary basis only to maintain the Musical Ride. The police-horse breeding farm was moved from Fort Walsh to Pakenham, Ontario, by the end of March, 1969, and the New York State Jockey Club donated the stallion Alton, grandson of the famous race-horse Man O'War, to the Force.

There were other changes too. Modern light-weight materials replaced heavier all-wools and cottons for uniforms. Boots and spurs remained, although sometimes they were obviously unsuitable, as when a young constable, hampered by his boots and spurs while pursuing a fleeing suspect, fired a shot which the fugitive claimed had hit him. The judge acquitted the constable of using firearms in a manner dangerous to the safety of others. But he commented: "The footwear was designed for riding horses . . . it has no place on the feet of policemen in an urban situation."

By 1969 a biennial pay review of several years' standing assured the Mounted Police that although they would presumably never be the highest-paid police in Canada, they would receive regular increases as the Treasury Board deemed advisable. It was a far cry from the early 1940s when a constable in Toronto working eighteen—and occasionally twenty-four—hours a day on a black-market squad earned two-thirds the wages of the man who delivered milk to his door. Like other government departments, the Force by 1969 was making a drive for bilingual persons. In March of that year it aimed to increase from twelve percent to nineteen percent the number of bilingual recruits.

In the fall of 1968 two widely separated events forecast a change in the rights of Indians to share in maintaining law and order in their own communities. In August, at Fort Good Hope in the Northwest Territories, Corporal R.J. Anderson swore in two Indians, Edward Cook and Noel Kakfwi, as the first Indian justices of the peace in Canada. In October the Caughnawaga Indian Band Council in Quebec received approval from the Department of Indian Affairs to form its own police department.

Five Indians from Caughnawaga, Quebec, took a two-week training course at "N" Division, Rockcliffe. Then they were sworn in as supernumerary special constables under the Royal Canadian Mounted Police Act. On returning home they received on-the-job training under the NCO in charge of the Caughnawaga detachment. In early 1969 they moved to their own quarters with two-way radio and police transport. Then, still under Mounted Police supervision, they began police operations by enforcing the Indian Act and by-laws. Later they were sworn in as special constables under the Quebec Police Act, and so could enforce Quebec provincial statutes and the Criminal Code.

Over the next few years, at the request of other Indian band councils, various Mounted Police divisional headquarters trained other Indians for similar police duties. The Department of Indian Affairs set up an internal task force to help the Indians establish their own police as an integral part of the various provincial police forces, including the Mounted Police. Retired Deputy Commissioner W.H. Kelly was engaged as a special advisor to the task force.

Service in the North had changed greatly by the time the thirteenth Commissioner retired. Perhaps that was one reason that by March, 1969, there was a shortage of unmarried volunteers for northern work, and so the Force had to send a limited number of recruits immediately after they had been trained.

Northern communications continued to improve, and mechanical transport—snowmobiles and power toboggans—gradually replaced sleigh dogs. In fact, for a time, some of the police who were required to maintain dog teams used their own snowmobiles part of the time.

The last dog patrol, on March 11, 1969, consisted of a constable and an Indian special constable driving two teams of Siberian huskies. The dogs were descendants of the thirty-four sleigh dogs which Walt Disney had donated to the Mounted Police after making the film *Nikki: Wild Dog of the North*. The police had gradually replaced their more vicious native dogs with the more amiable Siberians which they bred from the Disney dogs. Then they found that they no longer needed dogs of any breed.

This last dog patrol, from the small isolated Indian settlement of Old Crow in the Yukon to Fort McPherson two hundred miles away in the Northwest Territories, was as difficult and cold as many of the annual patrols over the same route since the 1930s. But this one was accompanied by a magazine writer-photographer team travelling on snowmobiles driven by Indian guides. And two of the dogs were later mounted by a taxidermist for historical display at the Regina Museum. The whole Force, even in the North, was moving toward a new era.

As the government pondered its choice of who would follow Commissioner Lindsay when he retired on September 30, 1969, it faced several problems. Each of the three previous Commissioners had been promoted from the rank of senior deputy. But Deputy Commissioner W.H. Kelly was already on extended service and due to retire soon, while the junior Deputy Commissioner, W.J. Fitzsimmons, was due to retire within a year. Moreover, some government officials believed that the Force was too ingrown and that an outsider should be chosen, particularly since the government had announced that it would not replace the Mounted Police security service with a civilian organization.

Serious consideration was given to a member of the armed forces as Commissioner. Instead, the government compromised by appointing a civilian as head of the Security and Intelligence Directorate, and by choosing the new Commissioner from within the Force. They announced that fifty-one-year-old John K. Starnes would become director general of Security and Intelligence on January 1, 1970, with rank equivalent to that of a deputy commissioner. Starnes was a distant relative of the sixth Commissioner, Cortlandt Starnes. As a senior official in External Affairs he had worked closely with the Mounted Police in security matters. He had also been ambassador to Germany and to Egypt. Later the name of the Directorate was changed to Security Service, but everything else remained the same—staff, methods, training and responsibilities.

On October 1, 1969, the government appointed the new Commissioner. He was fifty-two-year-old William Leonard Higgitt, a native of Anersley, Saskatchewan, who had joined the Force in 1937. After serving in his home province, he moved to the Intelligence Branch at Ottawa, where he worked on the Gouzenko cases. He was commissioned in 1952, and later became officer commanding Montreal Sub-Division, then spent three years at Ottawa as officer in charge of counter-espionage under the director of Security and Intelligence. After a three-year interval as liaison officer in London, he resumed his position at Ottawa, and in 1967 became an assistant commissioner and director of Security and Intelligence. After Kelly's retirement he became deputy commissioner, Operations for twenty-one days, then the Force's fourteenth Commissioner.

In May of the following year, the Mounted Police went to Japan. Commissioner Higgitt, the band under Inspector W.B. Smith, the Musical Ride led by Inspector P.J.C. Morin, and a security detail flew to Osaka, Japan, to take part in Expo 70. The security detail protected all government of Canada facilities and property during the six months of Expo 70, in liaison with Japanese police and security guards. In nine performances during Canada Week, the band and the Ride performed for enthusiastic audiences of a quarter of a million people, including some Japanese who had never before seen a live horse.

When Higgitt set out for home he travelled westward. By this time the Mounted Police had eighteen far-flung visa control posts, at Tokyo, Manila, Sydney, Hong Kong, New Delhi, Beirut, Athens, Rome, Vienna, Cologne, Stuttgart, Berne, Paris, Brussels, Stockholm, Madrid, London and Port of Spain. So the Commissioner finished his trip by flying around the world, making inspections as he went. Kingston, Jamaica, was added the next year. Two years later the Force's expansion of influence was again highlighted when Commissioner Higgitt was elected president of Interpol.

Although the Mounted Police have been criticized over the years, during the last two decades criticism has reached an all-time high. Members of Parliament constantly accused the police of keeping files on them, and refused to accept the fact that they are treated like other citizens. That is, if a file is kept it is not because a person is a member of Parliament but because he has been convicted of a traffic offence or has opened correspondence with the Force, and so on. Members of Parliament also accused the Mounted Police of tapping their tele-phones, in spite of police assurance that this was not true.

The NDP has accused the Force of not knowing the difference between socialism and communism, and of using inexperienced and uneducated men on investigations. Actually the Force has made a continuous study of communism for more than fifty years. And after Melville Watkins, an academic and one-time leader of the NDP

"Waffle" group, was interviewed by a Mounted Policeman concerning a security-classified government position, he told reporters that he felt he had been interviewed by a psychiatrist.

Ironically, another group criticizes the Force for sending men to university. Some members of the Canadian Association of University Teachers and many university students would like to keep the Mounted Police off campuses, and so deny them the right to higher education. Although the Mounted Policemen who attend university openly acknowledge that they are sponsored by the Force, some teachers and students accuse them of being undercover agents, planted to investigate subversive activities. These same people claim that Mounted Policemen should be prevented from conducting any investigations on campus. On this point Prime Minister Trudeau gave the Force the firmest support it has ever received from a member of the government during a decade of such criticism. He stated that Mounted Policemen do not go "fishing for trouble" on university campuses, but "when we have real cause to believe there is subversion, we will investigate."

The Force continues to encourage its members to upgrade their education. During the 1971–72 scholastic year, seventy-three Mounted Policemen were enrolled full-time at universities and technical colleges, and 730 took evening classes or correspondence courses. In addition, about fifty of each year's recruits have university degrees. One student told a news reporter, "I think attending university has made me more sophisticated in my judgment between what is social change and what may be subversion."

Justified criticism arose in July, 1971, when the public learned that thieves had broken into the Long Sault detachment in eastern Ontario two months earlier, presumably to destroy evidence against themselves. They stole confidential files, police weapons, and bonds worth $2,600, all kept in a locked strongbox but in a detachment office not sufficiently well guarded. The case was rare—the only one of its kind in the Force's history—but serious. Months later the stolen items turned up in Toronto.

Mounted Policemen have frequently been accused of mishandling Indians in admittedly difficult situations, especially under the liquor laws in the Indian Act. A constable was accused of causing the death of an Indian at Williams Lake, British Columbia, in November, 1971. Although two different coroners' juries cleared him of blame, the adverse publicity was widespread.

In another much-publicized incident, Prime Minister Trudeau criticized newly appointed Commissioner Higgitt for frankly answering a question with political implications. Late in 1969, the government was openly working for closer relations with China. But when Higgitt was asked at a news conference whether the establishment of a mainland Chinese embassy in Canada would result in an increase in subversive agents in this country, he said yes.

Higgitt's answer was based on sound knowledge. Much of his thirty-two years' service with the Force had been spent in security and intelligence work. He knew the history of Chinese intelligence from 350 B.C. As liaison officer in Europe he had learned how Chinese agents were working on the continent where China has been represented since World War II. He also knew the shocking state of Canadian immigration, and remembered the Chinese immigration scandal of the early sixties, when the federal government had allowed an estimated 11,000 illegal Chinese immigrants to remain in the country. And he was uncomfortably aware that Canada was a convenient base from which Chinese intelligence agents could supervise any agents among the Chinese illegally slipping into the United States via Hong Kong at the estimated rate of 4,200 each year.

But the government's main concern was closer relations with China. When a reporter questioned the prime minister about Higgitt's affirmative answer regarding the possible increase in subversive agents, he retorted sharply that the Commissioner was "allowed one mistake." Two years later, when Higgitt appeared before a Commons Justice Committee, he was saved from having to answer a similar question when the solicitor-general intervened and explained that our relations with Communist countries were excellent.

The bitterest criticism, as in earlier years, concerned the enforcement of drug laws. Public outcry over the stigma of criminal records given to young persons through their use of drugs forced the federal government to set up the LeDain Commission in 1969 to study the non-medical use of drugs. Three years later, changes in the Criminal Code made it possible for certain offenders to have their records "wiped clean" after a period of time. But until then, the government merely encouraged the courts to give lighter sentences, and the Mounted Police still had to enforce the law. The Force's use of undercover agents also continued to attract strong criticism, although that is the only effective way of combatting the widespread trafficking in drugs.

In the fall of 1971, a young Cornwall man who in 1968 had served a term in the Guelph reformatory claimed that the Mounted Police had used that fact to coerce him into acting as a paid drug informant. He also claimed that the coercion had occurred when he was a teenager, and that his parents had not known he was involved in informing. Several newspapers played up his story, and a CBC public-affairs program interviewed him at length on television. Newspaper editorials and the general public expressed shock and disapproval, while the Force, and Sergeant Lloyd G. Larose in particular, received much adverse publicity.

About a week later Solicitor-General J.P. Goyer reported the facts to the House of Commons. The "teenager" was eighteen years and eight months old and not a juvenile under Ontario law when he had first become an informant. He had volunteered his services, and his parents had been notified. The Mounted Police had paid him for his information, which had resulted in fourteen cases of "successful police action."

For the first time in history an unjustly accused Mounted Policeman fought back. Sergeant Larose instituted libel proceedings against the CBC, *The Globe and Mail*, The Toronto *Star*, the now-defunct Toronto *Telegram*, and the Cornwall *Standard-Freeholder*. In April, 1972, the CBC made retractions on two public-affairs programs, saying that its allegations against Larose were "completely untrue and without foundation," and the network later made a monetary settlement. The four newspapers also made retractions and monetary settlements.

But the drug problem was growing. In January, 1971, a French citizen was charged in Toronto with importing heroin, worth $12,000,000 at street prices. In May, hashish valued at $728,000 was seized at Montreal International Airport, and this was only the first shipment of what two young men had planned on a regular monthly basis. In June, Labrador police service dog Jennie had her first on-the-job experience with heroin. She sniffed out heroin with an estimated street value of $28,000,000 which was hidden in the rear panels and the rear fender of a Fiat shipped from Paris to Montreal aboard the Soviet luxury liner *Alexander Pushkin*. Later that year, while the Mounted Police at Ottawa headquarters were hosts to the annual conference of Interpol, a report stated that in spite of increased arrests and seizures, less than ten percent of the heroin and hashish directed to the rich North American market is actually intercepted. Thus every unit seized indicated that nine times that amount evaded the police of North America.

The most regrettable drug case ever, from the Force's point of view, involved two of its own members, Corporal Roger Mourant and Constable Orest Kwasowsky, both with the Montreal drug squad. They stole about twelve pounds of heroin from seized drugs which they were taking to Ottawa for destruction, and replaced the substance with milk sugar. They sold a small quantity to a narcotics ring in the United States for $500, and arranged to sell more. But the constable backed out of a second, larger sale, which the corporal then made alone, and the constable later reported the whole affair to his superior officers. The

Quebec courts sentenced the corporal to two years in jail and the constable to three years, but the Mounted Police appealed the "grossly inadequate" sentences. Mourant's sentence was increased to ten years, and Kwasowsky's to eight years.

By the beginning of 1972, it was obvious that the Mounted Police alone had insufficient resources to control the illicit drug traffic in the country. The Chiefs of Police Association of Ontario announced that various municipalities would henceforth conduct local investigations and so take some of the burden off the federal police. Montreal police formed their own narcotics squad, and the Mounted Police gave the members courses on drugs. Up to this time police forces across the country had been working closely with the Force, and some already had drug squads. Now others formed their own, but all continued to cooperate with the Force.

Commissioner Higgitt gave some depressing facts to a Senate committee in March. There were about 15,000 "hard-line heroin addicts" in Canada, he said, and many had to steal to support the habit. During the previous year police had seized heroin worth $75,000,000 on the illicit market. Addicts needing that amount of money to pay for the heroin would have had to steal articles worth three times that amount, or $225,000,000, as stolen goods usually bring no more than one-third of their value. Higgitt also linked the use of soft and hard drugs. Although not all users of marijuana progress to heroin, he said, most heroin users took soft drugs before they took heroin.

As the Mounted Police increased the strength of their drug squads to meet the challenge, drug offences climbed to an all-time high, especially those involving heroin and cocaine. The rate of arrests for importation of opiates was 150% higher in the first six months of 1972 than in the same period of 1971. Surprisingly, the number of offences involving marijuana and hashish during 1972 seemed to fall significantly. That was partly because the federal government changed the Criminal Code, effective July 15, so that persons convicted of lesser offences in this category could receive either conditional or absolute discharges. Also, according to Inspector Gordon L. Tomalty, a high-ranking drug-enforcement officer, the use of marijuana has apparently leveled off, and there is a shift to the use of more potent drugs. But, most significantly, the increase in hard drug offences and the number of addicts has forced the police to use their manpower to investigate hard drug offences at the expense of soft drug offences.

Other work of the Force has also continued to grow, and so has the strength of the organization. The Old Original membership of about three hundred men in 1874 had swelled by March, 1973, to 10,481 regular uniformed members, plus special constables, civilian members and public servants, to a grand total of 14,454.

Figures showing the amount of work done each year toward the end of the Force's first century are so high as to be difficult to comprehend. The following were chosen at random from only a few categories of the 1971 calendar year.

Criminal Code investigations	287,047
federal and provincial statutes and	
municipal by-law investigations	640,524
crime detection laboratories:	
(a) examination of exhibits	13,562
(b) experts' appearances in court	3,284
(exclusive of certificates accepted as evidence	
without appearance of expert)	
Identification services:	
fingerprints received	346,839
fingerprints identified	143,233
vehicles reported stolen and indexed	32,164
black and white photoprints, reproductions and	
colourprints	1,207,802
criminal records sent out	389,779

Lists of figures, however, cannot indicate adequately either the scope or the variety of Mounted Police work. During the last ten years of the Force's first century, the rate of crime in Canada almost doubled, and the work of the police increased accordingly.

Subjects of investigation varied from the customary illicit stills to rum-running by air, from bank holdups to the theft of rare coins, from ships' deserters to espionage. Organized crime continued in loan sharking, protection rackets and drug trafficking, and more organized criminals infiltrated into legitimate business, where it was more difficult for the police to check their activities. More criminals forged more cheques, which are easier to forge than bank notes. The Doukhobors continued to be a problem as they refused to obey certain laws, won release from jail through hunger strikes, and returned home to cause disturbances again. Guard duties at airports increased because of the danger of skyjackers. Inspector R. Carrière, unarmed, talked an armed skyjacker out of his plans to force an Air Canada Viscount to fly from Montreal to Cuba in 1968. Sub-Inspector Bruce Northrop, also unarmed, similarly dissuaded an armed skyjacker in 1971, when an American jetliner skyjacked over Alaska landed in Vancouver.

As crime increased, the Mounted Police developed new methods of combatting it. One of these was the videofile system of storage and retrieval of fingerprints established by the Identification Branch in 1971, one of the first in the world. All fingerprints are recorded on magnetic tape and can be retrieved by a computer and projected on a television screen for comparison purposes. This system drastically reduces storage space and manual handling, and provides a needed print within seconds.

The Force's greatest innovation, however, was the Canadian Police Information Centre (CPIC), which houses the $40,000,000 computer planned in 1966, and is operated by the Mounted Police as a national police service. The computer is a storage and retrieval system of police information about known criminals, motor vehicles of interest to the police, all registered firearms, and stolen property. This information is available almost instantaneously to all law-enforcement agencies linked directly to it through typewriter-like terminals in their own offices. By the end of 1972 all major police forces were linked with CPIC, and it is expected that eventually all police forces in the country will be so linked.

The computer began operating at noon on July 1, 1972. At 1:42 P.M. it made its first "hit." The Ontario Provincial Police at Burlington queried the licence number of a burned-out vehicle, and within a few seconds the computer answered that it was recorded as stolen from Hagersville, Ontario, on June 10, 1972.

During its second day of operation, CPIC received a query from the Hamilton city police about an allegedly stolen car. The computer correlated earlier information received from the detachment of the Ontario Provincial Police at Oakville, thus indicating to the police that the car's owner had abandoned it after a hit-and-run accident, and had complained that it had been stolen in order to throw the police off the scent. By 6:00 P.M. of July 3 the computer had made twenty-two hits, and by the end of the month, hundreds. During that first month of operation it processed 125,641 messages. A senior officer of the Force classifies the computer as the greatest single innovation in fighting crime since the introduction of fingerprinting.

As its first century ends, the Force continues to expand and to reorganize. Early in 1973 a position was created for a third deputy commissioner. Already serving were Deputy Commissioner M.J. Nadon as deputy commissioner, Operations in charge of all crime operations in the Force, and Deputy Commissioner P. Bazowski as deputy commissioner in charge of Administration. The newly created position was filled by Deputy Commissioner C.R. Eves, who as deputy commissioner of the National Police Services became responsible for the operation of the new Canadian Police Information Centre and its vast computer services, for the General Records Directorate, for all forensic crime laboratories and all Identification Branches, and for the Canadian Police College. Incidentally, two of these three deputy commissioners are university graduates whose higher education was sponsored by the Force, one a Bachelor of Commerce and the other a Doctor of Philosophy in chemistry.

In March, 1973, the first civilian head of the Force's Security Service, John K. Starnes, retired. The position of director general, equivalent to that of a fourth deputy commissioner, was then filled by Lieutenant-General M.R. Dare, former vice chief of Defence Staff, who was acting chief of the armed forces during the October crisis in Quebec. More recently Mr. Dare directed the Crisis Management Centre, attached to the Privy Council Office and responsible for a report, not yet made public, regarding contingency plans for insurrections and similar outbreaks.

The Force continues to plan for the future, usually over five-year periods. Anticipated developments range from the establishment of new Preventive Service Sections across the country to the establishment of commercial fraud liaison offices abroad; from building new offices and living quarters across Canada to using some fibreglass vessels for Marine Services and more helicopters and more short take-off and landing aircraft for Air Services. More helicopters will be added to the two already in service, one based in Newfoundland from July, 1972, the second based in Victoria for the policing of the Gulf Islands, from April, 1973. Existing police information in such areas as National Crime Intelligence Units (NCIU) will be converted for use in the CPIC computer. Improved and expanded telecommunications will reach as far afield as Inuvik and Frobisher Bay Sub-Divisions.

The Force plans for its own growth at the rate of more than a thousand recruits a year to 1979. These will include more French-speaking and bilingual men, more university graduates, and perhaps women. More regular members will receive advanced instruction, and special constables will receive in-service training. In accord with the project inaugurated in 1972, some English-speaking recruits will be taught French and some French-speaking recruits will be taught English before their regular training, which will be in both languages for combined groups.

Other innovations include compensation for overtime, which began only in 1972, and the adoption of a forty-hour week, scheduled to begin in 1974–75. Perhaps most notable is the organization's plan to deviate from its century-old stance as the "silent Force," through more communication with the news media and more frequent informal contacts between its members and citizens.

In spite of numerous changes, however, some things remain the same. Even the changes are based on the organization's life-long characteristic of adapting to meet new demands. Its members continue to risk and to lose their lives on duty. And it still retains the respect of the public it serves.

Recognition of the Force during its hundredth anniversary year includes two coins, three postage stamps, a slogan on Saskatchewan motor vehicle licence plates, and celebrations all over the country. But of equal significance is that when the government removed the initials RCMP from the organization's signs on offices and police cars, and substituted the more general term POLICE, public outcry forced the government to revert to the use of signs specifically identifying the Force. It seems reasonable to assume that the organization which was at first known simply as "a Mounted Police Force for the North-West Territories," and later became the North-West Mounted Police, then the Royal North-West Mounted Police, is now firmly entrenched in the hearts of Canadians as the Royal Canadian Mounted Police, and will remain so, far into the future.

Selected Bibliography

Annual Reports of the Commissioners, 1874—1972.

RCMP Quarterlies, July, 1933, to January, 1973.

Royal Commission Report on Espionage. The King's Printer, Ottawa, 1946.

_____. Commission Report (Lucien Rivard). The Queen's Printer, Ottawa, June, 1965.

_____. Commission Report (George Victor Spencer). The Queen's Printer, Ottawa, July, 1966.

_____. Commission Report (Gerda Munsinger). The Queen's Printer, Ottawa, September, 1966.

_____. Commission on Security. The Queen's Printer, Ottawa, 1969.

Allen, Ralph. *Ordeal by Fire*. Doubleday, New York, 1961.

Author unknown. *The Story of Louis Riel*. Rose Publishing, Toronto, 1885.

Berry, Gerald L. *The Whoop-Up Trail*. Applied Arts Products Co., Edmonton, 1953.

Berton, Pierre. *The Last Spike: The Great Railway*. McClelland and Stewart, Toronto, 1971.

Boulton, C.A. *Reminiscences of the North-West Rebellion*. Grip Publishing Co., Toronto, 1886.

Butler, W.F. *The Great Lone Land*. Hurtig Publishers, Edmonton, 1968.

Chambers, Ernest J. *The Royal North-West Mounted Police*. Coles Publishing Co., Toronto, 1972.

Dean, Burton. *Mounted Police Life in Canada*. Cassells, Toronto, 1916.

Dempsey, Hugh A. *Jerry Potts, Plainsman*. Glenbow Foundation, Occasional Paper No. 2, Calgary.

Denny, Sir Cecil E. *The Law Marches West*. Dent, Toronto, 1939.

Donkin, J.G. *Trooper and Redskin*. Sampson, Low, London, 1889.

Dwight, Charles P. *Life in the North-West Mounted Police*. National Publishing Co., Toronto, 1892.

Featherstonhaugh, R.C. *The Royal Canadian Mounted Police*. Garden City Publishing Co., New York, 1938.

Fraser, Blair. *The Search for Identity*. Doubleday, New York, 1967.

Gooderham, Kent (editor). *I Am an Indian*. Dent, Toronto, 1969.

Gwyn, Richard. *The Shape of Scandal: A Study of a Government in Crisis*. Clarke, Irwin, Toronto, 1965.

Hardy, W.G. *From Sea Unto Sea*. Doubleday, New York, 1960.

Harvison, C.W. *The Horsemen*. McClelland and Stewart, Toronto, 1967.

Haydon, A.L. *Riders of the Plains*. Hurtig Publishers, Edmonton, 1971.

Higginbotham, J.D. *When the West was Young*. Ryerson, Toronto, 1933.

Horrall, S.W. "Sir John A. Macdonald and the Mounted Police Force for the North-West Territories." *Canadian Historical Review*, June, 1972.

Kelly, Nora. *Men of the Mounted*. Dent, Toronto, 1949.

Leacock, Stephen. *Canada: The Foundations of its Future*. Private Printing, Montreal, 1941.

Lee, H.P. *Policing the Top of the World*. McClelland and Stewart, Toronto, 1928.

Longstreth, T.M. *The Silent Force*. Century, London, 1927.

MacBeth, R.G. *The Making of the Canadian West*. Briggs, Toronto, 1898.

––––––. *Policing the Plains*. Hodder and Stoughton, Toronto, 1922.

Morris, A. *The Treaties of Canada with the Indians of Manitoba*. Belford Clarke, Toronto, 1880.

Mulvaney, C.P. *The North-West Rebellion*. Hovey, Toronto, 1885.

Salerno, R. and Tompkins, J.S. *The Crime Confederation*. Eagle Books, U.S.A., 1969.

Sharp, Paul F. *Whoop-Up Country*. Historical Society of Montana, 1960.

Stanley, G.F.G. *Louis Riel: Patriot or Rebel*. Historical Booklet No. 2, Canadian Historical Society, 1954.

Steele, Harwood. *Policing the Arctic*. The Ryerson Press, Toronto, 1936.

Steele, S.B. *Forty Years in Canada*. McClelland and Stewart, Toronto, 1914.

Turner, John P. *The North-West Mounted Police*. (two volumes) King's Printer, Ottawa, 1948.

Zaslow, Morris. *The Opening of the Canadian North: 1870–1914*. McClelland and Stewart, Toronto, 1971.

Chronological Index

Index

French, Mrs. G.A., 55
Fulton, E. Davie, 232, 275
Fury, Sergeant, 76

Gagnon, H.A.R., 178, 205, 211
Gagnon, Sévère, 34-35, 65, 113, 178
Gammon, A., 222
Gendron, Fernand, 244-245, 248
Gerson, Harold Samuel, 207, 212
Goldstein, Morris, 195
Goldstein, Stanley, 195-196
Gouzenko, Igor, 203-212
Gouzenko, Mrs. Igor, 204, 207-208
Goyer, J.P., 298
Graburn, Marmaduke, 66-67
Grant, A., 145
Gray, Charles, 149
Griesbach, Arthur Henry, 21
Grizzly Bear's Head, 71
Grogan, Andy, 54-55
Grundy, Postmaster, 112

Hadley, E.D., 199
Hall, K.W.N., 221
Halperin, Israel, 207, 211
Hamilton, Alfred B., 12
Hamilton, R.W., 169
Hardwick Gang, 48-49
Hardy, W.G., 84, 111
Harling, Margaret, 286-287
Harrison, G.C., 178
Harvey, D.A., 251
Harvison, Commissioner C.W., 208, 233, 235-242, 275
Hayward, Edward, 122
Heipel, Harry, 185
Henderson, Jack, 86
Herchmer, Commissioner L.W., 87-88, 93, 95, 110, 111-115, 146
Herchmer, W.M., 83, 87
Herman, R.J., 215-216
Hersey, F.H., 170
Higgitt, Commissioner W.L., 284, 287, 294-295, 297, 299
Hockin, C.S., 112,
Hollas, K.E., 272
Holmes, Constable, 68
Hoover, J. Edgar, 291-292
Horrall, S.W., 13, 19
Hudson's Bay Company, 12-15, 20, 26-28, 35, 42, 50, 80, 139, 164

Hunt, J.C., 252-253
Hunt, P.G., 199, 200
Hutchinson, Constable, 87

"Idaho Kid," 118
I.G. Baker Trading Co., 40-41, 46, 64
Illvarnic, Interpreter, 136
Industrial Workers of the World, 148
Interpol, 234, 290, 295
Irvine, Commissioner A.G., 49, 56, 60, 69, 70, 72, 74, 78-79, 80-81, 86-87

Janes, Robert, 161, 163, 165
Jarvis, A.M. "Buz," 93, 125
Jarvis, W.D., 33-35, 50
Jensen, H., 285
Jennie, 298
Johnson, Albert "Mad Trapper," 170-171
Johnstone, H.M.C., 250
Joy, A.H., 161, 163-165, 167, 169, 170
Joyce, M.A., 128-129
Julien, Henri, 26, 37
Junget, Christen, 144

Kakfwi, Noel, 293
Kellock, Mr. Justice R.L., 208
Kelly, W.H., 193, 220, 233-234, 270-271, 293-294
Kemp, V.A.M., 167-168
Kemp, Mrs. V.A.M., 168
Kerr, Constable, 76
Kerr, J.R., 112
KGB, 270, 288-289
King, A.W., 171
King, Charles, 121-122
King Edward VII, 119
King George V, 145
King George VI, 181, 188
King, Martin Luther, 291
King, W.L. Mackenzie, 155, 206-208
Kinney, G.F., 133-134
Kirk, E.A., 187
Kirk, Mrs. E.A., 187
Kittson, J., 37, 59
Kodik, 106-107
Kourianov, Eugeni Ivanovitch, 288-289
Krassilnikov, Rem, 270
Kwasowsky, Orest, 298-299

Photo Credits

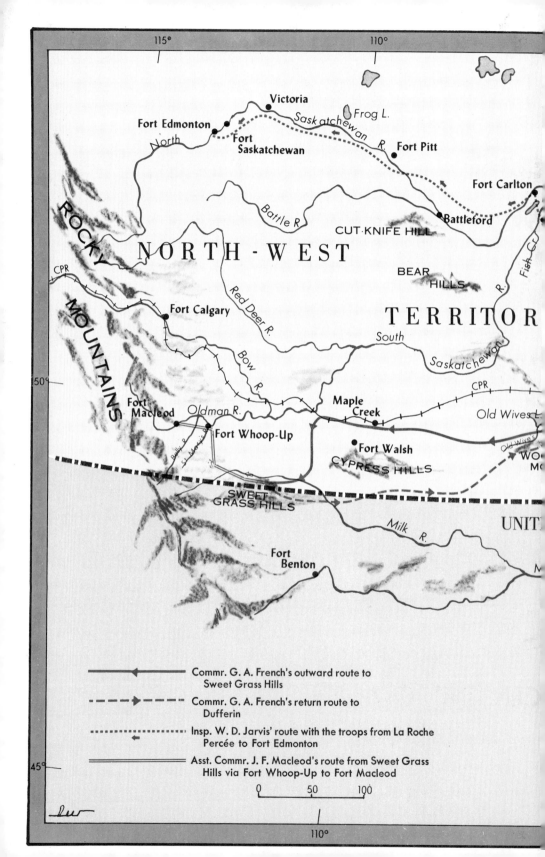

Map Legend

Commr. G. A. French's outward route to Sweet Grass Hills

Commr. G. A. French's return route to Dufferin

Insp. W. D. Jarvis' route with the troops from La Roche Percée to Fort Edmonton

Asst. Commr. J. F. Macleod's route from Sweet Grass Hills via Fort Whoop-Up to Fort Macleod

0   50   100